Reflecting the Past

Harvard East Asian Monographs 433

Reflecting the Past

Place, Language, and Principle in Japan's Medieval Mirror *Genre*

Erin L. Brightwell

Published by the Harvard University Asia Center
Distributed by Harvard University Press
Cambridge (Massachusetts) and London 2020

Printed in the United States of America

The Harvard University Asia Center publishes several monograph series and, in coordination with the Fairbank Center for Chinese Studies, the Korea Institute, the Reischauer Institute of Japanese Studies, and other facilities and institutes, administers research projects designed to further scholarly understanding of China, Japan, Vietnam, Korea, and other Asian countries. The Center also sponsors projects addressing multidisciplinary and transnational issues in Asia.

Library of Congress Cataloging-in-Publication Data

Names: Brightwell, Erin L., 1973– author.
Title: Reflecting the past : place, language, and principle in Japan's medieval mirror genre / Erin L. Brightwell.
Other titles: Place, language, and principle in Japan's medieval mirror genre
Description: Cambridge, Massachusetts : Harvard University Asia Center, 2020. | Series: Harvard East Asian monograph series ; 433 | Includes bibliographical references and index.
Identifiers: LCCN 2020003449 | ISBN 9780674247819 (cloth) | ISBN 9781684176182 (ebook)
Subjects: LCSH: Japan—Historiography. | Japan—History—Philosophy. | Japan—History—To 1600.
Classification: LCC DS834.7 .B75 2929 | DDC 952/.02072—dc23
LC record available at https://lccn.loc.gov/2020003449

Index by Do Mi Stauber

♾ Printed on acid-free paper

Last figure below indicates year of this printing
29 28 27 26 25 24 23 22 21 20

Contents

Figures

Preface

Reiwa 1 (2019).6.13. Around the hour of the Dragon, I set out for Urin'in Temple. When I arrived at the modest early eighteenth-century reconstruction, it was deserted, as usual. Despite the Urin'in's location near Kyoto's Kita-Ōji Dōri, a major thoroughfare, and its proximity to the famous Zen temple Daitokuji, it is off the beaten tourist path. (This being said, in an unprecedented surge of activity, three visitors passed through during the hour that I spent here.) Even the seemingly ubiquitous *omamori* (amulets) are nowhere to be found. The temple's present circumstances make it hard to remember that it has imperial origins dating back to the early ninth century. Even more so that it was once famous for lectures on the *Lotus Sutra* and so well recognized that the unknown author of *The Great Mirror* chose it as the setting for the first full-length narrative work to present Japan's history as driven by cosmological principles, marking the beginning of an entirely new way of writing about the past. In spite of the Urin'in's relative neglect today, because of its importance to the subject of this book, I thought that a return to it would provide the best setting to express my gratitude to those who have made this project possible. Or, to paraphrase one of the narrators who will appear in it, to reveal just how all of this has come about—for anyone who would but listen.

This book grew out of my dissertation, so I should begin by thanking my committee members, particularly Tom Hare, my advisor, and Ivo Smits. I am especially grateful for the intellectual latitude they allowed me. Although as a graduate student I was not always able to appreciate the value of this freedom, when it came time to sit down and write an actual book, I realized how important it was. Their guidance, along with support from Martin Collcutt, Thomas Conlan, Komine Kazuaki, and the late H. Richard Okada, has at a fundamental level made this book possible.

Despite its origins in my dissertation, however, most of the work for this project has unfolded at the University of Michigan, where I am lucky to have found intellectual camaraderie and friendship among members of the Department of Asian Languages and Cultures, as well as some interlopers from the History Department, thanks to the "Fragments" workshops hosted there. Micah Auerback, Ben Brose, Miranda Brown, Youngju Ryu, and Hitomi Tonomura each took the time to read chapters from (or in some cases, the entirety of) earlier versions of this work and offer constructive feedback. Don Lopez chaired an invaluable manuscript workshop for me as well as offering key advice about navigating numerous stages of the writing and publishing process. Chris Hill and David Rolston both provided useful reading suggestions that have found their way into this work. Juhn Ahn, SE Kile, and Emily Wilcox kindly assisted with sundry technical matters.

Farther afield (geographically speaking), I would particularly like to thank David Bialock and David Spafford for their generous feedback on this book. I have some sense of how much time and energy went into reading and commenting on an entire draft, and the benefit of having fellow medievalists engage so thoroughly with my work at a critical stage was immeasurable. In a related capacity, I would also like to express my gratitude to my two (recently revealed) reviewers—Terry Kawashima and Elizabeth Oyler—for their generous and constructive input, as well as my editor, Robert Graham, for suggestions and shepherding me through the publication process. And in more general matters of managing book writing (perhaps best classified as "aiding and abetting"), I wish to thank Anna Andreeva, Varuni Bhatia, Kevin Carr, Madhumita Lahiri, Levi McLaughlin, Matthew Stavros, Jolyon Thomas, Molly Vallor, and Jonathan Zwicker.

I have also profited from several opportunities to share my work as it was developing. The Kyoto Asian Studies Group supplied a venue for one of the earliest public presentations of my postdissertation research in 2016.

Subsequent opportunities for exchange have likewise been beneficial. In this vein, I would like to voice my appreciation to Matthew Fraleigh and Jason Webb for including me at "Loose Canons II," as well as Mack Horton for his comments; Angela Dragan, Magdalena Ciubancan, and the organizers of the 2016 "Japan—Pre-modern, Modern, and Contemporary" conference at Dimitrie Cantemir University for making me a guest speaker; Edward Kamens for giving me the chance to speak in the CEAS Japan Colloquium series at Yale University; Cynthea Bogel for bringing me to Kyushu University for a lecture; and the organizers of the Kyoto Lecture Series, Martin Nogueira Ramos and Silvio Vita, for giving me one last chance for feedback before my revisions were due.

Support for this project has been provided by multiple travel grants from the University of Michigan Center for Japanese Studies, as well as a Japanese Research Fellowship from the Hakuho Foundation, which has enabled a yearlong stay at Kyoto University under the auspices of the Graduate School of Education. Here, I would especially like to say thank you to Niels van Steenpaal for agreeing to host me, and all that has entailed in terms of offering feedback on chapters and pushback on presuppositions.

Acknowledgments (even when couched in a preface) are, in the end, a publicly oriented genre; but like a medieval scholiast, I believe that some information is better suited for limited circulation. I trust that the handful of people upon whom I have relied far more than their antiseptic recognition above suggests (as well as those completely behind the scenes) will understand if I deviate from genre conventions here and decide to keep some things beyond the realm of the written word. This in no way lessens my gratitude to each of you—I hope that you know who you are and that we can celebrate soon.

And with that, it is time to move back to the eleventh century.

Note to the Reader

A few words about the stylistic conventions of this book. For historical figures, names follow the traditional order of surname followed by given name. In the case of secondary scholarship, for texts in Japanese—as well as their translations—I follow the Japanese name order. Where the original language of publication is English, the given name is followed by the surname, regardless of the nationality of the author. All Japanese names are romanized in accordance with modified Hepburn style, save where a scholar has indicated an alternative romanization. There, I defer to the individual author. For Chinese historical figures, even within the context of Japanese texts, I romanize using pinyin to facilitate comparisons with non-Japanese sources.

Japanese place names are romanized in accordance with readings provided in the primary sources wherever possible. Where such readings are not indicated, as in the case of certain temples, I defer to the institution's current preference, although I indicate the possibility of multiple readings at the site's first appearance. When referring to specific dates, I follow the traditional dating system. Thus, they appear as "Reign Period year (Western year).Month.Day." The presence of a small "i" indicates an intercalary month.

Lastly, for Japanese and Chinese titles of and passages from primary sources, I use a hybrid approach. For Japanese works, I supply a romanization of the title followed by an English translation in parentheses. Although most of the works in this book have not been translated into

English, to reduce the burden on the reader, I refer to them after their initial appearance with the translated (English) title. Footnote citations will clarify the source language. For translated phrases, I provide a romanized rendering where needed in parentheses, following the translation. In a few instances, I also refer to specific works of Chinese poetry as part of my analysis. For those works, I supply the title in pinyin and characters followed by an English translation in parentheses. For translated phrases, I provide a pinyin romanization and characters in parentheses, following the translation. I appreciate that this compromise between the approach to Japanese and Chinese materials is a bit cumbersome, but I hope that it will give some sense of the very fluid (and contested) nature of linguistic categories in premodern Japan.

FIGURE I.1. *Ichi-no-tani, Hiyodorigoe sakaotoshi no zu* (Illustration of the Precipitous Descent at Hiyodorigoe Pass, Ichi-no-tani). Utagawa Yoshitora. 1845. Private collection.

INTRODUCTION

"Only one ignorant of the world could say that what we see before us now bears no resemblance to the past."[1] For a reader in a relatively stable or secure society, the sentiment may not elicit a strong reaction—perhaps only a sense of ennui. Or some sympathy with what sounds like dissatisfaction over a relentlessly presentist mode of analysis. Or even, with a bit of interpretive license, frustration at a lack of novelty. One response that it is unlikely to evoke, however, is that of relief.

But the above assertion is the product of a very different space and time, appearing in an elite courtier's—Nakayama no Tadachika (1131–circa 1194)—late-twelfth-century response to years of upheaval: *The Water Mirror.* For a courtier like Tadachika, the stability and security suggested by continuities with the past were precisely the message. He was writing for readers who had witnessed decades of violence. Not only would some of them have been through the Hōgen and Heiji Disturbances of 1156 and 1160, but nearly all of them would have experienced the recent civil war, the Genpei War (1180–85). Those based in the capital likely would have been able to recall how late in 1179, in a move interpreted as an expression

1. Kaneko et al., *Mizukagami zen chūshaku*, 28. This is the edition of Nakayama Tadachika's *Mizukagami* used throughout this book. There is some uncertainty as to whether Tadachika was born in 1131 or 1132. He refers to himself as being forty-nine (by the traditional count) in the diary entry for Jishō 3 (1179).2.23 (Nakayama, *Sankaiki*, 2:230), so I use the 1131 date.

of his "fury at the realm," Taira no Kiyomori (1118–81) marched in "several thousands of troops," striking fear into the city's denizens.[2] Many would have seen or heard about the warrior patrols of the capital that continued for months before war broke out. (Tonsured Prince Shukaku's (1150–1202) retrospective description of wartime Kyoto as "awash with blood" speaks to the impact of the violence.[3]) And 1185 saw the seven-year-old emperor "vanishing to the bottom of the sea" at Dan-no-ura, where he drowned in the arms of his grandmother (or wet nurse) during the final major battle of the war, a loss commemorated in 1191 with the founding of the nearby Akama Shrine.[4] Shortly after the war, the first shogunate, the Kamakura *bakufu*, was founded, over time expanding beyond its initial role as a semiautonomous, warrior-led regional power to one that could infringe on the authority of the court itself. For many, including Tadachika, these conflicts seemed to attest to the accuracy of widespread Buddhist beliefs that the country had entered an age of irreversible decline. Writing in the early thirteenth century, the monk Jien (1155–1225) would summarize the final decades of the twelfth century as a time in which "the Japanese realm's fate was exhausted, immense chaos broke out, and we were plunged into the age of the warrior."[5]

Such turmoil raised the question of how things had reached their present state, as well as, on occasion, what the future might hold. For over two hundred years—from the 1170s through the 1370s, roughly the life span of the Kamakura *bakufu*—writers turned to one type of text in particular to explain the logic of historical events: the *kagamimono* (mirror). The fountainhead for these *Mirrors* was the influential *Ōkagami* (The Great Mirror, written in the late eleventh century), the first full-length narrative work to present Japan's history as driven by cosmological principles (*dōri*).[6] A work that became a "must-read for medieval nobility and

2. Nakayama, *Sankaiki*, 2:312.

3. Shukaku, *Saki*, 665.

4. See Nagahara and Kishi, *Zen'yaku Azuma kagami*, 1:198, the entry for Genryaku 2 (1185).3.24. This is the edition of *Azuma kagami* used throughout this book.

5. Nakajima, *Gukanshō*, 608. For an alternative translation, see Brown and Ishida, *Future and the Past*, 216.

6. The dating of *The Great Mirror* is impossible to resolve with precision. For a discussion of the issues surrounding it, see chapter 1. Dating for each *Mirror* will be

intellectuals," *The Great Mirror*'s new approach to historiography, which I call "cosmological history," inspired a half-dozen similarly ambitious successors.[7] Their authors, including Tadachika, sought to narrate events in a way that made change sensible. And in so doing, they created a particular genre to engage with and order the past, one in which no matter what turn things might take, there was a potentially comforting cosmological regulation to historical events that a reliable informant was in a position to reveal.

This book will show that *The Great Mirror* and its successors form a body of texts that suggest specific interpretive strategies for coping with the past; that time and time again they offer a cosmological key to questions of the fate of the world. The result is a new, more complicated understanding of the medieval historiographic landscape—a landscape that has been eclipsed in part for reasons that will be discussed below—in which cosmological histories form a powerful, though today underrecognized, option for early medieval writers attempting to order the world around them.

---

addressed in the relevant chapters. Throughout this book, I use the terms "cosmology" and "cosmological" to refer to the notion of a supermundane system that regulates the universe. The texts under discussion in this book often refer to the world as subject to *dōri* (principles) that transcend worldly time or existence and are greater even than individual buddhas or *kami* (native deities). In other words, these are texts that reflect a universe that is ultimately subject to law, although specific texts interpret that law (or set of laws) differently. *Dōri* as a term is never defined in the *Mirrors* and is not listed as a compound in the extant dictionary dating from closest to *The Great Mirror*'s inception, the late-Heian *Ruiju myōgishō*. There, the individual characters *dō* and *ri* each can have the meaning of "path" (*michi*) or "law" (*nori*). Given this, I take *dōri* as a coordinate compound consisting of synonymous characters that together suggest the existence of a pattern or logic. See Masamune, *Ruiju myōgishō*, 1:64 on *dō*; 1:620 on *ri*; and 2:13–19 (of the afterword) on the dating. For a brief introduction to this dictionary, see Bailey, "Early Japanese Lexicography," 6.

7. Regarding *The Great Mirror*'s indispensability, however, Sakurai Hironori adds that this was for the information it contained rather than its literary quality ("'Ōkagami' ni hajimaru mono," 51). He later qualifies this assertion, stating that it is unclear how people read the work—that is, piecemeal or in its entirety (ibid., 57). Here and throughout, unless otherwise specified, I use "historiography" in the broad sense of the writing of history.

What Is a Mirror?

The cosmological histories that form the core of this study date from between the mid-Heian (794–1185) and early Muromachi (1336–1573) periods, with most concentrated in the final decades of the Heian period (the 1170s and 1180s) and the Kamakura period (1185–1333). The group consists of seven *Mirrors*—*The Great Mirror*, *Imakagami* (The New Mirror, 1174 or 1175), *Mizukagami* (The Water Mirror, late 1180s or 1190s), *Kara kagami* (The China Mirror, 1250s or 1260s), *Azuma kagami* (The Mirror of the East, 1290s), *Masukagami* (The Clear Mirror, circa 1368–75), and *Shinmeikyō* or *Shinmei kagami* (The Mirror of the Gods, circa 1434). *Nomori no kagami* (The Mirror of the Watchman in the Fields, 1295), though traditionally considered a text of poetic theory, will also be addressed.[8] In most cases framed as transmissions bestowed at temples or shrines, these works reflect a distinctive approach to narrating the past. I base this claim not so much on their more widely acknowledged recurring structural features, but on the existence of four concerns shared by all of the *Mirrors*: authority as derived from a particular site, the relationship between cosmic principles and historical progression, language or script selection as indicative of a given position vis-à-vis institutions, and the significance of ordering the past. These four concerns are the pillars of my analytical apparatus and, in turn, can be understood as products of gradual developments in Japanese historiography—in particular, both a discourse on the three-way relationship between language, history, and creativity, as well as changing uses of the mirror metaphor. A short overview of these developments will clarify some of the impulses that shaped the creation and consumption of the *Mirrors*.

When the first of the *Mirrors*, *The Great Mirror*, appeared roughly around the end of the eleventh century, Japanese historiography was in flux. Throughout the Nara (710–84) and early Heian periods, large-scale historiography had been the purview of the court, which meant it was

8. While I formerly translated *Kara kagami* as "The Mirror of China," I believe "The China Mirror" to be a more accurate rendering, as it reflects the role that China plays in the text as the medium for transmitting a message. In the translation of the title of *Nomori no kagami*, I follow Kimbrough, "*Nomori no kagami* and the Perils."

comprised of an imperial orientation, an "annalistic" format, and composition in *kanbun*.[9] The six "imperially commissioned" histories of the Nara and early Heian courts provided a model of orthodox historiography, and they would continue to operate as a referent in at least some of the eleventh-century discussions of what constituted the writing of history. Despite their status as official court products, however, the last of the six, the *Nihon sandai jitsuroku* (True Record of Three Reigns in Japan), was completed in 901. By the time *The Great Mirror* appeared almost two centuries later, the court had lost its monopoly on historiography.

In the early Heian period, official histories had appeared fairly regularly: the *Nihon kōki* (Subsequent Records of Japan) in 840, *Shoku Nihon kōki* (Continued Subsequent Records of Japan) in 869, and *Nihon Montoku Tennō Jitsuroku* (The True Record of Emperor Montoku of Japan) in 879. Had things proceeded apace, following the *True Record of Three Reigns* from 901, one might have expected another "installment" in the 930s at the latest. However, the 930s brought instead, in the form of two nearly simultaneous rebellions, ominous rumblings from the far reaches of a thinly stretched imperial polity. Off to the east, in distant Hitachi Province, Taira no Masakado (died 940) proclaimed himself emperor in 939 after four years of irregular armed clashes. At almost the same time, Fujiwara no Sumitomo (died 941) staged an insurrection in the west in the area surrounding the Setō Inland Sea. Masakado's "reign" was brought to an end with an arrow in 940, and Sumitomo's uprising likewise ended in failure in 941. Nonetheless, their defeats could not have been an easy or inexpensive matter for a court that lacked a regular conscription army. In the words of *The Great Mirror*, the fact that "Masakado's rebellion

9. This rudimentary summary of the following works, also known as the "six national histories," is based on Sakamoto, *Six National Histories of Japan*, 10–11. However, I follow Endō Keita in using "imperially commissioned" rather than "national" (see, for instance, "Chokusen shisho no seijisei"). This book has an intellectual affinity with Endō's article, which argues that an editorial position can be revealed in the selection and arrangement of the materials that constitute any given national history. In this book, *kanbun* refers to writing produced in Japan but modeled after Classical Chinese. *Wabun* is used to refer to texts primarily written in *hiragana* (a phonetic syllabary) that make use of traditional Japanese vocabulary and grammar.

and so forth occurred were too dreadful for [the Emperor], and he abdicated just like that."[10]

However, it would be simplistic to attribute the cessation of imperially commissioned histories entirely to events such as these. Nor did all court-based record keeping stop along with the official histories. Individual courtier diaries, for instance, and even scrolls such as the *Nenjū gyōji emaki* (Illustrated Scroll of Annual Events, produced in the late Heian period) continued to catalogue the workings and rituals of the Heian court. Thus, one should not interpret the lack of later imperially commissioned histories as indicative of a lack of courtly concern with record keeping. What can be said is that in the aftermath of Masakado's revolt, there is an early attempt—in a language (*kanbun*) and format (chronicle style) reminiscent of the traditional record-keeping practices of the court—at telling history from a nonimperial perspective: the *Shōmonki* (The Masakado Chronicle, written in the mid-tenth century).[11] Or, as David Bialock writes, "*Shōmonki*, in brief, represents what may well have been the first contestation of official history in Japan, appropriating the metaphorical center even as it speaks from a position outside of the court's geographical locus."[12]

If *The Masakado Chronicle* marked one of the earliest signs that the imperial monopoly on historiography was slipping, it nonetheless embodied only one of the approaches that emerged to narrate the past between the latter half of the tenth century and the writing of *The Great Mirror*. Roughly sixty years after the probable composition of *The Masakado Chronicle*, *The Tale of Genji* (circa 1008) famously posited a divide between official and unofficial historiography, suggesting that the true details of history were to be found in the latter—in the *monogatari*, or "tale."[13] In

10. The annotation to *The Great Mirror* specifies that this comment refers to both Masakado's and Sumitomo's revolts (Ishikawa, *Ōkagami*, 311n12). This is the primary edition of *Ōkagami* used in this book. The narrator follows up his comments with the observation that "It was quite strange that he [the Emperor] went that far." For an alternative translation, see Helen McCullough, *Ōkagami*, 221.

11. I follow Judith Rabinovitch for the translation of the title as well as the work's dating. For a short overview of the issues of dating and her conclusion, see *Shōmonki*, 50.

12. Bialock, *Eccentric Spaces*, 183.

13. In this introduction, the terms "tale" (*monogatari*) and "historical tale" (*rekishi monogatari*) appear frequently. "Tale" is a term indigenous to Heian and Kamakura

so doing, it suggested another potential alternative to the "official histories." This conversation, which pits "annals" against "tales" as two contrastive means of accessing the past, is suggestive of the intellectual environment in which *The Great Mirror* appeared.

The conversation that puts forth this claim occurs in the twenty-fifth chapter of *The Tale of Genji*, "Hotaru" (Fireflies). Genji is attempting to woo his adoptive daughter, Tamakazura, whom he has caught reading tales, and a mock debate over their merits ensues. Although Genji initially criticizes tales as "inconsequential" (*suzurogoto*) or "fabrications" (*itsuwari*) and "lacking" (*hakanashigoto*), he then backtracks to offer a more nuanced, if confusing, explanation of tales in contrast to the official histories.[14] After first discussing the nature of the creative license—as exaggerated but not implausible storytelling—that is supposedly characteristic of tales, Genji then rationalizes their content and function as akin to the Buddha's parables and their usage: "'There *are* differences between deep and shallow things, but to simply dismiss it all in one breath as lies would be to miss the point. In the Law, too, which Buddha in his grace set forth, there is something called *upāya*, and the unenlightened inevitably suspect errors in its seeming contradictions. Though there are many such things in the Scriptures, when they are all laid out, they speak to a single purpose. . . . In a nutshell, not a single bit of the entirety is superfluous!' In this way, he talked of tales as particularly essential."[15] Finally, in search of a convenient resolution to the argument, Genji offers the following formulation: "The official *Chronicles* of Japan provide but the outlines. *These* contain the real details!'"[16] That is, the chronicles offer a

---

writing, and using it throughout this book is an effort to be faithful to the primary sources' categories of analysis. In contrast, "historical tale" is an early modern neologism that has fostered a very particular view, both popular and scholarly, of Heian and medieval Japanese writing. The influence this term has had on the field of Japanese literary studies will be discussed below in the introduction, in the section titled "Challenging the Received Narrative." While "tale" will continue to be used in the chapters that follow, "historical tale" will not appear again until the epilogue.

14. In translating *itsuwari* as "fabrications," I follow Yanai et al., *Genji monogatari*, 2:438n9.

15. Yanai et al., *Genji monogatari*, 2:439–40; with reference to Tyler's translation: Murasaki Shikibu and Royall Tyler, *Tale of Genji*, 1:461.

16. Yanai et al., *Genji monogatari*, 2:439; translation (with modifications) from Murasaki Shikibu and Royall Tyler, *Tale of Genji*, 1:461.

government-endorsed, though adumbrated, account, and tales provide the instructive and exhaustive material required to flesh out that account. While this is often read as an endorsement of tales over chronicles, and by implication a contest between recounting the past in the officialese of *kanbun* or the less formal register of *wabun*, such value judgments may not be inherent in the text of the *Genji*. What the exchange clarifies is that both genres—the *kanbun* official histories and the *wabun* tales—can have the same subject matter but treat it in different ways.[17]

While there were certainly tales before the *Genji*, the above scene arguably sets the stage for tale writing as a potentially serious means of interrogating the past on a narrative scale in Heian Japan. At the same time, however, Genji's concern with rationalizing the use of material that was not strictly factual hints at one of the enduring concerns of tale writing in eleventh- and twelfth-century Japan: that it indulged in the sin of "false speech" (*mōgo*) or dissimulation. This tension between the potential for the "real details" and the risk of "fabrication" underlies some of the ensuing responses to Genji's invitation to take tales seriously as a means of historiography.

One of the earliest authors to use tales to provide "the real details" and to take up, as Takeshi Watanabe puts it, "the unprecedented task of writing a history in *kana*" was Akazome Emon (circa 960–circa 1040), author of *Eiga monogatari* (Tale of Flowering Fortunes, written in the early eleventh century).[18] The work, which spans fifteen imperial reigns and recounts the "flowering fortunes" of the Fujiwara clan, is a vast repository of information, despite what may strike some readers as a "lack

17. See Yanai et al., *Genji monogatari*, 2:439nn20 and 21. In an examination of the literary merits of *Tale of Flowering Fortunes*, Yamanaka Yutaka likewise refers to this passage in *The Tale of Genji*. He interprets it as Murasaki Shikibu's attempt to "relativize" the role of official histories and, in so doing, carve out a space for tales as a superior means of discourse (Yamanaka, "Rekishi to bungaku," 7). As Bialock has pointed out, the journal in which Yamanaka's piece appeared, *Kokubungaku: kaishaku to kanshō*, targeted a nonspecialist readership (personal communication, March 2018). Perhaps it is best to think of Yamanaka's comments in this context as offering a typical mainstream narrative for a Japanese audience.

18. Watanabe dates most of the text to circa 1027 ("Buried Mothers," 11). On the characterization of the work, see ibid., 87. For a discussion of earlier scholarship that ties *Flowering Fortunes*' genesis to the *Genji*, see ibid. 129–32.

of internal cohesion or narrative voice."[19] Unlike the vague lines with which the *Genji* opens—"Which reign was it?"—*Flowering Fortunes* specifies at once that its account begins in the reign of Emperor Uda (867–931). It proceeds to relate the content in chronological order through Chōwa 3 (1014), concluding with the safe delivery of a daughter to Empress Kenshi (994–1027).[20] In disambiguating the subject and providing exhaustive detail, *Flowering Fortunes* demonstrates that a "tale" could offer a thorough and presumably factual version of history.

Following close on the heels of *Flowering Fortunes, The Great Mirror* emerged in the latter part of the eleventh century as another attempt at writing an unofficial history. However, where *Flowering Fortunes* reveled in the potential to exhaustively relate "the real details," *The Great Mirror* emphasized the causality that governed events. As Matsumura Hiroji distinguishes them, "It is not necessarily the case that *The Great Mirror*'s description of [Fujiwara no] Michinaga or praise of his glory replicates that of *Tale of Flowering Fortunes*; in the resolve to reveal the *reasons* [my italics] for this florescence, it represents an advance over *Tale of Flowering Fortunes*."[21] I share this view that what sets *The Great Mirror* and its successors apart from a work such as *Flowering Fortunes* is their emphasis on explanation, which promises to render the events of the past as nonrandom. Moreover, unlike *Flowering Fortunes*, each of the *Mirrors* takes pains to establish at the outset the facticity of its contents as well, albeit through different means: narrative or not, nearly every *Mirror* seems to seek to evade the potential charge of sinful "falsification," the very problem that was dogging Murasaki Shikibu and *The Tale of Genji* just as the second *Mirror* appeared (a topic to be returned to in chapter 1). In other words, *Flowering Fortunes* and *The Great Mirror* are two very different endeavors at ordering the past. While *Flowering Fortunes* relates the past as a "tale," *The Great Mirror* complicates the two-way conversation that the *Genji* proposed by offering yet a third angle from which to narrate history: that of the *Mirror*.

19. Yamanaka, "Rekishi to bungaku," 16. Watanabe's dissertation offers a much more charitable reading of the work.

20. This discussion of the content of *Flowering Fortunes* is based on William McCullough and Helen McCullough, *Tale of Flowering Fortunes*, vol. 1.

21. Matsumura Hiroji, *Ōkagami*, 20.

That the "tale" continued as a productive mode of writing goes without saying. What is less frequently acknowledged is that *The Great Mirror* and its approach likewise spawned some half-dozen successors over the next three hundred years. Furthermore, the commitment to both a cosmological explanation and "true" content are not the only features that differentiate *The Great Mirror* and its successors from other works—including *Flowering Fortunes*—that take the past as their subject. Five of the seven historiographic *Mirrors* include prefaces set up along lines nearly identical to those of the preface of *The Great Mirror* (introduced in detail in chapter 1). Two of the *Mirrors* feature narrators who claim explicit ties to the narrator of *The Great Mirror*. All eight of the *Mirrors*, including *Watchman*, engage with the metaphor of the mirror as a means for understanding events and/or draw specific connections with earlier *Mirrors*.[22] In other words, not only do these texts share the four more abstract concerns I outlined at the beginning of the introduction, but they also do so via a multilayered intertextual web that further supports thinking of the *Mirrors* as a separate genre. Through such intertextual links and in their commitment to demonstrating past events as governed by cosmological principles, the *Mirrors* as intellectual projects suggest a fundamentally different priority than that of merely supplying the "details" that were elided from official histories.[23]

The eleventh-century "tales versus chronicles" conversation was not the only impulse that likely helped shape the project of writing history as a *Mirror*. The more general idea that a text could be a tool for reflection, correction, or general edification was not new in eleventh-century Japan. As Yamada Naoko has pointed out, Japanese were already well aware of continental modes of reading in which "history [was] presented in terms of knowledge, models, and admonitions as a 'mirror' to reflect actual society."[24] Not that the Japanese *Mirrors* were simply copies of Chinese

22. Yamada Naoko makes a similar point with regard to *The Great Mirror* and *The China Mirror* (*Chūgoku koji juyō ronkō*, 108).

23. One example of how successful efforts to establish *Mirrors* as credible authoritative texts can be seen in Yotsutsuji Yoshinari's influential *Kakaishō* commentary on the *Genji*. While Yoshinari draws on a dazzling variety of texts for the actual commentary, *The Water Mirror* is one of the few works cited by name in his general introduction to the work (Yotsutsuji, *Kakaishō*, 1 and 3).

24. Yamada, "'Kara kagami'-kō," 30.

textual conventions. Instead, they exhibited a synthesis of ideas from continental traditions and domestic writings. This suggests an ideal approach to construction not unlike that behind a famous flute described in *The New Mirror*: "The flute called Pipes' Passel was made by selecting for outstanding sound from among Chinese and Japanese bamboo."[25] Like the flute's makers, the *Mirror* writers were drawing on what they presumably found to be the best in both traditions, rather than using the either/or model suggested by the conversation in *The Tale of Genji*. To better understand how, in this respect as well, the *Mirrors* stand outside of a tales-chronicles binary, this introduction next looks briefly at how the mirror metaphor had been used in both China and Japan before the emergence of the Japanese historiographic *Mirror* as a particular type of writing.

Endymion Wilkinson traces this image in China back to the *Shijing* (Classic of Poetry), but the mirror used as a revelatory tool can also be found in the *Huainanzi*, which attracted an elite readership from the early days of the Japanese imperial court through at least the thirteenth century.[26] Invoking the mirror metaphor in a way that resonates with the models to which Yamada points, the *Huainanzi* enjoins the reader to "embrace the mindset of a great sage, using it as a mirror to illuminate the sentiments of the myriad things."[27] In a still more influential work for the

25. Takehana, *Imakagami*, 3:136. This is the edition of *Imakagami* used throughout this book.

26. On the first point, see Wilkinson, *Chinese History*, 604. For attestation of the *Huainanzi* in "Nara or Heian Japan," see Carpenter, "Chinese Calligraphic Models," 164. The continued relevance of the work in Japan is evidenced by Prince Shukaku's idiosyncratic rendering of a passage in his 1193 *Uki* (*Yūki*), 673. It also makes an appearance in the *Okanoya kanpakuki*, where it is among the texts cited by the father of the author of *The China Mirror* to support a proposed reign name in a 1249 debate (Konoe, *Okanoya kanpakuki*, 171).

27. On the second point, see Liu An, *Huainanzi*, 11.16. What we do not see in the early record, however, is any record of Sima Guang's 984 *Zizhi tongjian* (A Comprehensive Mirror for Assisting Governance). Terada Takanobu notes a Korean attempt to acquire this text as early as 1099. He points out that in the case of Japan, however, beyond the fact that it must predate a nineteenth-century printing, the date of its transmission is "unclear" ("Shijin no shiteki kyōyō ni tsuite," 8). More recently, Ri Yuri's work on the fifteenth-century Korean *Tongguk t'onggam* (Comprehensive Mirror of the Eastern Land) implies the following model of influence: *Zizhi tongjian* inspires *Tongguk t'onggam*, and the latter operates as a key source for *Honchō tsugan* ("Chōsenbon

male Japanese elite, in the early eighth-century *Zhenguan zhengyao* (Fundamentals of Governance from the Zhenguan era [626–49]), Emperor Taizong (598–649) of the Tang (618–907) is quoted as "using the past as a mirror" to "comprehend changing fortunes."[28] In Taizong's observations, in particular, the metaphorical mirror does more than reflect what is in front of it; it also reveals the logic behind the vicissitudes of the past. As even this brief nod to China shows, Chinese texts that relied on the metaphor of the mirror as instructional were indisputably a part of the intellectual landscape of elite male writers in medieval Japan.

However, the historiographic Japanese *Mirrors* that began to emerge in the late eleventh century were not drawing only on continental inspiration. In Japan, there were also domestically authored precedents for a text designated more broadly as a *Mirror* to have an explanatory function. This is visible, for instance, in Kūkai's (774–835) highly technical ninth-century work on Chinese poetry, *Bunkyō hifuron* (Disquisition, Comprising a Mirror of Writing and a Thesaurus of Rare Expressions, written in 819 or 820).[29] While Kūkai's *Disquisition* is not a narrative work, the "Mirror of Writing" it contains is intended to provide guidance. The *Disquisition* also features a short preface in which Kūkai clarifies the ultimately cosmic origins of literature and provides a brief personal account of how he came to transmit the following text.[30] Both the recourse to a supermundane framework for the material to follow and the personalized explanation of the author figure's motivations are features of the *Mirrors* that come into being roughly two hundred years after Kūkai's composition.

In *The Great Mirror* and the premodern historiographic *Mirrors* that followed it, elements from both the continent's and the archipelago's

'Tōkoku tsugan,'" 97). To my knowledge, there is as yet no direct evidence of the presence of Sima Guang's work in medieval Japan.

28. Wu Jing, *Zhenguan zhengyao*, 2.33.

29. Yamada Naoko also proposes awareness of Bai Juyi's (772–846) "The Hundredfold Mirror" (*Bailian jing*) poem (*Chūgoku koji juyō ronkō*, 108). Bai's poem tells of the presentation of a mirror engraved with Taizong's words to a ruler to guide his governance. For a complete text of the poem and explanatory commentary, see Okamura, *Hakushi monjū*, 1:661–64. The translation of the title *Bunkyō hifuron* is modified from Bodeman, "Poetics and Prosody," 168. My characterizations of the work also derive from Bodeman.

30. This discussion of the preface is based on Bodeman's translation (Poetics and Prosody," 162–69).

earlier *Mirrors* are visible.[31] *The Great Mirror* and its successors all subscribe to the mirror metaphor most clearly articulated by Taizong: the mirror as a medium for revealing a deeper logic for events. However, there are also echoes of Kūkai's implied linkage of the metaphor's explanatory function to Buddhist elements as well as his emphasis in the preface of the *Disquisition* on cosmic "patterns" (Japanese, *mon*; Chinese, *wen*). The legacies of both traditions play out in the *Mirrors* as "cosmological histories": a group of texts that, rather than simply importing and adapting continental models and discourses wholesale, draws on and reconfigures multiple traditions to create a distinctive collective site in which medieval ideas of cosmology, historiography, and authority intersect.

To summarize, Japan's *Mirrors* appeared in a world in which some people, at least, were questioning the nature of historiography. The fictional conversation in the *Genji* together with the appearance of *The Masakado Chronicle*, *Tale of Flowering Fortunes*, and *The Great Mirror* suggest an interest in articulating the past in new forms and languages, as well as from new perspectives, in the tenth and eleventh centuries. In the *Mirrors*, the forms that the answers to these questions take exhibit an ongoing negotiation between changing ideas of what constituted authoritative places, interpretive strategies, languages, and even narrative techniques for ordering the past in the late twelfth through the mid-fifteenth centuries, an age of unprecedented social and governmental change.

Challenging the Received Narrative

Arguing that the *Mirrors* deserve a central place in our understanding of medieval Japan challenges traditional binary narratives of Japanese historiographic and literary development. From the Meiji period (1868–1912) onward, Japanese historiography and writing more generally have been framed in terms of a shift from continental to indigenous models. In the case of historiography, this understanding presupposes, in its most basic

31. Many scholars have also pointed out the influence of the *Shiji* (Records of the Grand Historian) in the early *Mirrors*' use of the *kidentai* format: a combination of basic imperial annals, biographies, treatises, and charts. See, for instance, Matsumoto, "Rekishi monogatari to shiron," 26.

form, changes in format from annals to an anachronistically posited "historical tales" (*rekishi monogatari*) genre, the composition in Classical Chinese (or *kanbun*) giving way to texts in Classical Japanese (or *wabun*), and a gradual reorientation in subject matter away from the imperial court to the "rise of the warrior."[32] As Michael Brownstein has demonstrated, this narrative was a product of late nineteenth-century concerns surrounding the development of a "national literature" and was highly influenced by Western ideas about literary development as indicative of social evolution.[33]

In this version of Japanese literary history, the waning days of the Heian period were the age of a set of texts that are now known as "historical tales." Although Watanabe dates the term to the eighteenth century, I suspect that its use by the prominent nativist intellectual Haga Yaichi (1867–1927) has had the most influence on twentieth-century scholarship.[34] Haga's position is best understood in light of Susan Burns's work, which has demonstrated how Haga's ideas of a "new *kokugaku*" (or new nativism) were inseparable from his commitment to nationalism.[35] Burns's discussion of Haga's turn-of-the-century rhetoric of "pure Japanese thought" offers a helpful context for understanding the definition of "historical tale" preserved in his collected works.[36] There, he offers a formulation that revolves around domestic Japanese production and language selection: the "historical tales" are Japanese-language "tales of the past that originated in the Heian period."[37] Haga cites a double wellspring for

32. Haruo Shirane observed that "it was not until the establishment of *kokubungaku* (national literature studies) in the mid-Meiji period that Japanese literature was conceived largely, though not entirely, as kana-based literature" ("Introduction: Issues in Canon Formation," 5).

33. On likely influences, see Brownstein, "From Kokugaku to Kokubungaku," 439–40. For how this plays out in Mikami Sanji and Takatsu Kuwasaburō's 1890 *Nihon bungakushi*, see ibid., 447–52, especially 450–52.

34. On the earliest use, see Watanabe, "Buried Mothers," 107. Watanabe dates the modern iteration of the term to 1905 (ibid., 118). For a more thorough recapitulation of the emergence of the "historical tale" category with a special emphasis on *Flowering Fortunes*, see ibid., 107–39.

35. Burns, *Before the Nation*, 199–202.

36. Quoted in Burns, *Before the Nation*, 200.

37. Quoted in Fukuda, "Rekishi monogatari no han'i to keiretsu (jō)," 25. For the original, see Haga, "Rekishi monogatari to sono genryū," 293.

the genre: *Tale of Flowering Fortunes* and *The Great Mirror*.[38] By making allowances for additional Heian *Mirrors* and a handful of later compositions, Haga essentially creates a set of "historical tales" defined by supposed Heian origins. He then argues that their worth is in how they "relate history in the National Language in contrast to histories in Classical Chinese."[39] While this emphasis on the Heian origins and use of *wabun* are critical to his position, it is a move that obscures the very real differences between *Flowering Fortunes* and *The Great Mirror*, the two allegedly founding works of the "historical tales" genre.

Although Haga's formulation may have represented an extreme, in the version of Japanese literary history that he and similar thinkers helped create, once the age of court-centered Heian tales has passed, Japan arrives at the age of the so-called *gunki monogatari* (war tale), also a recently posited category that in turn, has come to occupy pride of place within medieval literary prose studies. This narrative of literary and stylistic development requires a commitment to progress through a succession of genres from court-centered narratives to war tales, which has implications for why the Kamakura *Mirrors* and the Muromachi-period *Mirror of the Gods* have been largely elided from any discussion of *Mirror* writing. Instead, the focus has often been on the idea of the rise of the warrior and warrior literature. The idea of the war tale's genesis has been neatly tied to the tenth-century *Masakado Chronicle* (mentioned above), the work that recounts Masakado's rebellion, with that unsuccessful uprising having been characterized as "the advent of an era: the coming of age of the order of professional fighting men in the capital and countryside that we know as the *bushi* or *samurai*."[40] The most famous "war tale," *Heike*

38. This discussion of Haga and the historical tale is based on Fukuda, "Rekishi monogatari no han'i to keiretsu (jō)" and "Rekishi monogatari no han'i to keiretsu (ge)." Fukuda is arguing for a broader category of "historical tale." Watanabe points out that Haga did not believe *Flowering Fortunes* to be the work of Akazome Emon ("Buried Mothers," 98–101).

39. Quoted in Fukuda, "Rekishi monogatari no han'i to keiretsu (jō)," 26. For the original, see Haga, "Rekishi monogatari to sono genryū," 293.

40. Rabinovitch observes, "*Shōmonki* is regarded as the earliest work in the influential and popular genre of *gunkimono*, or war tales, which reached their literary maturity in the fourteenth century" (*Shōmonki*, 5–6). For a short overview of the issues of dating and Rabinovitch's conclusion, see ibid., 50. I use *gunki monogatari* (rather than

monogatari (The Tale of the Heike), has even been translated into English multiple times and is the subject of much scholarly work.[41] The appeal and value of thinking about the war tale as a new way of conceptualizing and legitimating the experience of war is undeniable. But the identification of medieval narrative prose with "war tales" has resulted in the relative neglect of full-length narrative texts (such as those that make up the *Mirror* genre) that undermine the court-to-warrior trajectory.

Under this traditional schema, Japan's historiographic *Mirrors* fall into two categories, rather than the single genre this book proposes. The Heian *Mirrors* and the neoclassical *Clear Mirror* belong to the "historical tale."[42] The late-Kamakura-period warrior-centered *Mirror of the East* could be categorized as a "war tale," although it has more traditionally been set aside by scholars of literature and literary history as a historical work. And both the mid-Kamakura China-focused *China Mirror* and Muromachi-period *Mirror of the Gods* slip between the cracks.

Today, much of the field of Japanese studies recognizes the assumptions underlying this taxonomy as outmoded. Nevertheless, they continue to shape the way in which certain texts are read or not read, as can be seen in how the *Mirrors* are regarded or dismissed.[43] In scholarship of the mid- to late twentieth century, in both Japanese and Western languages, the primary result has been that those historiographic *Mirrors* that hew to standards similar to Haga's are the *Mirrors* that have been studied.[44]

---

gunkimono) as the Japanese term most commonly used today to refer to the texts at issue. For the description of the "era," see Friday, *The First Samurai*, 10–11.

41. On the anachronistic appreciation of the *Heike* and the rise of "war literature" more broadly, see Bialock, "Nation and Epic."

42. Indeed, Haga says as much (see Fukuda, "Rekishi monogatari no han'i to keiretsu [jō]," 25–26.) For an early example of scholarship that also groups the *Mirrors* along these lines, see Onoue, "Kaidai."

43. As Komine Kazuaki has pointed out to me (personal communication, August 2012), even the newer 1997 *Rekishi monogatari kōza* (Short Studies on Historical Tales) series replicates this category. The first volume is an introduction, and the final one is on "The Age and Culture." The other five volumes are ordered chronologically, with one per each of the following: *Tale of Flowering Fortunes*, *The Great Mirror*, *The New Mirror*, *The Water Mirror*, and *The Clear Mirror*. This is not atypical for the major Japanese series of classical literature.

44. See, for instance, Atsuta, "Rekishi toshite no kagamimono." While engaging with the idea of a "traditional Japanese historical consciousness" in this study, Atsuta discusses the problems with the "tales or history" categorization with regards to the

In other words, most work on the *Mirrors* to date treats them as historical tales, which has meant that with few exceptions, only *Mirrors* that are in Classical Japanese, about the court, and from (or reminiscent of) the Heian period have received serious attention by scholars of literature.[45] In Japanese-language literary studies, this has resulted in a more robust critical apparatus for those *Mirrors* that have been viewed as "historical tales": in addition to *The Great Mirror* and *The Clear Mirror*, both *The New Mirror* and *The Water Mirror* have annotated editions and modern Japanese translations. Moreover, each of these works has been the subject of literally hundreds of articles in Japanese.[46] Yet even now, the terms of the conversation are often implicitly inherited from these earlier conceptualizations of Japan's literary history. For instance, Kanō Shigefumi criticizes Haga's definition of the historical tales genre, but the analysis

---

Heian *Mirrors* (and *The Clear Mirror*), resolving to adopt "the perspective of Japanese historiography" and treat the works as the narrative successors to the *Six Imperial Histories* ("Rekishi toshite no kagamimono," 301). Fukunaga Susumu's more recent study comparing the *Mirrors* with *setsuwa* is primarily focused on *The Great Mirror*. On the *Mirrors* as a group, he suggests that other than a shared debt to *The Great Mirror* as generic progenitor, conventions common to the works' prefaces, and the possible significance of their shared title designation, the other three *Mirrors* (*New*, *Water*, and *Clear*) have very little of substance in common ("Kagamimono to setsuwa," 89).

45. Fukuda does note scholars who are exceptions to this trend and are willing to broaden the scope of the "historical tale" to include, among other works, *The China Mirror* ("Rekishi monogatari no han'i to keiretsu [jō]," 26). In a later study, he reenvisions the "historical tale" category as one defined in part by a focus on imperial succession, which permits him to include *Mirror of the Gods*, among other works ("Rekishi monogatari no katarite settei," 2). Perhaps the closest thing to an actual break from this, however, is Kawakita Noboru's earlier contention that the *Mirrors* constitute a distinct subset of historical tales. His discussion is limited to traditional *Mirrors* and does not include an analysis of what *Mirrors* as a subgenre might signify ("Rekishi monogatari no seiritsu to tokushoku").

46. Of course, that does not include books or chapters in edited volumes. In an example of a text with a relatively late "arrival," a search on December 20, 2017, of the National Institute of Japanese Literature's database for *The Water Mirror* yielded 192 articles, 78 of which were from 2000 or later. Even allowing for some false positives due to works with similar names, this suggests that scholarship on *The Water Mirror* is taking off. Komine earlier lamented the paucity of research on *The Water Mirror*, attributing it to the "low estimation in which it is held because of its dearth of literary interest" ("Chūsei no rekishi jojutsu," 162).

relies on canonical works.[47] Although Fukuda Akimichi has suggested an expanded notion of *Mirrors* that would accommodate some of the Kamakura texts as well, it still remains to interrogate the validity of the "historical tale" genre and the basic historiographical story in which Classical Chinese annals are replaced by vernacular Japanese tales. As a result, the Kamakura-era *Mirrors* have fared much worse on the whole, enjoying markedly less attention in literary studies circles. *The China Mirror* has neither an annotated edition nor a modern Japanese translation.[48] *The Mirror of the East* did not see Classical Japanese renderings (*kakikudashi*) or modern Japanese translations until the twenty-first century; historians have typically read the *kanbun* original. Scholarship on *The Mirror of the Gods*, the fifteenth-century *Mirror* reminiscent of *The Mirror of the East*, is almost nonexistent.

The same trends hold true for Anglophone scholarship, where—increasing numbers of investigations that cross languages, genres, and/or disciplinary boundaries notwithstanding—the field of literary studies has historically tended toward the conservative. This is in all likelihood the legacy of the same ideas about a literary canon worthy of study that informed the thinking of Haga and his peers. In the case of the *Mirrors*, *The Great Mirror* and *The Clear Mirror* boast complete English translations, but neither has been the subject of much secondary scholarship beyond that.[49] Excerpts of *The New Mirror* have been translated, but as with *The Great Mirror* and *The Clear Mirror*, engagement with the work remains largely at the level of the individual episode. While Anglophone scholars have mined *The Mirror of the East* successfully and repeatedly for information, and there are at least two English translations of excerpts from the text, the only book-length study in English that is entirely devoted to it is Minoru Shinoda's 1960 critical introduction and partial translation. The other *Mirrors* exist primarily in brief excerpts or not at

47. Kanō, "Rekishi monogatari no seikaku."

48. *Watchman*, too, lacks a modern Japanese translation.

49. One exception to the lack of English-language mention of the Heian *Mirrors* (and *The Clear Mirror*) is Brownlee, *Political Thought in Japanese Historical Writing*. Because that work offers only abbreviated treatments of the individual *Mirrors* and preserves the precise frameworks this study seeks to destabilize, it is left to curious readers to explore his analysis further.

all. In summary, a good portion of the *Mirrors* is largely unknown outside of Japan, and none of the *Mirrors*—Heian or Kamakura—has been treated in toto as the primary subject of an English-language monograph that moves beyond translation.

An uninformed reader whose ideas of Japanese literature rested on secondary scholarship (or translations) could easily mistake *Mirror* production as a primarily Heian phenomenon. However, despite what the lines drawn by mid-twentieth-century scholarship might suggest, historiographic *Mirrors* continued to be produced in the Kamakura period and beyond. Most of these *Mirrors* simply do not fit early twentieth-century standards of what a historical tale ought to be, nor do they align with the implicit vision of a thinker such as Haga, for whom their Heian-period production was definitive.

In place of vernacular Japanese tales about court life, the Kamakura-era *Mirrors* feature linguistic variation and new subject matter. More radical still is the fact that both court- and *bakufu*-based writers generated them. It is the Kamakura period that gave rise to *The China Mirror*, believed to have been written in Kamakura and set well outside the capital, as well as the voluminous account of the *bakufu*'s founding and development, *The Mirror of the East*. In the Kamakura period, *Mirrors* were shown, in short, to be a tool for ordering the past that appealed to both court- and *bakufu*-based writers. As will be demonstrated below, they were also likely read by courtier and warrior elites. Both of these discoveries trouble the simple distinctions between courtier and warrior culture, and court- and warrior-centered histories.

Given the potential misdirection that the category of "historical tales" invites, I propose to set it aside entirely and make an effort to address the *Mirrors* on their own terms—that is, as a group of texts that, despite linguistic and structural variation or retroactively posited disciplinary distinctions, engage broadly with common themes and, more specifically, intertextually with each other. This approach takes advantage of and builds on recent trends in Japanese studies, especially the ongoing reassessment of the place of Classical Chinese or *kanbun* and China itself in Japanese writing, the interrogation of the nature of writing and its relationship to reading and/or visual impact, and the emerging willingness to challenge the history-literature binary that has long informed ideas of which sources are appropriate for which fields.[50] I am also motivated by newer scholarship in Japan that pays serious attention to the ways in which historical writing in general is constructed and offers myriad examples of how factually derived materials, imagery, and rhetoric could all be manipulated in the medieval context to adhere to or advance particular agendas or perspectives.[51]

Although there is no perfect recovery of a twelfth- or thirteenth-century mode of reading or reception, doing away with retroactively posited genres of "historical" or "war" tales or ideas of language as the decisive factor in determining whether a work belongs to a particular category of analysis allows an approach to the *Mirrors* that is closer to taking them on their own terms. This enables an understanding of medieval historiographic writing that is not just about chronicles versus tales, court versus warrior, or even Japan versus China. It instead uncovers an alternative version of the historiographic landscape, one in which cosmological histories form a powerful third option for early medieval writers attempting to order the world around them.

Japan's (Mostly) Heian and Kamakura Mirrors *as a Genre*

Treating the *Mirrors* that are the focus of this book as their own genre enables the assemblage of texts not traditionally grouped together, revealing patterns suggesting that medieval categories of thought transcended the linguistic or disciplinary divides that often shape scholarship today. Once again, in chronological order, these works, which were produced during a period that corresponds roughly to the life span of Japan's first

50. In thinking through these questions, my work has particularly been inspired by the scholarship of David Lurie, Chino Kaori, Ivo Smits, Thomas LaMarre, David Bialock, and Elizabeth Oyler. I defer further discussion of these authors' particular works until the relevant portions of this book.

51. One work that has been instructive in this regard is Saeki Shin'ichi, ed., *Chūsei no gunki monogatari to rekishi jojutsu*. Sakurai Yoshirō is another scholar who effectively engages with Western theorists in his investigation of medieval writing (*Chūsei Nihon no shinwa to rekishi jojutsu*).

shogunate, are *The Great Mirror*, *The New Mirror*, *The Water Mirror*, *The China Mirror*, *The Mirror of the East*, *The Mirror of the Watchman in the Fields*, *The Clear Mirror*, and *The Mirror of the Gods*.[52] To readers familiar with the texts in question, this might seem at first a strange assortment—especially the inclusion of *The Mirror of the East*—with little to justify the grouping beyond the fact that each work has *Mirror* in the title.[53] Yet while scholars have frequently pointed to early discrepancies in the names of *The Great Mirror* and *The New Mirror*, and the diversity of texts upon which *The Mirror of the East* draws, the fact remains that all of these texts came to be read as *Mirrors* in the time period under discussion in this book.[54] To me, this suggests a common mode of reading. To refer once again to Yamada Naoko's characterization of continental precedents for reading *Mirrors* as works that show "history presented in terms of knowledge, models, and admonitions as a 'mirror' to reflect actual society,"[55] I would suggest that all of the historiographic *Mirrors* listed above, and even *Watchman*, lend themselves to this type of consumption.

Related to the notion of how the *Mirrors*, as cosmological histories, are read, one can also say that each lends itself to a reading as a "historical narrative," to borrow a turn of phrase from Paul Ricoeur's discussion of the "historian's presentation." ("Historical narrative" is not to be confused with the problematic genre of "historical tales.") As Ricoeur explains, a "historical narrative" is a work through which "the reader

52. For an early exploration of the *Mirrors* as *Great*, *New*, *Water*, and *Clear*, see Onoue, "Kaidai." See also Atsuta, "Rekishi toshite no kagamimono."

53. Komine is one of the few scholars to contend that *The Mirror of the East* deserves inclusion in such an inquiry, claiming that it is indispensable to any discussion of "medieval narrating of history . . . not as a historical source from the Kamakura *bakufu*, but rather as a text that narrativizes history through and through" as part of a larger argument for a more catholic treatment of historical tales ("Chūsei no rekishi jojutsu," 163). Fukuda, too, has acknowledged that *The Mirror of the East* shares features with the works he designates as historical tales ("Rekishi monogatari no han'i to keiretsu [jō]," 29), and recent Japanese work has begun to treat it precisely in this way.

54. On *The Mirror of the East*, a *Mirror* of relatively late provenance, Gomi Fumihiko points out that the title is already in existence by the fourteenth century (*Shomotsu no chūseishi*, 463).

55. Yamada, "'Kara kagami'-kō," 30.

expects . . . to reenter a world of events that actually occurred."[56] To return to medieval Japan, certainly this minimal criterion is met by the *Mirrors*. Through a combination of rhetorical devices—from claims to offer eyewitness testimony to textual citation and even the co-optation of the structural and linguistic patterns of official historiography—the *Mirrors* insist on their veracity. Yet it is not simply a question of true contents that shapes Ricoeur's ideas of the "historical narrative": there is also a prescribed mode of reading. As he elaborates, "What is more, in crossing the threshold of what is written, he [the reader] stays on guard, casts a critical eye, and demands if not a true discourse . . . at least a plausible one, one that is admissible, probable, and in any case honest and truthful."[57] If one thinks back to the discussion of Genji's ideas about what "tales" are supposed to offer—namely, plausible, detailed accounts—and considers his position as representative of at least some elite Heian thinkers, the *Mirrors* can be seen as subscribing to a relationship between the reader and the text such as the one Ricoeur describes. Bringing together all of the historiographic *Mirrors* then seems the next logical step in thinking about Heian and Kamakura historiography.

Reading the *Mirrors* as a genre is about more than shared title conventions and modes of reading, or about advocating for the collective recognition of the texts as a type of cosmological historiography. It is about identifying the tools that this group of texts uses to validate perspectives on and interpretations of the past, and then clarifying how the use of these tools develops over time. To do this, rather than focusing on a specific form or language as determinative of genre (as traditional scholarship on Japanese literature and historiography has tended to do), I delineate the *Mirror* genre along the four shared narrative preoccupations noted earlier: place, principle, language, and the relationship between ordering the past and narrative structure. Approached using this fourfold analytical apparatus, the *Mirrors* reveal how medieval thinkers navigated across and between these categories, the boundaries of which are now often taken for granted and seen as inviolable, rather than working within their constraints in the service of a singular perspective.

56. Ricoeur, *Memory, History, Forgetting*, 261.
57. Ricoeur, *Memory, History, Forgetting*, 261.

This book traces the four paths created by the abovementioned intertwined concerns across five chapters and an epilogue. The first path follows the imagined geography of the settings for the *Mirrors* to reveal an intimate connection between ideas of place and authority. Japanese scholars have long acknowledged that the setting plays an important role in the Heian *Mirrors*. Writing on *The Great Mirror* in 1990, Mori Masato emphasizes the importance of its narrative site by first bringing up the "tale's setting" in his introduction to *The Great Mirror* and then suggesting the following inversion as more appropriate given the significance of place: thinking of it as a "setting tale." He further points out the immense influence that this idea of setting has had on both later *Mirrors* and literature more broadly.[58]

When read across multiple *Mirrors*, an emphasis on setting sheds light on what types of sites or institutions are used to metaphorically ground the narrative (see fig. I.2). Moving from the earliest *Mirror*, set at Urin'in Temple, the narrative settings gradually spiral out from the capital, Kyoto, in an apparent parallel to the destabilization of court authority and the emergence of a major nonimperial center of power in the East. Completing the journey, the penultimate *Mirror* once again unfolds at a temple in the capital, just as the *bakufu* itself has relocated there. This is not merely a matter of geographical variation; the temples and shrines at which the *Mirrors* and their imitators unfold represent the interests of different agents. The correlations between a given *Mirror*'s narrative perspective and the changing configurations of real-world powers invite the reader to think about both physical and institutionally imagined geographies and their significance to medieval ideas of authority as grounded in "place."

The second path addresses the development of the cosmological principles that govern historical trajectories. Although *dōri* (principle) is now most famously associated with the monk Jien's treatise *Gukanshō* (My Humble Thoughts, circa 1219), Ishikawa Tōru has located a concept of history shaped by principles already present in *The Great Mirror* and even casts this earlier work as a *dōri monogatari* (principle tale).[59] Other scholars,

58. Mori, "Ōkagami ni okeru 'monogatari no ba,'" 15.

59. Ishikawa, *Ōkagami*, 386. I borrow the translation of the title of the *Gukanshō* from Bialock.

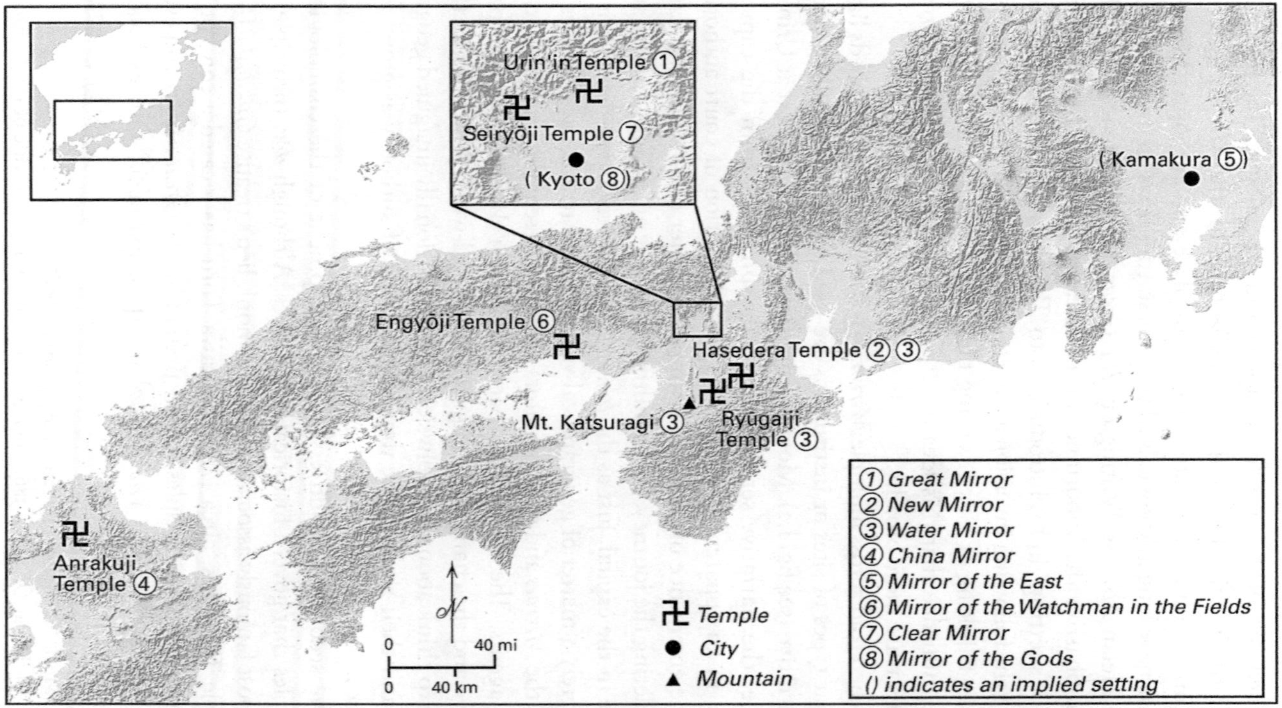

FIGURE I.2. Map of the settings for the *Mirrors*. Map by C. Scott Walker, Harvard Map Collection.

while not going so far as to explicitly identify a "principle" in *The Great Mirror*, have nonetheless insisted on a worldview in it that subscribes to a greater logic.[60]

The earliest *Mirrors* advocate a notion of history as driven by karmic causation. This is not a new notion in eleventh-century Japan, and how it works is accessibly explained by the monk Kyōkai (or Keikai, dates unknown) in Japan's oldest surviving collection of Buddhist *setsuwa* (exhortative tales), the *Nihon ryōiki* (Record of Miraculous Events of Japan, circa 822): "That which withers not is the seed of evil. That which is invisible is the root of good. Yet the speed with which recompense for evil comes is like water reflecting as a mirror: once you look into it, the reflection appears. The swiftness with which the reward for good arrives is like a valley echoing a call. Once you yell out, there is inevitably a response. Retribution in this age is exactly like this."[61] To paraphrase Kyōkai, historical events are a case of reaping what one sows. While evil may temporarily lie hidden, it will invariably result in payback. One may not see or understand the origins of favorable karmic recompense, but they necessarily exist, because karma governs all events. And much like Kyōkai's work, the early *Mirrors* seem to be primarily concerned with demonstrating that there is indeed an underlying cause-and-effect logic to the progression of the events they recount.

However, with the increasingly serious unrest that eventually culminates in the Genpei War, the *Mirror* narrators become ever more preoccupied with the question of the specific fate of the world. And the histories they relate grow to articulate more clearly—if not consistently—the implications of living in the final age of the dharma, the last stage in "a three part system . . . that was to become the most influential historical frame of reference in the Buddhist schools of China, Korea, and Japan."[62] Jan

60. From a slightly different angle, Fukunaga concludes that the typologization of anecdotes in *The Great Mirror* engages in the larger task of explaining Michinaga and his genealogy ("Kagamimono to setsuwa," 89).

61. Nakada, *Nihon ryōiki*, 258. For an alternative translation by Burton Watson, see Kyōkai, *Record of Miraculous Events in Japan*, 132. Because the connection between the ideas expressed in the first two sentences of my translation and the rest of the passage strikes me as awkward, I should mention that Watson's translation renders Kyōkai's similes as being about inevitability. However, from a strictly lexical or grammatical perspective, the original text is about the speed with which actions are repaid.

62. Nattier, *Once Upon a Future Time*, 65.

Nattier's general definitions of the three stages and their progress clarify what this might have meant for Heian and Kamakura audiences:

- a period of the "True Dharma" (Ch. *zheng fa*/Jpn. *shōbō*, corresponding to Skt. *saddharma*) immediately following the death of the Buddha, during which it is possible to attain enlightenment by practicing the Buddha's teachings;
- a period of the "Semblance Dharma" (Ch. *xiang fa*/Jpn. *zōbō*, a term patterned on but not identical to Skt. *saddharma-pratirūpaka*), during which a few may still be able to reach the goal of enlightenment, but most Buddhists simply carry out the external forms of the religion; and
- a period of the "Final Dharma" (Ch. *mo fa*/Jpn. *mappō*, a term for which no proper Sanskrit equivalent exists), during which traditional religious practice loses its effectiveness and the spiritual capacity of human beings reaches an all-time low.[63]

In particular for *The Water Mirror*, composed in the aftermath of the civil war, the fate of the world is articulated explicitly in terms of what it meant to exist within the "final age" (*mappō*). *The Water Mirror* attests to the ways in which this age of decline was something many understood not only as an abstraction, but as a condition that produced real-world manifestations in the form of social disorder.

This discourse gives way, however, once the *Mirrors* are positioned far beyond the capital to a more flexible discourse about historical events as subject to the forces of the buddhas and *kami*. The principle of the existence of a cosmic rationale remains, but the specific form that it grants to historical trajectories once again recedes from view. This suggests a gradual move away from a historiography driven chiefly by a concern with the decline of the dharma or the end of the world and toward a model in which otherworldly "divine" forces are still powerful. But rather than an

63. Nattier, *Once Upon a Future Time*, 65–66. For simplicity's sake, I have omitted two of Nattier's footnotes to these definitions that address Sanskrit terminology. I have also updated the romanization of the Chinese terms to reflect pinyin conventions. Readers interested in the emergence of *mappō* as a distinct term and its original relation to *masse* are referred to ibid., 101–3. In the *Mirrors*, these terms appear to be used interchangeably to refer to the "final age."

unmalleable cosmic law that determines the course of history, these forces can be manipulated or recruited to further one's cause.

The third path concerns language selection. Many scholars have called attention to the use of the vernacular in the early *Mirrors* and the importance of the eyewitness. However, once the *Mirror* group has been expanded beyond those traditionally seen as "historical tales," the potential meanings behind the ways that *kanbun* becomes increasingly prominent in *Mirror* writing over time must be taken into consideration. In this expanded set of *Mirrors*, the languages used range from *wabun* to linguistic hybrids to *kanbun*, with each choice of register enabling a different type of authoritative voice. These changes can be read as reflecting the different types of authority the respective *Mirrors* invoke, in which the appeal to the eyewitness is but one possibility: the choices range from drawing on the traditional prestige of the court orthodoxy to creating a voice that transcends worldly institutions.

In thinking through some of the possible functions of the language mixing that occurs in the *Mirrors*, I draw on Reinhart Koselleck's ideas of the role of the eyewitness in historiography (to be explored in greater detail in chapters 1 and 2). My interpretation of different modes of writing is also inspired more broadly by Mark Amsler's work on medieval Europe. Older views of language use in Japan typically talk about a decline in classical learning that, in addition to the rise of *wabun* writing, resulted in an increased production of texts in imperfect or *hentai* (variant) *kanbun*. Thus, medieval *kanbun* prose, which is frequently "variant" in one way or another, is often dismissed as being written in a deviant style. Amsler's discussion of a "marker model," however, presents a view of multilingual literacy that enables an alternative way to think about the deployment of "variant" Classical Chinese. Amsler explains the basic premise as follows: "Markedness is distributed throughout linguistic levels (phonological, grammatical, semantic). Dominant or normative forms and modes are unmarked, taken for granted or generally accepted in a general social context, whereas marked forms and discourses are exceptional or even disputed."[64] In the traditional narrative of language competence in Heian and Kamakura Japan, Classical Chinese writing corresponds to the unmarked prestige form, while "variant" *kanbun* occupies

64. Amsler, *Affective Literacies*, xviii.

the position of a marked form. Amsler continues: "The marker model helps us reaccess the absent and the unsaid or repressed in literate discourses and language use. By bringing written discourse's other back into the textual field, all language use becomes marked within a contested field."[65] Such an argument attributes an agenda or positionality to the selection of any language, Classical Chinese or otherwise. As Amsler states: "There is no fundamental or original language moment or grammatical form from which all other forms depart or derive EXCEPT as the products of ideological work. So-called unmarked, standard or given forms are products of ideological work, maintaining and governing regimes of power and truth. The generic, syntactic, and semantic oppositions of marked/unmarked structure the dominant social understandings of what is considered natural and deviant."[66] This contention has two important implications for the present study. First, it allows an understanding of textual production and reception as processes in which authors and readers, knowingly or not, assign values to choices of language or linguistic form. Writing in any form is not neutral in this framework. Second, and more significantly, it enables a destabilization of the narrative of language selection as simply a passive product of declining linguistic ability in Classical Chinese or *kanbun*. When no one form of writing is "natural," the choice to alter or combine forms becomes empowered rather than simply reactive. Ergo, it becomes possible—or even necessary—to think about multilingual or "nonstandard" texts as something other than linguistic or formal degenerates. Although I will not explicitly use the "marker model" in my discussions of language (or style) selection, my analysis of multilingual and multistyle writing as potentially deliberate choices clearly derives from Amsler's evaluation of language prestige and ideologies.

Lastly, the fourth path addressing the appeal of the ordering of the past can be understood in part through taking into consideration the larger historical context in which the historiographic *Mirrors* appeared, flourished, and then atrophied. In other words, if one asks why write *Mirrors* in the first place and then looks at when they are produced, *Mirrors* nearly always appear in times when the existing structures and institu-

65. Amsler, *Affective Literacies*, xviii–xix.
66. Amsler, *Affective Literacies*, xix.

tions of power have recently been exposed as vulnerable. *The Great Mirror* dates roughly to the beginning of the Insei period (when retired emperors became dominant figures of government); *The New Mirror* follows Japan's first capital-based rebellions; *The Water Mirror* is written in the wake of the civil war; and so on. At the same time, however, they rarely address or even acknowledge the most recent crisis. Thus, *The New Mirror* makes almost no reference to the Hōgen or Heiji Disturbances; *The Water Mirror* has plenty of political violence but ignores the Genpei War (and the twelfth century more broadly); the surviving two-thirds of *The China Mirror* confine the end of the world to China; *The Mirror of the East* omits the Mongol invasions; and *The Clear Mirror* elides the end of the Kenmu restoration (1333–36)—Emperor Godaigo's (1288–1339) abortive attempt at reestablishing imperial power—as well as the fracturing of the court that follows. *The Mirror of the Gods* is an exception in its inclusion of recent power struggles, if not in the prominence it gives to earlier violence.

One way to interpret this relationship between threats to stability and the nonnarration of the same in a given historiographic project is to see it as a corollary to the relationship between "historical consciousness" and historiography formulated by Hayden White:

> Where there is ambiguity or ambivalence regarding the status of the legal system, which is the form in which the subject encounters most immediately the social system in which he is enjoined to achieve full humanity, the ground on which any closure of a story one might wish to tell about a past, whether it be a public or a private past, is lacking. And this suggests that narrativity, certainly in factual storytelling and probably in fictional storytelling as well, is intimately related to, if not a function of, the impulse to moralize reality, that is, to identify it with the social system that is the source of any morality we can imagine.[67]

White's reading suggests, with some interpretive license, that a recognized societal order is a prerequisite for the authority to interpret, or narrativize, the past.

67. White, "Value of Narrativity," 14. His conclusion in this essay argues that narrativization and moralizing are inseparable.

I go somewhat further by reading works in a chronicle format as similarly validating and promoting a certain "moral" order, a function that White presents as a potential but not fully realized attribute of the chronicle. I suggest that this is, in part, possible because even the most chronicle-like of the *Mirrors*, *The Mirror of the East*, attests to an implicit cosmological structure behind events, and its final events suggest a morally sanctioned conclusion: an incompetent shogun is deposed, but the institution of the *bakufu* lives on, implicitly guarded by the buddhas and *kami* who have been behind it from its founding.[68]

In the case of the *Mirrors*, recourse to the chronicle format—as a partially integrated structural component or as the overarching framework—does not signal an abdication of concern with morality if, as I argue, the ultimate basis for a *Mirror*'s claim to authority is its grasp of and commitment to a larger cosmological order. One can even go so far as to say that in these works, there is always a presumption of cosmological order similar to White's demand for a "social system," but that its worldly analogue has been unsettled. Across the board, the *Mirrors* are texts that respond to potential (or real) crises by writing those very moments of uncertainty out of the histories they narrate. To repeat, the most recent civil wars, imperial uprisings, and internecine clashes are virtually absent from the very *Mirrors* composed in the immediate wake of each such event. Rather than confront specific political crises head-on, the early *Mirrors* offer ways to defer such moments through a recursive relationship to the past, while their later counterparts focus on the cosmological laws and/or worldly institutions that survive the threat elided from the narrative. In other words, the *Mirrors* can be understood as attempts to disambiguate the relevance of the cosmological order they advance through moralizing the historical trajectories they relate—the texts offer an order in which things have worked out as they were supposed to.

In addition to the four overarching lines of inquiry that drive this study, I also recognize that each *Mirror* is enmeshed in a "horizontal" synchronic context and that the innovations I locate in each are tied to concerns that may be specific to the individual text's context of production. Therefore, while the main trajectory of this book is one that charts the development of *Mirror* writing over time, each chapter also approaches

68. Compare White, "Value of Narrativity," 5 and 19–21.

specific features of the *Mirror* or *Mirrors* at its center and analyzes how they relate to contemporary concerns. This story begins in chapter 1, with the intersection of *Mirror* writing and questions of morality that surround the genre's origins and early stages: *The Great Mirror* and its first successor, *The New Mirror*. After introducing *The Great Mirror*, chapter 1 situates the production of *The New Mirror*, which takes place in a world that had seen unprecedented armed conflict in the capital, against a backdrop of growing concerns about social instability and a blossoming discourse on the immorality of "tales" (*monogatari*). It proposes that the author of *The New Mirror* saw in *The Great Mirror* a way to explain greater truths without recourse to either the waning genre of the official history or the morally fraught mode of the tale. Chapter 2 centers on the problem of contextualizing unprecedented violence, primarily looking at *The Water Mirror* in its role as the first cosmological history written after the Genpei War. The chapter argues that *The Water Mirror*'s major innovations—that is, the regular incorporation of *kanbun* and the focus on the distant, as opposed to the immediate, past—are attempts to normalize the civil war (a conflict that it never mentions) through the creation of a historical narrative punctuated by violence and articulated in a transcendent language of authority. Chapter 3 investigates the emerging uses to which narrating a Chinese past is put with the rise of the warrior; *The China Mirror* is analyzed as a product of a newly and violently consolidated Hōjō family rule in the east. The chapter contends that turning away from the Japanese court as subject matter and taking up the history of continental China is an intellectual power play, the ramifications of which are explored via coeval representations of China in two other didactic texts. Chapter 4 confronts the flowering and bifurcation of the *Mirror* genre. It interrogates the stylistic and thematic features of *The Mirror of the East* and *The Mirror of the Watchman in the Fields* as two very different projects that both appear in the wake of the attempted Mongol invasions in 1274 and 1281. Although *Watchman* is not a historiographic *Mirror* per se, its engagement with several of the elements found in the earlier *Mirrors* demonstrates the productive porousness of what are now often thought of as medieval categories. The fork in the *Mirror* road suggested by *Watchman* and the *Mirror of the East* speaks to the increasingly widespread appeal of the *Mirrors* as textual vehicles even as it simultaneously calls attention to the variety of agendas the genre is used to support. Lastly, chapter 5 examines the impact of the late Kamakura divergence of paths on the Muromachi *Mirrors*. It begins with an examination of the influence of *Mirrors* on non-*Mirror* historiography from the early to the mid-fourteenth century. *The Mirror of the Gods* and *The Clear Mirror*, the fruit of the division identified in chapter 4, are then read against the trends and concerns suggested by this experimentation. In light of how these last two *Mirrors*, as well as the contemporary *Mirror*-shaded historiographic efforts that come immediately before them, navigate the events of the early fourteenth century, I argue that both *The Clear Mirror* and *The Mirror of the Gods* reflect an engagement with their predecessors that is more nostalgic than productive. The epilogue reflects on the medieval *Mirrors*' legacies for the early modern period.

The result of bringing all of the *Mirrors* together is neither simple nor tidy. However, this fuller story of their legacy shows how problematic some of the hoary binaries—especially China versus Japan and literature versus history—are in discussions of medieval Japan. Furthermore, decentering the "tale" as the definitive prose category and introducing the *Mirror* genre as another major point of reference sheds new light on the complicated intertextual nature of medieval writing and the discourses that shaped it.

Conclusion

In the interest of full disclosure, there are no "smoking guns" in this study. I cannot offer a definitive account of why an individual writer chose to relate the past as he did. Rather, the aim of this project is a better understanding of the various general demands that people in the late eleventh through the mid-fifteenth centuries placed on the narration of the past. How did prominent thinkers present the past? Why? What worked? What did not? And how did all of these things change, depending upon the historical context in which works were written as well as the political allegiance of the presumed author? In other words, which permutations of attitudes, rhetorical tropes, and languages conveyed authority during the three centuries that saw some of the most significant reapportioning of institutional and actual power in Japan's history?

These questions, in turn, invite still more questions at an abstract level. Medieval Japan can be read as a case study for broader inquiries about the historiographic enterprise: What are the institutions people turn to when the world around them is in flux? How does the claim to interpret the past provide authority in the present? What balance of old and new preserves just enough tradition to be persuasive, yet is innovative enough to break free from the confines of a regime exposed as fallible? What are the symbolic centers that resonate despite social and/or political reorganization? And what cachet is provided by the claim that the gods (or buddhas) are on one's side? The answers vary with time and place, but these are issues that are no less relevant to understanding the twenty-first-century United States than they are to interpreting thirteenth-century Japan.

With respect to medieval Japan, the answers to these questions challenge narratives that continue to haunt the field today and compel us to always keep in mind what has been gained and lost in the interest of canonization. At the same time, I hope these answers will not only reveal more about intellectual developments in medieval Japan but also contribute more generally to an understanding of how historical realities can become casualties of a nationalist narrative of exceptionalism and remind us of the ever-present risks of accepting any version of the past as is.

CHAPTER I

New Reflections

Refuge in the Past during the Final Age

Main texts (in chronological order)

***Ōkagami* (The Great Mirror)**
Author: unknown
Date: late eleventh century
Language: *wabun*
Preface: yes
Setting: Urin'in Temple (Kyoto)
Time covered: the reigns of Emperor Montoku (827–58)–Emperor Goichijō (1008–36).

***Imakagami* (The New Mirror)**
Author: commonly attributed to Fujiwara no Tametsune
Date: 1174 or 1175
Language: *wabun*
Preface: yes
Setting: Hasedera Temple (Nara area)
Time covered: the reigns of Emperor Goichijō (1008–36)–Emperor Takakura (1161–81).

***Genji ippon kyō* (One-Volume Sutra on the Genji)**
Author: Chōken
Date: circa 1176
Language: *kanbun*
Preface: no
Setting: N/A

While conventional wisdom dated the beginning of the final age of the Buddhist law to 1052, for many of the court elite, it would take another century before things began to decline rapidly in a more immediate worldly sense.[1] However, after violence arrived in the capital in the mid-twelfth century, *The New Mirror* emerged only two decades later as the first full-length historiographic narrative to confront recent events. When the violence continued, *The New Mirror* was followed just ten years later with another related work titled *The Water Mirror*. Yet neither of these was the first historiographic *Mirror* to appear—*The Great Mirror* had been written over a century earlier. So why, after a hundred-year hiatus, did the idea of a *Mirror* suddenly seem to resonate with readers and writers in late twelfth-century Japan? Why turn back to this older model for making sense of twelfth-century events?

The seeds of the answers to these questions lie in *The Great Mirror*, so our journey will begin with an examination of those elements that had the greatest impact on subsequent *Mirrors*: *The Great Mirror*'s preface and its implications, the vernacular register, and the promise to lay bare a logic for the workings of the world. Then the chapter will turn to the late twelfth century to explore two contemporary factors that may have influenced the decision to return to the genre—social instability and the discourse on the "sinful" nature of fictional narratives—as a way to approach *The New Mirror*. The former factor can be tied to *The New Mirror*'s inscription of time and the latter to the work's "last words": a conversation on the morality of fiction. *The New Mirror*'s discussion of karma, creative writing, and sin suggests an intellectual world in which writing a *Mirror* could offer a way of narrating the past that sidestepped the problematic morality of "tales"—namely, as a historiography grounded in cosmology that thanks to an eyewitness narrator was decidedly not to be confused with fiction, despite using the classical *wabun* register of tales.[2]

1. For a more detailed summary of positions regarding the Buddhist units of time, see Marra, "Development of Mappō Thought in Japan (I)," 25–27. Marra completes his analysis in a second piece that focuses primarily on Shinran and has no overlap with the events under discussion in this chapter ("Development of 'Mappō' Thought in Japan (II)." For a similar and more recent characterization of the manifestations of *mappō*, see Rhodes, "*Ōjōyōshū* and Pure Land Discourse," 253.

2. The edition of *The New Mirror* upon which this study is based is Takehana, *Imakagami*. This, in turn, is based on a 1650 printing collated with early manuscripts, including the oldest surviving version—the Hatakeyama version. It includes as a postscript a

Origins of a Genre: The Great Mirror *and a New Approach to Writing History*

The Great Mirror is the foundation of the historiographic *Mirror* genre. Thus, this section examines the key features of narrative setting, history as subject to principles, and the use of the spoken register to establish the groundwork upon which later *Mirrors* build.

The Great Mirror is a work of unknown authorship, and its dating has proved elusive. Ishikawa Tōru, editor of the edition used for this book, has argued mostly on the basis of internal textual evidence that the work might date from roughly 1065–75.[3] Helen McCullough, whose English translation was first published in 1980, summarizes the scholarly estimates of likely production as "clustering around the years 1085–1125," while David Bialock has more recently drawn on Japanese work positing a range of 1086–1107.[4] As these analyses demonstrate, without a concrete authorial attribution, it is difficult to suggest a range narrower than the final decades of the eleventh century.

Things are further complicated by the fact that *The Great Mirror* seems to have initially circulated under different titles. Katō Shizuko groups them as follows:

- titles that incorporate the narrator's [Yotsugi's] name: *Yotsugi's Tale, Old Man Yotsugi's Tale, Yotsugi's Old Man's Tale, Shigeki and Yotsugi's Tale*, and *The Yotsugi Tale*
- titles that incorporate "*Great Mirror*": *The Great Mirror, Scrolls of the Great Mirror*, and *The Great Perfect Mirror*

---

short entry that is found in the Hatakeyama version but not any of the *rufubon* (popular editions). See ibid., 2:20. For a short introduction to the three complete manuscripts—the Hatakeyamabon, the Hōsa Bunkobon (the version that is also the basis for the *rufubon*), and the Maedabon—see ibid., 3:622–24. Takehana notes that there is some variation across the three, but does not go beyond that. For the appended Hatakeyamabon entry, see ibid., 3:612–14.

3. Ishikawa, *Ōkagami*, 356. But a short time later in the discussion, taking into account one theory of authorship, he suggests that the earliest end of this range is likely (ibid., 358).

4. Helen McCullough, *Ōkagami*, ix; Bialock, *Eccentric Spaces*, 167.

- titles that combine both: *Yotsugi's Great Mirror*, *Scrolls of Yotsugi's Mirror*[5]

There is no consensus about why *The Great Mirror* triumphed as the work's title. While Katō, drawing on the theories of Mori Masato, suggests that it was retroactively settled upon after the composition of *The New Mirror*, Ishikawa points out that the oldest titled manuscripts, dating from the early twelfth century, bear the designation *The Great Mirror*.[6] Both provide ample evidence that the title remained somewhat contested into the thirteenth century, and Ishikawa cites a Muromachi-period manuscript as evidence for the continued use of *The Yotsugi Tale*.[7] The fact that the *Mirror* designation was eventually victorious is particularly important, because it suggests that even if a *Mirror* did not necessarily have a historiographic function distinct from that of a "tale" when *The Great Mirror* first appeared, "Tales" and "Mirrors" subsequently came to be perceived as distinct genres.[8]

To return to *The Great Mirror* itself, what sets it apart from histories that preceded it, as well as what would most often be co-opted by its successors and/or imitators, is already apparent in the work's preface. Unlike an orthodox national history, *The Great Mirror* famously commences with a preface set at Urin'in Temple. When the work opens, the narrator/author has stumbled across Yotsugi, the ancient figure who will take center stage; his companion, Shigeki; and Shigeki's wife. As the narrator explains: "The other day, when I went to the Urin'in's Enlightenment Lectures, I ran into two strange, extraordinarily old men and an elderly woman who were sitting in the same spot. 'Huh! They're three of a kind,' I thought to myself."[9] The narrator next overhears the two men establishing their identities and ages with one another. Yotsugi is 190, and

5. Katō, "Kaisetsu," 450. Although Katō's classification of titles is quite convenient, Ishikawa's explication of the issue provides more concrete detail, and I rely primarily on his work.

6. Katō, "Kaisetsu," 452; Ishikawa, *Ōkagami*, 386.

7. Ishikawa, *Ōkagami*, 368–69. See also Matsumura Hiroji, *Ōkagami*, 6.

8. Yamada Naoko also sees the eventual dominance of the *Mirror* title as critical (*Chūgoku koji juyō ronkō*, 108).

9. Ishikawa, *Ōkagami*, 13. For an alternative translation, see Helen McCullough, *Ōkagami*, 65.

Shigeki is 180. They are soon joined by an attendant who is approximately 30. Having attracted an audience in the course of their conversation, the old men decide to while away the time before the lecturer arrives by talking about the past since, as Yotsugi reasons, "By talking of the past, we could let the people here grasp 'That's how it was. Long ago, *that*'s how the world was.'"[10]

With a sense of purpose, Yotsugi presses forward: "'I have only one thing of importance on my mind,' he went on, 'and that is to describe Lord [Fujiwara no] Michinaga's [966–1027] unprecedented successes to all of you here, clergy and laity of both sexes. It is a complicated subject, so I shall have to discuss a fair number of Emperors, Empresses, ministers of state, and senior nobles first. Then when I reach Michinaga himself, the most fortunate of all, [the matters of the world will be completely revealed].'"[11] And without further ado, Yotsugi launches into the narrative. What follows is a series of biographies, subdivided by office: the first scroll focuses on the imperial family, while scrolls 2–4 offer accounts of the elite Fujiwara clan whose ministerial successes paved the way for Michinaga. These are followed by the biography of Michinaga, which is spread over the last two scrolls, 5 and 6. "Tales of the Fujiwara Clan" (*Fujiwara uji no monogatari*) likewise appear in the latter half of the fifth scroll, and the sixth scroll closes with the motley "Tales of the Past" (*mukashi monogatari*), ostensibly offered as further information on Michinaga but actually closer to a series of disjointed anecdotes set at court.[12]

Most of the imperial biographies are fairly short. They provide basic biographical facts and the occasional anecdote. At the end of the scroll, the reason for this becomes clear: they are primarily intended as background for the true focus of the story. As Yotsugi explains: "I ought not to have spoken of imperial succession, but since I was thinking of the

10. Ishikawa, *Ōkagami*, 18; for an alternative translation, see Helen McCullough, *Ōkagami*, 67.

11. Ishikawa, *Ōkagami*, 19; the translation, other than the bracketed section, is taken from Helen McCullough, *Ōkagami*, 68. I have substituted my own translation for the bracketed section in place of McCullough's "you will understand just how everything came about."

12. Although there are both early six-scroll and three-scroll versions of the text, Ishikawa takes the six-part form as preceding the three-part (*Ōkagami*, 362). Compare Helen McCullough, *Ōkagami*, ix.

reasons for the Novice Chancellor's [Michinaga's] efflorescence, I first talked about the aspects of the emperors and empresses. Do not the planted tree's branches grow luxuriant and the tree itself bear fruit because we care for it that it might send out roots?"[13] A back-and-forth with Shigeki ensues, complete with a poetry exchange on mirrors (to which I will return), before Yotsugi makes the clearest pronouncement yet about the importance of his work by drawing parallels both to the lectures to follow and to orthodox historiography: "Rather than baseless matters, I shall speak of true affairs. Take heed and listen, everyone. As you think of today's sermon in relation to enlightenment, so should you think of what this old man says as listening to the official histories!"[14] Setting aside for now the link to the *Lotus Sutra* lectures that this claim establishes, in a move that will reverberate in *Mirrors* to come, Yotsugi has created a clear equation between the truth value of court histories and that of the information he recites.[15] His claim is that, unlike other unspecified writings, what *The Great Mirror* shows readers will certainly be true. And with this, Yotsugi moves on to his real interest, Michinaga.[16]

Scrolls 2–4, which recount the lives of the generations of the Fujiwara clan before Michinaga, feature much more detail. Although not all of the biographies are evenly developed, the longer ones often offer vivid glimpses of the highs and lows of the public and private lives of Japan's elite. In terms of relevance to later *Mirrors*, however, the account of Sugawara no Michizane (845–903), which is embedded in the narrative of

13. Ishikawa, *Ōkagami*, 47; for an alternative translation, see Helen McCullough, *Ōkagami*, 85.

14. Ishikawa, *Ōkagami*, 49; translation modified from Helen McCullough, *Ōkagami*, 86. By juxtaposing "trivialities" and "serious matters" rather than matters false and true in the translation of the first sentence, McCullough obscures the nature of Yotsugi's contrast.

15. Komine Kazuaki points to the parallel between the *Lotus Sutra* lectures and Yotsugi's account in ways that will be relevant later in this chapter ("Ōkagami-ron," 594).

16. In the course of the transition to his new topic, Yotsugi observes: "Just as it is well known that when you scoop up water, you seek its source, so should I start with the first bestowal of the highest [ministerial] office" (Ishikawa, *Ōkagami*, 54; for an alternative translation, see Helen McCullough, *Ōkagami*, 88). See Helen McCullough, *Ōkagami* 88n46: "Probably a popular saying: To understand everything about a river, we must not only sample the waters downstream but also trace out the source." In contrast, the Shinchōsha edition attributes Yotsugi's lines to a Tendai text.

Minister of the Left Fujiwara no Tokihira (871–909), is among the most fascinating. There the reader encounters Michizane at the height of his career, serving in conjunction with Tokihira, only to see him peremptorily exiled to Dazaifu in remote Tsukushi Province (modern-day Kyūshū). Through a series of melancholy poems, the text follows Michizane's progress until he reaches the ninth day of the ninth month, when

> he saw the chrysanthemum blooms of the Double Nines festival in Tsukushi, and he remembered how on this very night a year earlier, when he had still been in the capital, there had been a Chrysanthemum Banquet at the palace, and the emperor had praised a verse he had composed as outstanding, bestowing a robe upon him. He had brought the robe with him, and at the sight of it, he composed a verse:

去年今夜侍清涼	Last year, this night, I served in the palace
秋思詩篇独断腸	In my "Autumn Thoughts" poem, I spoke of secret anguish.
恩賜御衣今在此	The robe bestowed by Your Grace is here now
捧持毎日拝余香	Treasuring it, each day I bow before its lingering fragrance.[17]

Yotsugi then praises Michizane's poetry more broadly before moving on to relate his death and subsequent enshrinement at Kitano Shrine, adding that Michizane's former Tsukushi residence is now known as Anrakuji Temple.[18] Yotsugi grants Michizane the last word, with a nod to his deification and a poetic oracle that promises destruction "until the wound in Sugawara's heart/No longer gapes."[19]

Michizane's embedded biography captures many elements that would be familiar to Heian readers of courtly literature, prose and poetry alike. There is a career imperiled by personal tensions, a withdrawal from official life to become a monk, both *waka* (Japanese verse) and *kanshi* (verse

17. Ishikawa, *Ōkagami*, 69–70; translation modified from Helen McCullough, *Ōkagami*, 98–99.

18. Ishikawa, *Ōkagami*, 71; for the corresponding events in English, see Helen McCullough, *Ōkagami*, 99.

19. Ishikawa, *Ōkagami*, 71; translation from Helen McCullough, *Ōkagami*, 100.

in Classical Chinese) poetry as a vehicle for expressing emotions, and posthumous vindication. This incident—Michizane's memory of the height of his career in Kyoto and the verse he composes in response—is not simply a moving tribute to Michizane in the middle of Tokihira's biography. It is also a reminder of the centrality of the capital in the minds of the literary elite, not only in the early tenth-century imagination of Michizane but also for his late eleventh-century counterparts in the age of *The Great Mirror*'s production and even beyond, as will be seen in chapter 3.

The final two scrolls have much to say about Michinaga. In the fifth, one learns about his rapid rise to power and his numerous offspring. Yet as though sensing a need to remind the reader of how very atypical the degree of Michinaga's success is, Yotsugi suddenly announces that he is going to talk about the other Fujiwara, too, and this takes him back to the origins of the Fujiwara clan.[20] Here, not only is the present-day glory of Michinaga a recurring note, but so is the strategic use of Buddhist measures to confront problems. For instance, early in Yotsugi's recitation, Fujiwara no Kamatari (614–69), the clan progenitor, falls ill. The situation is exacerbated, Yotsugi implies, by the fact that "long ago, the Buddhist law had not spread widely in this country, and monks and the like were not readily at hand."[21] However, Kamatari apparently recognizes the indispensability of the Buddhist teachings, since "he ha[s] a nun come over from Paekche and perform *Vimalakīrti Sutra* offerings, and his illness abate[s] at once."[22] Even such a minor anecdote as this can be read as reinforcing the idea of long-standing connections between the Fujiwara and Buddhism, a testament both to the workings of karma in general and the deservedness of Michinaga's success in particular.

In the sixth scroll, things take a more circuitous turn after the young retainer mentioned in the preface enjoins Yotsugi to share his earliest

20. Ishikawa, *Ōkagami*, 266; for the corresponding events in English, see Helen McCullough, *Ōkagami*, 199.

21. Ishikawa, *Ōkagami*, 271–72; translation modified from Helen McCullough, *Ōkagami*, 201–2.

22. Ishikawa, *Ōkagami*, 272; translation modified from Helen McCullough, *Ōkagami*, 202.

memories.[23] The memories of all four (Yotsugi, Shigeki, the retainer, and Shigeki's wife) drift from anecdote to anecdote, seemingly driven by free association rather than any temporal scheme. Suddenly, however, Yotsugi takes things in a new direction when, apropos of nothing, he announces, "I've only been talking of the matters of the Fujiwara family, but I would also like to relate the rareness of the Minamoto lineage."[24] Yet despite the ostensible new focus, the stories gradually circle back to Michinaga via his daughters. Other than an extended digression on time and the truth of his narrative, to be returned to below in the section titled "Telling It Like It Was," the scroll remains an account of the sorrows and joys of life, to paraphrase Yotsugi—which draws to a conclusion with an account of two of Michinaga's daughters, Senior Grand Empress Shōshi (988–1074) and Kenshi (994–1027), sparring playfully if decorously at a public procession, and the formal donning of the robes of Michinaga's granddaughter, Princess Teishi (1013–94).[25] With their story done, Yotsugi and his band disappear into the crowd that has gathered for the lectures, never to be seen again.[26] Or, more accurately, with Yotsugi not to be seen until he resurfaces as a referent in later *Mirrors*, a seemingly definitive conduit to eyewitness legitimacy.

In terms of medieval historiography, the set of tools Yotsugi uses to reveal a logic to the events he relates is more important than most of the specifics of the biographies themselves. *The Great Mirror* creates its "definitive" claim by means of a skillful synthesis of concepts of place, principle, language, and ordering the past. All four are not only key to understanding how *The Great Mirror* works as a cosmological history; they are furthermore all issues that reappear in some form throughout the *Mirror* genre. But because the first two in particular are prominent from the beginning of *The Great Mirror*, we will now return once again to Urin'in Temple.

23. Ishikawa, *Ōkagami*, 301; for the corresponding events in English, see Helen McCullough, *Ōkagami*, 215.

24. Ishikawa, *Ōkagami*, 322; translation modified from Helen McCullough, *Ōkagami*, 227.

25. Ishikawa, *Ōkagami*, 345–46; for the corresponding events in English, see Helen McCullough, *Ōkagami*, 239–40.

26. Ishikawa, *Ōkagami*, 346–47; for the corresponding events in English, see Helen McCullough, *Ōkagami*, 240.

SETTING THE STAGE: THE GREAT MIRROR *AND THE IMPORTANCE OF PLACE*

The relationship between a specific geographic site and configurations of authority will emerge as a recurring and increasingly complicated issue for *Mirror* writing. From the genre's outset, the importance of narrative place in asserting the right to recount the past is clear. What is less clear on the occasion of the genre's founding, however, is what the invocation of this particular site means. Looking at the multiple possible readings for *The Great Mirror*'s narrative setting permits a greater appreciation of how unambiguously narrative setting is most often used in subsequent *Mirrors*.

The decision to set Yotsugi's account of Japanese history at the Urin'in can be interpreted in various ways. At one level, the preface plays with the relationship between the scheduled ritual event and the impromptu transmission that precedes it. Komine Kazuaki has argued that this creates a parallel between the eventual *Lotus Sutra* lectures briefly acknowledged in the preface and Yotsugi's intervening narrative, which effects a certain prophetic function with the narrative site enhancing Yotsugi's claims to veracity.[27] In a similar vein, Mori goes one step further and proposes a series of rhetorical and structural connections between *The Great Mirror* and the *Lotus Sutra*.[28]

One can attribute further significance to the Urin'in not only as the site of the famous lectures, but also because of its origin and geography. Bialock approaches the question from precisely this angle to contend that by repositioning a historical narrative at a venue beyond the traditional centers of court historiography, *The Great Mirror* occupies a distinctly

27. Komine, "Ōkagami-ron." Komine says that the linkage between the date and the location or ceremonies was "common knowledge" (ibid., 530). On the predictive aspect of *The Great Mirror*, see, for example, ibid., 538. On the relation between the setting and the work's truth value, see, for example, ibid., 542 and 577–78. It is important to note that Komine sees *The Great Mirror* as distinct from the other *Mirrors* because of the privileged function of the setting itself (see ibid., 552). For a brief summary of earlier arguments linking the setting with Buddhist thought, see Mori, "Ōkagami ni okeru 'monogatari no ba,'" 16–17. Mori (ibid., 17; see also 25) cites Komine.

28. Mori, "Ōkagami ni okeru 'monogatari no ba,'" 18–21. The remainder of the article focuses on locating similarities between the two.

heterodox position. This is achieved in both *The Great Mirror* and its successors through the use of the "wandering reciter" as a narrative source, a move that relocates historiographic production to "the margins of power."[29] In keeping with this reading of *The Great Mirror* as non-normative, Bialock casts the selection of the narrative site as subversive as well. Although he notes Urin'in Temple's prestige for the court elite, he also points to a more sinister underside: its setting for rites "to mollify the spirits of those alienated in the course of Michinaga's quest for power."[30] In short, Bialock is less concerned with the idea that *The Great Mirror*'s authority is derived from an implied relationship with the *Lotus Sutra* lectures than he is with the relocation of the historiographic voice to a figure outside of traditional (courtly) structures of power.[31] For Bialock, the narration of history and its implicit authority have been removed from the exclusive domain of the (static) center to a "nomadic" frontier region.[32] Thus, while both Komine and Bialock see the setting as conveying authority, in the latter's analysis, it becomes much more disruptive of conventional power relations.

I agree that there are contexts in which *The Great Mirror*'s choice of setting can be seen as a rupture with convention. At the same time, if the subsequent *Mirrors* can be used as a guide to the reception of *The Great Mirror*, the Urin'in came to be read as not quite as discursively far afield as it might now seem. In terms of its institutional pedigree, the Urin'in's origin as the detached imperial palace of Emperor Junna (786–840) and its official recognition as a state-sponsored temple in 869 constitute links, however temporally distant in the eleventh century, to the imperial court. Moreover, the temple enjoyed its heyday in the mid- to late Heian period.[33] Even if it was not geographically located in central Kyoto, it nonetheless played an active part in the court's ritual landscape. In describing

29. Bialock, *Eccentric Spaces*, 157.

30. Bialock, *Eccentric Spaces*, 158.

31. For a discussion of how *The Great Mirror* may be informed by Chinese historiography, see Bialock, *Eccentric Spaces*, 165–68. On the real-world echoes of what Bialock sees as *The Great Mirror*'s transfer of authority beyond the court, see ibid., 174.

32. In Bialock's lexicon, one quality of the "nomadic" is an implicit denial of the "hierarchical" (*Eccentric Spaces*, 12).

33. On the temple's late Heian florescence and medieval decline, see Ishikawa, *Ōkagami*, 13n1.

a poetic preface from this time—"Upon hearing the carriages returning from the Urin'in *nenbutsu* services deep in the night"—Edward Kamens characterizes the "famous" Urin'in as "a monastery that was often favored by visitors from the imperial court."[34] While it is impossible to be sure what the valence of the Urin'in would have been at the time of *The Great Mirror*'s composition, within the world of the text, the temple was at its peak.

Further complicating the Urin'in's significance is the fact that it also had ties to the popular courtly literature of the day, including *Ise monogatari* (Tales of Ise) and *The Tale of Genji*.[35] It is even possible to take the comparison Yotsugi draws between his own transmission of information and the official histories as a reference to the "Fireflies" chapter of the *Genji* discussed in the introduction.[36] The reference in *The Great Mirror* may be oblique or unintentional, but *The New Mirror* will leave no doubt that the *Genji* was part of the literary and intellectual landscape within which the long-term evolution of *Mirror* writing was unfolding. Although these connections may not have been what *The Great Mirror*'s author had in mind in selecting his or her site, their existence renders Urin'in Temple a multivalent setting in the larger world of *Mirror* writing.

The selection of the Urin'in thus resists a single reading, but as a narrative technique the setting of the preface there has a lasting impact. Regardless of whether it was originally intended as a disruptive or a conservative effort to locate *The Great Mirror*, it keeps the text within a geographic and social sphere that is connected to court culture. This arguably is not truly brought into relief until the appearance of works such as *The Water Mirror* (discussed in chapter 2) and *The China Mirror* (chapter 3), which both undertake to move their respective settings much farther away from a court-centered world, in terms of geography and orientation. But one thing is certain: the ways in which all of the later historiographic *Mirrors* navigate the role of the narrative "place" is central to their respective

34. The preface is to a poem by one of the female attendants of Imperial Princess Senshi (964–1035). I have modified Kamens's paraphrase of the preface slightly to provide a more literal translation. See Kamens, *Buddhist Poetry of the Great Kamo Priestess*, 47.

35. This information is from the explanatory placards at the Urin'in in 2017.

36. Ishikawa, *Ōkagami*, 49n15.

ideas of how to construct an authoritative position, and this is something they owe to *The Great Mirror.*

A HISTORY GOVERNED BY KARMA: THE GREAT MIRROR *AND ORDERING THE PAST*

Capitalizing on a particular place is not the only rhetorical tool that *The Great Mirror* uses to lasting effect. Common to both the readings that see parallels to the *Lotus Sutra* and the varied interpretations of the significance of the Urin'in is the assertion that the setting invites a reading that has implications beyond the transmission of historical events. Herein is another of *The Great Mirror*'s contributions: the intimation of history as governed by cosmological principles. As noted in the introduction, Ishikawa has called attention to how innovative *The Great Mirror* is "in emphasizing 'governing principles,'" dubbing it "a type of Principle-Tale or a work of literature with a strongly critical character."[37] Even though Yotsugi's promise to completely elucidate "the matters of the world" falls short of a clear statement of greater forces governing historical trajectories, *The Great Mirror* seems to be at pains to demonstrate that events are the result of karmic ties, or matters turning out "as they must" (*sarubeki*). In *The Great Mirror*'s lexicon, births and deaths as well as successes and failures are repeatedly attributed to "ties from a previous life" (*sukuse*), "karmic recompense from a previous life" (*mae no yo no gohō*), and factors that are "not of this lifetime" (*kono yo narazu*).[38] There is nothing in *The Great Mirror* that cannot be explained in these or similar terms.

The Great Mirror's commitment to cosmological principles is evident in more than just the frequent recourse to karma. One exchange from within the narrative illustrates this point particularly well. It occurs between Yotsugi and Shigeki as the work transitions from imperial to ministerial biographies (at the end of the first scroll and the beginning of the second). After an unexpected outburst from Shigeki about the wonders

37. Ishikawa, *Ōkagami*, 386. There has also been much debate about whether *The Great Mirror* is critical or laudatory of its subject, but since this has little bearing on the present analysis, I will omit any discussion of this problem.

38. For specific respective instances of these three terms, see Ishikawa, *Ōkagami*, 35 and 113; 145; and 265. For *sarubeki* (preordained), see, for instance, ibid., 73 and 319. *Gohō* (karmic reward) and *kahō* (karma) appear respectively in ibid., 105 and 192.

of Yotsugi's narrative, which he likens to looking in a brilliantly polished mirror, Shigeki composes a poem that implies *The Great Mirror*'s reflection of constant principles:

Akirakeki	Having encountered
kagami ni aeba	a brilliant mirror,
suginishi mo	past,
ima yukusue no	present, and future—
koto mo miekeri	all can be seen.[39]

In Shigeki's verse, the "brilliant mirror" (*akirakeki kagami*) reflects not only "bygone" (*suginishi*) events, but also "the present" (*ima*) and even "the future" (*yukusue*). This is an obvious analogue to how *The Great Mirror* is to be read. Its audience is enjoined to look beyond the superficial historicity of its contents to see the truth that the work actually reflects.[40] All of the later historiographic *Mirrors* will likewise lend themselves to this mode of reading, although rarely in such explicit terms. As with the use of a symbolically significant setting, in its promise to readers to reveal principles that govern history and beyond, *The Great Mirror* sets the standard against which its successors' decisions become legible.

TELLING IT LIKE IT WAS: THE GREAT MIRROR *AND THE VERNACULAR REGISTER*

The last important formal legacy of *The Great Mirror* is its exclusive use of a vernacular register. As numerous scholars have observed, the entire work is framed as a conversation between Yotsugi and Shigeki, with the occasional interruption by the attendant on the sidelines or remark from

39. Ishikawa, *Ōkagami*, 49; for an alternative translation, see Helen McCullough, *Ōkagami*, 85. I read the *-keri* here as indicating the sudden recognition of an ongoing state.

40. See also Ishikawa, *Ōkagami*, 49n8. Yotsugi's poetic reply is less interesting in this regard, as it primarily emphasizes the comprehensiveness of his account: "*suberagi no/ ato mo sugi sugi/ kakurenaku/ arata ni miyuru/ furuki kagami kamo* (Ah! A mirror of old/ that reflects anew/ the deeds of emperors/ age upon age, concealing nothing)" (ibid., 49; for an alternative translation, see Helen McCullough, *Ōkagami*, 86).

Shigeki's wife.[41] Komine's work has already drawn attention to the familiar tension in medieval Japanese discourse between spoken and written registers, and he sees the use of speech as an important gesture toward *The Great Mirror*'s project to "exaggeratedly claim its own meaning on equal terms with lecturers' preaching."[42] Indeed, one can see such bravado in a scene toward the end of the work, where Yotsugi explains to Shigeki: "However, there are probably young people who don't grasp the principles of what [we've related] thus and are assuming we must be 'prevaricating geriatrics.' May the Three Treasures of this temple and the bodhisattva appealed to by the preceptor of today's lectures stand as my witnesses as to whether I have purposely added even a single word of fabrication."[43] Such rhetoric, in addition to again emphasizing the importance of cosmological logic, fits well with Komine's reading, which proposes that this staged orality and the implied parallel it creates with the lectures to follow enables "a twofold challenge to previous fictional tales and narrations of history" as part of an "effort to overcome chronicles as such."[44] *The Great Mirror* seems to be asserting its veracity, as Komine claims. After a few additional remarks about his honesty, Yotsugi continues: "Basically, when the world began, the human life span was 80,000 years. This gradually declined, and when it had become 100 years, the Buddha appeared. However, thinking to demonstrate to people the fact that life and death are not fixed, he passed into extinction at the age of eighty, shaving off a further twenty years."[45] Yotsugi then talks about the extent to which human life span varies before concluding that "for the Final Age," he is "an old man possessed of an extraordinarily long life."[46] For Yotsugi, this short explanation of cosmic time centers on the need to sup-

41. Bialock offers another potential reading of the text as "polyvocalic" (*Eccentric Spaces*, 158–60). The roles of the narrators also play into his discussion of genre (ibid., 160–63).

42. Komine, "Ōkagami-ron," 594.

43. Ishikawa, *Ōkagami*, 337–38; translation modified from Helen McCullough, *Ōkagami*, 235.

44. Komine, "Ōkagami-ron," 594 and 595.

45. Ishikawa, *Ōkagami*, 338; translation modified from Helen McCullough, *Ōkagami*, 235.

46. Ishikawa, *Ōkagami*, 339; for an alternative translation, see Helen McCullough, *Ōkagami*, 235.

port his claims of having an unnaturally long life. In other words, *The Great Mirror* uses this rhetoric to support its status as an eyewitness account, rather than to enter into a discussion of time itself. Although subsequent *Mirrors* will make something more sophisticated of this discourse on time, for the moment it is enough to note that in the above passages, *The Great Mirror* clarifies that it has a larger truth at stake and, at the same time, vouches for the extraordinariness and reliability of its mouthpiece.[47]

Komine assesses these as real interventions made by *The Great Mirror* but dismisses their later use as being largely pro forma.[48] I argue, however, that the subsequent *Mirrors* will actively make use of several of these conventions—place, principle, and changing forms of language—and adapt them to make different messages palatable to a changing readership. The first manipulation of the standards set by *The Great Mirror* can be seen in *The New Mirror* (to which this chapter turns next), for *The New Mirror* is the first historical narrative to consciously model itself on and be in dialogue with Yotsugi's forms of ordering the past.

Signs of the Times: Instability and Anxiety in the Late Twelfth Century

Although the genesis of later *Mirrors* often appears tied to military events—wars, uprisings, invasions, and so forth—in the case of *The Great Mirror,* there is no such obvious violent historical catalyst that led to the decision to write the past as a *Mirror.* It seems a stretch to postulate an impending sense of military crisis leading to a need to reexamine history: while the late eleventh century was not free from armed conflict, most

47. Mori sees the role of the "eyewitness" as, in part, a way to differentiate the content of *The Great Mirror* from other texts in the written register. He explicitly states that Yotsugi is no Buddha and the work no *Lotus Sutra,* despite the suggestive parallels between the texts that occupy the bulk of his analysis ("Ōkagami ni okeru 'monogatari no ba,'" 26–27).

48. Komine adds that this may stem from the increasing prestige enjoyed by the written register ("Ōkagami-ron," 612).

fighting was taking place at the far edges of the realm.[49] Closer to home in the capital, however, there was a major change of another sort: the accession of Emperor Gosanjō (1034–73), whom Cameron Hurst characterizes as "the first emperor in almost two centuries not hampered by Fujiwara rule."[50] Between Gosanjō and his successor, Shirakawa (1053–1129), imperial power was reasserted in ways long unseen. The Fujiwara regency (970–1070) that had long dominated the imperial house and was so central to *The Great Mirror* was nearing its end, and at least some forty-odd years had passed since the death of Michinaga, *The Great Mirror*'s main subject. Michinaga had once famously versified that his grasp of power was absolute:

Kono yo oba	This world
wa ga yo to zo omou	I feel, is *mine*
mochizuki no	for like the full moon
kaketaru koto mo	I lack
nashi to omoeba.	nothing.[51]

However, that world was rapidly fading by the time *The Great Mirror*'s author had Yotsugi explain how it had come about. The late eleventh century was not, thus, devoid of potentially seismic shifts. Nonetheless, whether it was the waning of the regency, the reassertion of imperial authority, or something else entirely, it is impossible to pinpoint the impetus for narrating a Michinaga-centered version of the past in the closing years of the eleventh century. Yotsugi never says. And this, combined with the uncertainty surrounding the work's authorship and dating, makes it difficult to postulate in any meaningful way an original relationship between a specific historical context of unrest or paradigm-shifting event and the appeal of attributing a cosmological framework to the past.

This all changes with *The New Mirror*. Some fifty to seventy years after *The Great Mirror*'s composition, violence finally arrived in the capital, and concern about the fate of the world began to increase. The "strife and war" or "crimes and outrages" sometimes equated with the final age

49. See William McCullough's summary in "The Heian Court," 2:74.
50. Hurst, "Insei," 585.
51. Quoted in Fujiwara no Sanesuke, *Shōyūki*, 5:55, entry for Kannin 2 (1018).10.16.

of the Buddhist teachings took concrete form in the seventh month of Hōgen 1 (1156), when the short-lived Hōgen Disturbance struck.[52] For the first time, Kyoto became the stage for military conflict.[53] This was followed roughly three years later by the more substantial Heiji Disturbance, which broke out in the twelfth month of Heiji 1 (1160) and lasted three months. Within decades, these clashes proved not to be isolated manifestations of discord, but rather the beginning of a major upheaval that culminated in the 1180–85 civil war. This was a war that, for many, brought the end of the world—or the chaos of the 10,000-year "final age"—out of the realm of abstraction and into the realm of immediate possibility.

Not only were the Hōgen and Heiji events early sparks of the military conflict to come, but they also set the stage for *The New Mirror*, which heralded the first return of the historiographic *Mirror* and the first suggestion that a *Mirror* could be read as a way to process disorder. A closer look at the immediate impact of the Hōgen and Heiji Disturbances in the capital and the writings of its courtier elite—that is, the milieu from which *The New Mirror* emerged—as well as at how *The New Mirror* treats contemporary concerns, enables the discernment of a clearer position with respect to the project of ordering the past than was possible for *The Great Mirror*. The analysis that follows will show how *The New Mirror* represents an attempt at a "recuperative" history that capitalizes on the preexisting model of the *Mirror* to project order onto the past. Read from this position, *The New Mirror* becomes the first intimation of what looks to be a pattern in *Mirror* production: an intimate association between civil disorder and an impulse to turn to cosmological frameworks in the process of the narrative reordering of these events. As the first heir to *The Great Mirror*, *The New Mirror* solidifies the early standards of the genre, a backdrop against which all subsequent developments need to

52. Although vague in its citation of primary sources and largely lacking the annotation one would now expect, Hiraizumi's 1938 essay in the inaugural issue of *Monumenta Nipponica* provides an early overview of *mappō* thought in a Western language; I borrow the characterization of the age from that essay. See Hiraizumi, "Der Einfluss der Mappō-Lehre," 63. On the dating of the onset of *mappō* in two works, see ibid., 63–64.

53. Hiraizumi observes that it was the Hōgen Disturbance that occasioned the reintroduction of capital punishment after a hiatus of 340 years ("Der Einfluss der Mappō-Lehre," 65).

be understood: the structural conventions, the nature of the object under consideration, and the language(s) used to articulate the past.[54]

Unfortunately, although both the Hōgen and Heiji incidents would come to be celebrated in thirteenth-century tales, few twelfth-century records survive that offer a glimpse of the atmosphere in the capital. *The New Mirror*'s narrator claims both that she "doesn't even know how to put it [the Hōgen Disturbance] into words" and that "everyone probably already knows about it," before refusing to elaborate further.[55] (In addition, as will be seen below in "Ordering the Past to a New Purpose," she later provides a circumscribed account of events.) Therefore, even as she refuses to address it, the recurring asides and acknowledgment that "everybody" is familiar with it indicates that the Hōgen Disturbance constitutes an important reference point. To better understand the nature of the events that lurk in the background of *The New Mirror*, this chapter will look in some detail at one of the few extant contemporary accounts. While the disturbance lasted only a few weeks, it seems to have cast a long shadow.

Taira no Nobunori's (1112–87) *Heihanki* (Minister of War Nobunori's Logbook, also read *Hyōhanki*) is one of the few surviving sources that provides a contemporary perspective. Although there are no extant entries for Heiji 1 (April 1159–January 1160), the year in which the second rebellion occurred, the *Logbook* does contain a record of the brief Hōgen Disturbance that followed Senior Retired Emperor Toba's (1103–56) death on Hōgen 1 (1156).7.2. As a court diary, the *Logbook* is typically short on first-person analyses of events, but Nobunori's record nevertheless provides a sense of the violence and intrigue that surrounded the power struggle between forces loyal to the frustrated Retired Emperor Sutoku (1119–64) and the quickly victorious followers of the reigning emperor, Goshirakawa (1127–92).

Nobunori was among Goshirakawa's supporters, and in his account, the gravely ill Senior Retired Emperor Toba summoned high-ranking warriors to the capital to safeguard the palace in the month before his

54. Sakurai Hironori draws on Kanō Shigefumi to make the same point, arguing that it is "truly *The New Mirror* which establishes the *Mirrors* as a single genre" ("'Ōkagami' ni hajimaru mono," 53).

55. Takehana, *Imakagami*, 1:467.

death. Presumably, Toba was aware of the rumors that Retired Emperor Sutoku and his ally, Minister of the Left Fujiwara no Yorinaga (1120–56), "desired to be of service in the overthrow of the state," and he hoped to forestall unrest.[56] Yet despite such precautions, within three days of the senior retired emperor's death, Emperor Goshirakawa saw fit to issue an order to subdue unruly warriors in the capital.[57] Clearly Toba's efforts had not worked.

Goshirakawa's order failed to defuse the situation, and warriors flocked to both sides before matters came to a head. Finally, at nightfall on Hōgen 1 (1156).7.10, Goshirakawa's troops prepared for battle. Nobunori repaired to the Higashi-sanjō Compound to prepare for the secret relocation of Goshirakawa there.[58] Then, at dawn on the following day, a combined imperial force allegedly numbering over six hundred mounted warriors set out for Shirakawa Mansion, the base of the treasonous Retired Emperor Sutoku.[59]

Much of the fighting itself is elided—Nobunori is primarily concerned with the transport of Goshirakawa and the imperial regalia to the Higashi-sanjō Compound—but there are glimpses of it, such as mentions of the heavily guarded Shirakawa Mansion and of the fire and smoke that rise in the east when portions of the mansion go up in flames.[60] Although order is restored fairly quickly, with matters being carried out "just as at court" even on the day of the eleventh, the vulnerability of the imperial institution in this moment—particularly in its reliance upon warrior proxies—is unmistakable.[61] Nobunori's lack of comment on his allies' victory notwithstanding, it is difficult to imagine that he and his peers were unaware of their dependence on increasingly powerful warriors, especially Taira no Kiyomori (1118–81), the eventual antihero of the Genpei War.

Although the rebellion proper was short-lived, it took time to resolve matters, including the interrogation and pursuit of scattered enemies and

56. Taira no Nobunori, *Heihanki*, 2:115 (see also 2:114).

57. Taira no Nobunori, *Heihanki*, 2:115.

58. Taira no Nobunori, *Heihanki*, 2:116–17.

59. Taira no Nobunori, *Heihanki*, 2:117. I follow Royall Tyler in translating Shirakawadono as "Shirakawa Mansion" (*Before* Heike *and After*, 29).

60. Taira no Nobunori, *Heihanki*, 2:117–18.

61. Taira no Nobunori, *Heihanki*, 2:118.

the confiscation of conspirators' estates. Punishments and accolades were bestowed in the weeks following the disturbance, but a large-scale punitive exile was not enacted until Hōgen 1 (1156).8.3.[62] The warrior Minamoto no Tametomo (1139–70), a son of one of the central figures in the rebellion, was not captured until the twenty-sixth day of that month, six weeks after the defeat of the retired emperor's forces.[63] The fact that still more work remained to be done is evident in the "ecclesiastical business" conducted on Hōgen 1 (1156).9.25, which Nobunori glosses as "rewards for esoteric rites performed vis-à-vis the disturbance of the previous seventh month."[64] Perhaps it is not going too far to see the imperial edict issued on Hōgen 1 (1156).9.18 as a related attempt to constrain efforts to establish or expand authority that was not imperially sanctioned: the seven provisos all work to curtail private or independent enrichment and the accrual of other forms of support.[65] In short, the ripples of a failed rebellion that had lasted but a short time continued to be felt at court for more than three months afterward.

Unfortunately, though predictably, Nobunori, a fifth-rank courtier at the time of these events, offers no insight into the psychological impact of the disturbance or its consequences on either an individual or a broader social level. Yet even as the firsthand record of the rebellion remains silent on the matter of emotional wear and tear, in the contemporary literary work *Kara monogatari* (China Tales), one can observe a new concern with disorder. This short collection of anecdotes attributed to Fujiwara no Shigenori (1135–87)—who, like Nobunori, was a writer belonging to court circles—is in fact one of the few (nonpoetic) literary texts that can be fairly definitively dated to the latter half of the twelfth century. While the precise dating of *China Tales* has proved impossible, a study by Aoki Kengō that investigates Shigenori's poetics has proposed the fairly

62. Taira no Nobunori, *Heihanki*, 2:127.

63. Taira no Nobunori, *Heihanki*, 2:130.

64. Taira no Nobunori, *Heihanki*, 2:137.

65. Mikael Adolphson attributes a similar function to the edict, although he argues that the primary targets of these efforts were the increasingly powerful "religious institutions" (*Gates of Power*, 135–36). For a text of the edict, see Taira no Nobunori, *Heihanki*, 2:139–40.

narrow range of 1165–77.[66] This would put it after the author's temporary exile to Shimotsuke Province following the Heiji Disturbance in 1160 and the execution of his father, Fujiwara no Michinori (or Shinzei, 1106?–60), in the same year.[67] It would also predate the 1180 onset of the civil war, which may be why the work features violence but no rhetoric suggesting that things are in irreversible decline.

Despite its ostensibly foreign setting, *China Tales* sheds light on how writers with ties to the Japanese court interpreted the origins and impact of social disorder in the final years of the Heian period before the outbreak of war. In particular, the depictions of chaos in *China Tales* offer a potential indication of courtier understandings of where the world may have been headed in the mid-1170s in the wake of the Hōgen and Heiji Disturbances, just as Fujiwara no Tametsune (dates unknown) was returning to an old historiographic approach to anchor the recent past in *The New Mirror.*

China Tales is a collection of twenty-seven vignettes of varying lengths that are largely adapted from Chinese sources.[68] Both Kubota Jun and Komine have called attention to the tendency for Japanese authors to portray China in a negative light in this time period, and this impulse is at work here.[69] At the same time, however, many of the tales have a romantic element, and Asai Mineji and Ward Geddes have argued for various notions of "love" in the text.[70] Of greatest concern to the task at present,

66. Aoki, "Fujiwara no Shigenori nenpyō-kō." The annotated edition used as the base text for the current study takes a more circumspect approach, suggesting the period of 1151–88 (Kobayashi, *Kara monogatari zenshaku*, 296–97).

67. Aoki, "Fujiwara no Shigenori nenpyō-kō," 272–74.

68. For an early edition that includes Chinese "sources," see Asai, *Kara monogatari shinshaku*. For an English-language translation with a critical introduction, see Geddes, *Kara monogatari: Tales of China*.

69. Kubota proposes that the Japanese around this time were interested in China as a site of both politics and lechery (*Chūsei bungaku no jikū*, 169). Komine urges the reader of *China Tales* to remember its sociohistorical context: "In particular, at the root of the idea of incorporating ancient Chinese matters into *uta monogatari* [poem tales] and having the characters speak in *waka*, there was probably a strong anti-Chinese superiority complex; [this sentiment] had the striking Japan-Song relations of the Insei period as its background and a consciousness of having reversed an [earlier] inferior position" ("*Kara monogatari* no hyōgen keisei," 214). He opens his essay with a similar, but less explicit, challenge (ibid., 195).

70. Asai, *Kara monogatari shinshaku*; Geddes, *Kara monogatari*.

though, are the four stories (tales 6, 10, 17, and 18) that hint at how social disorder is perceived in the text, in terms of both its origins and impacts. Even though these tales constitute a small subset of the twenty-seven tales, because each of the four features elaborations on one or more aspects of war not found in the putative Chinese source texts, they are presumably suggestive of a type of information believed to speak to contemporary Japanese readers—who, in all likelihood, inhabited a post-Hōgen and Heiji world.[71]

Three of the four tales (6, 17, and 18) feature expanded material about the origins of military conflict, with editorial interventions in tale 6 that emphasize the role of passion as leading to war and in tale 17 that achieve a heightened narrative presence for social disorder. Nonetheless, it is tales 18 and 10 that offer the most fruitful examinations of large-scale instability.[72]

Tale 18, "The Tale of Emperor Xuanzong [685–762] and Yang Guifei [719–56]," explains explicitly, and in ways that are suggestive of recent Japanese events, what can cause the world to fall into disorder.[73] Although much of the story is devoted to the famous love between the emperor and his consort and the emperor's inability to recover from her death, the scene that leads up to her execution provides a summary of how the situation has become so dire:

> While the months and years thus went by, Minister of the Right Yang Guozhong [died 756], as the elder brother of Yang Guifei, came to hold the reins of government. Nevertheless, as the many ways in which he went

71. I am not the first person to suggest such resonances. See, for instance, Komine, cited in Morishita, "'Kara monogatari' no shinshō sekai," 29. Komine sees this primarily in terms of events connected to Shigenori's life (specifically, his post-Heiji exile), notwithstanding his general observation on the importance of war as a motif (cited by Morishita). See Komine, "*Kara monogatari* shōkō," 35 (on exile) and 36 (the general observation).

72. Kobayashi, *Kara monogatari zenshaku*, 42–47 and 121.

73. Kobayashi, *Kara monogatari zenshaku*, 139–210. In one of the more recent works on *China Tales*, Morishita has proposed taking this story as the most central to the collection, and to that end, he has probed it from several angles: Buddhist imagery and rhetoric, intertextuality and the reception of the Yang Guifei mythos, and correlations between the depiction of Yang Guifei and Shigenori's daughter ("'Kara monogatari' no shinshō sekai").

> against the will of the people accumulated, there came to be deep resentment in the world. In the midst of this, the adoptive son of Yang Guifei, one Minister of the Left An Lushan [703–57], resisted [Guozhong's] authority; and though the fury in his heart ran deep, there was no one at all to restrain it. Thus, when he suddenly amassed 150,000 troops to slay Yang Guozhong, the world fell into chaos, and there were great riots. Fear penetrated even as far as the palace, so the emperor fled elsewhere.[74]

In the Chinese source, Yang Guozhong is likewise depicted as a usurper "making a mockery of the country."[75] There is, however, no mention of the effect of misrule on public morale. Nor is there any attention paid to An Lushan's emotional state. While the mechanics of the retreat are recounted in greater detail, nowhere is there anything said about the world falling apart or mass unrest.[76] In short, the elaborations about the friction between the government elite and the people and about the threat of social collapse are extrinsic to the Chinese version. In ways similar to those that can be found in tales 6 and 17 (not discussed here), Shigenori has added material that foregrounds the danger to social stability posed by nepotism, misrule, and unchecked ambition—some of the very factors behind the recent Hōgen and Heiji Disturbances.

Tale 10, "The Tale of How Carrying a Split Mirror Enabled Deyan's Reunion with His Wife, Ms. Chen," best conveys how Japanese in the late twelfth century assessed the possible impact of war.[77] The familiar anecdote relates how a couple facing war decides to split a mirror in two so that they will be able to use the halves as proof of identity and reunite afterward should they lose track of one another. While the plot stays fairly close to that of the Chinese version, there is one striking difference: an insertion of how the war directly impacts society. After war's unexpected outbreak, "all people, lofty and lowly alike, hid in the mountains and forests, where they wandered about, lost. Even parents and siblings who were difficult to separate from each other dispersed in all four directions,"

74. Kobayashi, *Kara monogatari zenshaku*, 149–50.

75. For the Chinese text, see Kobayashi, *Kara monogatari zenshaku*, 181.

76. For the Chinese text upon which I base these observations, see Kobayashi, *Kara monogatari zenshaku*, 181.

77. Kobayashi, *Kara monogatari zenshaku*, 68–73.

with "everyone fleeing and wandering all about."[78] These lines are new, with the result that once again Japanese readers are treated to additional imagery that magnifies but does not explain the disorder. But their inclusion makes sense in a Japanese world that has recently weathered two rebellions and where tensions continue to mount.

These two roughly coeval courtier-authored texts—Nobunori's elliptical account of the Hōgen Disturbance and Shigenori's tales of love and disorder in China—offer tantalizing, though admittedly imperfect, glimpses into the intellectual world of the Japanese elite during the 1150s and 1160s. Nobunori's diary reveals warriors acting with increasingly ineffectual checks on their power, as well as hints of the physical destruction they could bring to the capital. At the same time, Shigenori's account slips in new passages of text that, however slender and few in number, suggest a recognition of or sensitivity to the causes and costs of war. Thus, both of these sources are critical to understanding the zeitgeist at court when, a few years later in 1174 or 1175, Fujiwara no Tametsune is believed to have written *The New Mirror*. As a history of recent events that encompasses the Hōgen and Heiji eras, even as it labors to ignore the rebellions in each, *The New Mirror* suggests that "once [people] know the origins" of things, it will be clear how and why they end as they do.[79]

Recovering Places and Principles en Route to the Past: The New Mirror

When Tametsune opens his story in *The New Mirror* with a temple pilgrimage and an unnaturally aged narrator who claims to be the granddaughter of Yotsugi, the celebrated narrator of *The Great Mirror*, he im-

78. Kobayashi, *Kara monogatari zenshaku*, 68. For the Chinese, see ibid., 72.

79. Takehana, *Imakagami*, 1:33; see also 1:37. Although the author of *The New Mirror* has not been absolutely identified, Takehana persuasively argues for Tametsune based on a collection of circumstantial evidence, including familial ties between Tametsune and the copyist of the earliest extant manuscript as well as a catalogue from the mid-Edo period that attributes *Shinkagami* (The New Mirror) to Jakuchō, Tametsune's Buddhist name (see ibid., 3:620–22). For a detailed discussion of the dating, including internal evidence suggesting that the work must date from late 1174 at the earliest and manuscripts from no later than early 1175, see ibid., 3:625–39.

mediately makes his work part of a specific conversation about ordering the past.[80] At the same time, however, his work also suggests a reorientation of some of *The Great Mirror*'s positions, including an active repositioning with regard to courtly loci of authority as well as the legacy of court literature. Because *The New Mirror* has no English translation, I will begin with a short summary of the work's content. Then I will look at the preface in greater detail, as the importance of both narrative place and cosmological principle are most explicit there. Lastly, I will turn to the body of the narrative proper to analyze two new problems that Tametsune's work has introduced: the relationship between court culture, narrative structure, and the past; and the issue of the morality of writing.

The New Mirror opens with a preface, to be returned to below, and consists of ten scrolls. In the first three scrolls, it focuses on the imperial family, covering the reigns from Emperor Ichijō (980–1011) through the ascension of Emperor Takakura (1161–81). In a meandering, often circular style, the narrative proceeds through successive rules, giving prominence to accounts of lineage and social events—typically those of the court, such as funeral observations or poetry contests and/or compositions.[81] One particularly long entry, that of "The Day of the Rat" (typically a reference to the first "rat" day of the new year), is representative of the breadth of concerns in *The New Mirror*. Taking place in 1026 just after *The Great Mirror* breaks off, the entry begins with the tonsuring of Fujiwara no Shōshi, Michinaga's daughter and the future Jōtōmon-in. After remarking on Shōshi's youth and how the decision was both "laudable" and "moving," the narrator reports that Imperial Princess Senshi (964–1035), the current Kamo priestess, has sent a poem on the occasion that speaks of her admiration for Shōshi, as well as her envy at Shōshi's chance to embark on the Buddhist path:

Kimi wa shimo	You, too,
makoto no michi ni	have entered the true path
irinu nari	I hear—

80. See Sakurai, "'Ōkagami' ni hajimaru mono," 53.

81. Matsumoto Shinpachirō provides a similar discussion of *Imakagami*'s content. He characterizes the work's structure as following the *kidentai* (transmitted biographies) format of *The Great Mirror*, a combination of basic imperial annals, biographies, treatises, and charts ("Rekishi monogatari to shiron," 26).

hitori ya nagaki	will I wander alone
yami ni madowamu	lost in the long darkness?[82]

But after briefly identifying Senshi, the entry then skips along to the next event: another of Michinaga's daughters, Empress Ishi (1000–36), giving birth to a princess whose eventual presentation to the future Emperor Goreizei (1025–68) also inspires a poem that makes a play on the "day of the rat."[83] This brings its reader forward to another new year, 1027, and the first imperial visit of the year to the Jōtōmon-in. Her home, described as even more "brilliant" (*haebaeshi*) than usual, is praised as being "like something from a Chinese painting—the color of the mountains, the green of the waters, the placement of the trees and stones were quite delightful," and the splendor of the robes and dancing are all "beyond words."[84] From there, the account moves directly to the eleventh month and Michinaga's death. Without preamble, it announces the intensification of his illness and recounts the rites and prayers undertaken on his behalf. Just before reporting his death, the narrator muses, "His descendants were the emperor and crown prince, so even in his time of illness, had there in the past ever been one who flourished such as he?"[85] This is followed by a short note on the birth of a new princess in 1029 and a longer reminiscence about the festivities for the seventieth birthday of Michinaga's widow, Minamoto no Rinshi (964–1053), in 1033. Among the guests is none other than Akazome Emon (the author of *Flowering Fortunes*, mentioned in the introduction), and she composes a celebratory verse. This, in turn, reminds the narrator of a different verse composed by Emon on "the day of the rat," bringing everything back full circle in terms of calendrical events.[86] The "Day of the Rat" concludes with the death of Emperor Goichijō (1008–36), which provokes memories of both a *kanshi* by the late emperor and a *waka* lamenting his passing.[87] In the repeated citation of poetry, the types of events with which the passage of

82. Takehana, *Imakagami*, 1:69.
83. Takehana, *Imakagami*, 1:72.
84. Takehana, *Imakagami*, 1:75–76.
85. Takehana, *Imakagami*, 1:78.
86. Takehana, *Imakagami*, 1:82.
87. Takehana, *Imakagami*, 1:86–87.

time is marked, and the wandering narrative focus, the "Day of the Rat" affords a good sense of how history is constructed and ordered within the world of *The New Mirror*.

With the conclusion of the royal biographies, the text arrives at the narrative present, only to return again to origins with the next set of biographies: the *Fujinami* (Wisteria Waves) of the Fujiwara family. Just as *The New Mirror* chooses a narrative setting (to be addressed below in "A Place with Prestige") with ties to both the imperial family and the Fujiwara elite, so too does its "historical" content demonstrate a double allegiance—in other words, much like *The Great Mirror, The New Mirror* is not solely an imperial history. In a structure that precisely duplicates the imperial biographies in the first three scrolls, the second three are devoted to relating the lives of the high-ranking Fujiwara. Once again harking back to *The Great Mirror* as well as to the rhetoric of causality suggested by a reference in *The New Mirror*'s preface that connects the origins and endings of events (to be explicated below in "Continuing Karma"), the first of the three scrolls commences with the explanation that "Yotsugi thought to explain the florescence of the Novice Chancellor [Michinaga] and elucidated those matters in detail; although I ought to speak of subsequent matters, since if one is unaware of a stream's fountainhead, its course is unclear, I need to first roughly relate the case of the [same] Novice Minister."[88]

The content of the Fujiwara biographies is fairly consistent with that of the imperial biographies, providing an image of the world in which the imperial and regent lines alike enable the cultural florescence that *The New Mirror* celebrates. In these accounts certain skills constitute the chief concerns: for men in particular, poetic and musical ability are especially favored. The most upwardly mobile men enter the court bureaucracy, though illegitimate or superfluous sons (in addition to those who are simply more piously inclined) often end up in ecclesiastical positions. For women, unsurprisingly, fertility is the most prized attribute; the best career prospects lie within the imperial household, ideally as empress. As in the case of the imperial family in the first three scrolls, charming individual anecdotes and asides surface, yet they are often nearly submerged in the ceaseless flow of the documentation of changes in rank and position

88. Takehana, *Imakagami*, 2:25.

and reminders of who is related to whom. The Fujiwara section closes rather abruptly with a reflection on the beauty of the lustration site at Ise, but *The New Mirror*'s work is far from finished, for the narrator's next task is to reveal the lesser but still impressive glory of the Genji lineage.

The Murakami Genji scroll, the seventh, opens with the assertion that it is "not the Wisteria Waves [Fujiwara] alone who flourish," and in drawing its conclusion it explains the success of the Genji by means of their ties to both Emperor Horikawa (1079–1107) and the maternal line of those holding the post of regent.[89] This scroll, too, is filled with genealogies interspersed with references to *The Tale of Genji* and *Tales of Ise*, as well as frequent citations of poetry.[90] The *Genji* and *Ise* references continue in the eighth scroll, "Noble Progeny," which relates the biographies of imperial descendants who can be traced to the Murakami Genji. The scroll focuses mostly on Minamoto no Arihito (1103–47), and the long account of him and his wife is followed by fragmentary biographies of other noble offspring. Anecdotes emerge amid the genealogical data, but the scroll's most striking quality is how the same people continually resurface: one begins to get a sense of just how interwoven the threads of power—imperial, regental, and ecclesiastical—are in the world of *The New Mirror*. The scroll concludes with an entry consisting of a short list of Emperor Nijō's (1143–65) children. The narrator summarizes it with the claim, "It would be quite overwhelming and very painful besides to continue talking about how things are now."[91]

In similar fashion to *The Great Mirror*, the final scrolls contain miscellaneous tales. Scroll 9 is comprised of tabloidesque accounts of various escapades, inclining heavily toward a virtuous Buddhist orientation at the end. The tenth also features this trajectory, though its anecdotes are more fragmentary "snippets" (*uchigiki*) that culminate in a discussion of the origins of the *Man'yōshū* (Collection of Myriad Leaves, circa 759 CE) and "the future of fiction" (*tsukurimonogatari no yukue*). The account

89. Takehana, *Imakagami*, 3:25; see also 3:210 on Horikawa and the regent connection.

90. Although this scroll includes a short entry for Emperor Nijō (1143–65), emperor during the Hōgen and Heiji Disturbances, there is no reference to either here. See Takehana, *Imakagami*, 3:204–5.

91. Takehana, *Imakagami*, 3:372.

suddenly breaks off with the narrator's realization of the late hour. Although she hopes to hear more, her elderly source demurs. As if to ensure that the reader understands the magnitude of what has just been related, the narrator closes the account by explaining: "Since she said things such as 'I hope we meet again somehow. Wouldn't it be nice if in the next life, we became buddhas beneath this tree and preached this kind of law to people that they might be able to hear it?' I don't think she was an ordinary mortal. Although I made inquiries in the area about her, I wasn't able to meet her again. 'Why didn't I have someone follow her to verify her whereabouts?' I ask myself, and I live with nothing but regret!"[92] By closing his work in this fashion, Tametsune has once again deployed the tools of *The Great Mirror*. With the monologue about the past concluded, the eyewitness informant vanishes, leaving narrator and reader alike to rue the lost opportunity.

These narrative contours of *The New Mirror* provide a context for understanding how Tametsune engages with the conventions of *The Great Mirror*: what he inherits unchanged, what he adapts to seemingly new ends, and what he inserts without precedent. A closer look at the preface will illustrate how *The New Mirror* manipulates the main rhetorical and stylistic conventions of *The Great Mirror*, including opening with a pilgrimage.

A PLACE WITH PRESTIGE: THE NEW MIRROR *AND ITS NARRATIVE SETTING*

Much like *The Great Mirror*, *The New Mirror* begins with an account of its origins that helps contextualize and clarify its priorities when it comes to narrating the past. The work opens this way:

> Sometime after the tenth day of the third month, I decided to make an excursion to Hase[dera] Temple accompanied by several like-minded friends and to take advantage of the opportunity to make a tour of various other temples. The days we wandered around Yamato, the road was long and the sun was hot; [at one point], thinking to rest, we approached a shade

92. Takehana, *Imakagami*, 3:594. Thomas Harper, however, takes the desire of the old woman to become a buddha as referring to herself alone ("Obsequies for *Genji*," 184).

> tree. While we were clustered beneath it, an elderly lady leaning on her walking stick and accompanied by a young girl—who had been breaking off bracken to put in the flower basket hanging from her arm—arrived at the base of the tree.[93]

Yet even as the preface resembles that of its predecessor, its choice of destination, Hasedera Temple, marks a significant change from *The Great Mirror*. Unlike the ambiguous status of the Urin'in—which, as seen above, could be read as both inside and outside of the established order—Hasedera was part of a popular elite pilgrimage route despite being well outside of Kyoto (and even Nara, to a lesser degree).[94]

That this tie to the court would have been part of the current imagination of Hasedera is supported by its representation in the roughly contemporary *setsuwa* compendium *Konjaku monogatarishū* (Tales of Times Now Past, written after 1120) as a temple with imperial and Fujiwara origins.[95] In the *Tales of Times Now Past* account, when Empress Genshō (680–748) learns of the mysterious origins of a famous Kannon image, she is inspired to have the temple built. Fujiwara no Fusasaki (681–737), progenitor of the powerful Northern House of the Fujiwara (which included Michinaga) springs to her aid, and the temple is completed in Jinki 4 (727).[96] The story acts as a perfect microcosm of Fujiwara and imperial cooperation in the founding days of the Nara state, and the temple becomes a symbolic nexus of Buddhist, imperial, and regental authority, a neat parallel to the world of *The New Mirror*.[97] In short, both in the popu-

93. Takehana, *Imakagami*, 1:27.

94. Anna Andreeva's focus is Miwa, but we can infer from her observations that Hasedera was a popular destination for "the Heian aristocracy, and noble women in particular" (*Assembling Shinto*, 63).

95. Yamada Yoshio et al., *Konjaku monogatarishū*, 3:116–18. The entry's title credits the Holy Man Dōtoku with the temple's founding, but as the content makes clear, Dōtoku is responsible for the Kannon image, while Genshō and Fusasaki provide for the actual temple construction.

96. On popular origin accounts of the temple and the rise in its cultural cachet, see Andreeva, *Assembling Shinto*, 86.

97. The narrator's unwillingness to speak of a Japan before this time may also reinforce an idea of imperial and Fujiwara cooperation as a prerequisite for a court worthy of discussion. When questioned about the possible Nara-period origins of the poetry anthology *Man'yōshū*, the old woman complains of feeling "quite dubious when you inquire in such detail about truly vague matters" (Takehana, *Imakagami*, 3:563).

lar imagination as reflected in the *Tales* and presumably in the elite choice of pilgrimage destinations, Hasedera was significant as a location with prestigious beginnings and contemporary cultural capital. Thus, despite its geographical remove from the court, it enjoyed a cultural proximity that connected it intimately to the world of elite society. Given this, whatever the leanings *The Great Mirror* has with regard to central authority, *The New Mirror* is unequivocally oriented toward the court in its site selection.

CONTINUING KARMA: THE NEW MIRROR'S *GUIDING HISTORICAL PRINCIPLE*

To return to the preface, *The New Mirror* is soon shown to be a faithful heir to *The Great Mirror* in terms not only of its court focus and cast of characters, but also of its specific commitment to karmic causation. The winding path the preface takes first establishes its social and literary worlds, deferring the revelation of its cosmological commitments to afterwards. After a lengthy exchange in which the old woman's age is discussed without arriving at any resolution beyond the fact that she is over 150, the conversation shifts to her lineage. When pressed for information, she responds: "My grandfather truly was a menial. He was employed in the empress's palace. His name was Yotsugi. You may perchance have heard of him. That story he blathered out is still around, it seems."[98]

The old woman then reveals that in her youth, she was in service at the palace in the retinue of one "Lady Shikibu." She reminisces about how Lady Shikibu inquired into the circumstances of her attendant's birth and considered various nicknames for her, including "little mirror" and "new mirror," the latter based on Bai Juyi's (772–846) poetry.[99] Here, *The New Mirror* seems to be marshaling a new type of authority—namely, a rich literary pedigree rather than the sermon parallels of *The Great Mirror*. Even though the pilgrimage setting continues to lend a sort of spiritual

98. Takehana, *Imakagami*, 1:31.

99. Takehana, *Imakagami*, 1:32. I have relied on Takehana's additional annotation regarding the poem (ibid., 1:43). While a more literal translation of Bai's line would be "reflecting on the past and reflecting on the present," having deferred to the conventional translation of *Imakagami* as "The New Mirror," I have rendered the poem reference in a way that reflects the allusion.

gravitas to the proceedings, the elderly narrator's ties to the "Lady" (who is soon revealed to be none other than Murasaki Shikibu) serve to enhance the prestige of the narrative in ways that will continue to resonate in later *Mirrors*. Indeed, in *The New Mirror*, the discovery of Murasaki's identity spurs the request that, in turn, results in the transmission of the past. After this unanticipated revelation, the narrator exclaims, "That's a person of high repute! She wrote the marvelous *Genji* tale, and since there was no one like her in the world, you must have heard ever so many things. What a lucky path that we could meet you and hear about her. Would you be willing to pass on the affairs of old?"[100]

After a small digression about the fates of her children and how their activities sometimes afford her additional information, the elderly woman reveals what is, in essence, the underlying principle of *The New Mirror*'s historical interpretations: "Once people know the origins, when they hear how things turn out, they will be filled with understanding."[101] In other words, like Yotsugi before her, the preternaturally aged informant of *The New Mirror* is positioned to explain not only what events have transpired since the time covered by *The Great Mirror*, but more importantly, to do so in a way that further attests to the interdependence of past and present, origins and endings. Her narrative will also subscribe to the same laws and principles as Yotsugi's: a trajectory defined by cause and effect. Although the preface devotes its closing lines to narrowing the timeframe of the narrative, the stage has now been set to answer the implicit question within it: to explain how karmic causation (although the text does not use this explicit term) has brought the world to where it is.

In setting things up in this way, Tametsune solidifies the foundation that many of the subsequent historiographic *Mirrors* will use. Most will frame their projects through a logic of place and principle, replicating the narrative setting to a greater or lesser degree by staging the narrative at or near a Buddhist temple, establishing explicit connections with earlier *Mirrors* (*The Great Mirror* in particular), and featuring a preternatural nar-

100. Takehana, *Imakagami*, 1:32.

101. Takehana, *Imakagami*, 1:32. Takehana, too, sees this sentence as the distillation of the author's "historical consciousness" (ibid., 1:40).

rator who promises to reveal something about the connections between past and present.[102]

Nevertheless, even though Tametsune has mobilized two of *The Great Mirror*'s defining tropes—the importance of location and the commitment to narrating historical trajectories in terms of cause and effect—the past in his presentation has very different contours than Yotsugi's relatively uncomplicated celebration of Michinaga's success as the fruition of his remarkable karma. While *The New Mirror* features a "packaging" that is similar to that of *The Great Mirror*, its contents reveal a different, more complex agenda.

Ordering the Past to a New Purpose: The New Mirror *and Recuperating the Past*

Although *The New Mirror* follows in the footsteps of *The Great Mirror* and addresses fairly recent events, many scholars agree that it has a different agenda regarding the past. Takehana Isao's work, for example, explores the boundary between succession and innovation. Takehana defines *The New Mirror* first and foremost as a successor to *The Great Mirror*,[103] but he nevertheless credits it with a distinct perspective: "The world *The New Mirror* describes is markedly qualitatively different from that of *The Great Mirror*. The age that *The New Mirror* takes as its narrative subject was one in which the regent government was essentially in its death throes, the system of rule by retired emperors had appeared, and moreover, the burgeoning might of warrior houses had arisen."[104] He adds to this the observation that politics, including the Hōgen and Heiji Disturbances, have virtually no presence in the work. For him, this is linked to the narrator's gender, and he concludes his appraisal by

102. Based on rhetorical parallels between *The New Mirror* and the twenty-fifth chapter of the *Lotus Sutra*, Suyama Yuko has argued that the narrator and Murasaki Shikibu are both incarnations of Kannon, while the work itself has a soteriological potential equivalent to that of the *Genji* ("'Imakagami' ni okeru Kannon shinkō").

103. Takehana, *Imakagami*, 3:615.

104. Takehana, *Imakagami*, 3:616.

characterizing the work as one primarily concerned with creating "a history of court customs or courtier culture."[105]

Although Takehana moves on after collapsing together the notions of the "female" voice and apolitical content, this claim can be unpacked to suggest that perhaps Tametsune's decision to use a female narrator is an escapist move.[106] Rather than assuming that this gambit is reflective of authorial interest in apolitical subjects, one might consider whether the selection of a female "informant"—in particular, one who is cloistered away in service to the palace in her youth—is itself a flight from the political realities of the present, a retreat to a world where the speaker cannot address these matters because of her gender. In any case, Takehana evaluates Tametsune's motivation for the nearly complete elision of current events as a decision inspired by the latter's awareness of the precariousness of *The New Mirror*'s world.[107] Takehana sees *The New Mirror* as a testament to a vanishing way of life,[108] and there is something to this claim. Although not mentioned in the preface amid the talk of "origins" and "endings," throughout the work there is a tension between the present and the past. The narrator repeatedly juxtaposes the past with more current events and often assesses the latter as in no way inferior.[109]

Yet I propose that we go a step further: like Ōki Masayoshi, I contend that Tametsune does not simply demonstrate the existence of court

105. Takehana, *Imakagami*, 3:617.

106. Sakurai states emphatically that this is not the case ("'Ōkagami' ni hajimaru mono," 54).

107. Takehana, *Imakagami*, 3:618–19.

108. Takehana, *Imakagami*, 3:619. This is not too different from the position taken by Sakakibara Kunihiko, who identifies a valorization of the past as one of the ideological positions informing *Imakagami* ("'Imakagami' no shisō"). His essay also discusses the influences of poetry, religion, and veneration of the royal house. In a piece on the state of the field, Kanō Shigefumi observes, "The debate on whether the text is about art or politics is a difficult question and central topic in [postwar scholarship]" ("Imakagami kenkyūshi," 66).

109. See, for instance, Takehana, *Imakagami*, 1:467. Ōki Masayoshi performs a detailed rhetorical analysis of passages comparing past to present in *Imakagami*. His work makes clear that *Imakagami*'s stance toward the past and present is not simply that the past is superior ("Imakagami no buntai"). For the most concise presentation of the conclusions of his argument, see ibid., 160–62. See also Matsumoto's observation that the arts are presented as lasting ("Rekishi monogatari to shiron," 28).

culture; rather, he writes a text in which the past is never lost.[110] Focusing on lexical items, Ōki sees *The New Mirror* as committed to a "continuation" of the positive aspects of "long ago," and he argues that the elision of the political is necessitated by the work's valorization of the past, which renders an "excavation of the true causes of political strife" impossible.[111] I suggest that this is also visible in the way that Tametsune maps chronological movement as fundamentally circular by means of his nonlinear narrative structure—a technique that provides another reason for seeing something more at stake than the survival of court culture. In other words, *The New Mirror*'s *plaidoyer* for the vitality of the past is not something that is achieved solely through rhetorical flourish, by the comments about the past or present, or even by the nearly complete refusal to address contemporary "reality." It is also embedded in the micro level of the narrative itself, where the text is broken down into units of court ceremony and/or poetic moments. Moreover, it is woven into Tametsune's narrative unfolding of a recursive representation of time, a construction that keeps past and present in close proximity, with both very much alive—endings invariably return the reader to beginnings—until the final stages, when the project collapses with the narrator's disappearance.

Put another way, Tametsune's nonlinear representation of time keeps an uncertain future at bay in the patterns he locates running across past and present. How this works becomes clearer if one turns to the ways in which historical events are scattered across the arrayed biographies in the narrative structure. In Ōki's more traditional view, *The New Mirror* is formally modeled on *The Great Mirror*, given its transition from imperial biographies to those of the "imperial mothers."[112] However, although the progression is similar, seeing *The New Mirror* as structurally parallel to *The Great Mirror* fails to take into account the different allocations of space given to the two categories of biographies. In *The Great Mirror*, the imperial biographies take up one scroll and the Fujiwara narrative

110. Ōki, "'Ōkagami' to 'Imakagami,'" 130. Ōki justifies this position based on the narrator's characterization of both herself and her audience as possessed of "yearning or nostalgia for the past" (*mukashi mo koishi*) (ibid., 128 and *passim*).

111. Ōki, "'Ōkagami' to 'Imakagami,'" 129–30. This is in response to an older argument by Kawakita Noboru. See also Sakurai, "'Ōkagami' ni hajimaru mono," 54.

112. Ōki, "'Ōkagami' to 'Imakagami,'" 127–28. On the use of biographies as inherited from *The Great Mirror*, see also Sakurai, "'Ōkagami' ni hajimaru mono," 53.

dominates the remainder of the work, so that the imperial biographies read almost like a second preface to the main narrative. In *The New Mirror*, the imperial and Fujiwara sections are allotted roughly the same amount of space (three scrolls each), which in a sense creates a double narrative. These two familial sets are then followed by the mininarrative of the Murakami Genji, which occupies a section roughly two-thirds the size of the narratives of the other two families.

This shift in structure results from the broadening of *The New Mirror*'s scope to fully encompass more than one family, which leads to an organization of the narrative along multiple genealogical lines in a manner that is much more pronounced than in *The Great Mirror*. Thus, in *The New Mirror*, a story about a member of the imperial family will be included most often in one of the "Emperors" scrolls, while an anecdote featuring a contemporary Fujiwara family member will occur in the Fujiwara-centered subsection titled "Wisteria Waves." However, only after reading through all of the imperial entries will the reader reach the entries for the Fujiwara. As a result, the narrative thread doubles back upon itself, and the reader repeatedly reexperiences time: along first the imperial trajectory, then the Fujiwara trajectory, and finally the Murakami Genji trajectory. Thus, rather than a side-by-side comparison of contemporaneous events, the reader retraces the same, longer temporal arc at work over the course of each family's narrative. In other words, if an event appears in the accounts of different houses, the reader will experience a given year over and over.

One clear instance of this type of redoubling is the treatment of the Hōgen Disturbance. The reader first encounters this event from an imperial perspective, where it surfaces in the account titled "Emperor Goshirakawa's Accession to the Throne." There, the reader learns: "At the end of the fifth month, the late Retired Emperor's ailment worsened and after he passed away in the seventh month, all sorts of rumors arose in the world. It felt most dangerous, and military events I don't even know how to put into words occurred. The imperial forces were victorious, and rewards were bestowed. Not only do I not know how to relate all of this, but everyone probably already knows about it. The governance of the realm was in no way inferior to that of the past."[113]

113. Takehana, *Imakagami*, 1:466–67.

At this point, the account takes up an issue of palace construction. However, the rebellion reappears in the "Wisteria Waves" scrolls, under an entry titled "Ceremonial Sword" that relates the rift between Fujiwara no Tadamichi (1097–1164) and his younger sibling, Yorinaga, two brothers who took different sides in the uprising. The relevant passages explain how their father Tadazane (1078–1162), the regent, turned against his oldest son before the disturbance, and the consequences of doing so:

> In the end, they turned against one another, and Tadazane and his younger son, Minister of the Left Yorinaga, allied with Retired Emperor Sutoku; Tadazane took the headship of the Fujiwara clan from Tadamichi and bestowed it on Yorinaga. . . . Around this time, Retired Emperor Toba died, and Retired Emperor Sutoku and Minister of the Left Yorinaga made a plan. When Goshirakawa ascended the throne, they engaged in battle at Shirakawa Mansion; but the Emperor was protected mightily by the *kami* and buddhas, and when Minister of the Left Yorinaga rode forth on horseback, he was struck by an arrow. (Who could have loosed it?) He escaped to Nara, but died there in no time.[114]

The entry then discusses Yorinaga's sons. Little is recorded about the oldest son beyond his pleasant (if slightly plump) appearance and character. The account notes that the second son, Moronaga (1138–92), was temporarily exiled but later recalled to the capital. The entry concludes shortly after relating how Moronaga's rank was restored at a command *biwa* performance for the emperor, and remarking upon how "sad" and "moving" both performer and audience must surely have found the deaths in exile of Yorinaga's other sons.[115] Neither version is particularly detailed, but the fact that events such as these become focal points in multiple anecdotes in the narrative invites the reader to ask: Why experience any event more than once?

114. Takehana, *Imakagami*, 2:300–302. The notes to this edition indicate that the wresting of the headship from Tadamichi also appears in "imperial" scrolls (see ibid., 2:303). I follow the modern gloss in translating *onmabori* as aid received specifically from the *kami* and buddhas rather than as protection more generally (see ibid., 2:302).

115. Takehana, *Imakagami*, 2:307–9.

Such repetition lends itself to two interpretations. On the one hand, *The New Mirror* subscribes to a logic of karmic causality, and it may be that patterns are more effectively presented when the reader sees how they consistently play out over multiple generations and across families. Adhering to a single chronology and moving back and forth between families would break the chain of events and could easily lessen the impact of the pattern on the reader. Given that the narrator spoke at the outset of a world of origins and suitable endings, repetition may thus be a way to elucidate the cause-and-effect relationship that informs her historical perspective.

On the other hand, the circular structure of the narrative may also be bound up with the attitude of the work toward its subject, an attitude identified in Ōki's "yearning for the past" and Takehana's claims that the work acknowledges a vanishing way of life as such.[116] In a universe governed by karmic causation, there is no guarantee that temporal progress is akin to advancement or any other sort of improvement. One might thus suppose that a general uncertainty about what karma portended for the future may have heightened the appeal of rendering the past, a known quantity, as not entirely lost.

Such evaluations of the historical perspective are not far removed from an understanding of, or desire for, the past as "recoverable" in a way that goes beyond mere preservation.[117] In the case of *The New Mirror*, however, this "recoverability" is not simply that of a "naked, unadorned, unequivocally reproducible truth," which Reinhart Koselleck contends is a hallmark of the premodern historian's understanding of the past.[118] Rather, in my analysis, *The New Mirror* implies that the favorable *conditions* of the past are recoverable. The work's circular structure permits the repeated narrative recuperation of bygone days, allowing the reader to ex-

116. Takehana asserts that this is the work's orientation—an awareness of the fragility of the world it depicts—based on its elision of current events (*Imakagami*, 3:619).

117. See Benjamin, "Über den Begriff der Geschichte," 252–53. I do not wish to engage with Benjamin's specific project(s) in this essay, but it is to this piece that I owe the abstract question of the "recoverability" of the past.

118. Koselleck, *Futures Past*, 132. This is part of a larger discussion of the *Mirror* metaphor in premodern European writing in chapter 2. Koselleck is a useful interlocutor here because he addresses the "premodern" world, although he does not allow for non-European cosmologies.

perience time as an endless series of loops. In other words, it is not a complete accounting of the past that is the aim of the historian here, but rather establishing the potential to return to a type of experience. In *The New Mirror*, this happens most obviously when an event is narrated more than once in different "lines," but the simple fact of returning to origins with each of its major genealogies is also a commitment to cyclicality.

At the same time, the patterns of cause and effect (karmic causation) revealed in these orderings of events demonstrate that society or the individual can influence subsequent events and conditions, thus making *The New Mirror* a fundamentally different project from the type of history that Koselleck identifies with the premodern. *The New Mirror* does not subscribe to the idea of "a present [that] in its forward movement collected the past without, however, being significantly able to change itself."[119] The principles at stake in *The Great Mirror* and *The New Mirror* are in direct opposition to that view: past karma shapes both present and future events. Thus, the disentangling of past and present suggested in Koselleck's discussion of premodern historiographic sensibilities is, at a basic level, impossible.

In my reading, this circular narrative and chronology are not an effort to recover the past in terms of its exhaustive representation; instead, they indicate a potentially more complicated appeal of *The Great Mirror* for Tametsune. By alluding to *The Great Mirror*, he recuperates an inherently conservative model for narrating history to recuperate a conservative vision of the past. However, whatever Tametsune's intent may have been, the import of this gesture resists a single interpretation. On the one hand, because *The Great Mirror* concludes its historical narrative on a positive note, by appropriating this historiographic vehicle from happier narrative days, Tametsune may have been enacting a recursive practice of optimistically narrating the past.[120] On the other hand, historical realities make reading the return to *The Great Mirror* as a purely celebratory gesture problematic. As Tametsune would surely have known, by the time *The Great Mirror* was written, Kenshi was long dead, and in 1074, Shōshi—who bore two emperors and was thus, by some accounts, the "origin" of Michinaga's success—had likewise died. In other words,

119. Koselleck, *Futures Past*, 133.
120. See Ishikawa, *Ōkagami*, 345–46.

The Great Mirror recounts a glory that was already on the wane by the time it was narrated. Therefore, rather than thinking that Tametsune turned to *The Great Mirror* only because of its promise to present a different kind of history, one might also consider whether he did so with a sardonic awareness that the past he was about to depict was gone. The Genji scrolls, in particular, lend themselves to this latter reading: their diminished scale (two rather than three scrolls) and the narrator's closing rejection of the present noted above can be interpreted as signs that the world of the past is receding. Nonetheless, whatever Tametsune's motivations, the result was the reanimation of an approach to the past that derived its authority from a combination of a powerful ritual narrative setting and a promise to present the past as ultimately subject to cosmological law.

Road to Perdition: Truth and Witness, Speech and Sin in Twelfth-Century Japan

The New Mirror also follows in the footsteps of *The Great Mirror* in its use of a style suggestive of spoken, rather than written, language. Just how loaded a choice that was becomes clear when put into the context of contemporary discussions about speech, writing, and morality—in particular, the morality of writing something that might or might not be true.

Social unrest was not the only source of anxiety for the Japanese court elite in the late twelfth century. There was also the troubling issue of how to avoid being reborn in a Buddhist hell in the next life. Lay practitioners followed rules that included observing the five precepts that prohibited the taking of life, thievery, wantonness, drunkenness, and false speech. The charge of false speech, in particular, had become a thorny issue for authors who engaged in creative literary production. One extreme manifestation of these concerns was the emergence during this period of a practice of making offerings for Murasaki Shikibu. This was tied to an increasing preoccupation with the supposed sinfulness of literature and mounting concern about the intensification of "the disturbances and uprisings that culminated in outright warfare in the capital region."[121] *The New Mirror* was facing a world in which not only was social unrest on the rise, but the morality of writing was increasingly called into question.

The *Genji ippon kyō* (One-Volume Sutra on the Genji, written circa 1176), a work by the Tendai monk Chōken (1126–1203, brother of the author of *China Tales*), is now the most famous of the textual condemnations of Murasaki.[122] However, for a broader sense of the world of sins that a twelfth-century audience had to navigate, there may be no better source than Taira no Yasuyori's (dates unclear) *Hōbutsushū* (Collected Treasures, written circa 1179), a work that bears an unmistakable structural resemblance to *The Great Mirror*.[123] Most striking of the similarities is the parallel that Yamada Shōzen identifies in how *Collected Treasures* unfolds at a temple as part of a three-way exchange between "narrator, audience, and scribe."[124] Yamada does not mention *The New Mirror*, but the similarity also holds true for it. If *Collected Treasures* speaks even indirectly to the world of *The Great Mirror*, then it speaks to the world of *The New Mirror*, too. This makes it a useful reference point in mapping a potential worldview for elite twelfth-century audiences.

To return to the issue of navigating a sin-free existence amid the worldly disorder of the day and with the knowledge of having entered the final age of the dharma, *Collected Treasures* takes up the question of keeping the five lay precepts as part of a larger discussion of twelve approaches to Buddhahood. The speaker first notes the necessity of proof of the efficacy of this method, and then the precepts are gone through

121. Harper, "Obsequies for *Genji*," 178. See also Harper's discussion of "false speech" as one of the "ten evils" (ibid., 177). On the beginnings of the characterization of Murasaki as sinful, see Marra, *Representations of Power*, 95.

122. Marra writes: "As early as the twelfth century, monk Chōken (1126–1203) accused Murasaki Shikibu . . . of immorality in a pamphlet entitled *Genji Ippon Kyō* (*The One-Volume Sutra on Genji*, 1168), condemning her to suffer the pains of hell because of the corruptive nature of her literary work" (*Representations of Power*, 96). In the dating, I follow Hakamada, "Genji ippon kyō," 217–18.

123. Koizumi and Yamada, *Hōbutsushū*, 510. Yasuyori was exiled for his involvement in the Shishigatani incident (discussed in chapter 2) but was later recalled to the capital.

124. Koizumi and Yamada, *Hōbutsushū*, 510. Yamada adds that like *The Great Mirror*, *Collected Treasures* relies on "numerous illustrative examples" to prove its points (ibid., 511). The relationship between the rhetorical conventions of the two works is a recurring point of analysis in this essay.

one by one, with each receiving a simple definition and illustrative examples.[125] The definitions, in particular, provide an indication of what might have been an elite reader's basic moral framework, including views on false speech, which is expanded upon at some length:

> The prohibition against false speech is such that you refrain from all lies, be it saying you didn't see something that you did or saying you did see something that you didn't. When we talk of the mouth as a tiger devouring a body or the tongue as a blade taking a life, this is enjoining against lying. The demon jailers instruct the sinners in hell, saying: "False speech often consumes the 'vast ocean' in flame. How much the more so must those who utter false speech burn—exactly like torches." They become the torches in hell. That is why we must be careful not to tell lies. In *Commentary on the Ten Stages*, in the third section it teaches that "even if a person dies, they mustn't lie," and in the *Sutra of the Great Assembly* there is the teaching: "Sweet dew and poison / all reside on the human tongue. / Sweet dew is true speech; / False speech turns to poison."[126]

This may not strike the reader as particularly surprising in its general formulation. A closer look at the specifics of wantonness and false speech, however, sheds light on where the lines were drawn when it came to determining which types of writing were sinful. The discussion of the prohibition against wantonness specifically lists the following as sources for proof of events having occurred: "diaries, *Flowering Fortunes*, and *Tales of Ise*," as well as the *Nihongi* (Chronicles of Japan), are all directly cited as sources of historical information, albeit in the dubious category of sources for information on illicit relations.[127] The speaker characterizes

125. On the need for proof as well as for a list of the precepts, see Koizumi and Yamada, *Hōbutsushū*, 193–94.

126. Koizumi and Yamada, *Hōbutsushū*, 225. Translated with reference to *A Dictionary of Chinese Buddhist Terms* (WE Soothill and Lewis Hodous, 2003 edition).

127. For the first three, see Koizumi and Yamada, *Hōbutsushū*, 215. The annotation suggests that "yotsugi," which I have here rendered as "Flowering Fortunes," is a catchall term for *The Great Mirror* and *Tale of Flowering Fortunes*. For the *Nihongi* (and its gloss), see ibid., 221. My reason for reading it only as *Flowering Fortunes* is Takeshi Watanabe's observation that this work is grouped with *Ise monogatari* and the *Genji* in a roughly contemporary text, Fujiwara no Sanefuyu's (1243–1303?) *Honchō shojaku mokuroku* (Catalogue of This Sovereignty's Texts) (Watanabe, "Buried Mothers," 108–9). I would

the first three as "extreme" (*katawashi*) but never calls their veracity into question and stops short of directly criticizing the works.

Murasaki Shikibu and the *Genji* stand in contrast to this. In the larger discussion of false speech, they are explicitly included among examples of how dying does not free one from the need for honesty. After citing an example from China, the speaker explains: "Near at hand, it's said that Murasaki Shikibu has appeared in people's dreams and related the suffering in hell she is enduring because she is guilty of the sin of using false speech in composing *The Tale of Genji*. Although she probably feels relief if poets gather, do a day of sutra copying, and make offerings for her."[128] *Collected Treasures* does not explain what makes writing the *Genji* so problematic. But it can be surmised that the reason is tied in part to the presumed effect of the text, as set forth in Chōken's contemporary *One-Volume Sutra*.[129]

In Chōken's reckoning, all tales are bad: "They do not transmit the virtues and vices of people of yore; nor do they heed the ancient matters of previous ages. In men and matters, they all present fabrications as gospel; and in establishing the age or era, they all clothe fictions as events. Although there are a thousand versions, they all come down to the Way of Fornication."[130] For Chōken, there is no room for "fact" in a tale. He goes on to identify *The Tale of Genji* as the most egregious offender among tales precisely because of the skill with which it was composed, including the "extreme beauty of its enticing language."[131] All of this is sure to enflame the desires of even the most stolid or inexperienced reader and trap her or him in the endless cycle of rebirth, leading Chōken to conclude that both the writer and readers of the *Genji* would inevitably

---

add that the same work, which dates to approximately within a century of *Collected Treasures*, also groups *The Great Mirror* (with this title) with the other extant *Mirrors*.

128. Koizumi and Yamada, *Hōbutsushū*, 229.

129. I assume that the text's effect is important, because the speaker closes the section with an explanation in which lying to a deer hunter about the presence of deer is specifically described as "not false speech" and something "the Buddha permits" (Koizumi and Yamada, *Hōbutsushū*, 229). Surely this white lie is allowed because of its effect: it spares a life.

130. Hakamada, "Genji ippon kyō," 221. For an alternative translation by Michael Jamentz, see Harper, "Obsequies for *Genji*," 190.

131. Hakamada, "Genji ippon kyō," 221. For an alternative translation, see Harper, "Obsequies for *Genji*," 190.

tumble into a hell of swords.[132] Chōken's condemnation suggests that not only is a writer to be truthful, but also she or he must plan ahead for a morally acceptable reception for her or his creation.

Although the imprecision of the dates make it impossible to definitively know the order in which *The New Mirror*, *One-Volume Sutra*, and *Collected Treasures* were completed, they were clearly part of a shared discourse. And since the final pages of *The New Mirror* are devoted to the question of Murasaki's posthumous karmic recompense, it seems that the question of morality and "fiction" weighed heavily on Tametsune's mind.[133] This becomes clear in the final "Future of Fiction" section, beginning with its subtitle: "Accounts That Shikibu Has Gone to Hell."[134]

The segment at once cuts to the heart of the matter, opening with the question: "Is it true? It's said that because in that long-ago person's work, *The Tale of Genji*, she pulled together completely baseless beautified and enticing things—[assembling away as though] gathering seaweed to burn to make salt—it's now she who is going up in flames in the afterlife."[135] Unlike the case in the *One-Volume Sutra* and *Collected Treasures*, however, the elderly narrator in *The New Mirror* assures her interlocutor that despite the proliferation of such rumors, "for those who understand the true nature of things, be it in Yamato or China, concocting texts has always been to stir people's minds and guide the benighted. It mustn't be mistaken for 'false speech.'"[136] That is, she contends that creative writing can do other than instigate sexual desire—that there is also

132. Hakamada, "Genji ippon kyō," 221–22. For an alternative translation, see Harper, "Obsequies for *Genji*," 190.

133. For a summary of the larger connections between Tametsune's household and offerings for Murasaki, see Itō Takako, "Murasaki Shikibu dagoku," 59. For a handy chart of people related to Tametsune who are also known to have had concerns about Murasaki's fate, see ibid., 64n9.

134. The following overview of the Murasaki segment shares much with Takehana's notes, since we coincidentally focus on similar sections of the text. For his overview, see Takehana, *Imakagami*, 3:605–11. For an alternative translation of this entry in *The New Mirror*, see Harper, "Obsequies for *Genji*," 182–84.

135. Takehana, *Imakagami*, 3:591. Takehana points out that this was a common belief "from the late Heian through the Kamakura periods," and he provides examples of texts that contain such imagery, including Chōken's work (ibid., 3:605; see also 3:606).

136. Takehana, *Imakagami*, 3:591.

well-established precedent for recognizing that creative writing can be used to salvific ends.

Without addressing a specific source, the narrator then proceeds to counter some of the more infamous charges against creative literary composition: "The sin lies in dissimulation—relating experiences one hasn't had as though true and persuading people that bad circumstances are good."[137] These are not the terms in which *Collected Treasures* defined "false speech," but they do shift the emphasis from the act of creation to its intent, a point to which she will return. Before that, however, she takes a detour to suggest a hierarchy of sins: "But ought we call this [the *Genji*] wanton? Even if it does contain 'ornate speech' or 'nonsensical prattle,' those aren't such serious sins. I've heard that killing all living things or stealing the treasures of all people and such are grave sins and can result in one sinking to the very depths of Hell, but while I haven't heard what Murasaki's lot was, in her case, that would be bizarre."[138] The old woman presses her case that producing works of fiction does not constitute a serious sin, despite the feelings it arouses and the challenges that those in turn pose to breaking free from the cycle of rebirth.[139] Citing both the soteriological power of the much-loved Chinese poet Bai Juyi's writing—indeed, pointing to his identification as an incarnation of Monju—as well as the use by the Buddha himself of parables that are not, strictly speaking, based in fact, she then points out that bodhisattvas such as Myō'on and Kannon have taken female form and led people to enlightenment, implying that Murasaki is such a figure.[140]

137. Takehana, *Imakagami*, 3:591. The similarities in Itō's and my independent analyses should support my reading of this portion of *Imakagami*. Itō is interested in reconciling the positive and negative views of the literature that she sees Tametsune as negotiating, while I focus on the logic that Tametsune's characters use to articulate his position and its implications. See Itō Takako, "Murasaki Shikibu dagoku," 60–61.

138. Takehana, *Imakagami*, 3:591–92.

139. See Koizumi and Yamada, *Hōbutsushū* (67), which likewise equates the degree of punishment with the severity of the sin. In short, *The New Mirror*'s narrator subscribes to the hierarchy of punishments within *Collected Treasures*; it is the classification of Murasaki's alleged sin with which she takes issue.

140. Takehana cites *The New Mirror* as the first place where Bai Juyi is thus identified. He suggests that the identification of Murasaki with Kannon, Myō'on, and the like is probably based on earlier *Genji* commentaries (*Imakagami*, 3:607). For a more typical take on Bai Juyi's solution to the problem of "floating phrases and fictive utterances" in

At this point, the old woman's young attendant interrupts. She acknowledges the precedents for female figures to awaken others to the truth of the Buddha's teachings but expresses doubts about whether Murasaki's writing actually has any salvific potential. After admitting that the tale's splendor can invite a sort of attachment, the old woman claims: "[The *Genji*] displays the depths of sin, causing people to chant His Holy Name; for those who would have offering services performed, it becomes a ladder to lead them [upward]; it speaks to the compassionate heart, and leads even those who would sink in the ways of this floating world to the paths of good; there can be none to whom it has revealed the impermanence of the world who have not left the ways of wickedness to pursue the path of the Buddha."[141] The discussion then turns to a list of the ways in which moments or characters from *The Tale of Genji* might, in fact, reveal Buddhist truths.[142] The old woman concludes by reiterating her assertion that the *Genji* can and should prove an aid to enlightenment, its superfluous or "sullied" words fading away like "dew and frost" at the approach of the "morning sun of the Law."[143] At this point, the characters all realize the late hour, and the party breaks up, as noted above, never to reassemble.

The reader is left with something of a mixed message.[144] On the one hand, the point has been acknowledged that writing the *Genji* may not have been entirely sin-free; on the other, the ends seem to justify the means in the narrator's assessment. The old woman never suggests that Murasaki is not punished; rather, she argues that burning in hell would be excessive. Fiction itself is likewise vindicated, but not entirely: making up stories is not inherently bad—the fault lies in making up stories that mislead people. The conclusion similarly falls short of a complete exonera-

---

medieval Japan, see LaFleur, *Karma of Words*, 8. Hakamada traces the connection between Bai Juyi's writings and Murasaki's to *Genji ippon kyō* ("Genji ippon kyō," 219).

141. Takehana, *Imakagami*, 3:593.

142. Takehana traces the origins of this rhetoric to a poem by Bai Juyi included in *Wa-Kan rōeishū* (Japanese and Chinese Poems to Sing, written circa 1013) (*Imakagami*, 3:608).

143. Takehana, *Imakagami*, 3:594.

144. Takehana similarly sees this discussion as not entirely resolved. However, he is more concerned with whether Tametsune wants to undertake a full-scale discussion of "tales," which he doubts (*Imakagami*, 3:609–10). Itō Takako, too, characterizes the pro-*Genji* argument as ultimately falling short ("Murasaki Shikibu dagoku," 63).

tion of the *Genji*, proposing instead that it is akin to a temporary, imperfect manifestation of the eternal truth of the Buddhist law.

It remains unclear throughout why Tametsune included this section at all, unless it was to highlight how *The New Mirror* does not take the liberties taken by *The Tale of Genji.* Where Murasaki admittedly fabricated (outstanding!) content, Tametsune's narrator relies on an eyewitness. If her elderly informant has been truthful, then there is nothing in *The New Mirror* that has not been observed at first or (via her family members) second hand.[145] Therefore, it does relate "the virtues and vices of people of yore" with careful attention to "the ancient matters of previous ages."[146] While Tametsune has presented an argument for fiction as an expedient means when it conveys Buddhist truths, it nevertheless appears that the charge of "fabrication" is one he seeks to avoid. This certainly makes sense in a time that Thomas Rohlich describes as "an age when many people believed that the reading and writing of *monogatari* [tales] led to neglect of important religious observations and the subsequent risk of eternal damnation. Evidence of this belief appeared as much as a century and a half earlier in the regrets the daughter of Sugawara no Takasue expressed in *Sarashina nikki* [which predates *The New Mirror* by just over a century] over the time she wasted on poems and tales rather than devoting herself to prayer."[147] It seems significant that despite his spirited and lengthy defense of Murasaki's work as something that certainly encourages people along the Buddha path, for his own writing, Tametsune sidesteps the fraught "tale" designation. Even as he uses the language most common to tales, *wabun*, to relate the past, with the emphasis on proximity to the sources, his narrator stresses that what she relates is true speech, not false. Especially if one considers Tametsune's apparent awareness of the logic reflected in a work such as *One-Volume Sutra*, which takes pains to distinguish between the production of histories and that of fiction, his decision appears deliberate.[148] In framing his account—*The New Mirror*—

145. Takehana also sees the final lines as an assertion of truth, albeit vis-à-vis the conclusion of *The Great Mirror* (*Imakagami*, 3:610–11).

146. Hakamada, "Genji ippon kyō," 221. For an alternative translation by Michael Jamentz, see Harper, "Obsequies for *Genji*," 190.

147. Rohlich, "In Search of Critical Space," 186–87; see also 203–4. I have removed the Chinese characters from the citation (ibid., 187).

148. For the distinctions, see Hakamada, "Genji ippon kyō," 221–22.

as something other than a "tale," he demonstrates an appreciation of the moral ambiguity of the genre at this time and, I suggest, makes a case for treating his work, a *Mirror*, as something different.

Conclusion

With the ambiguous circumstances of *The Great Mirror*'s production and even of its title, there is no way to be certain of the specifics it was intended to address beyond those articulated in the text itself: to lay bare "the matters of the world" that enabled Michinaga's rise.[149] This ambiguity also makes it impossible to argue that when Tametsune sat down to write *The New Mirror*, the first successor to *The Great Mirror*, he had a particular historical moment he hoped to reference or access in selecting a *Mirror* as his medium. What Tametsune did reveal through his crafting of the past in *The New Mirror* was the flexibility of the genre: how the selection of a narrative site and a particular language could work together with an explanation of the past as driven by cosmic principles and the structuring of the narrative itself to produce a persuasive interpretation of historical events for anyone able to use these tools well.

When Tametsune created *The New Mirror*, he co-opted characteristics of *The Great Mirror* that on one level seem to forestall an anticipated charge of "false speech"—namely, a prestigious narrative site that, as a temple, provided its narrator with moral authority; and a written language, *wabun*, that highlighted the nature of the account as an eyewitness oral transmission rather than as the personal (and potentially fanciful) reflections of an individual author. In the context of a larger medieval concern with the morality of creative literary production, one can easily imagine the possible appeal of writing a history as *The New Mirror* rather than as *The New Tale*.[150]

149. Ishikawa, *Ōkagami*, 19.

150. This being said, a century later, his grandson Nobuzane (1176–1275) is believed to have authored a work just so titled: *Ima monogatari* (more literally *Tales of Today*, but in keeping with the convention of rendering *Imakagami* as *The New Mirror*, *New Tales*.)

The morality of writing, however, was not Tametsune's only concern; he was also writing in a world increasingly marked by military unrest. Given this fact, the decision to co-opt the representation of history as driven by karmic causation is also legible. It provides a pattern for events at a time when social and governmental institutions faced growing challenges. At the same time, the narrative of the past as a recursive loop allows for its potential recovery, permitting the reader to infinitely defer the arrival of the day when the rules that governed Tametsune's world might be irreparably broken.

Such an escapist or reactionary position in light of the social unrest of the 1150s and beyond still could have made sense in the 1170s. Given the instability apparent in the *Logbook* and the tremors of unease detectable in *China Tales*, it should not be surprising that *The New Mirror*, a courtier-authored history, is a fundamentally conservative enterprise. Its mobilization of the morally "sin-free" and cosmologically endorsed position of *The Great Mirror* facilitates a reactionary attempt to write the recent instability out of the picture. However, its position was also soon revealed to be untenable, and its postwar successor, *The Water Mirror*, would face an irrevocably altered political landscape. Yet in the fallout from the Genpei War and subsequent challenges, authors of *Mirrors* would continue to exploit the flexibility into which Tametsune had tapped. This enabled a (re-)removal of historiographic authority beyond the exclusive reach of the court and different articulations of cosmological principles. These reimagined tropes would in turn allow integration into a larger and simultaneously both more urgent and more powerful effort to order Japan's past in a constantly changing present.

CHAPTER 2

Deviant by Design

Multilingual Writing in Postwar Medieval Japan

Main texts (in chronological order)

***Fusō ryakki* (Abbreviated Records of the Land of the Rising Sun)**
Author: conventionally attributed to Kōen
Date: conventionally dated to roughly 1094–1107
Language: *kanbun*
Preface: no
Setting: N/A
Time covered: presumably the reign of Emperor Jinmu (traditionally seventh century BCE)–Emperor Horikawa (1079–1107); sixteen of an original thirty scrolls survive

***Mizukagami* (The Water Mirror)**
Author: commonly attributed to Nakayama Tadachika
Date: late twelfth century
Language: *wabun* with regular insertions of *kanbun*
Preface: yes
Setting: Hasedera Temple; Ryūgaiji Temple (Nara area); Mount Katsuragi
Time covered: the reigns of Emperor Jinmu (traditionally seventh century BCE)–Emperor Ninmyō (810–50).

The civil war changed everything.[1] To be sure, unrest was already on the rise in Japan when Prince Mochihito's unsuccessful uprising in the fifth

1. Elizabeth Oyler's earlier assessment is: "It is impossible to overstate the significance of the Genpei War in Japan's history" (*Swords, Oaths, and Prophetic Visions*, 3).

month of Jishō 4 (1180) sparked what was to become a five-year conflict of unprecedented scope. In addition to enduring the Hōgen and Heiji Disturbances of 1156 and 1160, which hover at the margins of historiographic writings such as *The New Mirror*, the capital had also faced the abortive Shishigatani incident, an unsuccessful attempt in Angen 3 (1177) to displace Taira no Kiyomori.[2] This had been followed by Kiyomori's military coup in Jishō 3 (1179). In all likelihood, the escalation of this-worldly instability functioned as a sign that Japan had entered the latter days of the Buddhist law.

Although it is widely accepted that the Genpei War was not an effort to displace the imperial system, it both led to a certain restructuring of government and, arguably of more significance, occasioned a serious alteration in the worldview of at least some of the elite. With the establishment of the semiautonomous *bakufu* in Kamakura, victors and vanquished alike found themselves in a world in which imperial power was circumscribed in a way previously unthinkable. Not only was the court confronted with implicit and actual limitations to its authority, but also for the first time, a sitting emperor had been reduced to a battlefield casualty. It is not an overstatement to assert that the war irrevocably altered the political and sociocultural landscape of Japan.

In addition to the social and political reorganization that followed the war, there were also new demands made of those writing about the past. Japan had never before encountered a sustained or even semisuccessful attempt to establish an authority independent of the court. Thus, the war's violent reapportioning of power can be thought of as a rupture that invited or necessitated new ways of accounting for the events that led up to and followed it.[3] A *Mirror* that sought only to fetishize the culture of the court would have had very limited suasive ability in a postwar reality in which power apportionment continued to shift between the court and the *bakufu* as they negotiated their spheres of authority.

While the primary sources we used differ greatly, our evaluations of the war are very similar.

2. For a brief synopsis of the Shishigatani incident and some of its immediate implications, see Adolphson, *Gates of Power*, 154–55.

3. For war tales facing this challenge, Oyler suggests that the evolving depiction of Yoritomo and Yoshitsune's relationship in post-Genpei texts are among "attempts to shore up the new order with accounts of the rectitude of the Minamoto" (*Swords, Oaths, and Prophetic Visions*, 113; see also 114).

Presumably, this issue of how to interpret the immediate past was particularly pressing for the members of the court elite who were, as the old regime, faced with the task of making sense of something formerly unimaginable. From his base at Ninnaji, Tonsured Prince Shukaku looked back on the five years of the "chaos" of the Genpei War to describe it as a time of "streets . . . awash with blood and alleyways . . . buried under bodies."[4] Japan's imperial capital had become a site of violence, and the disorder extended to the uppermost reaches of society, as demonstrated by the drowning at sea of the child Emperor Antoku (1178–85) during the rout of the Taira at Dan-no-Ura. For Shukaku, this loss was certainly personal—Antoku was his nephew—but his subsequent remarks make clear its wider meaning, with the death of Antoku framed as an unprecedented disaster:[5] "Although both long ago and recently, there have been frequent examples of contention for the throne or of deposing a ruler and driving him from the Nine-Fold Palace, I had never before heard of a Dragon Countenance suddenly drowning beneath leviathan waves."[6] Shukaku does not address the wider implications of this loss, but they are immense. And while the specific subject of his concerns here is the tragic fate of the child emperor, the death can be read *pars pro toto* for the larger world that has itself become a casualty of the Genpei War. What is mourned is not solely the passing of Emperor Antoku, but also the obsolescence of a particular understanding of the world.

Looking back on the war years from his mountain retreat in 1212, Kamo no Chōmei (circa 1155–1216) provides a fuller account of the war's conditions and their psychological impact, describing the capital as filled with "more than 42,300 corpses" after the double wartime hardship of

4. Shukaku, *Saki*, 665.

5. Even the war tale *Jōkyūki* (A Record of the Jōkyū Years), from the mid-thirteenth century, is circumspect in its treatment of Antoku. Though this tale lists a series of twelve "royal wars" (*kokuō heiran*), Antoku is the sole emperor named without having any specific acts attributed to him. For a summary of various theories on the dating of the oldest textual lineage, the Jikyōji version, see Matsubayashi, *Jōkyūki*, 25–26. The catalogue of "royal wars" can be found in ibid., 178–80. In the translation of the title, I follow Tyler, *Before* Heike *and After*.

6. Shukaku, *Saki*, 665.

famine and plague.[7] He extrapolates: "Of course, many others died before and after this period, and if we include those on the Kamo riverbed, in Shirakawa, in the western half of the capital, and in the countryside beyond, their numbers would be limitless. How vast the numbers must have been, then, in all the provinces along the Seven Highways. I have heard that something of the sort occurred in the Chōjō era [1134], during the reign of Emperor Sutoku, but I do not know how things were then. What I saw before my own eyes was extraordinary."[8] Chōmei's essay then turns to a powerful earthquake that occurred just as the war was drawing to a close. After recounting the destruction in detail, he muses on what these experiences suggest: the impermanence and anxiety that characterize all human existence. Chōmei does not explicitly address the question of how to make sense of the past, but the lines that draw this segment to a close suggest that the conceptual frameworks for the prewar world had reached their limits: "Bend to the ways of the world and you will suffer. Bend not and you will look demented. Where can one live, and how can one behave to shelter this body briefly and ease the heart for a moment?"[9] The world to which Tametsune had clung so tenaciously in *The New Mirror* was in some ways now gone forever.

As discussed in the introduction, traditional literary histories have emphasized this period as an age marked by the rise of the war tale, in which military exploits and accomplishments came to occupy narrative center stage. However, while it is true that some of the greatest war narratives in the medieval corpus date from roughly this time, the "tale" was not the only way of reordering the past that was deployed in the wake of war. Rather, in the aftermath of the civil war, *Mirror* writing reemerged as a means of providing continuity with a traditional discourse sympathetic to the court while at the same time offering a locus of authority that was not contingent upon the power of the court. Two postwar *Mirrors*, *The Water Mirror* (for more on its dating, see below in this chapter) and *The China Mirror* (see chapter 3), suggest that some parties saw in

7. Takeda Kō, *Hōjōki zenshaku*, 174. For the corresponding events in Anthony H. Chambers's English translation, from which the brief quotation is also drawn, see Kamo no Chōmei, "Account of a Ten-Foot-Square Hut," 628.

8. Takeda Kō, *Hōjōki zenshaku*, 174. Translation from Kamo no Chōmei, "Account of a Ten-Foot-Square Hut," 628.

9. Takeda Kō, *Hōjōki zenshaku*, 217–18. Translation from Kamo no Chōmei, "Account of a Ten-Foot-Square Hut," 629.

the genre an opportunity to make their voices heard in a way that did not necessitate a complete break with the old order. Instead, these works feature a series of negotiations with the past, visions in which old and new markers of authority are deployed together or adapted to fresh ends as ways of processing and ordering new configurations of power.

This chapter argues that *The Water Mirror*, conventionally attributed to Nakayama Tadachika and the first *Mirror* to emerge after the war, marks a turning point in the genre that has an impact on both later *Mirror* writing and other disquisitions on the past. At the narrative level, *The Water Mirror* capitalizes on the place and principle rhetoric of the earlier *Mirrors* to advance a new position and relationship to the past. At the same time, its use of language—a regular alternation between *kanbun* and *wabun*—marks a significant development in the format of the *Mirrors*. In my reading, Tadachika's formal and thematic innovations to the genre collectively become a catalyst for an apparent reappraisal of *Mirror* writing, one that gradually moves the genre from the historiographic "margins of power" to the mainstream and has lasting legacies for medieval historiography.[10]

Identifying the Erased: *Origins of* The Water Mirror

In addition to the formal and thematic innovations just noted, *The Water Mirror* also breaks with precedent to turn to the distant past for its subject. Part of the work's power lies in what its author chooses to address, so before anything else, at least some sense of which events are being elided must be established. Unfortunately, the dating of *The Water Mirror* is murky. Often, it is simply given as being after 1170.[11] This dating means that it follows at least two significant armed uprisings, the aforementioned Hōgen and Heiji Disturbances of 1156 and 1160. But if the work was writ-

10. The "margins of power" are where David Bialock positions *The Great Mirror* (*Eccentric Spaces*, 157).

11. Gomi Fumihiko is representatively circumspect in dating it as in "the age of Tadachika" (*Shomotsu no chūseishi*, 177).

ten after the Genpei War, the significance of what it does and does not say about the immediate past is much greater, simply because of the magnitude of the events from which it turns away.

Based on developments suggested by Tadachika's other writings, I argue that *The Water Mirror* was written after the Genpei War, during the last decade of Tadachika's life.[12] Regrettably, there are no overt clues to be found within *The Water Mirror*. Nowhere is there a reference to specific current events that might provide a hint about the work's genesis. Like the two *Mirrors* before it, the work comes with a preface, but unfortunately that provides virtually no information about a reality external to the text other than to clarify that it postdates both *The Tale of Genji* and *The Great Mirror*.[13] The preface takes the form of the reminiscences of a seventy-three-year-old woman on a pilgrimage and also features a young ascetic who relates a historical transmission to her (that he has heard from an immortal), but there is no obvious narrative counterpart to the author. Neither the elderly woman nor the young ascetic is close to Tadachika in terms of age, although Tadachika's diary *Sankaiki* (A Minister's Logbook, written in 1151–94) attests to mounting physical woes that might resonate with the "pangs of old age" his septuagenarian narrator feels.[14]

Of course, it is perfectly possible that the figures Tadachika created were not based on any correspondence to his own autobiographical details. But since Tadachika's account of much of his time after the Genpei War is spotty, it is difficult to pin down the composition of *The Water Mirror* to this time period based on the factual record alone; the surviving

12. A recent annotated edition of *The Water Mirror* proposes in passing that it "is thought to probably be from the early Kamakura, and on top of that, around the Kenkyū era (1190–1198)" (Kawakita, "'Mizukagami' ni tsuite," 2).

13. Kaneko et al., *Mizukagami zen chūshaku*, 452. This critical edition is based on the oldest surviving manuscript of *The Water Mirror*, which dates from the mid-Kamakura period and is held by Senjūji Temple. See ibid., 3. Matsumura Takeo identifies the Senjūjibon and the Hōsa Bunkobon, dating from approximately the Ōei period (1394–1428), as the oldest and most reliable versions ("Mizukagami no shohon," 63). The other manuscript editions are the Yanase Kazuobon, from no later than 1652; the Edo-period Kunaichō shoryōbubon; the undated Ōkura Seishin bunka kenkyūsho edition; and the undated fragment held at Shinpukuji Temple (ibid., 70–76). The remaining three manuscripts he characterizes as "augmented" (*zōho*) editions (ibid. 76–87).

14. Kaneko et al., *Mizukagami zen chūshaku*, 11. For instances of Tadachika's ailments, see Nakayama, *Sankaiki*, 2:76, 289, 310, 311, and 327; and 3:244.

portions of his journal shed no light on the subject. In the entries covering the twenty-odd years between the earliest possible appearance of *The Water Mirror* and Tadachika's death, his journal is conventionally professional, focusing primarily on the court or court-related business. There is no mention of any of the *Mirrors*, or indeed of any private reading or writing.

Still more troublesome in a search for concrete evidence that *The Water Mirror* was a response to the war, there are no surviving entries in Tadachika's record from the months immediately after the final major battle at Dan-no-Ura, where Emperor Antoku was lost. A five-month gap exists between the entry for Genryaku 2 (1185).2.2 and those for the seventh month of the same year, the latter of which are dominated by an earthquake more severe than Tadachika had ever seen. Both Dan-no-Ura and the famous battle at Yashima are passed over in silence in the surviving record.

While the reason for this lacuna is unclear, it cannot reasonably be attributed to Tadachika's reluctance to address the Genpei War or violence itself.[15] Although he refrains from the lurid, Tadachika nonetheless vividly recounts the 1180 flight of the insurgent Prince Mochihito to Uji and the armed clashes that led to his death, complete with a limited enumeration of heads taken in front of the Byōdōin.[16] And in a similarly grisly instance, he notes that Kiyomori "ordered that the wife and the favorite child of the rebel Takeda of Kai Province be beheaded by night and their heads mounted on pikes before the gate of the Takeda [household]."[17] He is not an author who eschews the reportage of war.

Nor can the lack of extant entries on the closing days of the war be taken as indicative of these events' collective impact, or lack of impact, on Tadachika. Rather, the record that does survive suggests that the experience of the Genpei War deeply unsettled him. This becomes particularly clear in Tadachika's response to the earthquake on Genryaku

15. The record for the earlier Hōgen and Heiji Disturbances is similarly fragmented. No entries survive from the fifth month of Hōgen 1 (1156) through the sixth month of Hōgen 3 (1158). Nor are there any at all for the brief Heiji period (1159.4.20–1160.1.10). See Nakayama, *Sankaiki*, vol. 1.

16. For the events of Jishō 4 (1180).5.26, including Mochihito's death, see Nakayama, *Sankaiki*, 3:96–100.

17. Nakayama, *Sankaiki*, 3:149.

2 (1185).7.9—the quake also described by Chōmei—in an outburst that occurs in the midst of his catalogue of the resultant destruction: "My vision blurs, and my head hurts. My heart and senses are jumbled and chaotic, as though shipboard. Have we already arrived at the end of the world? With the war of late, none have known peace. And now there is this punishment, too. In a sullied age of wicked karma, the bitterness and suffering of sentient beings know no respite. Lamentable, lamentable!"[18] Despite earlier instances in which Tadachika bemoaned deviations from precedent, instances of decline, and other sources of distress, this is the only time in over two decades of writing that the reader is given such an intense expression of anguish about the state of the world at large. Between the war and the earthquake, the aftershocks of which would continue into the ninth month, Tadachika is moved to make his strongest recorded statement about the end of the world.[19]

Scattered utterances decrying "the decay of the realm" or characterizing the "transience of this world" as "beyond description," as well as juxtapositions of past matters with specific present practices from the eighth and ninth months of 1184, imply a gradual buildup of concern about the fate of the world during the closing months of the war.[20] Taken as an official's personal comments, such observations are not remarkable or atypical for a period that was widely believed to belong to an age of decline. However, when read in conjunction with the preface to *The Water Mirror*—the preface and the postface are the only parts of the work to refer to a "present"—Tadachika's concerns bring certain aspects of the position of *The Water Mirror*'s narrator(s) more sharply into focus. In particular, the preface expresses a repeated concern about the dangers posed by a romanticized fetishization of the past (to be discussed in detail in "Place and Principle Anew," below); this takes on greater meaning when

18. Nakayama, *Sankaiki*, 3:227.

19. I.e., the years 1170–94. His upset notwithstanding, Tadachika returns to form shortly thereafter with the inclusion of identified Japanese and Chinese responses to and interpretations of earthquakes. See Nakayama, *Sankaiki*, 3:228–29.

20. On Genryaku 2 (1184).9.9, Tadachika points out the "decay (*suihei*) of the realm," and on 9.28, after recording a death, he writes, "the impermanence of the world is something that cannot be put into words" (Nakayama, *Sankaiki*, 3:214 and 221). Explicit contrasts between past and present can be found, for instance, in ibid., 3:178, 180, and 204. Deviation from precedent in general is a much older theme for Tadachika.

the author was writing in a world turned, if not upside down, at the very least on its side.

Given that Tadachika's diary does not evince a preoccupation with the world in disarray or exhibit an implicit preference for the past over the present until near the close of the Genpei War, it makes sense to see *The Water Mirror*, which will be shown below to repeatedly engage with the characterization of the world as in decline, as a product of this concern that apparently emerged relatively late.[21] Simply put, if *The Water Mirror* reflects Tadachika's own aims—that is, if he means to dissuade his audience from clinging to the past by demonstrating that all ages are bad, as its preface argues—it makes sense to date the work to a time when a preoccupation with destruction and decline are visible in his other writings. The late prominence of the theme of the end or the decline of the world in *A Minister's Logbook*, as well as its importance to *The Water Mirror*, support treating the latter as a work written after the Genpei War. If so, *The Water Mirror* becomes a work that rejects the centrality of recent events—in particular, the war—and functions instead to provide a comprehensive framework for interpreting the past—a past in which violence and social disorder are instances of a larger cycle of rise and decline.[22] To understand how this works, after an overview of the content of *The Water Mirror*, this chapter will turn to the new twist given to "place" and "principle" in it, a twist that permits the creation of a meta-narrative of history that normalizes the otherwise abnormal experiences of the Genpei War.

Introduction to the Contents of The Water Mirror

The Water Mirror is not a well-known text, so before analyzing it, it will be helpful to gain some familiarity with its content. *The Water Mirror* consists of three scrolls, including a preface and postface that set up and reaffirm

21. "The vicissitudes of history" are also obliquely criticized in the introductory section of Nakayama Tadachika's *Kirei mondō* (439), which is believed to date from 1185–90.

22. Kaneko proposes that *The Water Mirror* is, at heart, a nostalgic work. This may be, but such an assertion is at odds with the work's self-professed position ("'Mizukagami' no setsuwa bungakusei shiron,"109).

the import of the work, driving home a lesson on the danger of attachment to the past. I will defer a close reading of the preface until the following section of this chapter; for now it will suffice to note that the framing story in the preface once again makes use of the conventions adopted in *The New Mirror.* To repeat the basics noted above, an elderly woman on a temple pilgrimage receives a transmission about the past from an ascetic. It is his account of the past—or, rather, his recitation of an account of the past that he had heard from an immortal—that the old woman in turn records and transmits and that makes up the main body of *The Water Mirror.*

In fact, the main body of the text derives much of its material from the Buddhism-inflected *Fusō ryakki* (Abbreviated Records of the Land of the Rising Sun, written circa 1094–1107), a *kanbun* history attributed to the monk Kōen (died circa 1169) that, though but partially preserved, seems to have covered the period from the reign of Emperor Jinmu (traditionally dated to the seventh century BCE) through most of that of Emperor Horikawa (1079–1107).[23] The relationship between *Abbreviated Records* and *The Water Mirror*, which this chapter will revisit more than once, is not one of the faithful translation of a *kanbun* source into *wabun.*[24] An anecdote-by-anecdote comparison of the two works falls outside the scope of this chapter, but one should bear in mind that Tadachika reshapes the material to his own ends, selecting, pruning, and rewriting in *The Water Mirror*—an account that spans the lives of the emperors from Emperor Jinmu through Emperor Ninmyō (810–50) and takes the form of a series of biographies. In terms of content, each ruler's age at death, the location of his or her tomb, identification of his or her parentage, date of designation as heir apparent and age at that time, date of and age at accession to the throne, and reign length are always included. Beyond that, there is a fair amount of variation. Many biographies give prominent space to narratives of violence, a point to which I will return below.

23. On the work's dating, Oyamada Kazuo's very brief article for the general reader offers a succinct summary. As he notes, this date somewhat strains the attribution to Kōen ("Shisen kokushi to wa nani ka," 158–59). The work is imperfectly preserved: of a presumed original thirty scrolls, only sixteen remain.

24. Oyamada also argues that *Mizukagami* is more than a translation. There is a long history of debate as to whether *The Water Mirror* is anything other than a mere translation of *Fusō ryakki*. Oyamada provides an able overview of these scholarly developments (see "'Mizukagami' to 'Fusō ryakki,'" 105–6, for his concluding argument on the translation).

Several include an occasional event with no obvious connection to a given ruler or the imperial house. At heart, however, *The Water Mirror* is a series of imperial biographies, and it is this commitment to the imperial house that provides the context for even those anecdotes of most dubious relevance.[25]

To turn briefly to these atypical inclusions, one especially fascinating case of the interweaving of such unexpected episodes into an ultimately imperial framework is the legend of Urashima Tarō. This is particularly interesting because of the contrast between the versions in *The Water Mirror* and *Abbreviated Records*, the presumed source. In *The Water Mirror*, Urashima Tarō is little more than a footnote, whereas in *Abbreviated Records*, he takes center stage. In fact, *Abbreviated Records* devotes a substantial two pages to Urashima Tarō (or Urashima-no-ko, as he appears there); two different versions of his adventures are recorded in the seventh month of the twenty-second year of Emperor Yūryaku's reign (traditionally dated to the late fifth century CE). In both, Urashima Tarō encounters a magical turtle that turns out to be a beautiful girl who dwells on Mount Penglai. She takes him there, and though the details of how they spend their time in the immortal realm differ in each version, both conclude with Urashima Tarō's decision to return to his home village and the promise not to open the box he is given by the girl if he wants to see her again.[26] Immediately after Urashima Tarō's homecoming, the entry ends with Emperor Yūryaku's death. In *Abbreviated Records*, the narratives occupy by far the greatest space and effectively dominate Yūryaku's biography, which otherwise consists of brief notations of various events—

25. See, for instance, the account of the etymology of *kitsune* under the reign of Emperor Kinmei (died 571), the entry on the preternaturally strong son that a man receives in recompense for helping Thunder during the reign of Emperor Bidatsu (538?–85), and aspects of the portrayal of the ascetic En no Gyōja in the time of Emperor Monmu (683–707)—none of which seems to have a direct bearing on the court, but all of which can be found in *Fusō ryakki*. In other words, Tadachika has not gone out in search of this seemingly incongruous content; rather, it is already present in the source material (Kaneko et al., *Mizukagami zen chūshaku*, 170, 186–88, and 267, respectively). Komine Kazuaki also notes the presence of these and other tales, arguing that such *setsuwa* are not consistent with the annalistic format (*Setsuwa no gensetsu*, 352–53). It is unclear on what basis Tadachika includes these tales, since he does not use all of those found in the *Abbreviated Records*.

26. Kuroita, *Fusō ryakki*, 18–19.

including anomalous encounters, the arrival of an emissary from Wu, and even wars on the Korean peninsula.

In *The Water Mirror*, in contrast, it is clearly the imperial biography that takes priority:

> The next emperor was called Emperor Yūryaku. He was the fifth son of Emperor Ingyō [traditionally circa 394–453]. He was seventy when he ascended the throne on the thirteenth day of the eleventh month of a *hinoe-saru* year. He governed the realm for twenty-three years. When this emperor was born, light flashed *inside* the palace.
>
> After he had become an adult, he grew impulsive and killed many people. The people called him the Wicked Emperor. In the seventh month of the second year of his reign, a woman he loved was seeing another man. The emperor was furious and summoned them both, and he bound their hands and feet to trees and burned them to death.
>
> In the second month of the fourth year of his reign, the emperor went hunting at Mount Kazuraki [or Katsuragi], and he encountered someone who looked exactly like him. When the emperor asked, "Who are you?" the other replied, "Tell me your name first. Then I'll tell you." The emperor said his name, and the other said, "I am the god Hitokotonushi [ruler of Mount Katsuragi]." Because they passed the day together hunting and the god Hitokotonushi even saw him off, people said, "He isn't an ordinary man, is he?"
>
> In the seventh month of the twenty-second year of his reign, there was the business of Urashima-no-ko going to Mount Penglai. Since everyone knows about this, I needn't go into detail.[27]

Every event in *The Water Mirror*'s version is also present in *Abbreviated Records*. But the reduction of Urashima Tarō to an aside in *The Water Mirror* is striking, and the elision of the longer story keeps the focus firmly on Yūryaku's reign. However, the matter does not end there. Urashima Tarō resurfaces in *The Water Mirror* in the biography of Emperor Junna (774–824). There the narrator observes: "This was the year in which Urashima-no-ko returned. When he opened the jewel box he had, he was enveloped in violet clouds, and afterwards, his youthful form suddenly turned into that of an aged man, and he couldn't even walk without

27. Kaneko et al., *Mizukagami zen chūshaku*, 129–34.

difficulty."[28] The fragmentation of this narrative into content for two separate imperial biographies suggests an extreme method for ensuring that despite the variation in the details of the individual lives recorded in *The Water Mirror* as well as the occasional digressions, the body of the text is a work that ultimately revolves around the fate of the imperial house.

The world of *The Water Mirror* is brought to a close with a postface that, though slight, implies that not only does *The Water Mirror* feature significant innovations, it also does so deliberately. The postface, discussed below in "Writing and Witness," raises questions about the role of writing as such, the tension between oral and written transmission and preservation, and the larger discourse on historiographic writing. The strategies that it suggests for addressing these issues leave the reader with the impression that Tadachika is presenting a work that is self-avowedly imperfect but nonetheless possessed of a larger mission.

Such are the rough contours and logic of *The Water Mirror*. The following section will demonstrate how the preface and postface show it to be a work that affords a way to make sense of recent events. Through them in particular, *The Water Mirror* establishes a cosmological framework that contextualizes and rationalizes the most extreme events, and it does so in part by its repeated innovative use of familiar sources of authority. In providing a larger governing principle to the universe, it continues the tradition of the earlier *Mirrors*. However, it also self-consciously deviates from older models, and it does so in ways that have a lasting impact on the meaning of and potential in writing a *Mirror* and, by extension, on medieval historiography.

Place and Principle Anew in The Water Mirror

Like *The Great Mirror* and *The New Mirror*, *The Water Mirror* has a narrative authority that is partially derived from the combination of place and principle. Both elements are on display in the work's preface, with the concept of cosmological principle undergoing continued elaboration

28. Kaneko et al., *Mizukagami zen chūshaku*, 429. Unfortunately, there is no surviving entry for Emperor Junna in *Abbreviated Records*.

and clarification throughout the work. Ultimately, the two familiar tropes combine in *The Water Mirror* to create a transcendent authority that goes above and beyond the traditional claims of court-generated narratives of the past to advance new positions.

To return to the preface in more detail, the larger setting is a religious pilgrimage, and it features an elderly narrator—a seventy-three-year-old woman. In the course of her devotions before the Kannon statue at Hasedera (the same temple that was the setting for *The New Mirror*), she chances upon an ascetic who is thirty-four or thirty-five. To help them stay awake until dawn, the ascetic submits to the aged pilgrim's request that he tell her about his experiences. As was the case in *The Great Mirror*, the tales of the world that are conveyed are part of a larger salvation-oriented performance: here, they are a coda to a sutra reading. To the extent that *The Water Mirror* replicates the salvific power it invokes, one can presume that the content to follow will provide the narrator and eventual reader with an enlightenment of some sort. Yet the mechanics and contours of its promises are very different, especially in how it mobilizes familiar ideas of place and principle.

DECENTERED AUTHORITY: THE WATER MIRROR *AND MULTIPLE NARRATIVE SITES*

One of the most noteworthy aspects of *The Water Mirror*'s preface is the way in which it invokes more than one site of authority. This adaptation permits the narrator to draw on multiple sites with different valences to synthesize a position of authority that has the potential to reach beyond the limitations of any one of the sites in isolation.

The specific setting of *The Water Mirror* is familiar yet distinctive. As just observed, in the preface, the encounter takes place at Hasedera Temple, which is already familiar from Tametsune's earlier work. However, the narrator explains that the real purpose of her trip is her annual pilgrimage to Ryūgaiji Temple (also known as Okadera Temple). This creates a two-part setting. On the one hand, there is Hasedera, which is both where *The New Mirror* was set and where *The Water Mirror*'s account actually occurs, but which is portrayed as a stop of convenience. On the other hand, there is Ryūgaiji, the ostensible goal of the pilgrimage, which (despite its relative geographical proximity to Hasedera) seems to occupy a different status in the network of temples in the area. Unlike Kyoto's Urin'in with its imperial origins or Hasedera with both imperial beginnings and a prominent place on the elite pilgrimage circuit, Ryūgaiji's roots are outside of the courtly system. Moreover, twelfth-century audiences likely would have been aware of this, given the portrayal of Ryūgaiji's founding in just such a light in *Tales of Times Now Past*:

> *The Tale of How Superintendent Monk Gien Founded Ryūgaiji Temple* (11.38)
> Long ago, in the reign of Emperor Tenji [626–71], there was a person known as Superintendent Monk Gien [died 728]. His lay surname was Ato, and his was a spontaneous birth.
>
> In the beginning, his father and mother had lived for years in a village in Amatsukami, [Kō]chi Commandery. They had lamented the fact that they had no children, and after some years of praying to Kannon, one night they heard the sound of a child crying from out back. Thinking this strange, they went to take a look—there was something atop the brushwood fence wrapped in a white blanket and emitting a boundlessly pleasing fragrance. At the sight of this, they grew afraid, but when they took [the bundle] down and looked, there was a splendidly beautiful newborn baby boy inside the white blanket.
>
> At that time, they both thought, "This has been granted to us because of our years of prayers to Kannon," and they rejoiced and took him inside, where the narrow home was filled with his lovely fragrance. They took care of him, and in no time, he was grown.
>
> The emperor learned of this and summoned him to adopt him as a prince. However, this child was possessed of wisdom and understood the Buddhist path. Therefore, he shaved his head and became a priest; he was a monk at Kōfukuji, and in Taihō 3 [703], he became superintendent, while his home, too, was made into a temple where a six-armed Kannon was enshrined.
>
> This is what is now known as Ryūgaiji. It manifests wondrous efficacy, and many people take the tonsure and go there; perhaps it has been thus handed down because prayers will surely be answered there.[29]

This account of Ryūgaiji's origins suggests that it is a site with a very different valence than that of Hasedera. Unlike the combined imperial and Fujiwara prestige behind Hasedera (discussed in chapter 1), Ryūgaiji's au-

29. Yamada et al., *Konjaku monogatarishū*, 3:125–26.

thority stems from its founder's otherworldly origins as well as his refusal to be co-opted into the worldly imperial system.

By invoking Hasedera as the setting while at the same time placing it within a larger journey to Ryūgaiji, a temple outside of the system, Tadachika engages with both familiar concepts of elitedom as well as sites of power that do not fall within the old system (the vulnerability of which the war had exposed). In his invocation of both sites, Tadachika presents a position that transcends familiar single-center models of authority. The narrator's movement between these two seemingly disconnected temples and the different social strata they represent implies an effort to reach beyond conventional social or worldly limitations.

This decentering is further complicated by the next development in the preface. In response to the old woman's request for information about his experiences, the ascetic decides to relate a mysterious transmission that he received while reciting sutras at Mount Katsuragi. There, he had been overheard by a mysterious "emaciated" immortal, dressed in a "robe of woven wisteria bark" and walking with the aid of a "bamboo staff."[30] This unidentified immortal is then explained as one who divides his time between Mounts Katsuragi and Yoshino. To readers versed in classical accounts of the miraculous, the locations and shadowy figure would likely have called to mind the famous seventh-century magician–lay practitioner En no Gyōja (or En no Ozunu, exact dates unknown).[31] Although the immortal does not directly correspond to En—they are later revealed to be acquainted—establishing the innermost layer of *The Water Mirror* as a transmission received from a figure not entirely of this world and at a correspondingly liminal location further undermines any notion of mapping authority to a single decisive site.[32]

The truths to follow belong both in the imperial realm of Hasedera and in the world of the humble but miraculous monk who refused the imperial call and instead founded Ryūgaiji—and even the liminal realm

30. Kaneko et al., *Mizukagami zen chūshaku*, 17. On the connections between specific mountains, *shugendō*, and En no Gyōja (discussed below), see ibid., 15nn42 and 43.

31. *The Water Mirror* includes an account of En no Gyōja that appears to have been largely derived from the contemporary *Fusō ryakki* (Kuroita, *Fusō ryakki*, 69–72).

32. For an overview of the development of En no Gyōja's symbolic meanings within the context of mountain pilgrimage and ritual practice in Nara and early Heian Japan, see Heather Blair, *Real and Imagined*, 24–29 and 253–54. On efforts to "recoup" Katsuragi in the late twelfth and early thirteenth centuries, see ibid., 262–65.

of wandering mountain ascetics. Together, they create a network-based vision of authority that is not tied to an individual site, functioning in a way somewhat similar to that which Terry Kawashima attributes to depictions of movement in one version of the medieval "origin narrative" of the "Suwa Shrine complex."[33] Kawashima argues that the manifestation of related deities across a broader area in this account "conceptualizes a matrix of power in which centers of authority matter far less than an all-encompassing sense of presence."[34] In *The Water Mirror*, this is less a matter of geographic than of status-based or institutional inclusivity, as suggested by the varying valences of the sites that appear in its preface. But the end results resonate with one another in that both deny the ability of a single prestigious site to speak for everywhere. Moreover, this multipronged approach to site in *The Water Mirror* is consistent with other techniques that Tadachika deploys in his narrative, each of which lends itself to an interpretation of *The Water Mirror* as a work that supersedes notions of authority as resting with any single worldly institution.

MORE THAN MERE KARMA: A PRINCIPLE TO PROMISE THE FATE OF THE WORLD

In addition to manipulating the conventions regarding the power of place, the preface also sets the stage for how *The Water Mirror* deviates from its predecessors in terms of principle. Although karma remains an important concept for understanding the interconnectedness of people and events, *The Water Mirror* has a new principle to promote—one that allows not only for the interpretation of the past, but also for the survival of the present and even holds a promise for the future.

To return again to the plot of the preface, the ascetic launches into the account of his fortuitous encounter with the mysterious immortal in the mountains. As he tells it, although the immortal initially claimed to marvel at the young man's "true" grasp of the Buddha's teachings, he also

33. See Kawashima, *Itineraries of Power*, for an overview of the different ways in which movement can be read in this context (158–59). ("Origin narrative" is Kawashima's translation for *engi* [ibid., 156].)

34. Kawashima, *Itineraries of Power*, 188. I will not engage with the idea of "elsewhere" that she posits as a part of this formation of power (ibid., 190–97), because it does not connect directly to how *The Water Mirror* positions its players.

criticized the ascetic's incomplete dismissal of the world, admonishing him for an undue valorization of the past: "Do not make the mistake of basically despising the present as worthless, but assuming that the past was different. You must think of all of the three realms [past, present, and future] as things to be shunned. The aspect of this very world changes this way and that over time. One must not praise the past and despise the present. . . . I would like to talk to you who single-mindedly eschew only the present and think that the past was not also thus; why not dispel but a bit of this fetish and help you along the Buddha path?"[35] The ascetic relates his eager acceptance of the above invitation, which provides the setting for an exposition on the nature of cosmic time, one that harks back to Yotsugi's remarks toward the end of *The Great Mirror* (discussed in chapter 1) but that contains much greater detail.[36]

The most significant feature of this explanation for the present undertaking is that time is portrayed as an endless cycle of rise and decline, sparsely punctuated by a few key events: the birth of the historical Buddha; the eventual birth of the future buddha Maitreya; and, at an unfathomably distant time, the appearance of 994 buddhas.[37] In the immortal's discourse, this is then tied to conditions in contemporary Japan through the contention that things long ago were uncertain in a way similar to the present.

35. Kaneko et al., *Mizukagami zen chūshaku*, 17. For an alternative interpretation of *sangai* (the three realms) as samsara—the realms of desire, form, and formlessness—see ibid., 19. Both meanings are possible in the premodern lexicon. However, the importance of a conceptualization of time as consisting of three realms is suggested by the performance of rites such as the *butsumyōe*, which expiated the sins of the three ages (past, present, and future). The first *butsumyōe* is even noted in *The Water Mirror* (ibid., 435). For a partial historical account of the rite from 1180, see Nakayama, *Sankaiki*, 3:148–49.

36. Rather than present this exegesis of the workings of cosmic time as an eyewitness account, the narrator in effect distinguishes between a larger account of the universe or universes and the specific historical account to follow. This contrastive positioning is unprecedented in the earlier *Mirrors*, and it is tempting to read it through Paul Ricoeur's analysis of the "transition from living memory to the 'extrinsic' positing of historical knowledge," whereby "it is as one of the formal conditions of possibility of the historiographical operation that the notion of a third-order time appears" (*Memory, History, Forgetting*, 153).

37. Kaneko et al., *Mizukagami zen chūshaku*, 22–23. This is a bit puzzling, since according to mainstream Mahayana teachings, after Maitreya's birth there should be 995 buddhas, not 994. See Jan Nattier, *Once Upon a Future Time*, 25.

The present decline is in keeping with a larger principle whereby the fading of the Buddha's teachings goes hand in hand with growing instability. The import of this is made clear with the immortal's enjoinder to the ascetic to take the long view: "Don't go deceiving yourself into thinking that this might become an absolutely awful age."[38] As the immortal has presented things, the current downward trend is but a phase in a vast, continuous unfolding.

Lest the immortal's audience remain unpersuaded, the preface closes with a final admonition before launching into the life of Emperor Jinmu: "When one doesn't fully understand the world, though one might single-mindedly despise the current age, on the other hand, that, too, would be a sin. Only one ignorant of the world could say that what we see before us now bears no resemblance to the past."[39] Here, then, is an explicit injunction against an uncritical celebration of the past such as the one in which, one might suppose, *The New Mirror* indulged. The present might be terrible, but the past was, too. In other words, the account in the body of *The Water Mirror* should convince its audience that the larger cycle of rise and decline notwithstanding, this world has always been bad, and, by implication, it will continue to be so for a while.[40] This suggests an emphasis on the workings of the cosmos and an insistence on the durability of the present condition that differ from the earlier efforts in the Heian-era *Mirrors* to prove karmic causality.

The specifics for how this update to the old principle model is achieved can be seen in the text's narrative structure. In a way reminiscent of *The Water Mirror*'s mobilization of multiple settings, it also deploys two distinct temporal levels to both contextualize and interpret the flow of historical events: an overarching macro-level discourse of time as endless within the framework of a four-*kalpa* (eon) worldview and a simultaneous

38. Kaneko et al., *Mizukagami zen chūshaku*, 23. Although rendering *aranu yo* as "awful age" relies on a less common meaning of *aranu*, it is consistent with the preceding talk of nonabsolutes.

39. Kaneko et al., *Mizukagami zen chūshaku*, 28.

40. Kawakita Noboru likewise identifies the continuity of human nature as a primary concern of the work, although he restricts himself to listing only a few examples, such as those of Fujiwara no Momokawa and Dōkyō ("'Mizukagami' ni tsuite," 4–5). Any similarities between his "twelve items" and my overview of the content of *The Water Mirror* are coincidental.

micro-level assertion that the present age is one that is subject to the law of decline. For Tadachika's readers, the most relevant takeaway lesson from this logic would likely have been that nothing is ever truly over: "Thus ending is beginning, and again ending is beginning. Nothing is [either] extreme."[41] This specific recourse to a larger macro-level cosmological narrative, though not taken up by later *Mirrors*, has undeniable similarities to the metanarrative of the four *kalpas* in the earliest manuscript tradition of *A Record of the Jōkyū Years*, a later narrative of the Jōkyū Disturbance of 1221.[42] A similar account of *kalpas* is likewise included in Kitabatake Chikafusa's *Jinnō shōtōki* (A Chronicle of Gods and Sovereigns, circa 1339–1343), a historiographic experiment that relates a version of the past sympathetic to Emperor Godaigo's Yoshino court (discussed in chapter 5), as part of a much more fully developed discussion of the origins of India, China, and Japan.[43] Thus, *The Water Mirror* affords an early look at what would become a popular medieval gambit: buttressing one's historical perspective with a well-developed and specific claim to understand the nature of the cosmos.

For *The Water Mirror*, this has a very specific result that is undergirded by the narrative structure: its position in terms of the relationship between past, present, and future is fundamentally different from the position suggested by the earlier *Mirrors*. To begin with the historiographic imperative—that is, the cosmological principle at issue—both *The Great Mirror* and *The New Mirror* subscribe to an idea of events as determined by karmic causality, as seen in chapter 1. In exegetical terms, this means that there is always an underlying logic to be decoded in the unfolding of historical events. The task of the historiographer or reader is to recognize

41. Kaneko et al., *Mizukagami zen chūshaku*, 23. The translation is based on the modern gloss in ibid., 27. The four *kalpas* are successive ages. In the immortal's highly detailed explanation, the universe is formed during a *kalpa* of becoming (*jōkō*); next is a *kalpa* of existence, in which life spans shrink (*jūkō*); then a *kalpa* of destruction (*ekō* or *egō*); and finally a *kalpa* of emptiness (*kūkō* or *kūgō*) (ibid., 21–23).

42. While Tyler likens the cosmological explanation of time that opens the work to later texts, he makes no mention of *The Water Mirror* (*Before* Heike *and After*, 196).

43. Iwasa Masashi, *Jinnō shōtōki*, 45–47. For the discussion of *kalpas*, I have relied on Kitabatake Chikafusa and H. Paul Varley, *Chronicle of Gods and Sovereigns*, 55–59. Ogawa Toyō also points to this shared rhetoric in his discussion of the creation myth at the heart of *A Chronicle of Gods and Sovereigns* ("Sangai o kenritsu suru kami," 45).

the constellation of things that have led to a given result. Provided that one has adequate familiarity with and understanding of events, this works perfectly well for interpreting the past. It does, however, limit one's ability to predict the future with any degree of specificity. While one can be certain that future events will likewise be subject to karmic logic, there is no way to project how that logic will be manifest. There is no pattern of events in which event type A inevitably produces result type B. In other words, a hermeneutics of karmic causality primarily functions by looking backward. It allows for the identification of patterns in the past and guarantees that there will continue to be patterns in the future, but it does not reveal the forms those patterns will take.

This works well for writings such as the earlier *Mirrors*, both of which seek to reveal to the reader the chains of cause and effect that have resulted in the events of the narrative present. In each of these earlier works, it is the existence of the pattern that needs to be proven. In the case of *The Great Mirror*, this pattern is straightforward: Michinaga's rise to power is explained. In *The New Mirror*, things are a bit more complicated, but its readers are assured in its preface of the inescapable relationship between cause and effect.

All of this is different in the world of *The Water Mirror*, where the focus is not primarily on karmic causality, but rather on situating the current age along a larger historical trajectory. This is visible on both of the temporal levels that Tadachika mobilizes. The work has a macronarrative that explicitly invokes a four-*kalpa* view in which time is an endless cycle, thus rejecting the possibility that the current age is the end of the world. At the same time, it also features a micro-level narrative of human experience in which "the loss of the Buddha's teachings and the gradual worsening of the world are principles [of the cosmos] in the current age."[44] It is this latter principle that the biographies within the body of *The Water Mirror* seem to illustrate most immediately.

Komine Kazuaki asserts that the cyclical perspective inherent in the four-*kalpa* view of the universe trumps the downward trajectory. However, rather than see these as contradictory impulses, they can be thought of as working toward a common end: an authoritative narrative of the larger progression of time at the level of the cosmos that also accounts

44. Kaneko et al., *Mizukagami zen chūshaku*, 23.

for the more immediate current experience of the readers.[45] It is tempting to argue that the larger narrative of the nature of cosmological time works primarily to enhance the perceived truth-value of the smaller claim about the temporal trajectory of the micronarrative. The ability to explain how all of time works imparts a certain authority to the immortal narrator that should, one can imagine, predispose the reader to accept the immortal's related premise: the current age is not the end of the world. At the same time, identifying the present age as one governed by the law of decline reinforces the larger claim of the operation of laws in all ages. If the present age does illustrate a principle, then why not accept that it is part of a larger logic that governs all of time?

This being said, it is at the micro level that the reorientation with regard to time is most readily observed. At that level, the biographies that form the core of *The Water Mirror* focus on a discrete chain of immediate events that are arranged in a single chronological progression, despite the ultimate lack of a beginning or ending to the cosmos. In other words, even if the late twelfth century is not the end of the world, and even if at the abstract level time is endless, because the narrative moves in one direction that follows a chronological progression, the reader effectively experiences the unfolding of events in a linear fashion.

Admittedly, this difference may in part be an effect of the shift in orientation from multiple families to a single family. In marked contrast to what was observed in *The New Mirror* in chapter 1, in *The Water Mirror*, with an imperial chronology that informs everything, events are presented only once. Yet this need not be only because of a more restricted genealogical focus; it also can be read as connected to the very different charge under which *The Water Mirror* operates. To repeat, the earlier *Mirrors* promote the recognition of the existence of a principle of karmic causation and thus emphasize histories in which events are connected and are not arbitrary. *The Water Mirror*, in contrast, seeks to persuade the reader of the existence of a historical arc that not only explains the past

45. Komine, *Setsuwa no gensetsu*, 349. On the present *kalpa*, see Kaneko et al., *Mizukagami zen chūshaku*, 23. Komine also sees the four-*kalpa* view in *The Great Mirror* (*Setsuwa no gensetsu*, 348–49). The position I take here is somewhat different from that in my earlier work, in which I concurred with Komine's argument (Brightwell, "*Mirror of China*," 278–80).

but also extends into the future and thus guarantees that the end of the world is not imminent. *The Water Mirror* is promoting a definite and specific pattern.

This change can be interpreted as signaling a basic realignment vis-à-vis the historiographic enterprise of *Mirror* writing and the cosmological framework supporting it. It is no longer desirable or sufficient to uncover or establish the existence of a relationship between past and present. Hence, there is no need for a recursive experience of the past. Instead, *The Water Mirror* offers a guarantee that the world is not ending—but to do that, it must implicitly look forward as well. Tadachika is attempting to persuade his readers that there is a larger pattern that can be seen across the entire trajectory of Japanese history, on the one hand, and a linear narrative that reinforces the idea that time moves unidirectionally along a single path, on the other hand. As a result of this clearly defined road, history's future course can likewise be inferred.

Here, then, is a shift in the nature of what a *Mirror* is supposed to demonstrate. While the narrators of both of the earlier *Mirrors* explicitly say that they are explaining how things have reached their current states, *The Water Mirror* offers basic indicators for where the world is headed. Through a vision clearer than that suggested by the subtleties of karmic causality, the reader is made to understand that there is a path for the past and the future that is both larger (in its *kalpa* orientation) and also more specific and immediate (in its guarantee that things are not going to improve any time soon). What it "models" is different: the earlier *Mirrors* tell their readers how they have arrived at the present, while *The Water Mirror* offers the reader a prognosis for the future.

Reading Tadachika's work as one that simultaneously employs two different but mutually reinforcing temporal scales does not require a dramatic shift in medieval understandings of the nature of time itself. Rather, it suggests an intimate connection between the narrative structuring of temporal progression and the historiographical imperatives to which different authors subscribed.[46] Admittedly, Tadachika never explic-

46. This is not entirely dissimilar to Hayden White's notion of emplotment, in which the form of a work determines how one is to interpret it (*Metahistory*). Like White, I see a connection between structure and readerly experience, which inevitably informs interpretation. However, for me, this is not dictated by genre.

itly states that the two narratives of time should be understood as working in cooperation. Indeed, the four-*kalpa* view does not reappear in the work's postface. Once *The Water Mirror* "downshifts" to "The Age of Men" with which Emperor Jinmu's reign commences, it never returns to the meta level of cosmological discourse. Nevertheless, the way in which Tadachika manipulates two superficially different temporal trajectories to arrive at a vision for the past and future arguably anticipates by forty or fifty years Jien's attempt, in the 1219 *My Humble Thoughts* (discussed in chapter 3), to maneuver between a downward trajectory and a divinely enabled possibility of forestalling decay.[47] Thus, *The Water Mirror* can be understood as part of a larger intellectual movement to reconcile inherent contradictions in contemporary cosmological thought.

This change from a history that explains the past alone to one that also implies a path for the future makes sense if one considers *The Water Mirror*'s position as that of a historiography intended to accommodate the realities of post-Genpei readers. As has already been suggested, albeit in different terms, the war can be expected to have produced an altered "horizon of expectations."[48] As a result, anyone who wished to write about the past would have been forced to do so in ways that addressed the postwar reality and at the same time accommodated the long-held conviction that Japan had entered the final age. Regardless of the limitations to the governmental restructuring that the Genpei War ultimately necessitated, the age was one in which, to borrow a phrase from Reinhart Koselleck's discussion of a European context, "an experiential space was bro-

47. On Jien's concern with the former, see Brown, "Buddhism and Historical Thought," 216 and 219, and *passim*. See also Brown and Ishida, *Future and the Past*, 4 and *passim*. On the possibility of the latter, see Brown, "Buddhism and Historical Thought," 217 and 222–25; Brown and Ishida, *Future and the Past*, 5–9 and, 13–14. Matsumoto Shinpachirō makes a similar point about *The Water Mirror*'s having a guiding principle that prefigures Jien's, giving *Mizukagami* and *Gukanshō* as examples of different developments of the *kidentai* "transmitted biographies" form ("Rekishi monogatari to shiron," 30). See also William H. McCullough and Helen McCullough, *Tale of Flowering Fortunes*, 29. Nishio Yōtarō has likewise argued for the work's status with regard to the *Gukanshō* ("Heian jidai gōki no rekishi shisō," 91–93). On the four-*kalpa* view, as well as *Mizukagami* and *Gukanshō*, see also Ozaki, "'Gukanshō' no hōhō to 'Mizukagami,'" 5–8.

48. My use of this term, as well as the subsequent discussion of its implications, is informed by Koselleck, *Futures Past*, 264–75.

ken up within a generation, all expectations were shaken and new ones promoted."[49] Or, as Jien succinctly puts it, "After Retired Emperor Toba's death on Hōgen 1 (1156).7.2, and after the rebellions arose in Japan, we had arrived at the age of the warrior."[50]

In the wake of the war, expectations were surely displaced or even overturned, and it fell to Tadachika and others like him to advance a cosmological logic that could anticipate and account for the new expectations that emerged. Tadachika's solution was to promote a world of absolute nonabsolutes: there is no beginning or ending in the grand scheme of things, nor is anything completely one way or the other. As a result, anything can be used to confirm nearly anything else. Even an event—such as the eighth-century planting of citrus trees on the recommendation of a dharma master—that might otherwise seem not particularly noteworthy is assessed as "a thing felt awesomely meritorious," thus confirming that despite the general threat of decline, good things happen: nothing is completely terrible.[51] Or, in a negative example, robbers who burn down Ise Shrine in the reign of Emperor Kanmu (737–806), although mentioned only in passing, attain significance as illustrative of the truth that "be it now or long ago, there is nothing as perverse as the human heart."[52] Ergo, the world has not been in good shape for a while, and by extension, current bad things are not indicative of the end's being nigh. Tadachika's principle of nothing being absolute is infinitely flexible. In short, provided that one accepts the logic of the four-*kalpa* worldview and the idea that there is nothing that is completely one way or the other, even in the present age of decline, Tadachika's framework is broad enough to contain all experience.[53] The real value of this framework lies in what it enables with regard to the recent events of the civil war, which I discuss next.

49. Koselleck, *Futures Past*, 264.

50. Nakajima, *Gukanshō*, 336. For an alternative translation, see Brown and Ishida, *Future and the Past*, 89.

51. Kaneko et al., *Mizukagami zen chūshaku*, 320.

52. Kaneko et al., *Mizukagami zen chūshaku*, 384.

53. This is in contrast to Christian prophecies, which could seem to be threatened by actual experience. See Koselleck, *Futures Past*, 265.

Eliding the Immediate: The Erasure of War and a New Purpose for Ordering the Past

The earlier *Mirrors* were conservative, fundamentally nostalgic works. The circular nature of historical movement as suggested by the narrative structure of *The New Mirror* in particular constituted a textual representation of the past as in some limited way recoverable. Yet for *The Water Mirror* to repeat this logic would have rung hollow: the reality of the civil war had demonstrated that the romanticized worlds of *The Great Mirror* and *The New Mirror* were irretrievable. Instead, Tadachika was left to create a logic in which things were moving somewhere other than backward or in impossible circles. The deployment of the *kalpa* cycle and its logic of nonabsoluteness and the integration of the micronarrative of decline suggest an effort to actively reimagine the cosmos in response to real-world events and, more significantly, demonstrate how a conservative genre such as the *Mirror* could be recast to meet the changing needs of its readership.

As one further way of achieving this, Tadachika shifts his focus to the distant past, a move that offers the most dramatic break with earlier *Mirrors* and permanently uncouples the genre from the need to recount events of a local, recent past. In *The Water Mirror*, a very specific function can be attributed to this maneuver. Paradoxical though it may seem at first, in eliding the recent war from the text's account of the world, *The Water Mirror* offers a worldview that both validates the general experience of war and simultaneously makes sense of what could otherwise be viewed as a devastating and unjustifiable loss, particularly to those who were defeated in the Genpei War. In more abstract terms, a focus on the distant past serves to deny the singularity of the war by demonstrating that it was consistent with larger historical patterns. Tadachika narrates a view of history in which the possibilities for the future continue to be delimited by the logic of the past.[54] In other words, he denies attributing

54. The idea of history as a "constant singularity" and the view of its impact on how history is understood that underlie this reading are based on Koselleck's discussion of this issue (*Futures Past*, 268).

to the Genpei War the power of a "rupture in continuity."[55] Appearances to the contrary notwithstanding, the disorder of the recent war does not mark the beginning of anything new.

To be sure, one could argue that Tadachika had nowhere to turn but the distant past, given that not much time had elapsed between the composition of *The New Mirror* and that of *The Water Mirror*. In terms of imperial reigns, the 15–23 years between the two works would have left Tadachika with a scant three "fresh" topics, had he confined himself to imperial biographies: the remainder of Emperor Takakura's reign through 1180, the short life of Emperor Antoku, and the first two-thirds of the reign of Emperor Gotoba (1180–1239). Nevertheless, Tadachika would not have been short of material had he been willing to consider families beyond the immediate imperial house, as the author of *The New Mirror* had done. The more serious difficulty, I suspect, is that given that the earlier *Mirrors* had focused explicitly on explaining how recent events had come about, Tadachika would have had to confront the war directly. And to take *The Water Mirror*'s immortal informant at his word that there is nothing uniquely bad about this age, to grant the war pride of place is precisely what *The Water Mirror* is trying not to do.[56] With this in mind, the alternative for an author unwilling to directly engage with the war, and thus epitomized by *The Water Mirror*, was to "go back to the beginning" to offer a new and totalizing historico-cosmological framework—one that could accommodate war without being overturned by it.

This return to the distant past can be understood in theoretical terms as a means of coping with what Paul Ricoeur identifies as the "heritage of founding violence" that the establishment of any new regime requires. In Ricoeur's analysis, "It is a fact that there is no historical community that has not arisen out of what can be termed an original relation to war."[57] This holds equally true for the reorganized communities born of the war in Japan. It was a civil war, after all, that had made the establishment of the *bakufu* in Kamakura possible. Even though the *bakufu* was not intended to entirely replace or usurp the court's authority, forcing the imperial state to share power produced five years of warfare (broken by famine),

55. Koselleck, *Futures Past*, 268.

56. For example, "Do not make the mistake of despising the present as worthless, but assuming that the past was different" (Kaneko et al., *Mizukagami zen chūshaku*, 17).

57. Ricoeur, *Memory, History, Forgetting*, 82.

a "founding violence" that gave rise to a reorganization of existing social and political structures.

One way that *The Water Mirror* creates a narrative in which contemporary warfare and unrest are rendered sensible is through the normalization of violence, in particular with regard to the imperial house. Matsumoto Shinpachirō, who likewise dates *The Water Mirror* after the war, sees "rebellions against the court and attendant issues of succession" as a defining concern of the text, arguing that it exhibits a clear break with works such as *The New Mirror*.[58] *The Water Mirror* is replete with accounts of treason, armed conflict, and, occasionally, imperial insanity. Proof of the wickedness of the world emerges in the first scroll, with a murderous plot by the elder brother of the future Emperor Suizei (traditionally circa 632–circa 549 BCE) to kill his younger siblings.[59] This is followed by accounts of a scheme by the empress and her brother to assassinate Emperor Suinin (traditionally circa 80 BCE–circa 70 CE), the famous abortive attempts by Emperor Ōjin's (traditionally 200–310) brothers to eliminate him, and the cuckolding of Emperor Richū (traditionally circa 339–405) and his revenge, to name just a few. A dramatic peak is reached in the depravity of Emperor Buretsu (traditionally 489–506), among whose misdeeds the cutting open of a pregnant woman to observe the fetus and the forced mating of women with horses are arguably the most disturbing.[60] The tide of wickedness slows temporarily in the second scroll, with much space devoted to chronicling the miraculous abilities and accomplishments of Prince Shōtoku (574–622). Yet in the midst of Shōtoku's rise, violence remains, including his and Soga no Umako's (died 626) war against Minister Mononobe no Moriya (died 587); Emperor Sushun's (died 592) assassination at the directive of Umako; and the slaughter of twenty-three of Shōtoku's descendants by Soga no

58. Matsumoto further contends that this is a critical shift in "historical tales" from biography-based accounts to those centered on events ("Rekishi monogatari to shiron," 29).

59. These traditional dates are based on a genealogy published by the Imperial Household Agency ("Genealogy of the Emperors of Japan") and the information provided within *Mizukagami* about the ruler's age at his time of death.

60. The editors point out that the description of Buretsu bears the rhetorical and thematic imprint of Chinese historiography; unfortunately, they do not elaborate on this point except to note that others have also observed it (Kaneko et al., *Mizukagami zen chūshaku*, 153).

Iruka (died 645)—who is himself later beheaded, with his body sent back to his father, Soga no Emishi (died 645), who then commits suicide. Nor does it stop there. Later military conflicts during the reigns of Emperor Tenmu (died 686), Empress Genshō (680–748), and Emperor Shōmu (701–56) extend Tadachika's catalogue of misfortune. The final scroll continues in the same vein. The immortal relating the events pronounces the behavior of Empress Kōken's (718–70) crown prince, "the deposed emperor" who is the subject of the scroll's first biography, "scandalous."[61] This is followed by a seemingly endless chain of armed conflicts: Fujiwara no Nakamaro (706–64) finds himself on the wrong side of the infamous monk Dōkyō (died 772); Fujiwara no Momokawa (732–79) ruthlessly manipulates imperial succession, killing others as needed; Prince Iyo (died 807) unsuccessfully attempts a coup and kills himself; Retired Emperor Heizei (774–824) rebels against his son; and so forth.

In the final scroll, more than any other, Buddhist achievements are acknowledged, in particular those involving the renowned monks Saichō (767–822), Kūkai, and Ennin (794–864). Nonetheless, in comparison to the information on Saichō and Kūkai found in *Abbreviated Records*, even these heroes of early Japanese Buddhism are granted relatively short shrift.[62] As a whole, although *The Water Mirror* dutifully records the occasional Buddhist miracle or demonstration of merit, Tadachika's assertion that the world has been bad from the start is consistently supported. The final biography in the scroll, that of Emperor Ninmyō, delivers a one-two punch to this effect in its closing lines:

> On Kashō 1 [848].3.26, Jikaku Daishi [Ennin] returned from China. While he had been in China, he had encountered a wicked king and seen many sad things. He met with a time in which the Buddha's sutras were burned, and nuns and monks forced to return to lay life; this Great Teacher, too, was forced to return to life as a layman and cover his [shaven] head.
>
> In the third month of Kashō 3 [850], the emperor's illness grew grave; he took the tonsure and died within the day.[63]

61. Kaneko et al., *Mizukagami zen chūshaku*, 313.

62. The biographies of the emperors under whom Ennin was active are largely missing from *Abbreviated Records*.

63. Kaneko et al., *Mizukagami zen chūshaku*, 446–47.

Having given so little attention to events outside of Japan, it is striking that Tadachika chooses the burning of Buddhist imagery in China as among the horrific things Ennin encounters. The inclusion of this incident, so out of keeping with much of Tadachika's content, suggests that it had a particular resonance for his audience. Taira no Kiyomori's much-censured wartime burning of the temples at Nara would have been an easy association for medieval readers to make, reminding them once again that even something as notorious as Kiyomori's behavior was not unheard of in earlier times (although in China).

In short, Tadachika has crafted an account of Japan's founding in which the world has always been beset by conflict and death and even the most impressive figures have a fleeting existence. In so doing, he presents a world in which the losses sustained in the Genpei War are not fundamentally extraordinary. The seeming rupture created by the war does not, after all, mark the start of something new. The reader is granted a narrative of the past in which the civil war is merely one example of unrest, albeit an extreme one, in a timeless series: it is no longer a moment of "foundational violence."

Looking back at *A Minister's Logbook*, Tadachika in 1185 probably spoke for many when he asked, "Have we already arrived at the end of the world?"[64] *The Water Mirror* provides his answer: "Don't go deceiving yourself into thinking that this might become an absolutely awful age."[65] The world has always been this way.

Writing and Witness: The Water Mirror*'s Use of a Hybrid Register*

It is not only in its alterations to the notions of place, principle, and the past that *The Water Mirror* marks a new strategy for processing historical change. In its linguistic forms—the regular recurring interpolation of *kanbun* in a largely *wabun* text—it literally inscribes a new, inclusive way of representing that change. Tadachika's use of language marks the be-

64. Nakayama, *Sankaiki*, 3:227.
65. Kaneko et al., *Mizukagami zen chūshaku*, 23.

ginning of a shift in the various written registers of subsequent *Mirrors* and one that I suspect plays no small part in the later co-optation of the genre by the Kamakura shogunate. Understanding this involves both an examination of how *kanbun* material is repurposed into a multilingual (or multistyle) text and an investigation into what the blending of registers in the resulting work enables—namely, a framework that rejects conventional worldly categories of orthodox versus deviant or oral versus written and implies an authority that transcends such dichotomies.

Approaching the text from this angle rests on certain assumptions about writing during this time period—especially the visual impact of arguably distinct scriptive forms—that I use to assess the linguistic forms in *The Water Mirror*. First and foremost, although I discuss these forms in terms of *kanbun* and *wabun*, this is not equivalent to using the categories of Classical Chinese and Classical Japanese. David Lurie's work in particular has demonstrated the inappropriateness of collapsing *kanbun* and Classical Chinese into a single category.[66] Lurie has reexamined the fundamental operations of writing and argues for a broader and simultaneously more nuanced notion of how texts were utilized in early Japan. By proposing that *kundoku* (Japanese readings of Classical Chinese texts) has been an element of writing in Japan from early on, Lurie's work undermines a long-dominant perspective that framed Japanese writing in terms of a foreign-native opposition.[67] Filtering "Chinese" and *kanbun* texts through the lens of *kundoku* practices relocates all forms of writing within the domestic Japanese realm.[68] Through an examination of passages from Heian texts, Lurie demonstrates how discussions of writing do not privilege the country of origin of the writing system: "Heian dis-

66. Lurie, "Origins of Writing in Early Japan." While Lurie's later *Realms of Literacy* further develops many of these points, it was his dissertation that directly led to my rethinking of the meaning of *kanbun*. For an explicit refutation of this Japanese-Chinese divide, see *Realms of Literacy*, 204; see also 324–34.

67. For an introduction to the mechanics of *kundoku*, see Lurie, *Realms of Literacy*, 175–80.

68. For a discussion of the traditional perspective and its problems, see Lurie, "Origins of Writing in Early Japan," 340–47, and *Realms of Literacy*, 207–12. Roy Andrew Miller also attributed a domesticating function to the *kundoku* practice, albeit as a factor in the "breakdown" of a clear division between Chinese and Japanese ("Writing Systems,"130–31).

cussions of written styles conceptualize them in graphic terms (*mana* versus *kana*, and so on) rather than linguistic ones."[69] A few lines later, he reiterates the point more strongly: "The meaningful category of difference among texts in this period—and for a long time afterward—is not linguistic, but rather graphic or stylistic."[70]

Lurie's point that Heian audiences did not see texts written in *kanbun* or *mana* as "foreign" is well taken. Nonetheless, two thirteenth-century texts suggest that closer to the time of the composition of *The Water Mirror*, even if everything could be read aloud using *kundoku*, writers attributed distinct aural and visual attributes to *wabun* and *kanbun* writing that tended to blur linguistic and stylistic boundaries. This is not to say that they were thinking of *kanbun* as an actual Chinese language and *wabun* as Japanese, but rather to point to how at this particular moment, the *kan* 漢 (China) of *kanbun* and *wa* 和 (Japan) of *wabun* could have oppositional valences tied to ideas of their respective origins. Both Jien's *My Humble Thoughts* and Tachibana Narisue's *Kokon chomonjū* (Notable Tales Old and New, written in 1254), texts discussed in chapter 3, expressly frame their writing choices oppositionally, with terms defined in the rhetoric of "familiar" and otherwise. For Jien, the dichotomy is between writing in "Japanese" (*kana*, *wago*) and "the Yamato tongue" (*yamatokotoba*), or "characters" (*mana*) and "Chinese characters" (*kanji*). Jien writes that he fears that were he to write in *mana* "there would be few who understood what they meant."[71] After listing various works in *mana* and bemoaning the scarcity of those who fathom them, he adds, "It is precisely by writing in *kana* that Yamato words are in their essential form, unconnected to characters."[72] Near the close of *My Humble Thoughts*, Jien once again lays out reasons for his decision to write in *kana* as opposed

69. Lurie, *Realms of Literacy*, 328.

70. Lurie, *Realms of Literacy*, 328.

71. Nakajima, *Gukanshō*, 180. As Ozaki Isamu observes, Jien seems to be saying that he has decided to write in *kana* to address a nonexclusive readership ("'Gukanshō' to 'Ōkagami,'" 19–20). Ozaki restates this point as part of a larger argument about the relationship between *Gukanshō* and *Mizukagami* ("'Gukanshō' no hōhō to 'Mizukagami,'" 34).

72. Nakajima, *Gukanshō*, 180. For an alternative translation that renders *mana* as "Chinese characters," see Brown and Ishida, *Future and the Past*, 348.

to *kanji*.[73] Here, however, he asks for indulgence for using such accessible language, which despite sounding "familiar to the ear" (*mimijikaku*) or "simple," nevertheless is "possessed of a 'deeply embedded' meaning" (*fukaku komoritaru koto*).[74] The implication is that *mana* or *kanbun* writing is neither of these things. Tachibana Narisue (thirteenth century) uses similar language, characterizing "Japanese characters" (*waji*) as "easy on the eye" (*meyasukaramu*) or "familiar to the ear."[75] "Things Chinese" (*Kanke*) in contrast, feature writing that is beset by "pointless rhetoric" (*munashiki kotoba*) and reserved for "writing on roadside monuments" (*michi no katawara no hi no fumi*).[76] While both of these texts identify the aural impact of their written registers as important, they also attribute distinct visual impacts to writing in *kana* versus *mana* or *kanbun*.[77] This point must be stressed, because regardless of how one might have read *The Water Mirror* aloud, it is a work composed in two different registers, and this is a difference that its readers would have recognized.

While *The Great Mirror* and *The New Mirror* were noted for their exclusive use of a vernacular Japanese register, *The Water Mirror* introduces *kanbun* into a *Mirror* for the first time.[78] This is visible in the man-

73. Nakajima, *Gukanshō*, 575. For the corresponding events in English, see Brown and Ishida, *Future and the Past*, 199.

74. Nakajima, *Gukanshō*, 579. The translation is modified from Brown and Ishida, *Future and the Past*, 202.

75. "Easy on the eye" is in the colloquial English sense. *Meyasushi* is more strictly defined as "not unsightly" and "pleasant," but the more literal translation captures the valences of the individual graphs, too.

76. Asami, *Jikkunshō*, 17–18.

77. Although I do not agree with some of the conclusions drawn based upon the mechanics of calligraphic brushwork, in thinking about the impact of distinct visual styles, I am inspired by LaMarre, *Uncovering Heian Japan*.

78. Some premodern editions of *The Great Mirror* also make use of a similar device. However, the numerous inconsistencies—in the presence or absence across variant lines, the contents of the lines, and its application within a given edition—all suggest that these are later additions to the text. The oldest complete manuscript of *The Great Mirror*, the Kamakura-period Tōmatsubon, features no such *kanbun* insertions other than the name of the emperor who is the subject of each biography (*Tōmatsubon ōkagami*). This is in contrast to *The Water Mirror*, where the content and format are largely consistent within an edition and are preserved across manuscript lines. My assessment of *The Water Mirror* manuscripts is based on Nakayama Tadachika's *Mizukagami* [*Senjūjibon*] and the unpublished *Mizukagami: Ōeibon* held by Hōsa Bunko.

uscript image, which is also representative in terms of content (see fig. 2.1). First, the ruler's name and position in the imperial chronology are provided. A two- or three-phrase synopsis, written in half-size *kanbun* in parallel columns, follows. This miniature recapitulation of an imperial reign typically includes the date of the ruler's death, his or her age, and the location of his or her tomb. This is followed by the main body of the biography, written entirely in *wabun*.

It would be too simplistic to attribute Tadachika's use of *kanbun* to more formally orthodox historiography and leave it at that. Rather, bringing *The Water Mirror* into dialogue with its most direct predecessor, *Abbreviated Records*, facilitates a deeper interrogation of this issue of languages and the impact of Tadachika's linguistic experimentation. Reading the two side by side reveals the ways in which Tadachika is manipulating language not in isolation, but rather together with the structure and content of the earlier *kanbun* history.

STRUCTURE(D) BORROWING: TADACHIKA'S UPDATES TO ABBREVIATED RECORDS

As noted above, to a large degree *The Water Mirror* contains information also found in *Abbreviated Records*. But the latter also boasts copious content that does not make its way into Tadachika's work. Moreover, there are certain patterns to the types of material that Tadachika never incorporates—patterns that highlight the new directions he takes with old materials.[79]

In the biographical material, Tadachika's mostly colloquial and not exactly court-centered history replicates the underlying structure of the entries in the more orthodox *Abbreviated Records*: name, fine-print synopsis, and main-body biography. This is immediately apparent when one sets the two texts next to each other, and it at once reinforces a structural link between *The Water Mirror* and *kanbun* historiography (see fig. 2.2).[80]

79. The following comparison is based on the surviving entries for rulers common to *The Water Mirror* and *Abbreviated Records*. The received version of *Abbreviated Records* is missing the biographies for Emperors Saga (786–842), Junna (786–840), and Ninmyō (810–50), the final three sovereigns included in *The Water Mirror*.

80. The format of *Abbreviated Records* is visible in the early Kamakura manuscript designated a national important cultural property and believed to have been the property

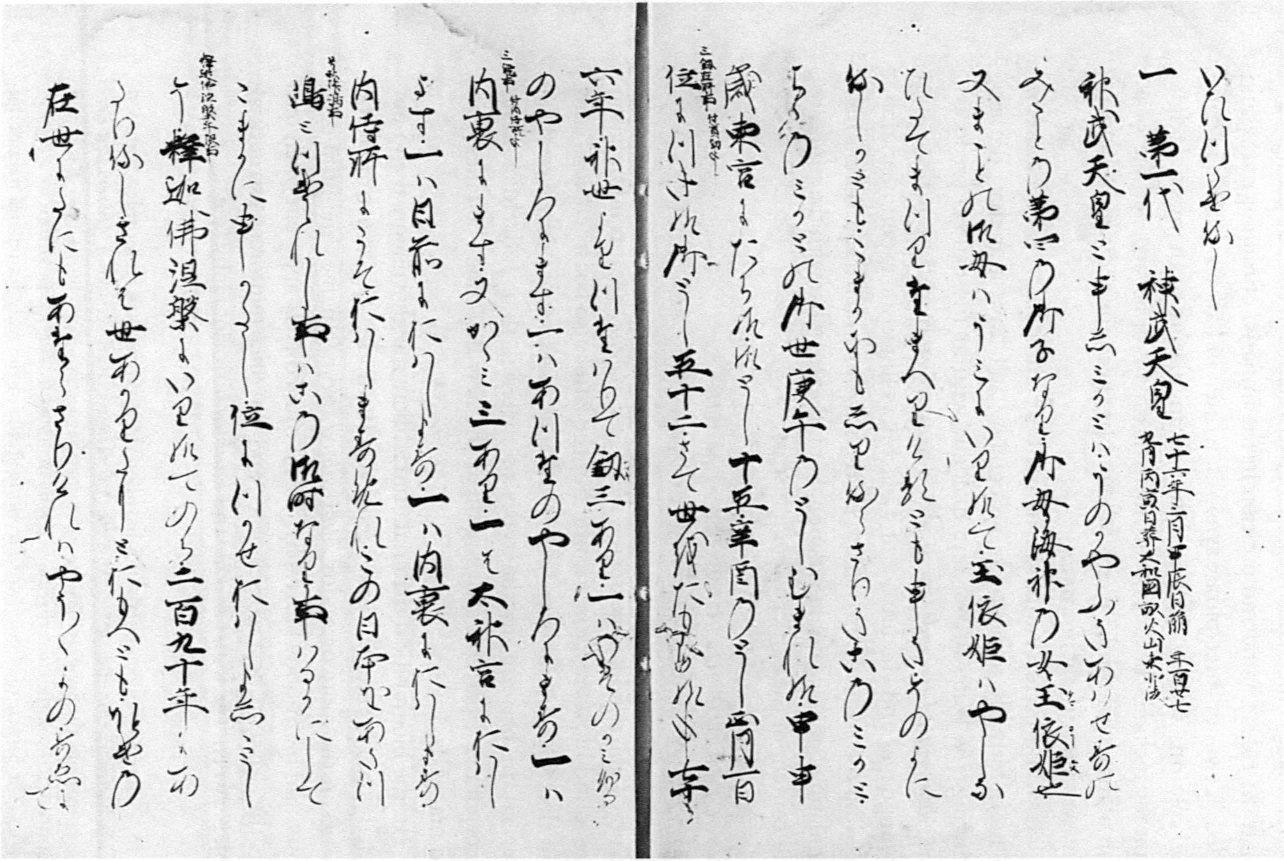

FIGURE 2.1. Example of script variation in the Senjūjibon manuscript of *The Water Mirror* from the late Kamakura period. The text shown is the opening of Emperor Jinmu's biography. Reprinted with permission from the National Diet Library Digital Collections—*Mizukagami* (frame 13).

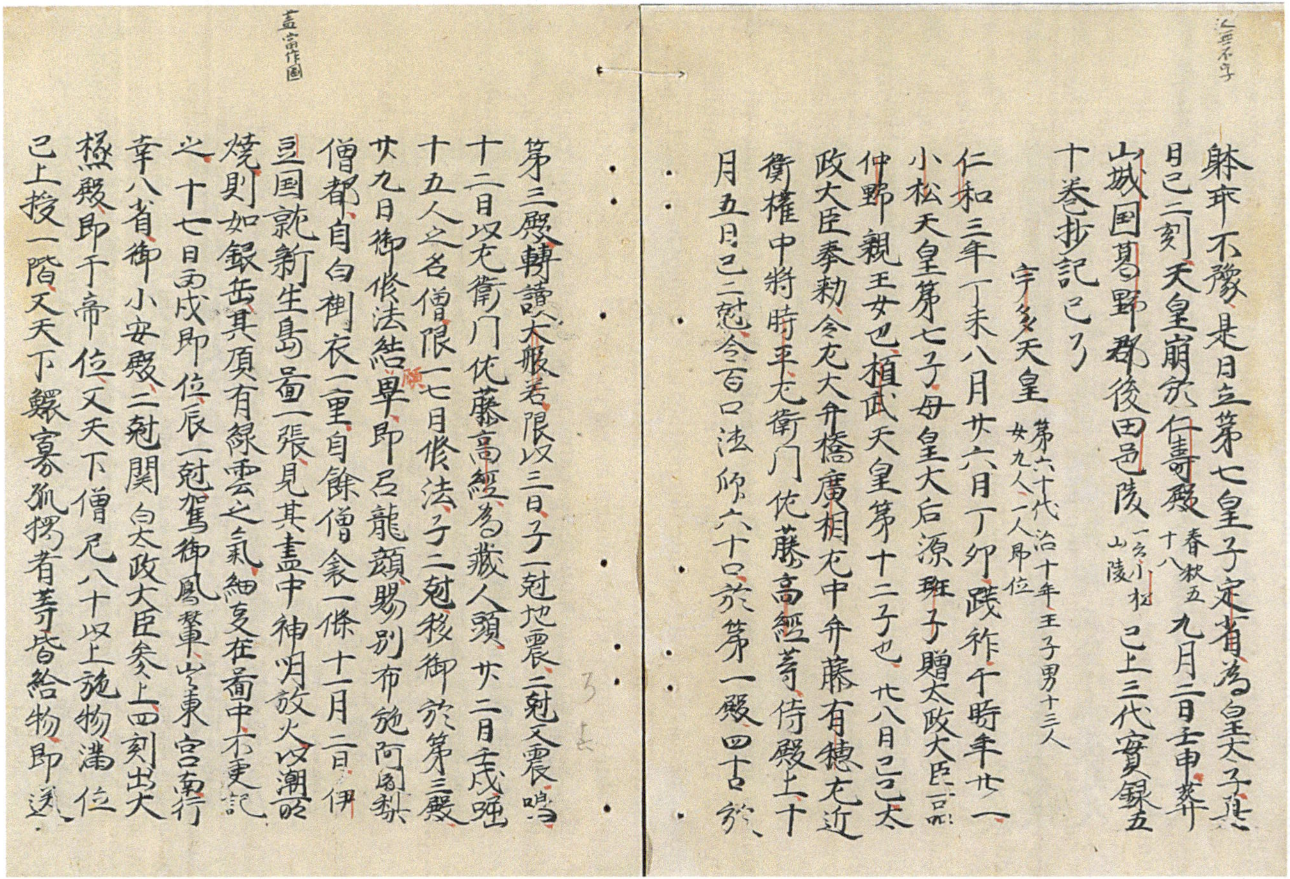

FIGURE 2.2. Example of biography format in a manuscript of *Abbreviated Records* from the early Edo period. The text shown is the opening of Emperor Uda's biography. Reprinted with permission from the National Diet Library Digital Collections—*Fusō ryakki* (frame 18).

In *Abbreviated Records*, each new entry opens with the subject's name, followed by a brief synopsis. This synopsis is written in a double row of smaller characters and typically concludes with a list of his or her progeny and an indication of how many of these ascended the throne. After Emperor Jinmu's name, for instance, the half-size text reads: "First [ruler] of the Age of Men. Governed the earthly realm for 76 years. Born [?] in a *kanoe-uma* year. [Begat] four princes. One ascended the throne."[81] The body of the entry follows these miniature biographies, with occasional double rows of commentary inserted. All of this is, of course, in *kanbun*.

Superficially, the format of the biographies in *The Water Mirror* resembles that in *Abbreviated Records*: emperor, half-size *kanbun* synopsis in double rows, followed by a fuller biography, albeit in *wabun*. However, the similarities in the synopses end at the formal level. In *The Water Mirror*, Emperor Jinmu's reign is (representatively) distilled in the double row of smaller *kanbun* text as follows: "On a *kinoe-tatsu* day in the third month of the seventy-sixth year [of his reign], he passed away. His age was one hundred twenty-seven. On a *hinoe-tora* day of the ninth month, he was interred in a tumulus northeast of Mount Unebi, the Land of Yamato."[82] While the synopses in *Abbreviated Records* emphasize the imperial institution and its continuity via the notation of accession and progeny, Tadachika presents the essential moments of any given reign as death and entombment. The recurring suggestion throughout *The Water Mirror* is that any individual life amounts to little more than its moment of extinction. To borrow the words of its immortal narrator, it reduces rulers to fleeting figures "but seen in a lengthy dream."[83] In both texts, the miniature synopses can be said to encapsulate a basic rule that

---

of Dōhan (1178–1252), *Fusō ryakki maki dai niju*. Agency for Cultural Affairs ("Kokushi bunkazai nado dētabēsu"). Regrettably, only the first and last pages are on display. However, the formal consistency across the late Heian or early Kamakura Kinshōinbon manuscript fragment held by Tenri Library and the National Diet Library's partial manuscript from the early Edo period suggests that this format is stable. For the former, see *Fusō ryakki: Kinshōinbon*, 46 of an appended "kaisetsu" (for description and dating); for the NDL partial manuscript, see *Fusō ryakki*: *Scrolls 22, 24, 25, and 28*.

81. Kuroita, *Fusō ryakki*, 1.

82. Kaneko et al., *Mizukagami zen chūshaku*, 31.

83. Kaneko et al., *Mizukagami zen chūshaku*, 449.

underlies the work—which, for *The Water Mirror*, is that nothing lasts forever.

LOCAL OUTLOOKS: EXTRICATING THE WATER MIRROR'S *CONTENT FROM A POLITICAL ASIA*

Tadachika's intervention in the tradition of *kanbun* historiography is not restricted to the structure of the individual anecdotes or the formal parallels he creates with that tradition via the use of *kanbun* synopses preceding *wabun* narratives. It also takes the form of reshaping its source material. *Abbreviated Records* replicates the content of orthodox histories. It is replete with information about the circulation of people and goods in northeastern Asia, including accounts of military involvement on the Korean peninsula, a record of the arrival of thousands of refugees from Paekche in the fourth year of Emperor Tenji's reign, and evidence of frequent diplomatic and economic exchanges with both the peninsular kingdoms and the Chinese mainland.[84] The "Land of the Rising Sun" in *Abbreviated Records* is firmly ensconced in a cultural, political, and economic network that, via its immediate geographical neighbors, extends well beyond the borders of Japan and all the way to India.

This changes in Tadachika's hands, however, when the source material from *Abbreviated Records* is reworked into the content of a *Mirror* written primarily in *wabun*, as the geographic scope of the narrative undergoes a sharp reduction simultaneously with the switch to a local idiom. In my reading, here too the hybrid register is doing subtle work to reinforce the narrative: the recurring refrain of impermanence that the *kanbun* synapses provide points outward, to a Buddhist frame of reference bigger than the polity itself, while at the same time the *wabun* narrative elevates domestic events to the center of the account. The result of this primarily inward orientation is that Japan comes to exist within a geographically unspecific Buddhist cosmology with little recognition of its this-worldly neighbors. "Real-world" geography is relevant only to the extent that it confirms transcendent cosmological rules. With the intrigu-

84. For this instance of refugees, see Kuroita, *Fusō ryakki*, 59. However, this is not unique: mentions of Japanese military involvement on the peninsula, embassies, or goods sent in tribute occur frequently and are too numerous to list here.

ing exception of the ability of En no Gyōja (an acquaintance of the immortal narrator, no less) to fly back and forth between Japan and the continent, Tadachika includes few references to "overseas" or interregional events other than the early building, burning, and rebuilding of temples in India.[85] Moreover, those figures who do move across borders are nearly all monks. Mobile Buddhist figures such as Kūkai, Saichō, and Ennin study or train on the continent and play key roles in the transmission of artifacts and knowledge, but they do not play overtly interregional political or economic roles.

One outstanding example of this tendency is the portrayal of Prince Shōtoku (574–622). *The Water Mirror* contains numerous anecdotes about his life, but most of them focus on him as a virtuous student of Buddhism or provider of wise counsel. The events related from his youth include the list of auspicious signs surrounding his birth and his recollection of a previous monkish existence in China.[86] Even the account of Shōtoku's alliance with Minister Soga to create an army to crush Minister Moriya in the military campaign mentioned above, which is an exception to the tendency to describe Shōtoku as politically disengaged, is framed as a result of Moriya's misguided disdain for Buddhism.[87] However, the extent to which *The Water Mirror* elides Shōtoku's secular achievements is most evident in the biography of Empress Suiko (554–628). Although Shōtoku is credited with ruling in the empress's stead from the fourth month of her rule onward, the narrator's focus is apolitical. Shōtoku has a mysterious piece of driftwood that has magical properties carved into an image of Kannon, and he rides a flying horse to Mount Fuji, but there is nothing to indicate his governmental duties.

The narrator's rejection of the overtly political aspects of Shōtoku's persona becomes most obvious in the account of the second decade of Suiko's reign. In the eleventh year, Shōtoku presents an image of the Buddha Maitreya to Hata no Kawakatsu (early seventh century), who then has Hachiokadera Temple built to house it. From there, the account skips ahead to the fourteenth year, in which Shōtoku holds lectures on the *Śrīmālā Sutra* at Empress Suiko's behest. In omitting the twelfth year,

85. On En, see Kaneko et al., *Mizukagami zen chūshaku*, 274–75.

86. Kaneko et al., *Mizukagami zen chūshaku*, 176–79.

87. Kaneko et al., *Mizukagami zen chūshaku*, 192.

The Water Mirror excises two of Shōtoku's best-known governmental achievements: the creation in 603 of the *kan'i jūni-kai,* a twelve-rank system of officials that was subdivided into "greater" and "lesser" grades based on six Confucian virtues, and the promulgation of his seventeen-article constitution in 604. Since both of these are included in *Abbreviated Records* (as well as in *Chronicles of Japan*), the omission implies a deliberate effort to reorient the reader away from a concern with secular institutions of governance.[88] This impression is strengthened by the account of Shōtoku's death, in which the narrator summarizes his life and achievements:

> On the twenty-second day of the second month of the twenty-ninth year [of the reign], he passed away. He was forty years of age. From the empress on down, all of the people of the realm were as sad as if they had lost their mother or father. I've only told you about one ten-thousandth of his deeds. Although there's no need to enumerate them afresh, and although everyone knows how laudable they were, I've been repeating them. Had the Crown Prince not appeared in this world, we would have passed from darkness into darkness, and long would we have spent in ignorance of the buddhas and bodhisattvas. It's said that three hundred years after Buddhism was transmitted from India to China it was passed on to Paekche, and after *one hundred* it reached this land. At that time, had it not been for the power of the Crown Prince, the people of this land would have followed Moriya's blasphemy![89]

Only Shōtoku's Buddhist accomplishments are acknowledged. This reaffirms *The Water Mirror*'s commitment, first and foremost, to a Buddhist cosmology rather than to the external realities of interregional politics. Figures such as Shōtoku, who participate in exchanges that allow them to interact with individuals from beyond Japan's borders or to move back and forth between Japan and other lands, are important in *The Water Mirror*, not for sociopolitical reasons but rather for their significance in the

88. For the record of these events that is the basis for my description of each, see Kuroita, *Fusō ryakki*, 41–43.

89. Kaneko et al., *Mizukagami zen chūshaku*, 212–13. The translated portion is from ibid., 213.

development of Japanese Buddhism. Thus, even exceptional figures do little that would tie Japan to a larger regional political reality.

That said, worldly political borders are not entirely erased. Two notable counterexamples exist in *The Water Mirror*: the arrival of emissaries from Silla during the reign of Empress Genmei (661–721) and Minister Kibi's (695–775) trip to China during the reign of Emperor Shōmu. The first is the most difficult to explain. There is no obvious reason for providing an account of the emissaries' presence in Japan, their unprecedented meeting with a minister, or their subsequent trip to the capital, although it was a "boundlessly happy and awe-inspiring matter."[90] As though to justify this digression, the immortal narrator chimes in at the close of the incident with the observation that "Princes and Ministers must, in keeping with the times, receive such visitors. Nowadays, I bet I could chastise them for not meeting with a single foreigner face-to-face."[91] With this inconclusive remark, the Korean peninsula again recedes beyond the boundaries of *The Water Mirror*'s world. Minister Kibi is less problematic. He is simply noted in the context of his detention by the Chinese, which is given as the reason for a ten-day period of darkness in Japan.[92]

The inclusion of such entries does not undermine the overall orientation of *The Water Mirror*. Rather, their very remarkableness attests to the near-complete absence of both the rhetoric and the institutions of this-worldly authority. Other than immediate issues of imperial succession, *The Water Mirror* gives very little space to the mundane matters of government that appear throughout *Abbreviated Records*, including numerous citations of imperial "firsts"—ranging from offices to clothing—or even most of the temple-building projects. All of this, in turn, reinforces the impression that *The Water Mirror*'s focus is a world independent of greater northeast Asian sociopolitical relations.

90. Kaneko et al., *Mizukagami zen chūshaku*, 281.

91. Kaneko et al., *Mizukagami zen chūshaku*, 281. The editors suggest that this anecdote marks a gesture on Tadachika's part toward Taira no Kiyomori's presentation of Retired Emperor Goshirakawa with continental representatives (ibid., 282).

92. Kaneko et al., *Mizukagami zen chūshaku*, 296. The specifics of what Kibi learned in and brought back from China are listed in *Abbreviated Records* (Kuroita, *Fusō ryakki*, 91) but not included in *The Water Mirror*.

The entries on Empress Jitō (645–702), though in both cases brief, are illustrative. The following excerpts from the *Abbreviated Records* biography contain several examples of the kinds of information and events that are excised from *The Water Mirror*:

> The empress assembled three hundred monks and had the previous emperor's royal garments made into *kasaya*, granting one to each. This year, a prince from the Silla court arrived. He presented gold, silver, rare gems, and Buddhist icons. Prince Ōtsu [663–86] plotted against Crown Prince Kusakabe [662–89]. In the eleventh month, he [Ōtsu] was executed. (He was twenty-four.) . . .
>
> In the second year, *tsuchinoe-ne*, the first day of countrywide mourning was established. This was the day on which the previous emperor had died.
>
> In the third year, *tsuchinoto-ushi*, on the first day, *kinoto-u*, of the first month, for the first time, the Bureau of Education presented a New Year's stave, setting a lasting precedent. . . . In the twelfth month, Sugoroku was banned. . . .
>
> In the sixth year, *mizunoe-tatsu*, . . . in the ninth month, emissaries were dispatched to the various provinces for a cadastral survey. The first Middle Counselor was named. Lord Isonokami no Maro [640–717] was the first to occupy this position. There was an imperial decree commanding the assessment of the temples in the earthly realm. There were roughly 545 temples. Each temple presented an allotment of lanterns and 1,000 bundles of rice. Daikan Daiji [Temple] presented various kinds of materiel and servants. The old hanging bell was remade. Several thousands of catties of copper were further submitted [in addition to the aforementioned goods and people], and it was recast.
>
> In the seventh year, *mizunoto-mi*, in the first month, a person of Chinese extraction first presented the Stomping and Singing Dance. . . .[93]

These excerpts provide an image of Jitō's court as administratively proactive and enjoying stable relations with Silla and having at least a certain interest in continental culture. The entry from *The Water Mirror*, in contrast, offers almost nothing beyond the standard information about her ascension to the throne. The same dance performance is noted (though

93. Kuroita, *Fusō ryakki*, 69. For *The Water Mirror*'s biography, see Kaneko et al., *Mizukagami zen chūshaku*, 263.

not its foreign origins), as is her retirement. In other words, because the bulk of the information in *Abbreviated Records* revolves around mundane matters of statecraft and religious ritual, it seems to hold little interest for Tadachika as he composes his narrative of continuous decline.

This disentanglement from the larger regional political context is even true about the types of imagery used: much (but not all) of the concern with celestial portents that is common to Chinese historiography and more orthodox Japanese works such as *Abbreviated Records* is absent from *The Water Mirror*. The only operative cosmological logic is that of decline.

In sum, reading the two texts against each other reveals *The Water Mirror* to be a work with a considerably narrower politico-cultural focus. On the one hand, this is not unexpected, given Tadachika's use of a more vernacular style—after all, the entire account is framed as the eyewitness testimony of a single figure, albeit an immortal one. The locally oriented eyewitness account is precisely the type of text one would expect to see written in a form of *wabun*. The fact that Tadachika's tale transforms a more externally oriented account written in the official language of this-worldly government and bureaucracy into a less grounded, internally focused work in a colloquial register is to be expected. The language and content reinforce each other in both cases.[94] On the other hand, what is critical to thinking about Tadachika's partial transformation of his source models is the fact that this transformation is deliberately incomplete. Despite the marked differences in content, the position of *The Water Mirror* is more complicated, because *kanbun* is also always present. The text is never a completely monolingual work. Tadachika's multilingual approach can be interpreted in at least two ways.[95] One of these readings is overtly suggested within the text, and it is also reinforced by a second more

94. As mentioned above, this type of internal (to Japan) focus seems to be one of the driving concerns behind Jien's slightly later decision to write in *wabun* in the *Gukanshō*.

95. To say nothing of not taking this multilingualism as a "linguistic patholog[y]." Regarding such a misdiagnosis of multilingual writing, see Amsler, *Affective Literacies*, 65. For a more thorough discussion of Amsler's analysis and its relevance to the study at hand, see the introduction. It should be noted that the *Shaku Nihongi* (Exegesis of The Chronicles of Japan) of the late thirteenth century frames its critique of Japanese histories in terms of legibility and the use of a "linkage via years and months"—that is, an

theoretical reading. Common to each of these readings is the idea that Tadachika is making a double gesture: in one case, to both orthodox and alternative histories; and in the other, to both the eyewitness and the archive as ways to legitimize his claims.

UNTANGLING THE DOUBLE GESTURE: ORTHODOXY, WITNESS, AND WRITING

Tadachika's linguistic double gesture is an act saturated with potential meanings. This section will consider how it can simultaneously constitute engagement with ideas of orthodox and unorthodox histories, changing notions of the role of the eyewitness, and a twelfth-century discourse on writing preoccupied with access to the past.

The first way to interpret this regular, recurring insertion of *kanbun* is as a way to blend the languages of two styles of historiography—namely, works in *kanbun* with (or perhaps aspiring to) official status and works in varying styles of *wabun* that are unmarked by officialese and have more diverse orientations. By deploying two distinct linguistic forms rather than rejecting the orthodox language of court authority (*kanbun*) in favor of an entirely different idiom (some variant of *wabun*), Tadachika creates a linguistic amalgamation of these two typically separate spheres and thus claims mastery over mainstream and marginal forms of historiography alike.[96] Such a position is commensurate with both the mobilization of multiple sites of authority in the preface and the use of a double-layered approach to the narration of historical trajectories. At a time when the limitations of the traditional center(s) had been exposed and the structure

---

annalistic format (Onoda, *Shaku Nihongi*, 16–17). It does not explicitly prohibit the mixing of *kana* and *mana*.

96. Kokubota Kaaki's recent comparison of *kanbun* and *wabun* vocabulary and reading pattern usage in the four *Mirrors* proposes that one reason *The Water Mirror* has a relatively high percentage of *kanbun*-derived vocabulary is to "heighten its expressive effect." However, given its emphasis on vocabulary, the study appears not to include the recurring interpolation of *kanbun* as such among its data ("Shikyō no bunshō," 25; the journal in which this article was published has two sets of page numbers, and I use the Japanese numbers). Despite a 1998 assertion that this mixing of styles merits research (Kaneko et al., *Mizukagami zen chūshaku*, 456), Kaneko's subsequent article on *The Water Mirror* argues instead that the text creates a more or less continuous spoken narrative (Kaneko, "'Mizukagami' no setsuwa bungakusei shiron," 115–16).

had been dismantled to a degree, the appeal of a "greater" vision of the universe suggested by this multilingual (or multistyle) approach is not difficult to imagine.

Within *The Water Mirror*, too, there is a clear indication of a larger discussion of writing and genre that supports a reading of Tadachika's linguistic hybridization as intentional. Specifically, in the final pages of the text, Tadachika invokes a much earlier (though still relevant) debate about the meaning of writing history. He does so by having his narrator liken her position and work to that of Murasaki Shikibu and *The Tale of Genji*.[97] However, it must be noted that in so doing, Tadachika—unlike Tametsune in *The New Mirror*—makes no reference to Murasaki's posthumous fate or to views of her work as sinful. As a result, *The Water Mirror* does not appear to directly engage with the question of whether its content might be mischaracterized as "false speech," perhaps signaling that for Tadachika, a *Mirror* was well enough established as something distinct from a "tale" that there was no need to belabor that particular point.

This nod to Murasaki instead invites (or instructs) the reader to think back to the exchange within the *Genji* in which the difference between "chronicles" and "tales"—posed as contrasting categories with regard to recounting the past—is spelled out. As explained in the introduction, the conversation occurs in the "Fireflies" chapter and takes the form of a discussion between Genji and his adopted daughter in which the truth-value of "tales" is the core issue. Because it sets forth the issue so clearly, Genji's attempted summary bears repeating: "The official *Chronicles* of Japan provide but the outlines. *These* [tales] contain the real details!'"[98] As noted above, this conversation advocates a position from which both official and unofficial historiography (the former as "chronicles" and the latter as "tales") can claim to relate a "true" past.

This is important here not so much for any supposed hierarchy between tales and official histories, but rather because it posits a correlation between form and content. In this worldview, chronicles do one thing (in *kanbun*) and tales do another (in *wabun*). Yet now, in a *Mirror*, Tada-

97. Kaneko et al., *Mizukagami zen chūshaku*, 452.

98. Yanai et al., *Genji monogatari*, 2:439. The translation is modified from Murasaki Shikibu and Royall Tyler, *The Tale of Genji*, 1:461.

chika has invoked the languages of both, suggesting a perspective that transcends the limitations of either type of writing and by extension transmits a more comprehensive truth. On the one hand, he has made use of the language of the chronicles, implicitly invoking their "official" authority (which Genji cites earlier in the "Fireflies" exchange). On the other hand, he has also provided "the real details" by rendering large swathes of his content in the language of tales. The linguistic hybridity of his text thus embodies a simultaneous mobilization of contrasting types of authority: the authority of the orthodox chronicle, with its transcultural (*kanbun*) pedigree and court orientation; and the authority not only of the tale but also, more importantly, of the earlier *Mirrors*, with their local (*wabun*) idiom, nongovernmental focus, and implicit ties to truthful sources. By invoking the *Genji* with its binaristic view of writing about the past, Tadachika leaves his reader with a final reminder of the role of writing in communicating different types of truths. He has both orthodoxy and comprehensive accuracy in his arsenal. Read in this way, using two linguistic forms is neither insignificant nor an error—it becomes empowering. Moreover, although his logic is quite different from that of *The New Mirror*'s author, in claiming this new authoritative voice that is independent of the limitations of tales or chronicles, like Tametsune before him, Tadachika implies that his writing is something else.

At a more abstract level, the interpolation of a distinctive written register (*kanbun*) suggests a new position vis-à-vis the authority of the eyewitness. As discussed in chapter 1, the *Mirror* genre previously made exclusive use of a colloquial register to record the firsthand observations of its narrators, with their accounts bolstered by their embedded narrators' claims to have lived through the times of which they spoke. With *The Water Mirror*, however, this is no longer the case. The written register has suddenly become part of the text's means of self-presentation. As a result, its content is certified by both the eyewitness reportage of its embedded immortal informant (the original source of the information that the ascetic then relays to the elderly female narrator) and the linguistic authority of orthodox historiography. *The Water Mirror* marshals the power of both the firsthand observer and text as such, in effect co-opting two traditionally contrastive positions.

The Water Mirror's use of language(s), and the authority or authorities invoked as a result, can also productively be understood as connected to the shift in content from the immediate to the distant past and the difficulties this poses for the figure of the eyewitness as a conduit for or guarantor of truth. Whereas the earlier *Mirrors* rely on preternaturally elderly figures to vouch for the events of relatively recent generations—in *The Great Mirror*, Yotsugi is 190, and his sidekick Shigeki is 180; while in *The New Mirror*, the narrator is an unspecified age over 150—*The Water Mirror* turns to the distant past for its subject, choosing to rely in the preface on an ascetic mediator positioned between the immortal narrator who is the "source" of the testimony and the audience. Without going so far as to accept Komine's suggestion that this insertion of an extra layer of transmission through the setting of the story within a story is intended to create distance as well as "avoid [the question of] the narrator's responsibility," I propose that it does destabilize the authority of the alleged eyewitness.[99]

As mentioned in chapter 1, Koselleck ties the significance of the eyewitness to a premodern notion of history as recording "a naked, unadorned, unequivocally reproducible truth." In the European tradition, the historiographic mirror is a common metaphor for this approach to truth. Koselleck adds that "such metaphors involving a naïve realism draw primarily on eyewitnesses (less on 'earwitnesses') whose presence guarantees the truth of a history."[100] Even in this reduced form, Koselleck's argument intersects at several points with problems posed by the changes *The Water Mirror* makes to the Japanese *Mirror* genre, all of which circumscribe the traditional eyewitness authority of the *Mirror* in early medieval Japan.

To begin with, there is the nature of what the *Mirror* itself reveals: Tadachika's elderly female narrator—the figure who is closest to the reader in the layers of embedded narrative—characterizes *The Water Mirror*'s content as fundamentally different from the content of *The Great Mirror*. Moreover, she argues that both fall short of an exhaustive account of the truth, as is made explicit in the final lines of *The Water Mirror*: "*The Great Mirror*, too, was the work of a benighted layperson, so it's certainly not a 'mirror' like the Buddha's mirror of absolute wisdom. Comparing this [*The Water Mirror*] to *The Great Mirror*, I thought, 'Even if that vis-

99. Komine, *Setsuwa no gensetsu*, 347.
100. Koselleck, *Futures Past*, 132; see also 130.

age [of wisdom] isn't truly visible here, why, isn't [what we can see] as clear as a reflection on the water?' "[101] In other words, the narrator of *The Water Mirror* describes not only her own work but also *The Great Mirror* (the genre's progenitor) as imperfect limited representations of the truth. Even if the principles espoused within the works by the preternatural informants—Yotsugi in *The Great Mirror* and the nameless immortal in *The Water Mirror*—hold true for the cosmos, the historical events that illustrate them are never "naked" (completely exposed) or "unequivocally reproducible" because their representation is always clouded by the fallibility of human memory, both that of the ascetic who passes on *The Water Mirror*'s content initially and that of the old woman who records it.

This is a marked change from the earlier *Mirrors*, neither of which suggests that their content is anything short of a complete recounting of events. In both cases, the otherworldly informant vanishes at the end of his or her recital, but the regret that this occasions in the narrator is not due to the fear of having forgotten or misrepresented the original transmission, but rather simply the regret of being deprived of additional information. In *The Great Mirror*, when the arrival of the preacher interrupts Yotsugi's recitation, the narrator laments her later inability to locate Yotsugi again because she wants to hear more, not because she is unable to remember what she has already heard.[102] The narrator of *The New Mirror* finds herself in a similar situation: "And she thus continued talking, so that I forgot that I was headed somewhere; there was still much that I wanted to hear, but to my great regret, it was evening, and we made our farewells."[103] The final lines show her regretting her failure to meet the narrator again, but make no mention of anxieties over imperfect transmission. These avowed sentiments are very much in keeping with Koselleck's description of a certain premodern sensibility: the historical content that readers enjoy secondhand is the (more or less) unedited truth provided by eyewitnesses as recorded verbatim.

Yet in *The Water Mirror*, the immediacy is lost. Or rather, the narrator suggests that it has never really been there. There is a break between an actual truth, as represented by the Buddha's mirror of perfect wisdom,

101. Kaneko et al., *Mizukagami zen chūshaku*, 452.
102. Ishikawa, *Ōkagami*, 346–47.
103. Takehana, *Imakagami*, 3:594.

and the inherently imperfect historical accounts, none of which can completely reflect things as they really (or absolutely) were. To be clear, this is not the same break that Koselleck posits. In Koselleck's analysis, historians became aware of the impossibility of a truly exhaustive account.[104] In *The Water Mirror*, the concern seems to be not so much with objectivity as with a failure to correctly (or perhaps one might here translate *tadashiku* as "righteously") transmit a deeper truth of which historical events are but a superficial manifestation.

Somewhere between *The New Mirror* and *The Water Mirror*, the authority of the eyewitness—or earwitness, since all of these early *Mirrors* are presented as secondhand narratives—has been compromised. On the one hand, it still clearly holds a powerful sway. Some kind of authority is still derived precisely from a text's being represented as a speech-based work, particularly one that unfolds in settings closely associated with preaching and an oral transmission of truth.[105] Otherwise, there would be no need to have an immortal informant present the work's content as based on a supposed eyewitness account, despite its temporal distance.

On the other hand, the fact that this is not enough is suggested by the integration of the smaller *kanbun* texts. The insertion of a distinct written register differentiates *The Water Mirror* from the realm of pure testimony, moving it into "the archive."[106] It interweaves text as such throughout the testimony to form a mutually reinforcing narrative of spoken and written word. I suggest that this recourse to the written register speaks to a perceived insufficiency of the eyewitness and his or her colloquial style. Despite the testimony and the sacred setting, something is missing: here, too, Tadachika's turn to the language of orthodox historiography—a register that is inseparable on one level from the notion of writing as such—can be understood as a means of marshaling additional authority.

Thomas Conlan's work on the connection between a text and its oralization as pertains to medieval Japanese documents posits a sort of

104. Koselleck, *Futures Past*, 134.

105. Komine has argued that the setting for *The Great Mirror*—Urin'in Temple before religious services honoring Empress Seishi—has this effect ("Ōkagami-ron," 542 and 577–78). I accept this and assume it to correspondingly apply to the other *Mirrors* with similar settings.

106. Ricoeur, *Memory, History, Forgetting*, 163–65.

symbiotic relationship between the two that can shed light on some of the dynamics that may be at work in *The Water Mirror.* While for Conlan the emphasis is on the spoken realization of the texts and the authority this conveys, his treatment of the relationship between documents and reading nonetheless credits writing with a certain heft. He observes that "in Kamakura times . . . written words when read had a formality and weight missing from regular conversation."[107] Working with several examples of texts that, though intended to be read aloud, also foreground their identity as written documents, Conlan enjoins the reader to remember that "writing was not . . . an end unto itself."[108] Nevertheless, though documents might have required being read aloud to be recognized as bearing meaning, Conlan's analysis implies a state of documentary affairs in which neither oral testimony nor written record alone was sufficient. In a similar light, although the texts Elizabeth Oyler draws on are from a slightly later period, she, too, locates a coordinate relationship between reading and writing.[109] In both analyses, the authorities of speech and writing reinforce one another.

In a more extreme contemporary example, the woman known as Fujiwara no Shunzei's daughter (circa 1171–circa 1251) argues that writing is the most effective means of conversation with the past.[110] A short section on *fumi* 文 (writing) in her work *Mumyōzōshi* (Nameless Writings, circa 1196–1202) speaks of a desire to engage with a wider past, one that is not available simply through eyewitness (or earwitness) accounts. Her opening salvo is fairly tame, as she begins by remarking on the value of letters as "repeatedly mentioned" in the classic *Makura no sōshi* (The Pillow Book, written in the late tenth or early eleventh century). She recounts

107. Conlan, "Traces of the Past," 31.

108. Conlan, Traces of the Past," 23; quotation from ibid., 29.

109. This is particularly true in her analysis of "Kanetō's Oath" in the *Heike.* Oyler's focus is the presentation of texts as texts within the larger narrative, both here and in her study overall, and is thus slightly different from the central issue of the present chapter. Nevertheless, her emphasis on the navigation between speech and writing is germane (*Swords, Oaths, and Prophetic Visions,* 69–71, especially 70). For a similar conclusion regarding the depiction of Kakumei and "the increasing importance of writing," see ibid., 83–85.

110. She is actually his granddaughter, but she was raised as his daughter and is commonly designated as such.

their worth in remembering those of "long ago" or the deceased, an ambition of modest scale. Then, however, she moves on to the significance of written characters—that is, writing in relation to the past or unfamiliar: "Not only ancient matters of the splendid Engi [901–23] or Tenryaku [947–57] eras, but also those of unknown lands such as China or India—were it not for writing, how would we record and pass on even the slightest bit? When I ponder such things, I feel that there is nothing at all more wonderful than it."[111] In Shunzei's daughter's reflections, we see an argument for the importance of writing as such. Its value lies precisely in its ability to transmit information across time and distance: an ability to broaden the scope of accessible materials beyond what any one eyewitness could hope to provide.

More importantly, writing is not presented as a shoddy substitute for a firsthand oral transmission; on the contrary, there is "nothing at all more wonderful." This is in direct opposition to the hierarchy familiar from earlier tale collections such as *Tales of Times Now Past*, in which oral transmission—the direct conduit to the eyewitness—marks veracity and/or authority. Where once "thus it was told, and thus it has been handed down"[112] constituted the literal last word, Shunzei's daughter closes her work by referring those who would speak of the affairs of emperors and other men to *Yotsugi* and *The Great Mirror*—that is, to texts.[113] In short, while *Nameless Writings* is written as a conversation between characters, it invests texts and writing with a unique position vis-à-vis access to the past.

Tadachika was an inveterate chronicler, as the surviving portions of his diary attest, and his frustration when recorded precedents proved impossible to locate, inconclusive, or contradictory suggests that he felt the medium of writing ought to have been a reliable means of preserving history. Thus, even though Shunzei's daughter's position may have been at the extreme end of the spectrum, it was not so far removed from Tadachika's.

Shunzei's daughter's insistence on the superlative nature of writing differs from the attitude toward text suggested by Conlan's more broadly

111. Higuchi and Kuboki, *Mumyōzōshi*, 184.

112. This phrase, or a variation of it, is a closing refrain for many of the tales in *Tales of Times Now Past*.

113. Higuchi and Kuboki, *Mumyōzōshi*, 249.

based evaluation, but to a certain extent, the end result is the same. In either case—be it as a way to bridge temporal or geographical divides or as a guarantor of gravitas—the unique potential of writing is acknowledged. It is writing that certifies (or at the very least enables) the accuracy of the transmission, and writing has a function that cannot be fulfilled by vernacular speech (or its replication). In the logic of the world of documents as well as that of Shunzei's daughter's literary imagination, writing carries a different kind of weight. Read against this larger backdrop, it makes sense to suppose that by using the registers of both speech and writing, Tadachika has mobilized at once the authority of the eyewitness and the heft imparted by the suggestion that there is text that confirms his account.

Nowhere does Tadachika state that harnessing different types of authority is his agenda. However, understanding his choice to combine styles in this way provides a consistent interpretation of the interventions he makes in the *Mirror* genre that are otherwise unexplained. Examining Tadachika's multilingual maneuver from the perspective of the problem of the eyewitness highlights different issues from those exposed in the discussion of *kanbun* and *wabun* spheres of authority. Nevertheless, in either investigation, the inclusion of *kanbun* can be interpreted as a way to supplement another notion of legitimacy, buttressing the authority already implicit in the colloquial-style *Mirror* principle or reinforcing the implied truth claims of the eyewitness account. Not only has Tadachika woven together a narrative of decline that accounts for the Genpei War, but he has also done so in a hybrid idiom that moves between the language of the old authority of the court and that of the earlier *Mirrors*, creating a work that reaches far beyond the purview of the traditional elite.

Conclusion

It is true that many of the concerns of Tadachika do not seem to have spoken to the popular imagination in the way that more literary or artistic renderings of the warriors of the Genpei War did. The *Hōgen* (circa 1223) and *Heiji* (1230s or 1240s) tales relate the vicissitudes of war, allotting space to both valor and sorrow, as well as the machinations for power behind both disturbances,[114] and the thirteenth-century scroll *Heiji monogatari ekotoba* (Illustrated Scroll of the Tale of the Heiji) renders the Heiji Disturbance in frightening yet beautiful strokes.[115] Dramatic representations of romanticized warriors likewise later flourished in *nō* drama, doubtless inspired at least in part by warrior patronage. The great playwright Zeami (circa 1363–circa 1443) composed at least three plays on Taira casualties from the Genpei War: "Atsumori," "Tsunemasa," and "Sanemori." The only play that "stars" a contemporary courtier is "Teika," the work of Zeami's son-in-law Konparu Zenchiku (1405–circa 1470), and it is scarcely a flattering depiction; rather, the poet has become a vine that entwines the ghost of his lover, creeping around her grave and preventing her release from the bonds of attachment.

Nevertheless, despite an apparently wider audience for warrior-oriented works, *The Water Mirror* did make an impact in the world of *Mirror* writing and perhaps even beyond. As shown above, similar metanarratives of the four *kalpas* are present in *A Record of the Jōkyū Years* and *A Chronicle of Gods and Sovereigns.* Though neither of these later works mentions *The Water Mirror*, the similarities in the ways in which they structure their respective narratives in terms of cosmological explanations are too striking to be mere coincidence. Moreover, the explanation in *A Record of the Jōkyū Years* of the connection between Buddhism and the understanding of time makes it clear that medieval thinkers saw the power of including this kind of metanarrative to enable a reimagining of history—as a way not only to reflect on the past but also to understand events to come: "Since then [the Buddha's death] more than two thousand springs and autumns have passed like a dream, yet his [the Buddha's] teaching flourishes still. Those who master it, laymen and clerics alike, understand both past and future."[116]

114. I follow Tyler in these dates (*Before* Heike *and After*, 9 and 106).

115. Ikeda Shinobu argues that, unlike the manuscripts for the *Heiji* tale, the scroll represents a courtier perspective that unfavorably depicts warriors and that its beautification of events may be an attempt to render them as "the past" ("'Heiji monogatari emaki,'" 255–57). Matsubara Shigeru offers a fairly narrow date range for the scroll's composition: circa 1249–55 ("'Heiji monogatari ekotoba,'" 100).

116. Matsubayashi, *Jōkyūki*, 177. The translation is from Tyler, *Before* Heike *and After*, 198.

Within the scope of the later *Mirrors*, the factors this chapter has discussed as innovations in *The Water Mirror* are present in the next cosmological history to take up the *Mirror* mantle: *The China Mirror*. A linear historical trajectory, the integration of *kanbun*-derived passages, and the overt use of a textual archive to support contents presented primarily as oral testimony all appear in *The China Mirror* in ways that suggest they are further modifications of *The Water Mirror*'s techniques. In other words, *The Water Mirror* may well have had an impact on the perception of a *Mirror*'s uses and, by extension, on the purposes to which narrating the past can be put.

Lastly, understanding the significance and power of Tadachika's unorthodox alterations helps make sense of the sometimes cold reception of his work. When the fourteenth-century *Clear Mirror*, the final and most conservative of the well-known medieval *Mirrors*, dismisses *The Water Mirror* as "something I but cursorily looked through," we can guess why.[117] Even though *The China Mirror* and eventually *The Mirror of the East*, written in the late Kamakura period, appear to build on *The Water Mirror*'s changes (and the Muromachi *Mirror of the Gods* overtly cites the work), *The Clear Mirror* largely brushes them off, suggesting that subsequent medieval authors saw in the very sites that have been the foci of this chapter's analysis (those points at which Tadachika demonstrably and strategically deviates from earlier norms) the power to innovate or threaten the way people articulated and processed the past.

117. Kidō, *Masukagami*, 7.

CHAPTER 3

Containing China

The Continent as Medieval Object of Knowledge

Main texts (in chronological order)

***Gukanshō* (My Humble Thoughts)**
Author: Jien
Date: circa 1219
Language: *wabun*
Preface: yes
Setting: N/A
Time covered: the reigns of Emperor Jinmu (traditionally seventh century BCE)–Emperor Juntoku (1127–1242).

***Jikkunshō* (Ten Teachings)**
Author: Sugawara no Tamenaga
Date: circa 1252
Language: *wabun*
Preface: yes
Setting: Kyoto (Higashiyama)
Time covered: N/A

***Kokon chomonjū* (Notable Tales Old and New)**
Author: Tachibana no Narisue
Date: 1254
Language: *wabun*
Preface: yes
Setting: none specified
Time covered: N/A

***Kara kagami* (The China Mirror)**
Author: Fujiwara no Shigenori
Date: 1250s or 1260s
Language: *wabun* with semiregular insertion of *kanbun* style
Preface: yes
Setting: Anrakuji Temple (Dazaifu)
Time covered: the reign of Emperor Fuxi (traditionally twenty-ninth or twenty-eighth centuries BCE)–presumably the Song (960–1276); the first six of an original ten scrolls survive

Although the Japanese had witnessed the fall of the Northern Song in 1127 and were aware of the Southern Song's (1127–1279) ongoing challenges, mastery of things Chinese garnered cultural capital like little else in thirteenth-century Japan. Long the domain of the court nobility, acquisition of such knowledge had more recently become an objective of members of the new eastern warrior elite in their quest for legitimacy. As Tonomura Hisae has shown, "the correct inheritance of Japanese culture" was indispensable for a warrior authority looking "to position itself vis-à-vis the Kyoto court and nobility and establish a new governmental authority that included the same."[1] This included, as Tonomura points out, familiarity with Chinese history.[2]

In such an environment, few gestures encapsulated the ideal of the culturally sophisticated warrior more successfully than Taira no Kiyomori's presentation of the *Taiping yulan* (Imperial Readings of the Taiping Era, written circa 983) at the palace on Jishō 3 (1179).2.13, on the eve of the war that would lead to the founding of the Kamakura *bakufu*.[3] Nor was the significance of this donation lost on the audience of the time, as is visible in the recording of the event (the only noteworthy occurrence of the day) by the courtier Nakayama Tadachika in his journal: "Professor of Mathematics [Miyoshi] Yukihira [dates unknown] came and told

1. Tonomura, "Kamakura bushi to Chūgoku koji," 107; see also 103–6. For a similar depiction of warriors' desire for knowledge, see Ogawa Takeo, "Fujiwara no Shigenori-den no kōsatsu," 36.

2. Tonomura, "Kamakura bushi to Chūgoku koji," 107.

3. Moreover, as Ivo Smits points out, foreign sales of the *Taiping yulan* were forbidden, and Kiyomori's copy was incomplete ("China as Classic Text," 196–97). David Bialock also notes this acquisition in passing in a larger discussion of Kiyomori's trade activities (*Eccentric Spaces*, 200).

me that the (Rokuhara) Novice Chancellor had proffered a Chinese text at the palace. Its name was *Imperial Readings of the Taiping Era*. It consisted of 260 books. The Novice [Kiyomori] wrote in the book that it must be donated to the palace as a collectanea. This text had never before been brought to our court."[4] Clearly, even in its incomplete form, this assemblage of previously unseen Chinese writings was a substantial and presumably not inexpensive tome. As a gift to the palace—home of Kiyomori's daughter and grandson, the crown prince—it was surely not to be taken lightly. Rather, Kiyomori's bestowal of a new Chinese text in all likelihood constituted a powerful gesture, an assertion of his own belonging at court not only as a martial leader who now happened to be related to the imperial family, but also as an individual possessed of cultural savoir faire.

Over the following decades, knowledge of things Chinese continued to provide a certain cachet, even as the eastern warrior elite grew in power. The flow of knowledge from west to east, and from court to *bakufu*, that enabled this is embodied in the figure of Minamoto no Mitsuyuki (1163–1244), who relocated from the capital to Kamakura, where his Chinese expertise allowed him to "play an important educational role in warrior society."[5] In the small world of houses specializing in Chinese learning, Mitsuyuki was a former pupil of "the leading China scholar" Fujiwara no Takanori (1158–1233).[6] The activities of Mitsuyuki and scholars like him provided a certain amount of intellectual groundwork and audience appetite for later China specialists who relocated to the east, including Takanori's grandson Fujiwara no Shigenori (circa 1204–circa 1294). Like his grandfather before him, Shigenori was a prominent China scholar, and like Mitsuyuki, fortune took him east to Kamakura, where he authored *The China Mirror* (in the 1250s or 1260s), the next of the historiographic *Mirrors* to appear.[7]

4. Nakayama, *Sankaiki*, 2:225. Kiyomori's presentation seems to have hit a nerve with Tadachika, for he comments on it again in the twelfth month of the same year (ibid., 2:328).

5. Tonomura, "Kamakura bushi to Chūgoku koji," 104.

6. Tonomura, "Kamakura bushi to Chūgoku koji," 104.

7. Tonomura also notes this relationship ("Kamakura bushi to Chūgoku koji," 111). In dating the work to this decade, I follow Ogawa Takeo, "Fujiwara no Shigenori-den no kōsatsu," 32.

Despite the intellectual continuity suggested by the enduring value placed on Chinese learning, the world that was the backdrop for *The China Mirror* was in many ways very different from the one that had inspired *The Water Mirror* a mere eighty years before. By the time Shigenori's work appeared, Yoritomo, the founder of the Kamakura *bakufu*, had been dead for roughly half a century, and in 1221 the *bakufu* itself had weathered an unsuccessful rebellion led by Retired Emperor Gotoba. Although *Matsuranomiya monogatari* (The Tale of Matsura), the fantasy set in China and written in the late twelfth century by Fujiwara no Teika (1162–1241), portrayed warrior skills as within the grasp of even the most inexperienced courtier—and thus depicted a world in which the court's reseizure of power was only a few well-aimed arrows away[8]—the reality was that Gotoba's abortive efforts had resulted in a stronger, not a weaker, hold on power by the warrior elite. On top of this, the de facto rulers of the *bakufu*, the Hōjō family, had consolidated their position in the east after eliminating their last remaining rivals, the Miura family, in the Hōji Disturbance of 1247. One clear manifestation of this state of affairs was the unprecedented appointment of the child Imperial Prince Munetaka (1242–74) as the sixth shogun—a position he held from 1252 to 1266.[9] Munetaka's shogunal tenure was the direct result of a clandestine *bakufu* request to depose his predecessor and send an imperial prince in his stead.[10]

It should come as no surprise, then, that even as *The China Mirror* builds on the precedents established by the earlier *Mirrors*, it takes the genre in new directions, targeting different readers and focusing on an unprecedented subject.[11] This chapter argues that *The China Mirror* is a

8. At one point, the hero (Ujitada) claims, "At home, in my country, I never even learned to tell which way an arrow should fly" (Higuchi and Kuboki, *Matsuranomiya monogatari*, 59; translation from Fujiwara Teika and Wayne P. Lammers, *The Tale of Matsura*, 103). Needless to say, this does not prevent him from being a formidable archer on the battlefield.

9. For a more thorough overview of the shifting power dynamics of this period, see Hurst, "The Kōbu Polity."

10. On the original request, see the entry for Kenchō 4 (1252).2.20 in Nagahara and Kishi, *Zen'yaku Azuma kagami*, 5:139. On the decision to send Munetaka, see the entry for Kenchō 4 (1252).3.5 in ibid., 5:143–44.

11. Yamada Naoko is, at the time of writing, the Japanese scholar who has worked most recently and thoroughly on *The China Mirror*. On this matter, she observes that

site where two strands of medieval thought intersect: the issue of China's place (or places) in the medieval imagination and the issue, familiar from the earlier *Mirrors*, of narrating the past. To put it another way, there are two larger questions that *The China Mirror* invites. At the more immediate narrative level, one can ask what the "China" is that is being taught, and how that does or does not resonate with contemporary discourses on China. *The China Mirror* reflects at least two positions vis-à-vis the continent, which is imagined as a wellspring of cultural prestige but also as an irredeemably declining civilization. The latter is a position that allows Japan to occupy what Charlotte Eubanks describes as "the cutting edge of Buddhist expansion, the current location of the Buddhist event horizon."[12] At the meta level one can also ask what the use of China and Chinese history as a teaching tool—as a means, rather than an end—enables, for the *Mirror* genre in particular. The shift in focus away from a narrative centered on the Japanese court has profound implications for the types of lessons (or principles) that can be taught, as well as for the narrative geography of sites that have the power to legitimate such teachings.

To first interrogate what Shigenori's treatment of China signifies in terms of medieval readers concerned with "things Chinese," the present chapter examines how Shigenori and two contemporary authors create an image or multiple images of something "Chinese." Following a brief overview of the China created within *The China Mirror*, I compare that China with the China(s) of the 1252 work *Jikkunshō* (Ten Teachings, also read *Jikkinshō*) and the 1254 composition *Kokon chomonjū* (Notable Tales Old and New). After investigating the ways in which *The China Mirror* participates in medieval narratives ostensibly about Japan's neighbor to the west, especially narratives that find warrior readers, I then turn to the theoretical implications of Shigenori's particular reimagining of the Chinese past as a geographically, linguistically, and temporally contained

---

"in handling Chinese history, [*Kara kagami*] draws a line between itself and other *kagami*, including *Ōkagami*" (*Chūgoku koji juyō ronkō*, 109). Tonomura places *The China Mirror* in a lineage with *Mōgyū waka* ("Kamakura bushi to Chūgoku koji," 114).

12. Eubanks, *Miracles of Book and Body*, 66. This is especially relevant, since Eubanks is analyzing a similarly didactic mode of writing, *setsuwa*, and how the position of Japan relates to those of China and India in collections with a multipolity frame of reference.

unit to argue that Shigenori's innovations signify a fundamental change in the ends to which *Mirror* writing, or the past itself, is being used. To better understand how *The China Mirror* fits into a larger picture of medieval historiographic possibilities, the chapter closes by considering—especially in light of Jien's thirteenth-century history, *My Humble Thoughts*—the elements of *The Water Mirror* that Shigenori did or did not choose to incorporate. In this light, *The China Mirror*'s reconfigurations of the *Mirror* genre outlined above—object, scope, language, and rhetoric—point to fault lines that will play out in a fracturing of the genre in chapter 4.

Locating The China Mirror*: Authorship*

The China Mirror is the first of the historiographic *Mirrors* believed to have been composed far from the capital. It is also the first of the *Mirrors* to be set far from the capital, although the site of composition and the narrative site are not the same (the significance of the latter will be analyzed below, in "Far from the Capital"). Its author, Fujiwara no Shigenori, was a member of a well-established line of scholars and moderately successful courtier bureaucrats.[13] A denizen of Kyoto, Shigenori was a rising star of the academy when in 1253 he received the order to join the young Prince–Shogun Munetaka in Kamakura as his tutor. By Kenchō 5 (1253).11.25, Shigenori had provided a draft of the *kakikudashi* (Japanese rendering) of Shogunal Regent Hōjō Tokiyori's (1227–63) vow to accompany the offerings at the newly completed Kenchōji Temple.[14] In all likelihood, it was in Kamakura that Shigenori composed *The China Mirror*. Ogawa Takeo, who has conducted the most thorough research into Shigenori's biography to date, is circumspect on the question of the work's

13. These cursory observations on Shigenori draw on the work of Ogawa Takeo unless otherwise noted ("Fujiwara no Shigenori-den no kōsatsu," 28–32).

14. Nagahara and Kishi, *Zen'yaku Azuma kagami*, 5:215–16. Only the information pertaining to Shigenori's involvement with the offerings draws on my own reading of *Azuma kagami*—the remainder is derived from Ogawa Takeo's previously cited work. As though foreshadowing the preface to *The China Mirror*, the *Azuma kagami* entry also notes that the event was presided over by Daolong, a monk from the "Song court."

readership. He first opines that it "could have been for the education of nobility" or "written at their behest," before suggesting that "its original target reader might have been Imperial Prince–Shogun Munetaka."[15] Eventually, however, considering it within the context of Eastern warriors' demands, he concludes that *The China Mirror* may well have been written with warriors' needs in mind.[16] With Tonomura Hisae reaching a similar conclusion about a warrior readership, it seems reasonable to think of the work as one that resonated strongly with Kamakura concerns.[17]

Shigenori's tenure in Kamakura concluded in 1264, but he maintained ties to the east after his return to Kyoto.[18] Indeed, his last brief trip there took place in 1287, when he was in his eighties; in 1294, he took the tonsure, at which point he vanishes from the record.[19] As Ogawa demonstrates, however, these connections with an eastern base outlived Shigenori: his descendants also used the east and their ties to its warriors as an alternative power base, enjoying professional successes as a result.[20] Using similar reasoning, Tonomura has even gone so far as to suggest the involvement of Shigenori's "house" in the later composition of *The Mirror of the East*.[21] This multigenerational connection with the eastern warrior elite suggests a level of commitment to the east that reinforces the idea that *The China Mirror* was written at least in part with an eye to a warrior audience.

Forging a link between biography and creative content, Shigenori's experience seems to have occasioned at least one change to the basic premise of the *Mirror* genre. Shigenori sets *The China Mirror* away from the

15. Ogawa Takeo, "Fujiwara no Shigenori-den no kōsatsu," 32. Nevertheless, in Hirasawa Gorō's catalogue of works that refer to *The China Mirror*, it appears in the fifteenth-century diary of Tonsured Prince Sadafusa (the *Kanmon gyoki*), the *Taishiden gyokurin shō* (written in the early fifteenth century), and the courtier diary *Nobutanekyō ki* (late fifteenth or early sixteenth century). As Hirasawa's work indicates, *The China Mirror*'s appearance in the two court diaries suggests that it enjoyed at least some prestige ("*Kara kagami* no denpon oyobi shutten kō," 310–12). It is clearly not being read only by warriors.

16. Ogawa Takeo, "Fujiwara no Shigenori-den no kōsatsu," 36.

17. Tonomura, "Kamakura bushi to Chūgoku koji," 112.

18. Ogawa Takeo, "Fujiwara no Shigenori-den no kōsatsu," 32–33.

19. Ogawa Takeo, "Fujiwara no Shigenori-den no kōsatsu," 34.

20. Ogawa Takeo, "Fujiwara no Shigenori-den no kōsatsu," 35.

21. Tonomura, "Kamakura bushi to Chūgoku koji," 115.

capital in Dazaifu (modern-day Kyūshū), a traditional site of courtier exile. In other words, the temporary physical relocation of Shigenori to Kamakura coincides with both a literal and a narrative uncoupling of *Mirror* writing from former sites of authority and, perhaps, audience. While the authors of the earlier *Mirrors* (to the extent that they are known) were based in or near the capital, Shigenori has been sent to the east, to the site of the warrior government. His resulting *Mirror* is a work that explores a new seat of power in geographic and thematic terms.

Indeed, as becomes clear in the remainder of this chapter, *The China Mirror* turns out to distance itself from the world of the earlier *Mirrors* in multiple ways that continue the relocation of this type of text from the "margins" to the center of power. Not only does *The China Mirror* situate power in a new geographic location away from traditional Japanese court institutions, just as the founding of the *bakufu* had done, but the work also adopts an unprecedented focus for a *Mirror*: China. This departure from the traditional theme of the Japanese court has major implications, both in terms of how a *Mirror*'s historical object could be conceptualized and for the notion of what constituted an appropriate subject or even a "principle" for a *Mirror* at all.

An Introduction to The China Mirror

In 1994, Chino Kaori's now-famous essay argued that in Heian art, the category of "China" (or rather, *Kara* 唐) designated a domestically produced construct rather than "the actual (or former) Tang empire across the sea."[22] This holds true not only for Japanese art, and Ivo Smits has gone a step further to assert that in terms of literature, too, for Heian Japanese intellectuals the imagined China was at least as real or important as the China of the real world.[23] These understandings (of the importance of China as an analytical category with little or no basis in reality and of the relative significance of this image) are central to any consideration of

22. Chino, "Nihon bijutsu no jendā," 526. For an English translation of this essay, see Chino Kaori, "Gender in Japanese Art," 17–34.

23. Smits, "Way of the Literati," 109.

the implications of the China that is assembled in *The China Mirror*—namely, China as an entity pieced together from selected texts to serve a certain purpose.[24]

However, because there is no critical edition or modern Japanese translation of *The China Mirror*, I will begin with an overview of its content to shed light on what the China is that the text "teaches."[25] Such an overview is inevitably incomplete, given that the received version is presumably missing roughly half of the text: only six of the original ten scrolls survive. If its introduction is to be believed, however, *The China Mirror* originally covered the period from the Sage Emperors through an unspecified more recent age—some point in the Song.[26] While the six extant scrolls cover only through the Jin (265–420), the work is substantial even in its partial form.

As with each of the *Mirrors* that precedes it, at its most basic structural level, *The China Mirror* is composed of a preface set at a temple and a series of biographies. The preface unfolds at Anrakuji Temple and features an encounter between the narrator and two Chinese monks who have fled the impious Song court and come to Japan. The senior of the two monks identifies a worthy audience in the figure of the narrator and offers to "roughly relate the aspect of the land of Cīnasthāna, if [he] would but listen."[27] Of course, the narrator accepts, and the story proceeds from there.

The rest of scroll 1, which runs through the end of the Yin (Shang, sixteenth century–1045 BCE), takes the reader to the origins of Chinese

24. Otagiri Fumihiro has done meticulous work on the first section of *The China Mirror*, demonstrating that Shigenori did not draw exclusively on Chinese official histories, or even on Chinese texts alone ("'Kara kagami' ni okeru Kanseki juyō" and "'Kara kagami' ni okeru Kanseki juyō [zoku]"). The earlier work of Hirasawa was much more centered on the orthodox histories ("*Kara kagami* no denpon oyobi shutten kō," 371–73).

25. This summary is based on Hirasawa and Yoshida, *Kara kagami: Shōkōkanbon*. This edition provides an introduction to and a typeset version of the text, as well as detailed descriptions of manuscript lineages to which I will return. However, its punctuation is limited to breaking clauses with commas. Nor are voicing marks or any annotations included.

26. The latest of the citations of *The China Mirror* that Hirasawa identifies in the *Taishiden gyokurin shō* deals with the Tang. See Hirasawa, *Kara kagami: Kōi hen*, 247–48 and 253–54.

27. Hirasawa and Yoshida, *Kara kagami: Shōkōkanbon*, 9–10.

civilization and the appearance of the earliest rulers: Fuxi, Nüwa, and Shennong.[28] The content of each entry is fairly brief, providing the basics of each ruler's biography. More significant than the concrete details of any given figure's life is the way in which the reader is immediately confronted with an indication of one of Shigenori's methods for reworking the material, a technique that resembles those found "on the fringe of Chinese Buddhist literature."[29] For each of the primeval divine rulers, Shigenori introduces commentary that universalizes his or her identity. Fuxi is equated with an incarnation (*gonge*) of Ōsei Daishi and described as having been charged by two bodhisattvas, Hōōsei and Hōkisshō, with making the sun and moon.[30] Nüwa is designated as an incarnation of Hōkisshō, and the two are subsequently compared to the bodhisattvas Seishi and Kannon, respectively. Lastly, Shennong is matched to both the Medicine Buddha and his (Shennong's) Japanese counterpart, "the Bull-Headed Sovereign of Gion."[31] Thus, at the same time as this trio of founding figures is introduced within the narrative of Chinese history, each is specifically placed in a Buddhist frame of reference. This links them to a broader identity that defies state or sovereign boundaries, making them simultaneously Chinese entities and something more.[32] Or, to put it another way, turning the founders of Chinese civilization into manifesta-

28. I render the names to reflect modern Mandarin pronunciation primarily for practical concerns: first, to facilitate cross-referencing with Western-language scholarship on Chinese history, and second, for the simple reason that Chinese has more sounds than Japanese has morae. Using Chinese thus makes it easier to distinguish between the sounds.

29. Zürcher, *Buddhist Conquest of China*, 308.

30. Hirasawa and Yoshida, *Kara kagami: Shōkōkanbon*, 12–13. Erik Zürcher points to the idea in Chinese "Buddhist apocrypha" of "even the rulers of the legendary era being qualified as Bodhisattvas" more than once (*Buddhist Conquest of China*, 309 and 313–14). On the Chinese texts in which this occurs, see ibid., 318–19. See also Otagiri, "'Kara kagami' ni okeru Kanseki juyō," 189–94.

31. Hirasawa and Yoshida, *Kara kagami: Shōkōkanbon*, 15. Itō Satoshi denotes this deity as "a figure of markedly amalgamatory characteristics," adding that "this deity's history in Japan was shallow, and his roots are thought to lie in Chinese traditions of Yin-Yang thought and astrological divination" ("The Medieval Period," 78).

32. What is striking is that India plays almost no part in *The China Mirror*. Thus, the text does not seem to subscribe to a three-country worldview, which Willy Vande Walle implies is coming into its own around the time of *The Mirror of China*'s probable composition ("Japan," 90–91). Given that essay's brevity, it does not delve deeply into

tions of a greater non-Chinese system turns China into an instructive case study intended to illustrate a larger logic, rather than an end unto itself.

While the origins of rituals and customs are included in abundance and are clearly significant information, perhaps the most important specific lesson for a reader to take away from this part of his or her study of China—in particular, a young reader hoping to govern—is the lesson on governance found near the end of the scroll. The implied message is that the ultimate responsibility for government lies with the ruler, who would do well to listen to both his advisors and his subjects. Shigenori clarifies this with concluding commentary that summarizes the import of the *Mirror*'s content. His first point is that Emperors Yao (traditionally twenty-fourth century BCE) and Shun (traditionally twenty-third century BCE) are the "archetypes of the sagely ruler" (*shōshu no hajime*), while Emperors Jie (traditionally late eighteenth or early seventeenth century BCE) and Zhou (traditionally eleventh century BCE) are the "original wicked kings" (*akuō no moto*).[33] Perhaps in anticipation of the charge that the heavens ought to have given a sign that telluric events were spiraling out of control rather than to allow either of the latter to take the throne, Shigenori's final didactic pièce de résistance is an exchange between Duke Ai of Lu (reigned 494–468 BCE) and Confucius (551–479 BCE) that explains the lack of celestial portents as occasioned by the complete deviation from the Way on the part of both Jie and Zhou. Essentially, when rulers have gone so far astray, Shigenori–Confucius suggests, the heavens are no longer bound to give fair warning of imminent change.

Scroll 2 runs from the Zhou (eleventh century BCE–756 BCE) through the Qin (221–206 BCE). Much of the scroll revolves around imperial succession or governance, with the first three rulers, Kings Wen (eleventh century BCE), Wu (reigned circa 1046–1043 BCE), and Cheng (reigned circa 1042–1021 BCE) predictably most remarkable for their ability to take good advice. Kings Wen and Wu both benefit from wise council, but it is King Cheng, with his famous regent Zhou Gong (eleventh century BCE), who both has the most extraordinary advisor and takes the longest to learn his lesson. In a particularly charming entry,

---

the specifics of Buddhist cosmology or cosmologies, but it does provide an accessible overview.

33. Hirasawa and Yoshida, *Kara kagami: Shōkōkanbon*, 42.

Zhou Gong teaches the young king that words have consequences: "King Cheng was playing with his younger brother Tang Shuwu beneath a paulownia tree. King Cheng wanted to play a joke, and he stripped off a paulownia leaf and made a seal, enfeoffing Shuwu as Marklord of Ying. When he heard this, Zhou Gong offered congratulations. When King Cheng said, 'I was joking!' Zhou Gong said, 'The Son of Heaven does not make jokes.' And because of this, Tang was indeed made Marklord of Ying."[34]

Although King Cheng needs time to realize the value of his councilor, he comes to appreciate Zhou Gong's sagacity in the end. King Cheng outlives his mentor, and when his rule comes to an end, so, too, does a golden age for the Zhou. The Zhou is followed by the Warring States period (457–221 BCE), and the scroll concludes with violent entries on the Qin and its destruction—including the third emperor's weeklong stewing alive of his conniving and traitorous advisor Zhao Gao (died 207 BCE).[35]

At the same time, Buddhism continues to make scattered appearances, reinforcing the links established in the first scroll. In this regard, the most noteworthy events concerning the Buddha are his birth during the reign of King Zhao (reigned 977–957 BCE),[36] his death in the fifty-third year of King Mu's reign (reigned 956–918 BCE),[37] and an omen of the Buddha's birth referred to in the reign of King Zhuang (reigned 696–682 BCE).[38] Further emphasizing Buddhism's centrality to understanding

34. Hirasawa and Yoshida, *Kara kagami: Shōkōkanbon*, 49–50.

35. Hirasawa and Yoshida, *Kara kagami: Shōkōkanbon*, 83.

36. Hirasawa and Yoshida, *Kara kagami: Shōkōkanbon*, 51.

37. Hirasawa and Yoshida, *Kara kagami: Shōkōkanbon*, 53. For an account of this entry that ties it to larger Tang debates on Buddhism versus Daoism, see Morita, "Jidō setsuwa to gohō riron." The article also provides an easy-to-digest background on some of the rhetorical sleight of hand taking place that helps make sense of other events Shigenori notes here—Laozi's and the Buddha's respective births, in particular (see especially ibid., 55).

38. Hirasawa and Yoshida, *Kara kagami: Shōkōkanbon*, 58. Since both King Zhao and King Mu are believed to have reigned during the tenth century BCE, and King Zhuang's reign is likewise believed to have predated the Buddha's birth, this account at first appears confusing. Shigenori in fact seems to be drawing on two distinct traditions. For possible sources for these theories of dating the Buddha's birth, see Zürcher, *Buddhist Conquest of China*, 271–74.

Chinese history, Laozi (sixth century BCE) is identified as "an incarnation of Kashō"[39] and Confucius as "an incarnation of the bodhisattva Judō," subsequently rumored to have left China for Japan.[40] Confucius's famous disciple Yan Hui (521–circa 481 BCE) is revealed to be none other than the Kōjō bodhisattva,[41] while Crown Prince Jin (circa 567–circa 549 BCE) is reborn in Japan as the Kumano incarnation (*gongen*).[42] As with the primeval figures of the first scroll, Shigenori again links "stars" of Chinese civilization—most especially Confucius—to a framework that is not restricted to China.

The abovementioned preternatural events culminate in the arrival of Buddhism in China, where it has a hostile reception under the first Qin emperor (circa 259–210 BCE): "Despite things being like this [the Qin burning of books and mass deaths have just been noted], at this time, an Indian monk arrived, bringing Buddhism. Since the First Emperor did not believe, he [the monk] was imprisoned. A six-*zhuang* Vajra being came and smashed the jail gates, and the monk departed."[43] The scroll makes short work of the remainder of the Qin, concluding with the arrival of Liu Bang (circa 256–195 BCE) and the destruction of the Qin tombs, mirroring the destruction at the end of scroll 1.

A discussion of the rise of the Western Han (206 BCE–25 CE) through Emperor Jing (188–141 BCE) occupies the third scroll. As with the earlier scrolls, violence and war feature prominently. The central cast of characters shrinks dramatically in number, but those who are featured often get extensive accounts of their exploits. The three most prominent characters are Emperor Gaozu (circa 256–195 BCE); his rival, Xiang Yu (232–202 BCE); and his wife, Empress Lü (241–180 BCE). Gaozu is the fallible hero who founds the dynasty yet cannot maintain his own

39. Hirasawa and Yoshida, *Kara kagami: Shōkōkanbon*, 59.

40. Hirasawa and Yoshida, *Kara kagami: Shōkōkanbon*, 60–62.

41. Hirasawa and Yoshida, *Kara kagami: Shōkōkanbon*, 60–62.

42. Hirasawa and Yoshida, *Kara kagami: Shōkōkanbon*, 61. Morita Tsurayuki also calls attention to how tales of the crown prince as an incarnation suggest a transmission "far earlier than the eastward flow of Buddhism in the time of the first Qin Emperor or Emperor Ming of the Eastern Han" ("Jidō setsuwa to gohō riron," 71). For an in-depth discussion of the Chinese texts in which this schema and others like it appeared, see Zürcher, *Buddhist Conquest of China*, 313–15 and 317.

43. Hirasawa and Yoshida, *Kara kagami: Shōkōkanbon*, 80.

household entirely in accordance with ritual propriety; he is too deferential to his own father and unable to stand up to the machinations of his wife.[44] Xiang Yu, the conniving yet romantic warrior who attempts to defeat Gaozu but ultimately chooses an honorable defeat and cuts off his own head, is treated somewhat sympathetically in the text.[45] As one would expect, the notorious Empress Lü likewise occupies a central position; the account of her persecution of Lady Qi (late third century–194 BCE), a story that was well known in Japan at the time (and a version of which is also contained in *China Tales*), is gleefully gruesome.[46] The scroll concludes with the efforts of Dowager Empress Dou (ca. 205–135 BCE), whose appearance is followed by ominous portents. Her efforts to manipulate the imperial succession result in brutal murders before ending in failure. The scroll closes a few lines later with the regnant emperor's death.[47]

The fourth scroll relates the lives of the rulers from Emperor Wu (157–87 BCE) through Gengshi (died 25 CE), lingering over images of the simultaneous cultural florescence and latent decadence of the later Western Han. Subtle ties to the Heian court are also present in nods to the origins of both linked verse and the Way of Kickball (*kemari*; Chinese:

44. On these events, see Hirasawa and Yoshida, *Kara kagami: Shōkōkanbon*, 101 and 102–4.

45. The account of their rivalry can be found in Hirasawa and Yoshida, *Kara kagami: Shōkōkanbon*, 88–99. Liu Yuan-ju has pointed out to me that the Chinese reception of Xiang Yu is similar (personal communication, June 2010).

46. I propose that it is not just the particularities of her rule that Shigenori highlights here, but also the larger problem of women in power. After all, it is not just Empress Lü who causes problems with her stratagems. Combined with earlier remarks by Shigenori on how the infamous Meixi, Daji, and Baosi "occasioned the destruction of kingdoms and the deaths of lords," the narrator appears to come down strongly against the idea of having women in proximity to power (Hirasawa and Yoshida, *Kara kagami: Shōkōkanbon*, 57). A reconstructed section from *The Mirror of the East* explicitly likens Hōjō Masako (1156–1225) to Empress Lü in the entry that records her death on Karoku 1 (1225).7.11 (Nagahara and Kishi, *Zen'yaku Azuma kagami*, 3:415). For a sense of just how involved Masako was in the highest levels of politics, see Gomi, "Kyō, Kamakura no ōken," 70–72 and 86–87, and *passim*. (The point resurfaces throughout Gomi's essay, but it is most clearly made in the section "Nyonin jugan," 70–72.) Tonomura also attributes just such a comparison to Yoritomo's son Sanetomo ("Kamakura bushi to Chūgoku koji," 110). For a contemporary criticism of Masako's position, see Nakajima, *Gukanshō*, 177–78.

47. Hirasawa and Yoshida, *Kara kagami: Shōkōkanbon*, 119–22.

cuju).[48] Citations from the poetry of Emperor Wu, Empress Wei (died 91 BCE), and Favorite Beauty Ban (circa 48–circa 6 BCE) enhance a sense of artistry as appreciated in the early years of the dynasty.[49] Whereas *The China Mirror*'s previous originary accounts have tended to dwell on ritual or the institutions of statecraft and have at the same time been less evocative of Japanese courtier life, its account of this stage of the Han resonates with medieval Japanese depictions of high culture.

Yet even amid the glory of this golden age, there are seeds of its dramatic decline. Shigenori gives ample space to anecdotes of female jealousy and further plots to manipulate imperial succession, and the perils of excessive beauty are also well documented. Concurrent with the valorization of Han arts, there is a distancing from the increasingly marked political corruption. Emperor Wu's fascination with Daoism and the occult is noted on more than one occasion, but never without proof that they are fruitless: his trusted occultist, Shao Weng (died 117 BCE), is revealed to be a fraud, and the emperor's quest for immortality is written off as a failure.[50] Reminding readers of the futility of non-Buddhist religious pursuits, the entry on Shao Weng draws to a close with the wry observation that "all matters of love of the Way of Immortality are like this."[51] The scroll ends on a particularly damning note after the usurper Wang Mang (45 BCE–23 CE) has been destroyed: "All together, the throne was stolen for a period of nineteen years."[52]

Scroll 5 ranges from Emperor Guangwu (5 BCE–57 CE) of the Eastern Han through the early Three Kingdoms period (220–80). In a predictable pattern, the early days are the glory days of the dynasty, and the latter are its decline. Given this, what is most striking about the entries is the type of figure who takes the helm. These accounts do not provide a simple celebration of imperial leadership, but rather an account of extraordinary men who lead well because of military or religious vision. In the dawning days of the dynasty, Guangwu surfaces as a brilliant mar-

48. Yamada Naoko also repeatedly calls attention to *Kara kagami*'s depiction of origins, including that of the Way of Kickball ("'Kara kagami'-kō," 35–38).

49. For Emperor Wu's verse, see Hirasawa and Yoshida, *Kara kagami: Shōkōkanbon*, 126. For Empress Wei's, see ibid., 129; and for Ban's, see ibid., 141.

50. Hirasawa and Yoshida, *Kara kagami: Shōkōkanbon*, 125 and 128.

51. Hirasawa and Yoshida, *Kara kagami: Shōkōkanbon*, 125.

52. Hirasawa and Yoshida, *Kara kagami: Shōkōkanbon*, 153.

tial mind and Emperor Ming (28–75) as an advocate of Buddhism—there is even a mass conversion of over 1,000 men, 620 Daoists, and 230 women.[53] However, even in the reign of the fourth emperor things are beginning to go downhill, including the Yellow Turban Rebellion (184–circa 204), multiple famines, and the destruction by fire of the imperial palace in Jian'an 1 (196). Shortly thereafter, Cao Cao (155–220), Liu Bei (161–223), and Sun Quan (182–252) each proclaim themselves emperor, with the final result that "the sub-celestial realm was divided in three, ending up just like a tripod."[54]

Moving on to the final sixth scroll, which provides a tripartite narrative of the Three Kingdoms, what stands out is how little content of consequence there actually is.[55] Whereas the earlier scrolls contain substantial narratives of superhuman or extraordinary figures, by the time of the Three Kingdoms, events are portrayed as revolving around vastly reduced characters in settings far less grand than the cosmological level implied at the founding of the empire. Gone are the figures belonging to transcendent frameworks. The reader has descended from the temporally distant origins of civilization and an idealized culture that spans court-bounded sociogeographic entities to the trivial specificities of their later manifestation, which exhibits diminishing institutions and narrative figures and is subject to an accelerated pace of political decline. Shigenori makes no efforts to tie any of these figures to a greater-than-China frame.

However, political decline is not the only thing occurring in the sixth scroll. There are also two lengthy episodes featuring confrontations between Buddhism and other beliefs. Both take place in the entries on the Kingdom of Wu. The first is an unproblematic account of the conversion of its ruler, Sun Quan.[56] The second is more colorful, occurring during

53. Hirasawa and Yoshida, *Kara kagami: Shōkōkanbon*, 165. Morita discusses the significance of Emperor Ming's encounter with Buddhism in terms of the idea of Buddhism as transmitted to China in waves. With regard to its function vis-à-vis King Mu's earlier supposed exposure, see Morita, "Jidō setsuwa to gohō riron," 64–65. Morita specifically credits *Kara kagami* with a view of Buddhism as "moving east in stages" (ibid., 67). On the sources for this episode, see also Morita, "'Kara kagami'-kō (shōzen)," 43–45.

54. Hirasawa and Yoshida, *Kara kagami: Shōkōkanbon*, 180.

55. For a similar conclusion, see Yamada Naoko, *Chūgoku koji juyō ronkō*, 112.

56. Hirasawa and Yoshida, *Kara kagami: Shōkōkanbon*, 188. On the sources for this account, see Morita Tsurayuki, "'Kara kagami'-kō (shōzen)," 45–47.

the reign of Wu's final ruler, Sun Hao (242–84) and ominously foreshadowing what can happen to a dynasty when Buddhism is not taken seriously:

> After that, when [Emperor Hao] was wandering around the park with palace women, there was a golden figure that had been excavated from beneath the earth in the course of landscaping the grounds. It was of a dignified and beautiful appearance. The emperor set this figure against the side of the privy. On the eighth day of the fourth month, he urinated on top of the figure and laughed, saying: "Since this is the eighth day of the fourth month, there is an anointment." While he was diverting himself with palace women, suddenly, his scrotum swelled and ached painfully. The inflammation was unendurable, and it went on from night until morning, so he decided to lie down for the pain. Even the medicines and techniques of renowned physicians were insufficient. The Grand Astrologer conducted a divination and said: "You have wronged the Great Lord." Though there were prayers in the temples, there was no sign [of improvement], and no one, high or low, could figure out what to do. One of the women in the Inner Quarters had faith in the Buddha. She loved the emperor, so this palace woman said to him: "Your Highness, ask the Buddha for salvation." The emperor asked: "Is the Buddha then the Great Lord?" The palace woman said: "Of all that is worthy in heaven above or in the sub-celestial realm, none should surpass the Buddha. The Buddha figure Your Majesty got is still next to the privy. If you make offerings to it, your swollen parts will surely return to normal." The emperor, since his illness was becoming urgent, bathed the hands and eyes of the figure with perfumed water, and placed it in the palace. He kowtowed and apologized for his transgressions. With all his heart, he sought pity. On that night, the pain ceased, and the swelling, too, abated. He had Kang Senghui [died 280] administer the Five Precepts to him, erected a large marketplace temple, and had crowds of priests make offerings. In Yuankang 4 of the Jin, at the age of forty-two, he died. The four Wu leaders in total [ruled for] fifty-nine years.[57]

The entry suggests that political and religious (here, Buddhist) decline are inextricably linked. In fact, the founding of temples, installation of

57. Hirasawa and Yoshida, *Kara kagami: Shōkōkanbon*, 196–97. The translation of *taishi* as "Grand Astrologer" is from *Dictionary of Official Titles* (Charles O. Hucker, 1985 edition).

monks, and even condemnation or support of Buddhism are among those few phenomena, other than plots to manipulate succession or overthrow an emperor, that merit inclusion in the scroll. Perhaps most striking of all, the dynasty is summarized in terms of its Buddhist achievements: "The Eastern [317–420] and Western Jin [265–317] were legitimate for one hundred forty (thirty?)-two years. During this period, 1,768 temples were built; twenty-seven people translated 263 sutras; there were 204,000 monks and nuns."[58] In other words, by scroll 6, the fate of Buddhism under a specific ruler, or its treatment by a powerful individual, is intrinsically valuable as a historical event in Shigenori's work. Perhaps as a result, religious accomplishments have also become a way to measure the worth of a dynasty. Nevertheless, despite the Buddhist achievements of the Western and Eastern Jin, it is the reapportioning of the kingdoms and the extinction of the last remnants of the Jin that draw the scroll and the surviving portion of *The China Mirror* to its close.

Without the final four scrolls, it is impossible to speak conclusively of an overarching message for the work or to pin down an ultimate composite image of China. There is instead an unresolved tension between two noncomplementary images. On the one hand, this is a civilization founded by Buddhist incarnations, at least some of whom have counterparts in Japan. Moreover, the origins of many Japanese ritual and social institutions (even amusements) are also located in this China.[59] Thus, it offers a legitimating source for sociocultural and religious phenomena.[60] On the other hand, this is a China that is indisputably in decline. Even though the work is incompletely preserved, and despite the narrative prominence of Buddhism in the last extant scroll, the reader knows from the preface that the China constructed by Shigenori will eventually reach such an unfortunate stage that the monks who bring its history to Japan in *The China Mirror* will be forced to leave their homeland. Taken together with the repeated pattern of a downward trajectory for the earlier

58. Hirasawa and Yoshida, *Kara kagami: Shōkōkanbon*, 213–14.

59. Although *suguroku* or *sugoroku* (a board game) is explicitly identified as coming from India (Hirasawa and Yoshida, *Kara kagami: Shōkōkanbon*, 53).

60. Bialock cites an observation by Hirano Satuski that posits a similar position vis-à-vis the image of China in the Engyōbon version of the *Tale of the Heike*: a "double-bind of simultaneously invoking China as an exalted realm of precedent and 'othering' it to safeguard Japan's own prestige" (*Eccentric Spaces*, 207). Hirano's characterization is similar to what I see in the works under examination in this chapter.

dynasties in the surviving portions, it seems reasonable to suppose that the remaining dynasties were presented in a way consistent with the surviving scrolls—that is, with space for Buddhist developments but trapped in a downward trajectory.[61] In short, in the world created by the text, even if selected moments or individuals from Chinese civilization can be outstanding or praiseworthy, Chinese history equals a downhill journey.

Because the text is incomplete, certain questions are unanswerable—in particular, the question of whether an ultimate underlying principle was made clear in a final segment of or postface to the work. All that can be said definitively is that China within the received version of *The China Mirror* is a place that simultaneously affords validation and is going from bad to worse. In my reading, a chronological progression serves as a scaffold for the entire narrative and creates an account of temporal progress that goes hand in hand with social or institutional decay. In other words, decline in the end is the dominant "message."[62] Yet I also suggest that China is certainly not only about its own decay. Otherwise, why study it at all?

Instead, I propose that the China(s) of *The China Mirror* are part of a larger bifurcated—or even more fractured—narrative of China emerging in the thirteenth century to suit different audience needs. This is in some ways reminiscent of David Bialock's characterization of "China in the Medieval Imaginary," which emphasizes the "ambiguous" nature of the continent's representation in medieval literary texts.[63] Here, however, I will focus on three texts from the 1250s and 1260s to examine the intersection of ideas about "China" and "history" at a moment when the *bakufu* under the Hōjō was in a stronger position than ever before. In this context, China occupies multiple positions, but

61. I owe a considerable debt to Morita's works in demonstrating how firmly embedded the Buddhist developments are as a narrative strand.

62. In part, decline is wrapped up in the sources from which Shigenori draws, because retrospective orthodox histories relate the establishment and fall of an earlier dynasty. Nonetheless, as noted above, Otagiri's work decisively undermines any claim of the theme of dynastic decline as a simple reflection of the priorities of China-composed source material. In other words, decline is an aspect of the tale told in *The China Mirror*, not merely of its sources ("'Kara kagami' ni okeru Kanseki juyō" and "'Kara kagami' ni okeru Kanseki juyō [zoku]").

63. Bialock, *Eccentric Spaces*, 177–216.

there are patterns to the forms that these take. Thus, *The China Mirror* affords a chance to see not only how *Mirror* histories evolved to serve new audiences, but also how the treatment of China, especially the theme of dynastic decline, could vary depending upon presumed medieval audiences.[64]

A Constellation of Chinas: Teaching the Continent in the 1250s

To anyone familiar with *Ten Teachings* or *Notable Tales Old and New*, these texts might seem an unlikely starting point for creating a constellation of China images in medieval Japan. After all, *Ten Teachings* opens with the following claim regarding Chinese material: "I privileged *kana*—I did not at all exert myself with numerous brush strokes. It was because I thought this would be easier on the reader's eyes. As for the topics, I relegated things Chinese to second place, and I did not widely roam the path of [Chinese] letters. It was because I wanted things more familiar to my listeners. I did not use pointless rhetorical ornaments; I just collected true exemplars. I don't aspire to the [Chinese] writing on roadside monuments."[65] *Notable Tales Old and New* takes an even more hard-line approach with regard to recourse to continental culture: "I did not take a single peek at the Chinese classics or histories—[this is] the work of the mores of [our] world. Now, with all of Japan, old and new, at my disposal, it contains the affairs and events of conversation in the streets

64. I have decided to limit the texts under discussion to those that are primarily prose, since opening up the field to consider verse on Chinese topics would make the discussion impossibly unwieldy. Similarly, I have stayed away from collections or "matches" framed along Wa-Kan lines. These are projects that strike me as fundamentally dissimilar to narrating China as such. One of the most intriguing, if inconclusive, English-language studies of the Wa-Kan issue remains Thomas LaMarre's *Uncovering Heian Japan*.

65. Asami, *Jikkunshō*, 17–18. For an alternative reading ("As for the words I used, I privileged *kana*; the *kanbun*-style rhetorical flourishes are few and far between"), see ibid., 17.

and alleyways."[66] Protestations notwithstanding, however, both collections interact with "China" to a greater or lesser degree and, moreover, do so in ways that help shed light on the imagery in *The China Mirror* and its ostensible appeal. As *Ten Teachings* is the text that tackles China most directly, I will first consider the issue of China in it before turning to the more circumspect representation of China in *Notable Tales Old and New.*

Ten Teachings, a collection of *setsuwa* that appeared around 1252 with the promise to guide young readers along a proper path, is of particular value in ascertaining whether Shigenori's China is representative of anything beyond an individual vision. Admittedly, there is a basic difficulty in determining whose interests the text initially represented, and conflicting theories about its authorship abound. For example, Asami Kazuhiko has made a tantalizing case for attributing the work to a Kamakura-based individual with an eye for a warrior readership.[67] He even goes so far as to speculate that its original "target audience" could have been the young companions of Imperial Prince–Shogun Munetaka.[68] All of this would mean that *Ten Teachings* was written to reach and teach the same (or similar) readers as *The China Mirror.*

However, more recent scholarship demonstrates that the issue is far from resolved. Working largely from circumstantial evidence, Gomi Fumihiko argues that Sugawara Munenaga (thirteenth century) is the most likely author.[69] In contrast, Uwayokote Masataka finds the attribution to Yuasa Munenari ("a warrior with deep connections to Kyoto") most "enticing," but in the end he rejects it as unlikely and abandons all efforts to identify an author.[70] Uwayokote's retreat forestalls a need for further discussion of his study in this context, but should Gomi be correct, *Ten Teachings* would be the work of an author based in Kyoto at the time. This in turn would mean that *The China Mirror* and *Ten Teachings* would have less similar initial contexts of production than Asami's work sug-

66. Nishio and Kobayashi, *Kokon chomonjū (jō)*, 28. My analysis is based on the entirety of this two-volume set (*Kokon chomonjū (jō)* and *Kokon chomonjū (ge)*).

67. Asami, *Jikkunshō*, 502 and 506.

68. Asami, *Jikkunshō*, 502.

69. Gomi, *Shomotsu no chūseishi*, 388–98.

70. Uwayokote, "'Jikkunshō' no hensha o megutte," 70–71; see also 76.

gests. Nevertheless, as Gomi also points out, the colophon to *Ten Teachings* indisputably signals *bakufu* readership.[71] Thus, regardless of original intended audience, both *Ten Teachings* and *The China Mirror* are texts that offer ideas of China that resonated with warrior readers. Therefore, to read *Ten Teachings* and *The China Mirror* together should help clarify what Japanese in the middle of the thirteenth century (particularly members of the rising warrior elite) saw as the essential or desirable China.

Indeed, within *Ten Teachings*, Chinese people, texts, and occasionally history are present in significant numbers. Specifically, of the 293 sections (the general preface cited above, individual prefaces to each of the ten scrolls, and 282 anecdotes), 92 (31 percent) make a direct reference to a Chinese proper noun of some sort, typically a person or a text.[72] Given these figures, it is worth considering how and to what ends these explicit acknowledgments of China are made and invoked.

Upon closer inspection, things are not as simple as the numbers might suggest. Although *Ten Teachings* contains nearly two hundred mentions of individuals or compositions from China, only approximately seventy-five contain specific additional information that actually grounds them in China as such.[73] That is, fewer than half of the invocations of things "Chinese" provide either a Chinese location (be it something as broad as *Morokoshi* or as specific as the name of a city) or any sort of recognizably Chinese temporal frame of reference (such as the name of a particular

71. Gomi, *Shomotsu no chūseishi*, 389.

72. In making these calculations, I included only instances of the direct mention of a Chinese person, text, or place within the body of *Ten Teachings*. As a result, a line such as the following (which despite ultimately referring to the *Wenxuan* makes no obvious reference to its source) would not be included: "The mountain does not give away tiny clods of earth—that's why it's tall" (Asami, *Jikkunshō*, 23). Tallying the actual nouns cited, there are approximately 180 references—ranging from a passing mention in a list of exemplars or an allusion in a poem to a full-fledged anecdote. In instances of listing, I have counted each "item" as a separate reference. At the risk of stating the obvious, a mention of a person and a place or time was counted as a single item.

73. In fact, there are doubtless more that can be inferred as being about and/or set in China, simply due to their location within the text—that is, as part of a list of Chinese precedents or in proximity to an anecdote clearly set in China. However, while my insistence on an actual "signal" for each item does reduce the overall numbers somewhat, to be less rigorous in the application of this standard would have resulted in a more approximate impressionistic discussion than seemed productive.

dynasty). In other words, most of the episodes about or allusions to what one might think of as China lack substantive "reality-signals" that locate the content on the continent.[74] What this means is that there are two different types of China in the text.

For the majority of the text, there is an unmarked China. For instance, in a more extreme example, Confucius appears in *Ten Teachings* nine times. Only once, however, is he mentioned in a way that foregrounds a Chinese origin—as Confucius of Lu.[75] The same can be said of the wildly popular Tang poet Bai Juyi, who likewise appears nine times and is identified only once as living during the Tang (and, thus, as Chinese). On the one hand, one might argue that this is because it is self-evident that Confucius and Bai were Chinese, so there was no need to spell it out for the audience. On the other hand, one could as easily propose that given the far-reaching influence of both figures in Japan, there was probably neither a widespread particular need nor a desire to emphasize their continental origins as such. This latter reading makes more sense when one bears in mind the previously encountered explanation from *The China Mirror*, in which Confucius relocated to Japan on a raft with his disciples in tow, as well as Shigenori's repeatedly used device (mentioned above) of identifying Japanese incarnations of Chinese cultural heroes as their implicit culminations.[76] In this logic, identity is less a question of origins and more one of ultimate destinations.

In fact, such erasure of overtly Chinese elements to create a placeless or timeless China that lingers as a semi-acknowledged cultural touchstone is a recurring maneuver within literary representations of China from the late twelfth and the thirteenth centuries, a point I will revisit in this chapter's conclusion. For now, suffice it to say that this "unmarked" image of China that lacks specific Chinese features is consistent with Chino Kaori's emphasis on a disconnect between imagined and actual Chinas and reflects a common medieval method for narrating Japan's neighbor. One might think of it as an idea of a China one knows to be China but that is nevertheless not marked as such.

74. I borrow the term "reality-signal" from Reinart Koselleck (*Futures Past*, 207).

75. Asami, *Jikkunshō*, 295.

76. On Confucius's fate, see Hirasawa and Yoshida, *Kara kagami: Shōkōkanbon*, 8.

However, this is not the only China to emerge in *Ten Teachings*. In contrast to the placeless or timeless China that operates as a cultural touchstone, there is a China that is specifically and clearly tied to the continent. This becomes visible in a significant number of stories—just over seventy "episodes" contained in roughly fifty distinct entries—that include Chinese locations and dates in ways that suggest that the setting itself is important.[77] They offer a China that is marked as such. It is to these that I turn next to investigate whether there is any particular lesson that can be drawn from taking these stories as a set—in other words, whether China as a construct has a specific meaning when it is deliberately framed in a Chinese historical context, and if so, how this might or might not tally with how China (or Chinese history) works as an object of knowledge in *The China Mirror*.

To be clear, there is no handy or obvious trajectory in terms of how the stories are ordered within the text. That is, China does not start out grandly and then end in disgrace as one moves through the work. As one progresses through time, however, it is a different story. Not unlike *The China Mirror*, the dynasties that receive the most attention are not the contemporary Southern Song but rather the Western and Eastern Zhou (collectively, eleventh century BCE–256 BCE), the Western and Eastern Han (collectively, 206 BCE–220 CE), and the Tang.[78] Early China fares particularly well; the years between the founding of the Zhou and the establishment of the first Qin emperor are peopled almost exclusively with worthy exemplars of humble rulers and competent advisors. Other than the tale of Duke Yi of Wei (died 660 BCE), who relies on cranes for his retainers and is eaten by barbarians when he proves unable or unwilling to rally human troops, and the haunting account of Duke Ling of Wei's (540–493 BCE) insistence on hearing the music of a vanished state, the bulk of the material presents early China in a positive light.

77. In other words, a single numbered entry can contain multiple unnumbered episodes that nonetheless appear as discrete units. When China is marked as such, it typically does not appear as part of a catalogue—hence, the closer correlation between instances in which the historical China is mentioned (seventy-five) and the number of anecdotes that feature Chinese history (fifty-three).

78. For clarity's sake, I group events from the Spring and Autumn period with the Zhou entries, although the protagonists hail from several kingdoms.

The treatment of the Han material is somewhat different. While on balance, the models are presented as positive, the few stories set in the Han that appear later in *Ten Teachings* (which does not follow a chronological order) offer a darker image. Empress Lü's disfigurement of Lady Qi, Zhu Maichen's impatient wife's refusal to stand by his side through hard times, and Emperor Wu's resentment at the premature loss of Lady Li are all noted in the later lessons, albeit briefly.

The Tang incidents, too, follow a similar, though less pronounced, arc. Most of the examples are from the rule of the second emperor, Taizong, and he is clearly set up as a figure to emulate. Marring the golden image of the Tang, however, there are also three stories of the later Emperor Xuanzong. While two are fairly neutral—one features an imaginary (or Daoist-enabled) trip to the inside of the moon and the other the emperor's unearthly talent at playing the flute—Emperor Xuanzang has the dubious distinction of being one of the few rulers in the entire work who is called "foolish."[79]

Still, one could not truly talk about a pronounced historical trajectory were it not for the Song entries. It is in them that present-day China is indisputably shown as having sunk far below its lofty origins. Although there are only two Song entries, they stand out from the bulk of the China entries in both length and narrative development. Significantly, neither has an attested Chinese source. In other words, preexisting textual evidence seems to have been less important than making a point, and surely it is not a coincidence that the two "fabricated" stories of Chinese history are examples of contemporary China's fall.

In the first story, for which the annotation simply observes that in earlier sources the account is framed as being about Koryŏ,[80] the tale centers upon an unsuccessful attempt by the Chinese court to entice the physician Tanba no Masatada (1021–88) to journey to China to treat the empress's illness. Minamoto no Tsubenobu's (1016–97) gruff reply ("What's it to us Japanese if the Chinese empress dies?") is translated by Ōe no Masafusa (1041–1111) into a poem so well crafted that all parties, even the Chinese, are impressed.[81]

79. Asami, *Jikkunshō*, 286.

80. Asami, *Jikkunshō*, 62n34; see also 514.

81. Asami, *Jikkunshō*, 62. Bialock offers an analysis of the version of this tale that appears in the Engyōbon edition of the *Heike* (*Eccentric Spaces*, 214–16).

The other entry is more representative of *Ten Teachings'* Buddhist orientation in that it is placed in a context in which both China and Japan must take care. As a story, it stands out as the longest and most complicated China-centered narrative in the collection, and it presents an unflattering version of contemporary China. The story follows in its entirety:

> Recently, there was a Chinese emperor known as Huizong [1082–1135]. This was in the reign of our Retired Emperor Toba. That emperor was a fool at heart, and he fancied what Daoists said while doing away with the Buddha's words. Thereafter, the country's strength gradually waned and the people grew unruly. It was customary [at the time] for merchants to sell wares outside of the city, but the emperor prized gems and summoned merchants within the palace and had them do business there. The merchants casually approached the emperor and received his patronage. It was self-evident that the imperial heart was devoted to profit.
>
> At some remove from the capital, there was a land called Khitan. Because they had a great deal of gold, they were called the "Great Jin [Gold]." In the case of Japan, it was like the province of Michinoku, which is a land that contributes gold to the court. In that place [Khitan], there was a king. He was brave of heart and a clever strategist. The merchants went to the [Khitan] king and told him about the emperor's foolishness and devotion to material wealth.
>
> Thereafter, the king decided to raise a rebellion. It was about thirty days' journey to the Great Jin. However, this was by the major thoroughfare that wound through the land over great distances. If one were to go through the steep mountains, it would probably take around seven or eight days. That route was short, but there were numerous tigers and wolves, so no one used it.
>
> The land on either side of the [mountain] route was known as the Thousand-*Liang* Pine Wilderness. Long ago, a person of immense wealth lived in that area and he had buried a thousand *liang* of gold in the wilderness. That's why it was thus dubbed. The king secretly hatched a plan with the merchants, having them take a great deal of gold and present it to the emperor. The emperor asked them, "What sort of gold is *this*?" to which they replied, "On the way here from the Great Jin, there is a place known as Thousand-*Liang* Pine Wilderness. It's said that long ago, a rich man buried gold there. We went there and when we tried our hands at digging, we happened upon this [gold]."

The emperor was stirred with pleasure and said, "Bring me more." As instructed, they reported to him again. The emperor was dissatisfied. He instructed the king of the Great Jin to dig up the gold. By nature, this king was possessed of vigor, and he took many people to have them dig up the gold. Because of this, the steep peaks were leveled, and the fierce mountains were cut away, making the land just like a vast road.

Thereafter, the king of the Great Jin let word leak out that he was plotting a rebellion.

The emperor was incensed and dispatched numerous troops. None of them knew of the [newly made] good route. They set off via the main thoroughfare. After about twenty days had passed, the king of the Great Jin, having reckoned that there would be few soldiers left in the capital, took his troops instead via the newly made road and entered the city. They overthrew the capital, seized the emperor, and returned to the Great Jin [capital].

Thereafter, all of the countries fell in line behind the Great Jin, paying taxes and reparations. After the emperor [Huizong] passed away, it fell to his son to rule. Although he fought against the Great Jin, since not only were they brave to begin with, but also by this time had grown stronger, it was impossible to defeat them. Of three hundred sixty territories, roughly one hundred seventy were taken by the Great Jin. The remaining one hundred ninety were left to the emperor. Famous places such as Wutai Shan and Chang'an were taken by the Great Jin.

As a result of this, the current emperor is not in the capital—he lives at an approximately three-day remove from Mingzhou, the site of the district administrative offices. Although it's unusual for an emperor to live in the country, which he is doing since he's in the mountains, it is because he lacks the power to live at [the site of] the district administration.

There are two district government offices in Japan: the Chinju Office in Michinoku province and the Dazai Office in Tsukushi. In China, there are government offices like this in all of the provinces. The current imperial residence is now one of them. As for the River Shu, it's the site in poems on "washing brocade." Like Japan's Sunomata, it's a place where the river is wide and swift, and people don't cross it. The river acts as a border and is part of the territory of the Great Jin.[82]

82. Asami, *Jikkunshō*, 329–33. Ron Egan has suggested that despite the lack of an identified Chinese source, this representation of Huizong is not inconsistent with continental discourses (personal communication, February 2018).

This is the only entry in *Ten Teachings* to deal directly with Song China, to say nothing of the Jin (1115–1234), and it is significant for at least two reasons. First and foremost, its lack of an attested Chinese source notwithstanding, it is awash in "reality-signals." Not only is the Chinese emperor named, but his reign period is specified in terms meant to resonate with local readers by indicating his Japanese counterpart. Sites are identified, and distances between concrete locations are measured in terms of days. Supposed current political realities—the present emperor's location among them—are likewise explained. In other words, this is the most "real" image of China as China that the reader encounters. Secondly, with its colorful recounting of the fall of the Northern Song and Huizong's part in it, the account completes a path from glorious distant origins to present decline that can be assembled out of the entries that feature China as such.

To be sure, the pains the author takes to make connections to Japan support an interpretation in which events in China can represent issues that transcend the boundaries of a particular state. The parallels between China and Japan—forced though they may be at times, as in the equivalence postulated between Dazaifu and the displaced Song emperor—are noteworthy both within this particular tale and in the rare instances in the remainder of *Ten Teachings* when the author offers commentary that specifically pairs China and Japan. For instance, within the "teaching" of which this tale is a part, the author observes, "On the whole, there are numerous examples of the habit of deceiving others, both in China and Japan."[83] A similar sentiment can be seen in the remark that concludes an earlier "teaching": "The Chinese kings who despised and belittled the gods did not rule for long. The rebellious retainers of our court who looked down on Buddhism and withdrew [thence] have been unable to avoid punishment from heaven. How much more so the common people?"[84] Rather than working to create a narrative of Japanese superiority to China as sometimes seen in more "secular" cultural products of the day, commentary such as this suggests that the downward trajectory of Chinese history should serve as a warning. Yet relative or not, there is no mistaking that the direction in which the historical China is headed is bad.

83. Asami, *Jikkunshō*, 334.
84. Asami, *Jikkunshō*, 145.

To summarize, and to the extent that one can speak about a text that is only partially preserved, *The China Mirror* and *Ten Teachings* appear to take similar positions with regard to the continent and what it has to offer as an object of instruction. China is both a placeless and timeless locus of cultural authority (or the elements worthy of appropriation are so temporally distant as to seem timeless) and a sociohistorically delimited site moving along a trajectory of decline. Of course, this bifurcation of the image of China happens at different narrative levels in the works. In *Ten Teachings*, the overarching image of China is one of an amorphous cultural grab bag from which exemplars, primarily good but occasionally bad, are conveniently extracted. The historical narrative is present, but in disjointed fashion, and its reconstruction in all likelihood probably requires a reader who is looking for it.

In contrast, as noted above, the ultimate organizing principle of the surviving portion of *The China Mirror* is chronological. Thus, even as the specifics of each scroll or dynasty often lend themselves to different interpretations or imply a variety of priorities, it is the overarching framework—the primarily forward-moving unfolding of historical events—that suggests the takeaway message: that it is a civilization where the Buddhist teachings are in decline. What is common to both works, however, is that when history is brought into play, what it reveals is a downward trajectory.

In attempting to understand the significance of this narrative of Chinese history as decay, Tachibana no Narisue's *Notable Tales Old and New* provides a valuable counterpoint. Yoshiko Dykstra has assembled the scant information available about Narisue's life and proposes that "Narisue was a cultured and musically inclined government official of the junior fifth rank, who had some leisure after his retirement from being a provincial governor and began to collect elegant stories about aristocratic Heian life, music, and poetry."[85] His collection is an array of anecdotes that relate matters concerning the Japanese *kami*, Buddhist teachings, etiquette, literary and cultural acumen, and so on, and it primarily deals with the court nobility, as Dykstra points out. What makes it relevant to the present discussion is the disavowal in the preface to the work of interest in

85. Dykstra, "Notable Tales Old and New," 471. I follow Dykstra in the translation of the title.

the Chinese canon (noted above): "I did not take a single peek at the Chinese classics or histories—[this is] the work of the mores of [our] world."[86]

However, this claim does not mean that the work contains no references to Chinese texts, figures, or poetic topoi. In fact, these appear in abundance—in particular in the section on "literature," in which numerous *kanshi* draw on the Chinese tradition or earlier works. What sets the work apart from *Ten Teachings* and *The China Mirror*, however, is that these images are nearly always devoid of anything that would tie them to a specifically Chinese origin or context. Thus, Bai Juyi can appear in a dream (as when Ōe no Asatsuna [886–957] encounters him but awakens before learning why) or as an author Japanese poets draw on, but typically not as a Chinese writer per se, as when the same Asatsuna and Sugawa no Fumitoki (899–981) are made to select the best poem from the *Hakushi monjū* (Collected Works of Master Bai).[87] To the extent that it in no way treats the subject of Chinese history or historical development or decline as such, *Notable Tales Old and New* does not present China as a sociohistorical entity at all. China appears only as the vaguest of constructs, more consistent with the "cultural grab bag" image in parts of *Ten Teachings*.[88]

Moreover, this particular styling of China is largely consistent with that of the earlier court-oriented collection of China-centered pieces, *China Tales* (discussed in chapter 1). There, too, while the setting is obviously intended as China, it is likewise without historical detail: of the twenty-seven anecdotes, only one provides an exact year, and a mere four others by default provide the historical context of a reign because they feature specific emperors. Otherwise, everything is simply "long ago."[89]

86. Nishio and Kobayashi, *Kokon chomonjū (jō)*, 28.

87. For both stories, see Nishio and Kobayashi, *Kokon Chomonjū (jō)*, 160–62. Bai does make one appearance explicitly in China as the originator of a practice continued in Japan (see ibid., 173), but this is the exception.

88. The other exception to this is entries 722–25. However, these, as well as the final entry (726, taken from *Ten Teachings*), were added later. See Nishio and Kobayashi, *Kokon chomonjū (ge)*, 414–19. For a chart that identifies the sources of tales interposed after the initial composition, see ibid., 436–37. The issue of interpolations is discussed in ibid., 433–42.

89. Three additional anecdotes identify figures as hailing from Chu, Jin, and Qin, but I would suggest these are fairly vague designations with which to locate the tales on

As with *Notable Tales*, the most desirable China for a court audience seems to be one that is marked as little as possible.

The apparently different orientation toward China exhibited by a work such as *Notable Tales Old and New*, with little or no concern for a particular Chinese past, and that by collections such as *Ten Teachings* and *The China Mirror*, with their inclusion of explicit references to historical events, may be related to their different intended audiences. Given its subject matter, *Notable Tales Old and New* was in all likelihood written for readers very much like its author, those with the background and education to appreciate court-centered reminiscences and for whom a lesson that empires decline would have been neither surprising nor congenial.[90] In contrast, as both Ogawa and Tonomura have suggested, *Ten Teachings* and *The China Mirror* probably ultimately targeted a warrior readership (or one sympathetic to warriors). Furthermore, Tonomura has pointed out that "despite the fact that it was another country," Chinese history provided valuable precedents for warriors, whose own position was unprecedented in Japan.[91] I assume that the most striking of these is the idea that the mandate to rule moves, and that its relocations are contingent upon virtue rather than bloodline. As seen most explicitly in *The China Mirror*, each ruler who eventually loses the mandate does so because he deserves to, and each upstart who founds a new regime is able to do so because he is favored by heaven. According to this logic, the Hōjō may not have been the original founders of the *bakufu*, but they had to be divinely backed, or else they would not be in a position to control it. If this is a lesson that Chinese history can teach to a warrior audience, it is not incongruous to have Chinese history playing a more prominent role in texts that found warrior readers, such as both *Ten Teachings* and *The China Mirror*.

I would like to go a step further and suggest that a narrative of imperial decline could convey two messages. The first is that just discussed—a more immediate lesson that nonecclesiastical (imperial) authority never

---

a historical trajectory. And as is the case with all other tales, they nevertheless begin with *mukashi* (long ago).

90. See Dykstra's summary of the work's "purpose" ("Notable Tales Old and New," 471–72).

91. Tonomura, "Kamakura bushi to Chūgoku koji," 110.

lasts and the mandate to rule will inevitably move. The second is the lesson that within a Buddhist framework, all worldly institutions are impermanent. One could extrapolate from this second lesson that there is nothing inherently aberrant in a change in the institutional configurations of power, such as the establishment or increasing prominence of a shogunate working in tandem with the imperial house. In this way, the dual-pronged notion of a movable imperial mandate as embodied in narratives of the Chinese past could serve as both a cautionary example and, perhaps more indirectly, a potential validation for nontraditional (that is, nonimperial) players' participation in power.[92]

Needless to say, none of the works discussed here ever explains just what it is that China is intended to teach a reader; nor does any of them feature an image that was necessarily a true or accurate representation of Chinese history. Rather, the varied nature of the Chinas seen here demonstrates that there was more than one sort of China being imagined in the medieval period and that, moreover, these different types of China could fulfill vastly different purposes. The consistent treatment of Chinese history in particular, though limited to two works here, suggests that narrativizing the Chinese past, regardless of the repackaging this required at times, constituted a different sort of project from the creation of an ahistorical China devoid of most of the attributes that would link it to continental civilization.

Delimiting the Continent as a Historiographic Enterprise

Having identified two medieval perspectives on China and speculated on their appeal for different audiences, I will conclude the treatment of the "immediate" questions of the nature of the "China" being taught and its medieval resonances by reflecting on the intellectual position that delim-

92. It was precisely this message against which Kitabatake Chikafusa was writing when he unfavorably contrasted Chinese history to Japanese history in the imperially oriented *Jinnō Shōtōki* (A Chronicle of Gods and Sovereigns) (Shimokawa, "'Jinnō shōtōki' no rekishi jojutsu," 440 and 446–48).

iting the continent as something to be taught suggests. This is an important corollary to the bifurcation of China that one can observe in texts such as *The China Mirror*, because it hints at a positionality, whether aspirational or actual, for medieval thinkers who engaged with the Chinese past—with Chinese history—as such.

To be able to "teach" China as *The China Mirror* does implies a power relationship in which the author or teacher renders what is being taught the "object of knowledge," to borrow from Michel de Certeau.[93] In Certeau's analysis, having a dissociation from the object or a distance between it and the writer is an integral step toward the ability to render that object comprehensible to another. The following section will show how Shigenori inserts multiple reminders of just such a distance, resulting in a China that is kept continually at bay or, more strongly still, contained. Such reminders can be read as reinforcing a position in which the Chinese past—as something that can be learned—is subordinate to its teacher and even student.

Revisiting the preface in a little more detail will clarify how this works. Once again, the narrator is on a pilgrimage. This time, however, the transmission of the *Mirror*'s content is enabled by a seemingly chance encounter at a Double Nines banquet and poetry contest, events that follow the completion of the narrator's vow to perform a thousand sutra readings. As noted above, two Chinese monks have been waiting on the sidelines the entire time, and they approach the narrator with the following explanation (reminiscent of Eubanks's "cutting edge"):[94] "Buddhism is languishing at the Song Court, and people who venerate this teaching are rare, so we have come to Japan; our first stop was this temple, where we heard it [the *Lotus Sutra*] being read a thousand times. . . . Though India is the land of the Buddha's dwelling, its shores are distant. [But] I could roughly relate to you the aspect of the land of Cīnasthāna, if you would but listen."[95] Thus, *The China Mirror* is born.

More than simply setting the stage in a familiar yet different manner, the preface also works to create multiple layers of distance between Shigenori and his subject matter that are not present in the earlier *Mir-*

93. Certeau, *Writing of History*, 36.
94. Eubanks, *Miracles of Book and Body*, 66.
95. Hirasawa and Yoshida, *Kara kagami: Shōkōkanbon*, 9–10.

rors. Most obviously, there is the geographic remove between writer and subject matter. While India is, to paraphrase Shigenori's informant, too far away to speak of, China is also framed as a place that people leave to go elsewhere—that is, Japan. The significance of this distance (the demarcation of a boundary between China and Japan) can also be seen in the preliminaries to the above exchange when Shigenori observes: "One was quite a great priest. His speech was impossible to decipher. The other, who was [his] disciple, did the honors of passing on the master's words, translating them, and so on."[96] China is "foreign," an incomprehensible other without the proper mediator.

Although Shigenori uses deferential language toward the monks, the work's attitude toward the Chinese present reflects an unspoken power relationship. Specifically, the narrator's lack of facility with the contemporary spoken idiom in no way compromises his ability to provide a history of China to his readers: it is not just the "words" of the monk, but also texts, that are cited. While these ostensibly fall within the monk's narrative, it is difficult to see them as anything other than a display of a text-based knowledge of China. In other words, to the extent that one can read the narrator as a stand-in for Shigenori, direct access to contemporary China or Chinese is superfluous for someone in his position—namely, an authority on or translator of things Chinese. One might go a step further and infer that it is contemporary China as such that is rendered largely irrelevant by such a move: the "China" worth knowing about is temporally contained. China is not only foreign, it is also the past. Such an interpretation is justified by the lines with which Shigenori's narrator closes the preface: "Since I have heard that there is a practice whereby one takes the *past* [emphasis added] and uses it to reflect on things, I ought to call this *The China Mirror*."[97] Unlike the popular "antiquity and today" (*kokon* or *kokin*) pairings in many classical and medieval texts suggesting that their lessons are drawn from both current and bygone events, Shigenori will draw only on the latter.

China's "pastness" is still further compounded by the selection of Chinese texts quoted or acknowledged within Shigenori's work. In addition to scattered references to sutras, he overtly cites the writings of Zheng

96. Hirasawa and Yoshida, *Kara kagami: Shōkōkanbon*, 9.
97. Hirasawa and Yoshida, *Kara kagami: Shōkōkanbon*, 11.

Xuan (127–200 BCE) and Kong Anguo (206 BCE–8 CE), as well as the *White Tiger Propagations* (circa 79 CE).[98] He also notes *Records of the Grand Historian* and *The Sayings of Confucius* (late third or early fourth century CE), as well as the Mao *Odes* and one General Li's *Laws of Attack* regarding kickball.[99] Even Zhang Heng's (78–139) "Rhapsody on the Eastern Capital," which Shigenori also obligingly notes is in the *Selections of Refined Literature* (circa 530 CE), appears.[100] Yet nowhere in the surviving scrolls does Shigenori draw on more contemporary works. Chinese textual authority ends in the Liang Dynasty (502–87).[101] And in what may be an accident of preservation, the effect of temporal distancing is multiplied by the reception of the work itself and its incomplete surviving form: the past to be preserved and transmitted runs only through the fifth century. For Shigenori's readers, then, China was desired as something kept at both a geographical and temporal distance, as a doubly othered entity.

This emphasis on distance is what enables the application of the concept of "object of knowledge"—along with some of the processes implied by this—to China in this text. Although Certeau writes of the emergence of a "modern Western" historiographic enterprise, the following can productively be thought of as a prerequisite inherent in Shigenori's writing, too: "[The rupture between present and past] assumes a gap to exist between the silent opacity of the 'reality' that it seeks to express and the place where it produces its own speech, protected by the distance established between itself and its object."[102] For Shigenori, the establishment of the remoteness of the Chinese past renders it a distinct

98. Hirasawa and Yoshida, *Kara kagami: Shōkōkanbon*, 15 and 59. Kong Anguo and Zheng Xuan appear again in ibid., 29.

99. Hirasawa and Yoshida, *Kara kagami: Shōkōkanbon*, 29, 73, and 142. The *Laws of Attack*, possibly a Western Han text, is now lost.

100. Hirasawa and Yoshida, *Kara kagami: Shōkōkanbon*, 160 and 163. Shigenori also quotes from several verses without giving titles (see ibid., 19, 126, 141, and 183).

101. Smits has argued that earlier Heian attitudes toward the importation of nonreligious texts primarily privileged the past products of China, which is consistent with what can be seen here ("China as Classic Text"). In this respect, Kiyomori's earlier gift of the *Taiping yulan* may have seemed still more extraordinary.

102. Certeau, *Writing of History*, 2–3. However, I do not wish to suggest here that Shigenori subscribes to the other tenets of Certeau's description of interrelated operations that inform Western history, or even the concept of "a rift between *discourse* and *body*" (ibid., 3). What is relevant here is the function of the distancing.

and discrete "body" that he is in a position to make "legible" for his readers.[103] Similarly, he can be said to be engaging in the very sort of "selection" that underlies the process of creating something with "present intelligibility."[104] Although no firsthand accounts of how Shigenori's work was interpreted by medieval readers survive, his manufacture of distance and containment of China may have worked to alleviate some of the tensions created by using China as an object of instruction, in that it could signal the possibility of a Japanese experience that was not inevitably or completely continuous with Chinese models. With a China that was narratively predetermined to decay—in terms of both sociopolitical institutions and Buddhist teachings—one can conjecture that this sort of escape hatch might have been appealing for any reader, warrior and courtier alike.

Fitting In: Innovations Incorporated and Abandoned

At this point, I will turn to the meta-level interrogation and the implications of using China as the medium of a *Mirror*'s message. Some of the effects are short-lived: the emphasis on the past as past discussed in the preceding section, for instance, is an aberration. Others have more lasting legacies. The most striking developments of this type can be seen in how moving the focus to China reorients the geographic imaginary away from the Japanese court as well as in the eschewal of specific "principle" rhetoric. Shigenori relocates his tale to Dazaifu and all but abandons any overt concern with cosmological principles beyond the fact that the world is in a state of decay. The rhetoric of principles has vanished. At the same time, despite its unprecedented foray into continental subject matter, *The China Mirror* does feature continuities with the earlier *Mirrors* beyond the shared conventions of their prefaces. The most obvious is the linguistic patterning it shares with *The Water Mirror*. All of these developments

103. On the body and legibility, see Certeau, *Writing of History*, 3.
104. Certeau, *Writing of History*, 4.

are ultimately conducive to the genre's continued movement toward new centers.

FAR FROM THE CAPITAL: NARRATIVE PLACE AT SEA

In the preface to *The China Mirror*, for the first time, there is a setting far from the capital. In addition to the remote location, *The China Mirror*'s speaker draws parallels to famous mobile and misunderstood figures such as Sugawara no Michizane and Bai Juyi (to whom I return below). Together, these combine to suggest that this is an account that will unfold at great remove from the court at more than one level.[105] In short, even as Shigenori makes recourse to the familiar notion of "place" as indispensable for a proper *Mirror*, he enacts a major change by setting his *Mirror* far beyond the established territory of the earlier ones. And he does so at a site that for him clearly does not represent a celebration of the imperial court. In contrast to the setting of the earlier works in proximity to Kyoto or Nara—Urin'in in *The Great Mirror*, Hasedera in *The New Mirror*, and the double invocation of Hasedera and Ryūgaiji, as well as the embedded nod to Mt. Katsuragi, in *The Water Mirror*—*The China Mirror* has a narrator who speaks from a place of exile.

To return to the preface one final time, the very first lines are the narrator's explanation of his long-cherished desire to go on a pilgrimage. Yet similar to the aged narrators of the earlier *Mirrors*, he finds himself in a state where "[much as] the grasses of spring go by, wasted, and the winds of autumn easily surprise [one], the days of my prime had waned."[106] After professing his diligence in the spiritual pursuits of his dotage, the narrator says: "Around the first third of the fifth month, I proceeded from

105. The relocation of the narrative site from one in proximity to the capital to one at a remove from it bears some resemblance to a maneuver that Elizabeth Oyler identifies in the Kakuichibon of the *Tale of the Heike*. In her discussion of the figure of Yoshinaka, she observes, "There is a clear (original and originary) center, but imbalance at the axis causes dispersal and shifts narrative attention to alternative power configurations and new power-holders like Yoshinaka dotting the landscape beyond the capital's perimeter" (*Swords, Oaths, and Prophetic Visions*, 63). I argue that while *The China Mirror* similarly moves away from traditional loci of authority, its significance lies less in a specific reconfiguration and more in what the act of uncoupling enables in terms of the selection of a subject.

106. Hirasawa and Yoshida, *Kara kagami: Shōkōkanbon*, 8.

the Southern Sea to the Western Sea. The route through the 'banks of clouds' and 'billowing waves' was 'vast,' and the 'thousand-league' view from the 'solitary sailboat' was 'boundless.' More than ten days passed as we headed toward Anrakuji Temple."[107] There, the surroundings are likened to "the autumn sky over Mt. Goushi" and "the lake by night at Wuzi Temple."[108] Shigenori's narrator then muses on the fact that the Double Nines festival is occurring and reflects, "At the memory of that composition—'Last year, this night, I served in the palace./ In my "Autumn Thoughts" poem, oh, such anguish'—several rivulets of tears bathed the words of the Buddha's teaching."[109] At this point, the narrator's poetic reminiscence breaks off with the observations that "the cool night had gradually deepened" while the "autumn wind 'soughed mournfully,'" whereupon he is joined by the two Chinese monks who offer the transmission of *The China Mirror*, if he "would but listen."[110]

In heading to Anrakuji, the journey in the preface that launches *The China Mirror* relocates the narrator beyond the borders of the *kinai* (the provinces that made up the core of the *ritsuryō* state) to the outpost of Dazaifu (in present-day Kyūshū), a move that resonates on multiple levels. From a historical perspective, Dazaifu is the "logical" site for a China-focused narrative. Dazaifu and Hakata Bay marked the official entry for foreign traffic (the bulk of which was from the continent) into Japan for much of the polity's history through the twelfth century.[111] Although historically Dazaifu had lost its monopoly on sanctioned ingress by the time of *The China Mirror*, setting the narrator's encounter there creates a plausible setting for an exchange with Chinese monks.[112] In this regard,

107. Hirasawa and Yoshida, *Kara kagami: Shōkōkanbon*, 8. I am grateful to Li Shenzhi for calling my attention to the fact that this surely refers to the Anraku Temple in Dazaifu (personal communication, 2014). See also Tonomura, "Kamakura bushi to Chūgoku koji," 111.

108. Hirasawa and Yoshida, *Kara kagami: Shōkōkanbon*, 8.

109. Hirasawa and Yoshida, *Kara kagami: Shōkōkanbon*, 9. Shigenori has a slightly different rendering from that found in Chapter 1. Poem translation modified from Helen McCullough, *Ōkagami*, 99.

110. Hirasawa and Yoshida, *Kara kagami: Shōkōkanbon*, 9–10.

111. For a concise overview of this history, see Batten, *Gateway to Japan*.

112. On this change in circumstances, see Batten, *Gateway to Japan*, 120–23.

Shigenori's decision to stage *The China Mirror* at Dazaifu can be understood as a gesture to enhance the work's veracity.

It is well known, however, that this was not the only position that Dazaifu enjoyed in the medieval Japanese imagination. It also had a lengthy history as a site of exile, particularly of the unjust sort, and the most famous example of this was the maligned China scholar Sugawara no Michizane.[113] In fact, when the narrator recalls the "verse on autumnal reverie," the passage reproduces almost verbatim one from *The Great Mirror* in which Michizane in exile recalls the Double Nines banquet of the previous year and thereupon composes the verse that opens with the couplet Shigenori cites.[114]

In invoking Michizane I presume that Shigenori was not looking to overtly criticize the decision to assign him to the role of tutor to Imperial Prince–Shōgun Munetaka, although the defining feature of Michizane's exile was its injustice. The Kamakura posting may well have been frustrating, but it seems too obvious and risky a move for Shigenori to have cast himself as a slandered and vengeful exile. Rather, he takes advantage of the preface to gesture not only to Michizane but also to famed Chinese poets. Thus, the preface becomes a plea for sympathy as well as a literary tour de force that demonstrates Shigenori's mastery of the Chinese poetic tradition.

One author Shigenori thus engages with was a poet-bureaucrat who more than once found himself on the wrong side of disputes and, as a result, posted far from the cultural center: Bai Juyi. Although Bai's career had its ups and downs, the esteem in which he was held in medieval Japan is well known. Therefore, a gesture to Bai creates the possibility for a more auspicious reading of the poetic undertones of the preface, even an eventual vindication and appreciation. What the three figures—Michizane, Bai, and Shigenori's narrator—have in common in this type of interpretation is the distance between the loyal scholar–bureaucrat/literatus and the capital, rather than a fatal and unjust exile.[115]

113. On the broad topic of the trope of exile, see Stockdale, *Imagining Exile in Heian Japan*, 9–11. For a short overview of Michizane and other cases of exile in literature, see ibid., 74–75. Stockdale also touches on Michizane's depiction in the *Gukanshō* in ibid., 73.

114. Ishikawa, *Ōkagami*, 69. For a lengthier discussion of this scene in *The Great Mirror*, see chapter 1.

115. For a theorization of distance as regards the distinction between court and noncourt life, see Stockdale, *Imagining Exile in Heian Japan*, 12–13. Shigenori's ties with

Indeed, Shigenori's allusions to Bai's writings play on this distance. To return to the narrator's journey, he travels across a sea that is "vast" (*manman to shite*), moving through the "banks of clouds" (*kumo no nami*) and "billowing waves" (*kemuri no nami*), a trip that unfolds in the language of Bai's *Hai manman* 海漫漫 (Vast Is the Sea) ballad. The opening lines of the latter read:

海漫漫，	Vast is the sea,
直下無底旁無邊。	Its floor without fathom, its reaches without end.
雲濤煙浪最深處，	In the depths of its banks of clouds and billowing waves,
人傳中有三神山。	Legend has it there are three divine mountains.[116]

Admittedly, the poem Shigenori draws on here is not a joyous one, and its futile journey is not a cause for celebration. Shigenori stops short of citing more explicitly unhappy lines, but were this the only work he cited, it would be hard to read any hope in his preface. However, the lines that immediately follow complicate this somewhat. When the narrator speaks of the "boundless" (*byōbyōtari*) "thousand-league" (*senri no*) view from a "solitary sailboat" (*kohan*), it suggests a work by the famous early medieval recluse Tao Yuanming (365–427), *Shi zuo zhenjun canjun jing Qua zuo* 始作鎮軍參軍經曲阿作 (Composed upon Passing Through Qua, Having Been Named General), which enables a less pessimistic reading. On the one hand, Tao's poem, which is written from the perspective of Liu Yu (363–422), is an unambiguous expression of reluctant service to a cause beyond one's control and a desire to return home. On the other hand, its subject is the eventual founder of the Liu-Song dynasty (420–79), and although the current journey is a hardship, all ends well. This does not make the speaker's longing for home less affecting, but it does allow a reading of travel as a necessary evil en route to eventual success. The lines, from the middle of the poem, are:

Prince Munetaka (and the growing power of the shogunate) complicate Stockdale's reading of exile as being in part about access to the center. Perhaps it can be said that Shigenori's narrator is being distanced from an old world order.

116. Okamura, *Hakushi monjū*, 1:557–58. For the entire poem and an annotation, see ibid., 1:557–62.

眇眇孤舟逝	Boundlessly journeys the solitary boat,
綿綿歸思紆	Continuously binds my desire to return home.
我行豈不遙	How could my journey be other than distant
登降千里余	When I have scaled and descended over a thousand leagues?[117]

When Shigenori's narrator frames his journey in similar terms, it can be read not only as a complaint about isolation and distance, but also as an expression of the hope that, like Liu Yu, the narrator will emerge triumphant. Invoking this particular poem lets Shigenori incorporate both the reimagining of Liu Yu (a reluctant but capable general and eventual emperor) and the figure of the well-known reclusive poet, Tao: Shigenori may be in a sort of enforced reclusion as a result of his skill, but with luck, it will be temporary.

This is the imagery that brings Shigenori's narrator to Anrakuji, where he takes up the language of Michizane, as noted above. Before he turns to the Chinese monks and the contents of his *Mirror*, however, the narrator's thoughts once more are framed in language evocative of Bai: the narrator's allusion to the landscape of "the lake by night at Wuzi Temple" (*Goshibyō no yoru no ushio*) calls to mind lines from Bai's poem *Hangzhou chunwang* 杭州春望 (On the Spring View in Hangzhou), a celebration of the spring scenery at dawn at Hangzhou's famous West Lake, in which the speaker notes the "sound of the waves by night entering Wu Yun Temple" (*taosheng ye ru Wu Yun miao* 濤聲夜入伍員廟).[118] There, the temple is still under cover of night, in contrast to much of the rest of the scene. Since Shigenori positions this line directly after an apparent reference to Goushi, the birthplace of the famous Chinese monk Xuanzang (circa 602–64), perhaps the intent is to gesture to both his benighted state in terms of religious endeavors and his isolation, alone but for the waves.[119] At the same time, in Bai's piece, it is spring, and it is dawn—both of which seem laden with positive potential as tropes.

117. Matsueda and Wada, *Tō Enmei zenshū (jō)*, 166. For the entire poem and an annotation, see ibid., 164–67.

118. Okamura, *Hakushi monjū*, 4:397. For the entire poem and an annotation, see ibid., 4:397–99.

119. I borrow Okamura's reading of this line as regards the solitude of the temple. See Okamura, *Hakushi monjū*, 4:398.

At this point, Shigenori invokes Michizane's wistful poem, as noted above, and then abruptly discontinues his reminiscences about the court, returning to the present. Shigenori's "autumn wind" (*shūfū*) with its "mournful soughing" (*shōsatsu*) in these lines is once again reminiscent of one of Bai's quatrains. The "mournfully soughing chill wind" (*xiaosa liangfeng* 蕭颯涼風) arrives with "autumn" (*qiu* 秋) and old age in the form of "thinning side locks" (*cuibin* 悴鬢) in Bai's short melancholic poem *Liqiu deng Leyou yuan* 立秋登樂遊園 (Upon Ascending to Leyou Park on the First Day of Autumn).[120] Presumably Shigenori (or his narrator) hopes that he will not end up aged and alone like the speaker in this poem. Yet despite the gloomy air of the latter piece, it shares with "Spring View" a plum location: Hangzhou. Thus, it may be possible to read into Shigenori's citation of these two pieces a glimmer of hope that he, like Bai, has the possibility of being recalled to the capital.

Last but not least, Shigenori invokes one final prestigious, and notably nonexiled, source when he closes his preface with the lines cited above that are widely believed to be an allusion to Emperor Taizong: "Since I have heard that there is a practice whereby one takes the past and uses it to reflect on things, I ought to call this *The China Mirror.*"[121] The particular import of this citation for a *Mirror* is addressed below in "Principles Past"; here it should be sufficient to remark on the aspirationally upwardly mobile nature of Shigenori's citations.. By journeying via the language of Bai and Tao to reach the destination of Michizane, and eventually even drawing parallels to Taizong, Shigenori is able to activate multiple associations with three gifted poets and masters of Chinese verse—all of whom find themselves, either in actuality or in a poetic pose, removed from their respective capitals—as well as an exemplary Chinese emperor.[122] Shigenori positions the narrator as in the same set as these

120. Okamura, *Hakushi monjū*, 4:268.

121. Hirasawa and Yoshida, *Kara kagami: Shōkōkanbon*, 11. I follow Hirasawa in taking the *Zhenguan zhengyao* to be the source for these lines ("*Kara kagami* no denpon," 312). See also Tonomura, "Kamakura bushi to Chūgoku koji," 115.

122. Although my focus here is limited to the narrowest of implications of Shigenori's citations of two of Bai's particular works, this does not foreclose the possibility of a much more complicated engagement with Bai. For an intriguing glimpse into the broader world of what a gesture to Bai might have indicated, see Anna Shields, "Remembering When."

famed literati and thinkers, allying him with the topos of the loyal expert and gifted individual who serves at a remote locale (to say nothing of the wisdom of an emperor). It is a complicated and lonely journey Shigenori creates, but given the allusions beyond Michizane, the possibility of eventual success and recognition emerges.

Thus, in terms of both the historical and literary associations it evokes, Dazaifu proves to be a highly charged narrative site, one that taps into not only Japanese history and literature, but also China and Chinese learning in multiple ways.[123] To reiterate, it heightens the plausibility of the transmission from Chinese informants, while at the same time connecting the narrator to familiar tropes from the both the Japanese and Chinese traditions. Furthermore, it achieves one other thing with regard to the broader project of *Mirror* writing: in removing the setting from the home provinces and turning its gaze to China, in addition to creating the possibility for a noncourt focus, it opens the door for *Mirrors* to be set outside of the confines of the court's immediate reach. Consciously or no, this uncoupling from sites in relatively close proximity to Kyoto or Nara echoes a real-world redistribution of power, especially after the failed Jōkyū Disturbance of 1221, and shifts in institutional authority. As chapters 4 and 5 demonstrate, subsequent *Mirrors* and *Mirror*-inspired writings will continue to exploit new possibilities for narrative sites that speak to each author's particular loyalties.

PRINCIPLES PAST: RHETORICAL LIMITS AND CONCEPTUAL SHIFTS

Although Shigenori has created a China removed from contemporary Japan in *The China Mirror*, this is not to imply that China's past is somehow irrelevant. China—or, more precisely, Chinese history—is a medium for reflecting a lesson, just as Japanese history has been in the earlier *Mirrors*. Yet unlike the earlier *Mirrors*, *The China Mirror* makes no explicit mention of "principles" or cause and effect. All the reader is told is that things are deteriorating in China. On the one hand, it is possible to take decline itself as the principle that informs *The China Mirror*; on the other

123. Stockdale observes, "In this Heian imagination of exile, any divide between history and fiction was thoroughly blurred" (*Imagining Exile in Heian Japan*, 2).

hand, it is noteworthy that the rhetoric of principles is entirely absent from the surviving portion of *The China Mirror*, including the preface (the typical site of exposition on a *Mirror*'s principles). This move away from explicitly articulated principles reflects a shift in the ways in and ends to which the past is being read in *The China Mirror*. The two developments are connected: it is impossible to understand the rhetorical realignment of *The China Mirror* independent of the particular form Shigenori's engagement with the past takes. The decision to shy away from an explanation of the workings of the universe is in some ways unexpected, particularly since this rhetoric is picked up by other historians of the age (see chapter 2). However, at least two possible reasons suggest themselves. A comparison with the roughly contemporaneous *My Humble Thoughts* suggests the limitations of "principle" discourse. And at the same time, Shigenori's emphasis on a Chinese precedent for the mirror metaphor in the preface to *The China Mirror* invites a reexamination of what it is that a *Mirror* is supposed to teach. Together, these developments render the lack of a clearly stated principle in *The China Mirror* less surprising. The rhetorical change is the more obvious, so the following discussion will begin there and then conclude by turning to Shigenori's use of Chinese history and its impact on *Mirror* writing.

The China Mirror and *My Humble Thoughts* share a few basic features. While both were written with an initial imperial reader in mind (Munetaka in the case of *The China Mirror*, and Gotoba in the case of *My Humble Thoughts*), each work was in all likelihood intended to eventually reach a larger audience. In his provocative analysis of Jien's narrative "stance," Fukazawa Tōru argues, based in large part on Jien's use of *kana*, that Jien was writing for warriors; at the same time, however, he proposes the "children of those with ties to the Kujō house" as the "target audience."[124] In other words, both *The China Mirror* and *My Humble Thoughts* may assume or aspire to a warrior readership as a part of their greater respective audiences.

Furthermore, in addition to being pitched to similar readerships, *My Humble Thoughts* and the earlier *Mirrors* have a common preoccupation with Japanese succession and the promotion of a rule-governed cosmos. Indeed, Jien's positioning of his work in regard to "Succession Tales" and

124. Fukazawa, "Rekishi no 'gaibu' ni tatsu koto," 141; see also 125 and *passim*.

"Succession Mirrors" suggests that he saw his work as in some way a response to works that included, at the very least, *The Great Mirror*: "There aren't people who have continued to write *Succession Tales* that deal with the Hōgen Disturbance or affairs thereafter. There may be rumored to be a few [that deal with later matters], [but] I haven't been able to see them. I suspect that those all just record good things, and since everything from Hōgen on is chaos, people foolishly think it is all bad and are ashamed to bring it up."[125] Jien, in other words, saw himself as writing in the tradition of the earliest succession tales, of which *The Great Mirror* was almost certainly one.

Most significantly, however, there is the shared recourse to the idea of the universe as governed by principles. While explicitly invoked earlier in *The Water Mirror*, it is in *My Humble Thoughts* that this rhetoric is most fully and elaborately developed.[126] Although a full analysis of Jien's notoriously complicated work is beyond the scope of the current discussion, a closer look at the ways in which Jien uses the rhetorical device of the principle (*dōri*) reveals limitations to the concept's ability to accessibly frame the past.

My Humble Thoughts presents at least three major difficulties: structural, rhetorical, and conceptual. Unlike the earlier *Mirrors*, the structure of *My Humble Thoughts* offers little in the way of consistent guideposts for the reader. It does not begin by laying out what principle its

125. Nakajima, *Gukanshō*, 184. For an alternative translation see Brown and Ishida, *Future and the Past*, 19–20. The notes to the Japanese edition simply suggest that "succession tales" include those like *A Tale of Flowering Fortunes*, *The Great Mirror*, and *The New Mirror* (Nakajima, *Gukanshō*, 185). The English note does not include *The New Mirror* (Brown and Ishida, *Future and the Past*, 20n2). The "Scrolls of Yotsugi's Mirror" mentioned in chapter 1 as one of the alternative titles of *The Great Mirror* appears in Nakajima, *Gukanshō*, 238. The notes propose that this refers to *The Great Mirror* and possibly also to *The New Mirror*, although the possibility of *The Water Mirror* is not entirely dismissed (ibid., 240).

126. These similarities notwithstanding, Fukazawa points out that the position of Jien with regard to his material is fundamentally different from those of the writers/narrators of the *Mirrors* ("Rekishi no 'gaibu' ni tatsu koto," 134). Despite Jien's nod to the *Succession Tales*, contemporary readers likewise did not see them as belonging to the same category. The thirteenth-century catalogue *Honchō shojaku mokuroku* reveals the four *Mirrors* to date as falling under the heading of *kana*, while *My Humble Thoughts* is listed under the immediately preceding "Miscellaneous Works" (*zasshō*) (Fujiwara no Sanefuyu, *Honchō shojaku mokuroku*, 179).

content will illustrate. Nor does it supply a comprehensive definition for the term "principle." After two scrolls of imperial annals—the first Chinese, the second Japanese—Jien abruptly takes up a more narrative mode, simply opening the third scroll with the statement that "the passage of time" has led him to "ruminate single-mindedly upon the principle of things."[127] Delmer Brown and Ichirō Ishida make clear in their invaluable translation and study of Jien's work that this central principle consists of two interrelated parts: Jien ultimately views both the decline characteristic of the final age and the hundred-reign vow of the *kami* to protect the imperial line as the guiding transcendent principles that inform all of Japanese history through his present.[128] Nevertheless, Jien himself does not stop in his preface to elaborate on what *dōri* means.

The overall structure of the remainder of *My Humble Thoughts* does little to alleviate this ambiguity. The bulk of the five narrative scrolls is a recounting of historical events, irregularly interspersed with exegetical commentary that primarily relies on the rhetoric of *dōri*. Most often, Jien identifies the operative principle at the conclusion of a passage or event that illustrates it, but without much elaboration as to how it works or what it might illustrate beyond the immediate. The following passages from early in the third fascicle provide a representative sense. The first follows a short overview of the first thirteen imperial reigns, before concluding with the death of the fourteenth emperor, Chūai (traditionally 149–200 CE): "First, when we consider this sequence of events, the original Principal of Imperial Succession continued along the Correct Path through the thirteenth reign, that of Emperor Seimu [traditionally 82–190 CE]; the sovereign ruled the land completely and without assistance, and nothing was lacking. In the reign of Emperor Chūai, because there was no Imperial Prince, the Principle emerged whereby a grandson could be used."[129] Jien next explains that Chūai's death was due to his failure to

127. Nakajima, *Gukanshō*, 184. The translation is modified from Brown and Ishida, *Future and the Past*, 19.

128. As Ishida puts it at one point, "Let us think of *Gukanshō* [*My Humble Thoughts*] thought as having a religious superstructure made up of two elements: Buddhist eschatological thought, and the Shinto belief that ancestral Kami protect their descendants" ("Structure and Formation of *Gukanshō* Thought," 421).

129. Nakajima, *Gukanshō*, 187. For an alternative translation, see Brown and Ishida, *Future and the Past*, 21.

heed the gods, before quickly summarizing Empress Jingū's (traditionally circa 170–circa 269 CE) reign, to which he appends the interpretation below:

> These must have been successive manifestations of the Principle that nothing is absolute. The Principle that natural aptitude must take precedence over sex, the Principle that in the event of a mother as empress, one must follow her with filiality. Since I aim to inform others of these Principles in the final age, this [Principle] is one in which [karmic] cause and effect are in harmony. Not a soul understands this Principle! Next, in the age of Emperor Seimu's predecessor Emperor Keikō [traditionally 12 BCE–130 CE], Takeshiuchi [traditionally second through fourth centuries CE] was first named Minister. This, for its part, was due to the Principle that ministers must appear.[130]

Passages such as these imbue Jien's principles with the air of a posteriori explanations. Principles are identified, but elaboration is minimal. They are both too vague to reveal much new ("cause and effect are in harmony") and too specific ("ministers must appear") to offer any basis for extrapolation beyond asserting that there must be a principle for everything. The cumulative effect is to persuade the reader via inductive reasoning that there is presumably a principle for each and everything that occurs. But most of the principles do not suggest a historical trajectory of the same coherence or duration as those suggested in the *Mirrors* to date.

The ambiguity of "principle" in the above context is exacerbated by the fluidity of the term as used by Jien. His concept of *dōri* is more open-ended than that of the *Mirrors* and serves multiple purposes. In some instances, such as when Jien explains his rationale for writing in *kana*, it lends itself to an interpretation of "reason" or "rationale."[131] In others, it is called upon in an abstract capacity similar to that of the principles found in *Mirrors*. In contrast to the authors of the *Mirrors*, Jien is committed to applying principles at both the macro and micro levels. This leads to a seemingly endless proliferation of principles, in which the "principle" be-

130. Nakajima, *Gukanshō*, 188. For an alternative translation, see Brown and Ishida, *Future and the Past*, 21–22.

131. For this instance, see Nakajima, *Gukanshō*, 183.

comes a rhetorical deus ex machina that allows it to be extricated from the thorniest of interpretive situations. Even violence in the name of the protection of Buddhism is legitimated through a postulation of dominant and subordinate (literally, "light" and "heavy") principles.[132]

That said, Jien anticipates some of the difficulties his theories present, and in the seventh and final scroll of his work, he announces that he will present the idea of the principle in a "manner that is slightly easier to grasp."[133] Here, he offers seven different refractions of principles, most of which can be mapped to discrete historical periods. Yet this schema, too, falls into redoubling and abstract rhetoric that does not make Jien's concepts much more accessible. Even in his short summary, principles are variously manifest or obscured and implementable or not. The sixth is extreme in its circularity but is particularly germane in that it applies to the present (the thirteenth century): "In this way, principles are impossible to classify (*kubetsushigataku*); they are argued about this way and that, or people go along thinking they are unresolved, and finally in an age of erroneous implementation, those inclined to wickedness will evilly calculate that the lack of principles is the principle (*mudō o dōri to ashiku hakaraite*), and erroneousness will be the Principle of the Principle (*higaggoto ni naru ga dōri naru dōri nari*)."[134] This passage reflects the abstruseness that bedevils Jien's writing, especially when it comes to classifying and ordering "principles." The imprecision and frequency of the use of *dōri* almost slip into parody in a passage such as the one quoted above, where "principles" become a rhetorical device not only of Jien as author, but also of those he criticizes.

The rhetorical slippage of Jien's "principles" and the confusion his unbounded use of the term can occasion points to the deeper issue of the conceptual difficulties with *dōri* in *My Humble Thoughts*. On the one hand, to return to Brown and Ishida's useful clarification, Jien is trying

132. Nakajima, *Gukanshō*, 200–204. For a slightly different reading, see Brown and Ishida, *Future and the Past*, 27–28.

133. Nakajima, *Gukanshō*, 587. The translation is modified from Brown and Ishida, *Future and the Past*, 206.

134. Nakajima, *Gukanshō*, 588. For an alternative translation, see Brown and Ishida, *Future and the Past*, 207–8. For the seven refractions of principles and the ages to which they correspond, see Nakajima, *Gukanshō*, 587–89; Brown and Ishida, *Future and the Past*, 206–8.

to reconcile what Brown identifies as "the inevitable decline of history" with the possibility of forestalling the decay.[135] In working to synthesize these two apparently contradictory positions regarding historical progression, Jien has undertaken a historiographic project of serious magnitude. A statement at the end of the sixth scroll offers a sense of the gravity with which he takes his task, as well as one of the most explicit clarifications of how his hierarchy of principles works. Jien explains that he has written *My Humble Thoughts* "that later generations might exercise restraint in governing the world, that they might distinguish between heterodox and orthodox, good and wicked principles, and adhere to the Principle of the Final Age, and benefit from the buddhas' and *kamis*' protection of sentient beings," adding that "Buddhist Law will protect Imperial law, and this is the true intent of this eternal protection."[136] In short, Jien is laying out his plan to save the world based on these two principles, and presumably all of the other principles that appear in *My Humble Thoughts* are subordinate to this greater logic.

That said, even Jien seems aware at times that his argumentation is not for everyone. At the conclusion of the summary of the seven principles referred to above, and after a brief rumination on the relationship between principles and *kalpa* within a Japanese context, Jien admits that he is "not in the least able to teach people how to be in accord with principles" and adds that he has written the work primarily to aid those who are already predisposed to be sympathetic to principles.[137] The section closes with an apparent disclaimer about his treatment of the past as "impossible to relate in detail, since everything appears entirely speculative and no one today will believe it."[138] Jien then turns his attention to the

135. Brown, "Buddhism and Historical Thought," 216 and 219. See also Brown and Ishida, *Future and The Past*, 4 and *passim*. On the lattermost point, see Brown, "Buddhism and Historical Thought," 217 and 222–25. For a similar conclusion, see Brown and Ishida, *Future and the Past*, 5–9 and 13–14. For Jien's brilliant metaphor that illustrates how this works as akin to partially replenishing a stack of paper each time you draw from it, see Nakajima, *Gukanshō*, 219; Brown and Ishida, *Future and the Past*, 36.

136. Nakajima, *Gukanshō*, 572. For an alternative translation, see Brown and Ishida, *Future and the Past*, 198.

137. Nakajima, *Gukanshō*, 591. For an alternative translation, see Brown and Ishida, *Future and the Past*, 209.

138. Nakajima, *Gukanshō*, 592. For an alternative translation, see Brown and Ishida, *Future and the Past*, 209.

theme that dominates the remainder of the work: the problem of stable government and the importance of cooperation between the court, including the regency, and *bakufu*.

In a conventional sense, Jien's historiographic endeavor was a failure. Not only did it fail to forestall the Jōkyū Disturbance, but it also does not seem to have attracted much of a contemporary readership.[139] If the author's demanding prose was not the only explanation for its limited circulation, another reason might be the limitations of the principle-based discourse it suggests. In *My Humble Thoughts*, Jien tasks the rhetoric of principles with both driving and curtailing historical change. His solution is a proliferation of principles, allowing them to become tools that simultaneously explain history as both inevitably in decline and not—or not really. Yet what is one to make of the fact that many of Jien's principles seem to be finite in scope and applicability? Or of his conclusion that the present is an age without principles?[140] Even if the reader of *My Humble Thoughts* stops short of agreeing with the memorable characterization of the work as something "which today serves mainly to illustrate the confusion of its author's mind," the rhetorical and conceptual gymnastics that Jien's approach requires did not spawn imitators.[141]

But if one thinks of Jien's conundrum as symptomatic of broader societal trends, then his failure has more to say about changing intellectual currents than "bad" writing. It demonstrates that the principle had become an unsuitable means of explaining historical trajectories, once the historian was charged with doing something other than presenting a relatively straightforward narrative of decline.[142] *The Water Mirror* had narrowed the focus on the principle-driven past to promote a specific unilinear movement through time, but in Jien's attempt to expand the focus to accommodate a flexible future, the rhetoric of principles had hit a limit. Once principles were called upon to accommodate every bump in the his-

139. On its reception in the traditional narrow sense, see Fukazawa, "Rekishi no 'gaibu' ni tatsu koto," 151. However, Fukazawa argues that it had more indirect influence.

140. Nakajima, *Gukanshō*, 589. This closes his discussion of the seven historical stages and their principles noted above. See also Brown and Ishida, *Future and the Past*, 208.

141. Quoted in William H. McCullough and Helen McCullough, *Tale of Flowering Fortunes*, 29.

142. On Jien's insistence on the necessity of human ability to comprehend and manipulate these workings, see Brown and Ishida, *Future and the Past*, 12.

toriographic road, on the level of overarching discourse, they were reduced to an often contradictory or incoherent muddle. Because they could explain everything, in the end, they explained nothing. Although the subsequent *Mirrors* continue to depict events as subject to cosmological laws, none of them returns to the rhetoric of principle.

However, principles are not the only rhetorical touchstone to disappear from the *Mirrors*. In a phenomenon that can scarcely be unconnected, the very idea of the final age (*mappō* and its synonyms) also recedes ever further from center stage in the *Mirrors* as Japan moves into the Kamakura period. To be sure, the final age can probably be assumed to be what drives the decline of the Buddhist teachings in China that inspires Shigenori's narrator's informants to travel to Japan, but this is never stated. There is no overt final age in *The China Mirror*. As chapter 4 will demonstrate, *mappō* does not play an informing role in *The Mirror of the East* either. This contrasts not only with *My Humble Thoughts* but also with the earlier *Mirrors* more broadly. Court-focused, they are all preoccupied with a decline, implicit or explicit, that comes to a head in *The Water Mirror* and its repeated avowals that the present moment does not mark the end of the world—despite what the never openly addressed Genpei War might suggest. In that context, "principles" provide an antidote to the final age, proving that there is a world beyond the present. Yet once *mappō* (or at the very least, the decline of the imperial court) no longer dominates the narrative of the *Mirror* writers, mapping historical change to a single decisive force or path also garners less attention. This is not to say that history is no longer subject to cosmological laws or forces in the Kamakura historiographic *Mirrors*, but rather that those laws and forces are articulated largely in a language other than that of *dōri*.

To return to *The China Mirror*, as mentioned above, Shigenori's focus on China indicates a repositioning with relation to the metaphor of the *Mirror* that may also be linked with his nonuse of "principle" rhetoric. The earlier *Mirrors* had all claimed that they would reveal an order to historical events: cause and effect, origins and endings, or even simply finite decline. *The China Mirror*'s new perspective is hinted at in the line from the preface mentioned above in which Shigenori speaks of "us[ing the past] to reflect on things."[143] This becomes more readily apparent if

143. Hirasawa and Yoshida, *Kara kagami: Shōkōkanbon*, 11.

one considers the following remarks of Emperor Taizong of the Tang (mourning the loss of his trusted advisor and former tutor, Wei Zheng, 580–643 CE) to which Shigenori is alluding:

夫以銅爲鏡，　Those who use bronze as a mirror
可以正衣冠；　can set to rights their robes and caps.
以古爲鏡，　Those who use the past as a mirror
可以知興替；　can comprehend changing fortunes.
以人爲鏡，　Those who use man as a mirror
可以明得失。　can understand gains and losses.
朕常保此三鏡，　We always maintain these three mirrors
以防己過。　to guard against transgression.[144]

The past here is part of a catalogue of materials that can be used in a corrective or preventive capacity. Rather than turning to the past for a revelation of the existence of Buddhist principles that drive historical change, the ruler looks to it as one means among many for self-regulation—"to guard against transgression." This is quite different from the purpose of *The Water Mirror*, but as Yamada Naoko has argued, it is consistent with the continental conceptions of a *Mirror* noted in the introduction as "history presented in terms of knowledge, models, and admonitions as a 'mirror' to reflect actual society."[145]

What is not included in either Taizong's enumeration of the uses of mirrors or Yamada's list of *Mirror* functions is the ability to guarantee or predict future developments (unlike *The Water Mirror* in particular). Although the past is surely intended to guide the future conduct of the astute reader or ruler, it is not suggested as a pattern for future events along a trajectory. In other words, *The China Mirror* is a *Mirror* that serves up the past. The preface makes no promises to reveal anything other than the approximate contours of Chinese history, remembered fragments of "matters of the worthy kings of Cīnasthāna and the governments of the

144. Wu Jing, *Zhenguan zhengyao*, 2.33. I follow Hirasawa in taking the *Zhenguan zhengyao* to be the source for these lines ("*Kara kagami* no denpon," 312). See also Tonomura, "Kamakura bushi to Chūgoku koji," 115.

145. Yamada Naoko, "'Kara kagami'-kō," 30. Yamada sees this as also applying to *The Great Mirror* and limits her discussion here to it and *The China Mirror*.

Sage Emperors, the ages of governance and those of chaos, . . . things outstanding and ignoble."[146] There is none of the by now familiar emphasis on the hows and whys of history that characterize the earlier *Mirrors*.

In some ways, this makes sense, given the subject matter. It is easy to suppose that many readers would not have been overly eager for an account of Chinese decline that was intended to predict the Japanese future. This would doubtless have been particularly true in an age in which part of China was again (partially and for the moment) under foreign rule. In other words, Shigenori's choice of subject matter may have effectively limited the uses to which the past he was narrating could be put. Nevertheless, the fact remains that neither it nor any of the subsequent medieval historiographic court-oriented *Mirrors* makes explicit promises about the future.[147]

The above developments make sense, too, considering that Shigenori was writing in the east and, ultimately, for the de facto lords of the land, the Hōjō. This marks the first time that a *Mirror* is written for an ascendant or established authority, rather than as a recuperative or recentering undertaking by a shaken or displaced elite. The principle-based rhetoric of *The Water Mirror* in which violence is both inevitable and awful could easily have been read as censorious of the violence—most recently, the Jōkyū Disturbance—that had enabled the Hōjō family's rise. Moreover, as noted, Chinese history offered precedent for a movable mandate to rule. In tracing the history of the Chinese imperial mandate, Shigenori was killing two birds with one stone: he offered novice readers (whatever their age or background) the basics of Chinese history that were still sought as cultural capital, while at the same time presenting a version of history as a teaching tool for immediate implementation, rather than a necessarily gloomy prognostication of things to come.

MORE MULTILINGUALISM: THE CHINA MIRROR *AND WRITING*

The last thing to consider in this chapter is the linguistic legacy of *The Water Mirror* for *The China Mirror*. As I argued in chapter 2, *The Water Mirror* usurps the traditional linguistic form of legitimacy to position

146. Hirasawa and Yoshida, *Kara kagami: Shōkōkanbon*, 10–11.

147. The one possible exception is *The Mirror of the Gods*, which breaks off in the present. This text is discussed in chapter 5.

itself as a synthesis of elite language and a vernacular that transcends worldly court-centered discourse. *The China Mirror* maintains a similar distinction in written styles, which approximately reproduces the format of *The Water Mirror*.[148] It also affords an opportunity to complicate the relationship between the two registers, in particular because at some level, it presumably represents a reworking of Classical Chinese–language texts.[149]

Even if not directly inspired by *The Water Mirror*, Shigenori's use of language is reminiscent of Tadachika's linguistic innovation in *The China Mirror*. A like movement between languages or registers is visible in the preserved fragment of the oldest surviving manuscript of *The China Mirror* (see fig. 3.1), which is attributed to Nijō Tameuji (1222–86).[150] While

148. However, it is impossible to pinpoint a "trigger" for this, since the *Ōkagami* Tōmatsubon imperial biographies, in particular, are similar in appearance. No complete manuscript of *Ōkagami* that predates the Kamakura period exists, however, so establishing the text's original form would be nearly impossible.

149. The identity of these texts is a subject of some debate. There is no annotated edition of *The China Mirror* at the moment, nor has the debate advanced beyond Otagiri's forays into the first scroll ("'Kara kagami' ni okeru Kanseki juyō" and "'Kara kagami' ni okeru Kanseki juyō [zoku]").

150. The ascription to Tameuji makes sense when one considers the high regard in which Munetaka held his father, Tameie. Munetaka asked Tameie to annotate five hundred poems of his own composition on Kōchō 3 (1263).7.23. See Nagahara and Kishi, *Zen'yaku Azuma kagami*, 5:490–91. If this work, a section of which can be seen in fig. 3.1, is genuine, the manuscript dates to within twenty or thirty years of *The China Mirror*'s composition. Regrettably, only the fourth scroll survives. The discussion of this manuscript is based on my inspection of Document 108–67, property of Hōsa Bunko. Hirasawa offers a thorough account of the surviving manuscript lineages in Hirasawa, *Kara kagami: Kōi hen*, 201–22. To summarize, Hirasawa divides the extant manuscripts into three categories. The first group (of which there are three examples) contains only the fourth scroll and are derived from the Tameuji manuscript. The second group (four copies) contains somewhat newer, longer versions, with the next in terms of age the six-scroll Shōkōkan version. This version uses a unique scriptive form of mixed logographs and *katakana*. Like the Shōkōkan line, the Matsudaira version (from the seventeenth century) also contains six scrolls. Its format—a combination of characters and *hiragana* for the first five scrolls with characters and *katakana* for the sixth—and mere minor textual differences from the Shōkōkan version suggest to Hirasawa that the sixth scroll derives from the "Shōkōkan lineage," though the obvious stylistic differences and abovementioned discrepancies imply different models for the bulk of the remainder. Hirasawa concedes that the final group (a single copy) has somewhat murky origins, and he posits it as slightly predating the Matsudaira line. After a

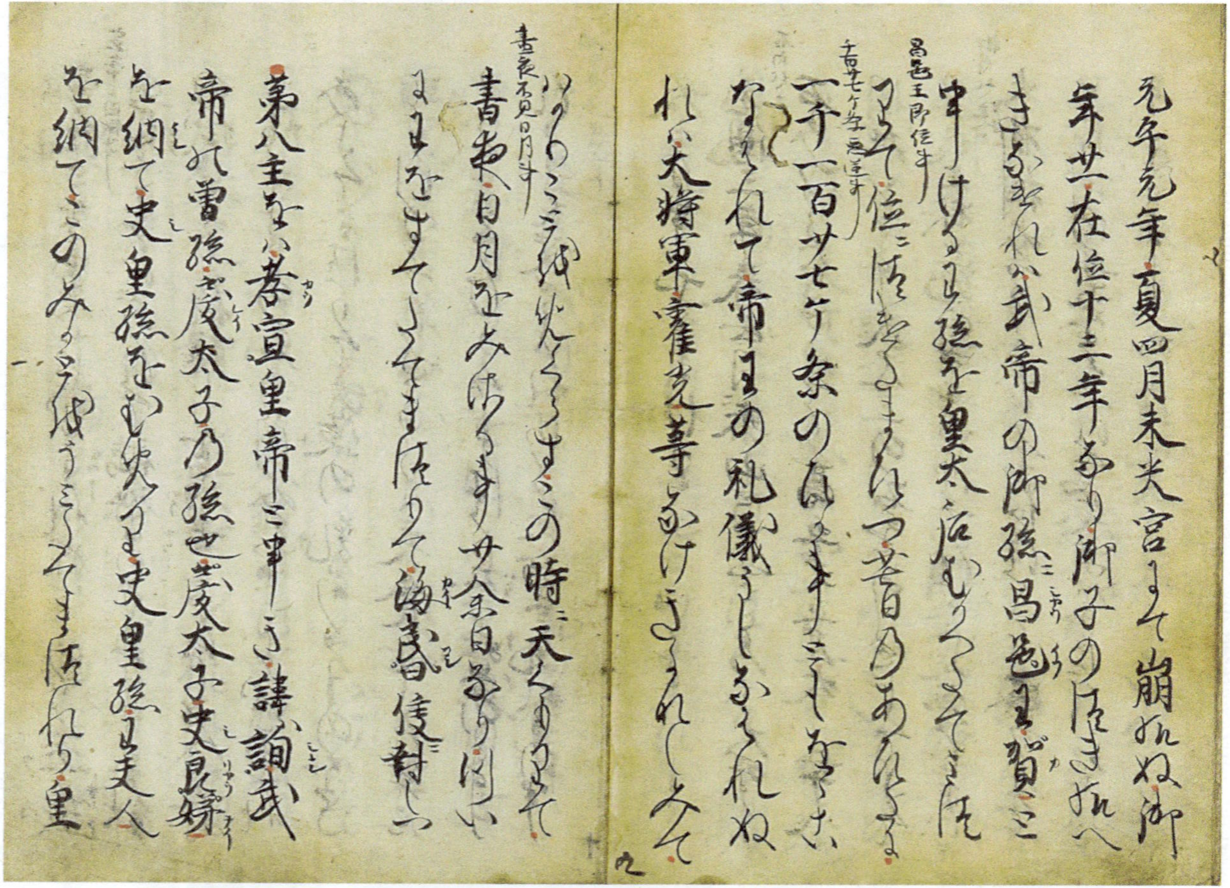

FIGURE 3.1. Example of script variation in the Tameujibon manuscript of *The China Mirror*, possibly from the late Kamakura period. The text shown covers the usurpation of the throne by the King of Changyi, followed by the opening lines of the biography of Emperor Xuan. Property of Hōsa Bunko. Imaging by Nakasha Creative and reprinted with the permission of Hōsa Bunko–*Kara kagami* (14b–15a of unnumbered pages of text).

there are no longer the smaller discrete passages of *kanbun* seen in *The Water Mirror*, there are nonetheless two distinct styles. Most entries open with a line (or lines) in "mixed character and *hiragana*" visually similar to *kanbun*.[151] These segments are primarily in Chinese characters, with Japanese readings and word order indicated through glosses. Entries may or may not close in like fashion. The rendering in such sections resembles the idiom(s) of the official histories. Yet between such visual anchors, the bulk of the remaining text is in a distinct cursive script much closer to that of "literary" manuscripts—namely, "character-interspersed *hiragana*."[152] In portions of the text such as these, with the exception of proper nouns, nearly everything is written in *hiragana*. Thus, the text of *The China Mirror* has two distinct visual registers in its earliest extant form, not unlike *The Water Mirror*. In employing a similarly recurring insertion of *kanbun*-like text between larger intervals of more "Japanese" script, *The China Mirror* replicates *The Water Mirror*'s formal inscription of the union of the languages of official and unofficial historiography.

Moreover, the explicit use (noted above) of Classical Chinese textual citations to validate or elaborate Shigenori's narrative, though sparse, continues to imply that a *Mirror* need not (or should not?) be grounded in oral testimony alone. This is striking in the case of *The China Mirror*, because of the two forms that Shigenori's demonstrations of having mastered Chinese traditions take. The first is the form of direct citation. Shigenori provides quotations from several Chinese poems, the *Records of the Grand Historian*, and multiple sutras.[153] When he does this, the Chinese

painstaking comparison, Hirasawa assesses this last subset of versions as representing a blending of textual lineages, a "corrected and supplemented [version] rather than variant." This summary is based on Hirasawa, "*Kara kagami* no denpon," which provides a rough grouping and overview on 315–19 and analyses of group 1 on 319–25, group 2 on 325–43, and group 3 on 343–59.

151. I borrow this designation from Misumi Yōichi, whose 2007 survey of Heian and medieval writing styles breaks *hiragana* writing into two categories and *katakana* into three ("Kanbun-tai to wabun-tai no aida," 103). This enables a much more nuanced discussion of script styles than the typical *kanbun-wabun* binary.

152. Ibid.

153. Hirasawa and Yoshida, *Kara kagami: Shōkōkanbon*, 19, 58–60, 73, 126, and 141. For the two exceptions that feature *kundoku*, see ibid., 129 and 163. This preservation of Classical Chinese citations as visually distinct can also be observed in the Matsudaira line of manuscripts, although a *kundoku* is provided next to the original text.

word order is typically undisturbed. In most instances, there is no indication of how the characters would need to be transposed to produce a *kundoku*. In short, these citations are visually indistinct from Classical Chinese. What is more intriguing, though, is that Shigenori does not consistently use this fidelity: in the preface, both Taizong's and Bai Juyi's phrases have been transformed via *kundoku*. (Michizane, in contrast, is quoted in *kanbun*.) In short, while the selection of China as the field of study plausibly paves the way for this increased presence of *kanbun*, the blurring of linguistic boundaries with which Shigenori tantalizes his reader complicates the matter. This testament to the ability to preserve and present *kanbun* strategically reinforces its potential to register upon the reader in a way distinct from *kana*.

Indeed, this persistence of *kanbun* within these later *Mirrors* is one of the ways in which the genre seems to be drawing closer to more traditionally mainstream ideas of official history. This makes the appearance later in the century of a would-be mainstream historiographic *Mirror* written entirely in *kanbun*—such as *The Mirror of the East*—less sudden or surprising. In terms of linguistic prestige, *Mirrors* are headed toward the traditional center even as their narrative settings take them farther afield.

Conclusion

The legacies of *The China Mirror* are more difficult to "prove" than those of the previous *Mirrors* in many ways. After all, *The China Mirror* is not referred to in any of the later medieval historiographic *Mirrors*. Nevertheless, the fact that it did survive in some form into the Edo period (1603–1867), when it was copied and in some cases highly edited, suggests that it was a text that continued to be read. Moreover, it is a text in which two significant currents in medieval thought—depicting China and narrativizing the past—converge in ways that have implications for subsequent historiographic productions.

For the undated manuscript used as the basis for this comparison, see National Institute of Japanese Literature ("'Kara kagami': Hizen Matsudairabon").

Looking at *The China Mirror* in terms of what type of China it presented and how that China resonated with or differed from contemporary depictions of China suggests that the narrative of Chinese decline found a receptive audience in the east. This is not to say that only warriors were interested in narratives in which China was portrayed as implicitly inferior to Japan. There are, after all, few more distinctive images or fantasies of Japanese superiority than the scene in *Kibi no Otodo nittō emaki* (An Illustrated Scroll of Minister Kibi's Trip to China), a scroll from the late twelfth or early thirteenth century, in which Chinese officials search through Minister Kibi's feces in an ultimately fruitless effort to prove that Kibi has cheated at Go.[154]

By and large, however, the narratives of China from this time constitute a more complicated set. Rather than a single imagined China, there is a tendency toward a bifurcation. On the one hand, the China suitable for cultural appropriation was carefully and thoroughly cleansed of anything that tied it to the sociopolitical entity across the sea, as in the case of the court-oriented *Notable Tales Old and New* and those tales in *Ten Teachings* that, despite featuring things known to be Chinese, did not mark them in any way as such. On the other hand, accounts that were specifically grounded in China hewed to a narrative of decline, as in the episodes in *Ten Teachings* that were explicitly marked as Chinese and the overarching narrative of *The China Mirror*. Unpacking the China of *The China Mirror* and analyzing it via contemporary texts helped clarify the thematic importance of Chinese history—in particular, its significance for a warrior audience.[155]

154. In a discussion of the somewhat earlier depiction of Minister Kibi in the *Fusō ryakki*, Kubota Jun opines that "it is true that in the wake of the destruction of the Tang and the fall of the Song, there was a popular shift in perception [toward] overcoming an inferiority complex vis-à-vis China. But, if one goes a bit further, were not such posturing of enhanced national prestige or such consciousness of resistance warped manifestations of this very sort of inferiority complex?" (*Chūsei bungaku no jikū*, 176). This interpretation is certainly possible but ultimately difficult to prove. Nonetheless, Kubota's observation is useful for noting the fascination this historical moment held for Japanese. My understanding of the Minister Kibi scroll derives largely from Komatsu, *Nihon no emaki 3: Kibi no Otodo nittō emaki.*

155. Tonomura, "Kamakura bushi to Chūgoku koji," 110 and 112.

To reiterate the second major point of this chapter, the selection of China as subject matter also enabled (or perhaps necessitated) changes in the treatment of history. In general, history, or at least Chinese history, was written as something that was completely distinct from the Japanese present. In contrast to *The Water Mirror*, in which the past was portrayed as having a reach that extended into both the present and future, in *The China Mirror* the past became a contained object. One corollary of this containment of the past, in particular when considered together with the elision of abstract cosmological discourse on the nature of time, is the solidification of the presentation of the past in *Mirrors* as unidirectional. None of the later *Mirrors*—even the conservative *Clear Mirror*—inscribes time as anything other than linear.

Perhaps the most significant change wrought by *The China Mirror*, however, is the departure from a genealogical orientation. The groundwork for this was arguably laid in *The Water Mirror*, when Tadachika opted to focus solely on the imperial family: there, genealogy and institution occupied essentially the same space. Completing this move, *The China Mirror* chronicles the movement of the mandate of heaven rather than the generations of any single family. In terms of a constant focus, it is the history of an institution rather than of its representatives. In summary, it is a didactic narrative that features the permanence and mobility of the authority to rule—the mandate—while at the same time illustrating the decline of individual imperial (genealogically driven) lines. Given this, it is tempting to suppose that such an account would have been of greater appeal to a warrior elite in the east than to readers based in a court on the wane.

Taken together with the continued use of Chinese-like *kanbun* writing and the foregrounding of text in *The China Mirror*, these changes paint a picture in which the subsequent appearance of an "official" *kanbun*-language *Mirror* to recount the founding of the Kamakura *bakufu* makes a great deal of sense. As chapter 4 will demonstrate, much as the early *Mirrors* afforded court writers a way to order the wars and rebellions that shook the late twelfth century, their mode of engagement with the past would again exert an appeal—this time on court and *bakufu* writers alike—in late thirteenth-century efforts to address change in the wake of the Mongol invasions.

CHAPTER 4

Moving *Mirrors*

Ordering the Past in the Wake of the Mongols

Main texts (in chronological order)

***Azuma kagami* (The Mirror of the East)**
Author: unknown
Date: circa 1290s
Language: *hentai kanbun*
Preface: no
Setting: none stated; the implied center is Kamakura
Time covered: the beginning of the Genpei War (1180)–the abdication of the sixth shogun, Munetaka (1242–72); fifty-two scrolls survive, with some gaps in coverage.

***Nomori no kagami* (The Mirror of the Watchman in the Fields)**
Author: often attributed to Minamoto no Arifusa
Date: 1295
Language: *wabun*
Preface: yes
Setting: Engyōji Temple (Harima)
Time covered: N/A

The Mongol fleet arrived in Japan in 1274, after diplomatic overtures to establish "friendly relations" (*tsūkō*) proved futile.[1] According to the account

1. For a distillation of the epistles and embassies from the Mongols and their peninsular support, see Saeki Koji, "Mōko shūrai ikō no Nihon no tai-Kōrai kankei."

contained in one version of the *Hachiman gudōkun* (A Simple Teaching on the Hachiman Deity), they struck first at Tsushima, on the fifth day of the tenth month, mere hours after flames had spontaneously and ominously burst forth from the Hachiman deity's local "temporary shrine" (*karidono*).[2] Nine days later, Mongol forces attacked at Iki Island and then moved on to Chikuzen, where fighting broke out on the twentieth of the following month. There, the account reports that Japanese forces met a deafening noise of drums, gongs, and launched projectiles that threw their horses into confusion, as well as deadly weapons that included poison-tipped arrows.[3] It describes the Mongol warriors as able horsemen, trained to respond to drum summons, and "strong and brave, galloping freely about."[4] The *Mōko shūrai ekotoba* (Illustrated Account of the Mongol Invasions) of the late thirteenth century offers a similar, if smaller-scale, account, featuring vividly rendered bloodied corpses, a wealth of weaponry, and severed heads.[5] And although Japanese forces famously triumphed in both the 1274 and 1281 invasions, the landings in Hakata were violent, bloody, and presumably horrific affairs.

If the Genpei War and its aftermath suggested limitations to imperial authority and a shift in the horizon of expectations for the survivors, similar reorientations likely occurred in the wake of the multiple failed efforts by the Mongols to breach Japan's borders. Among the vicissitudes of the late thirteenth century, it is these two attempted invasions—above

Needless to say, "friendly" is a euphemism. For an English-language overview of these events, see Zuikei and von Verschuer, "Japan's Foreign Relations," 414–16. For a translation of one of the letters to Japan, see ibid., 428.

2. Hagiwara Tetsuo, "Hachiman gudōkun (kō)," 183. Although *Hachiman gudōkun* is a hagiography, it nonetheless provides one sense of how the Mongol invasions were memorialized in the Japanese imagination in the early fourteenth century. On the date, see ibid., 169. Komatsu Shigemi, who also cites this work, dates it to the fifteenth century (*Nihon no emaki 13: Mōko shūrai ekotoba*, 134–35).

3. Hagiwara, "Hachiman gudōkun (kō)," 183–84.

4. Hagiwara, "Hachiman gudōkun (kō)," 184.

5. Even allowing for artistic license and the possibility of some self-promotion, since the scrolls were commissioned as proof of their subject's loyal service, the Mongols and their conscripts were surely formidable. I follow Komatsu in the dating of the scrolls, and my understanding of them—both text and image—derives from Komatsu's edition. On the date, see Komatsu, *Nihon no emaki 13: Mōko shūrai ekotoba*, 1. Thomas Conlan's work remains the definitive English-language monograph on the subject (*In Little Need of Divine Intervention*).

all, the fact of their absence—that haunt the two *Mirrors* to appear the soonest after their conclusion: *The Mirror of the East* (circa 1293–99) and *The Mirror of the Watchman in the Fields* (1295). *The Mirror of the East*'s narrative concludes just a year and a half before the arrival of the first Mongol epistolary overture was brought to the attention of the court and *bakufu* in 1268.[6] Unless the *Mirror* was completed almost immediately after the final events it records, this omission seems deliberate, and it is consistent with the earlier *Mirrors*' lack of narration or minimization of recent threats to stability. The Mongols lurk more explicitly in the background of *Watchman* as a threatening foreign force, but not one capable of seriously jeopardizing Japan. Outside of the world of the texts, even though the Mongol invasions were unsuccessful, the jockeying for rewards that followed each one revealed how thinly stretched the *bakufu* in particular was. And the fact that a foreign invading army had reached Japan not once, but twice, and had made major inroads into Southern Song territory before overthrowing it entirely in 1279 was surely not lost on those close enough to the centers of power to be writing would-be official histories or boasting about that foreign power's defeat.

Despite their coeval production, the final two Kamakura *Mirrors* reflect nearly oppositional worldviews. The differences are manifested in their contrasting linguistic forms, structural conventions, and attitudes toward their subjects, marking a divide that the historiographic *Mirrors* of the fourteenth century will inherit and replicate (a legacy addressed in chapter 5). The current chapter focuses on the moment of this dramatic fork in the road. I propose that even as the commitments that have characterized the *Mirrors* thus far—the strategic use of place, language, principles, and the past—remain central to both paths taken by subsequent historiographic *Mirrors*, the polarity of their specific manifestations results in completely divergent trajectories. That is, the *Mirrors* of each fork ally themselves with a particular embodiment of authority and its prospects. On the one hand, *The Mirror of the East* completes the genre's journey to the institutional mainstream, where it is aligned with the interests of warrior authorities to create a forward-oriented aspirational *Mirror*. On

6. Charlotte von Verschuer points out that news of this document was already circulating among Japan's elite in 1267 (Zuikei and von Verschuer, "Japan's Foreign Relations," 415–16).

the other hand, *Watchman* takes the reader back to the home provinces of the Japanese state, where it recommits the genre to a celebration of traditional court culture (albeit in the form of an attack on innovations), even as it seems to admit the ultimate impossibility of long-term success.

The fact that the *Mirror* is the textual vehicle selected for both positions attests to its continuing flexibility and appeal as a mode of reading and writing. Nevertheless, an examination of the two iterations from the late Kamakura will also point to where the genre seems to be moving away from some of the attributes that were indispensable to its early claims to authority—in particular, a clearly demarcated cosmological framework and a geographically unambiguous relationship to power.

Intersecting Mirror *Worlds*

Both of the *Mirrors* that appear shortly after the Mongol invasions, *The Mirror of the East* and *Watchman*, exhibit greater differences from the earlier *Mirrors* than any of their genre predecessors did with their respective antecedents. However, when viewed in a greater context, it is evident that both speak to the same larger world that their forebears did. To help clarify this greater web of texts, tropes, and even the occasional people who move between the *Mirrors*, I will briefly highlight some of these intersections, moments of contact that in some cases are historically attested and in others only speculative.

The issues of authorship and literacy mark one of the more complicated nexuses, particularly in the case of *The Mirror of the East*. The work's authorship is an unresolved question (and will be discussed at greater length in the "Embracing Orthodoxy" section below), but there is no doubt that the ability to author and/or edit a text of this size in a language resembling *kanbun*, even in a nonstandard form, required a fair amount of education. This being said, it is impossible to prove that the cultural literacy of the one or more unidentified authors or compilers who worked on *The Mirror of the East* included any of the other *Mirrors*. There are no explicit indications within *The Mirror of the East* of direct textual models or inspirations of any kind. However, it is beyond dispute that men from the court, at least, knew *kana* narrative texts.[7] Records also clearly indicate that some such educated figures, including the author of *The China Mirror*, traveled back and forth between Kyoto and Kamakura, human agents in the circulation of texts and learning between the two poles.

What is likewise evident is that the worlds of these *Mirrors*—even those set outside the court—overlap: the poets at the center of *Watchman* were, at least in some cases, on familiar terms with the shogunal elite of *The Mirror of the East*, and these poets and warriors will appear again in *The Clear Mirror* (including the putative author of *Watchman*).[8] Moreover, educated men were reading, or fairly familiar with, the earlier *Mirrors*. To the extent that their authorship has been established, all of the earlier *Mirrors* are the works of male authors, and most demonstrate an awareness of other *Mirrors*. Not only do the four earlier *Mirrors* each use the same overarching format first seen in *The Great Mirror*, the coordinated chronological span of each suggests an awareness of the other *Mirrors* even when they are not overtly acknowledged. To recapitulate, *The Great Mirror* covers the period from Emperor Montoku (827–58) through Emperor Goichijō (1008–36); *The New Mirror*, picking up where its predecessor left off, covers the period from Emperor Goichijō through Emperor Takakura; and *The Water Mirror*, turning to the earliest part of Japanese history, covers the period from Emperor Jinmu through Emperor Ninmyō. These three collectively provide nearly seamless coverage of the imperial line from Jinmu through Takakura. And, as seen above, both *The New Mirror* and *The Water Mirror* make explicit references to *The Great Mirror*. In other words, the *Mirrors* were circulating to some extent among educated male writers.

7. Not only does the *Honchō shojaku mokuroku* (mentioned in the notes to chapters 1 and 3) contain several such texts, but Prince Munetaka, while shogun, received lectures on *The Tale of Genji*. See Nagahara and Kishi, *Zen'yaku Azuma kagami*, 5:244, the entry for Kenchō 6 (1254).12.18.

8. For instance, Nijō Tameie, who appears in *Watchman* as an example of a good poet, was held in high esteem by Prince–Shogun Munetaka. Munetaka requested Tameie's input on his poetry in the seventh month of Kōchō 3 (1263); the feedback arrives in the tenth month of the same year (Nagahara and Kishi, *Zen'yaku Azuma kagami*, 5:490–91 and 509).

More explicitly, Gomi Fumihiko and Tonomura Hisae have separately postulated connections between *The Mirror of the East* and *The China Mirror*. Gomi proposes that the former's title is in all likelihood "influenced" by the title of *The China Mirror*.[9] Tonomura goes one step further to postulate the involvement of the "house" of *The China Mirror*'s author, Fujiwara no Shigenori, in the composition of *The Mirror of the East*.[10] It is true that the author (or editor) claims familiarity with the Chinese classics, which are the intellectual specialty of Shigenori and his lineage.[11] Thus, the hypothesis is tenable. Although all of the evidence is circumstantial, it is surely worth considering that whoever was behind a project of the size, scale, and language of *The Mirror of the East* could also have been familiar with at least one of the earlier *Mirrors*.[12]

Watchman is a similar case in that its connections to the earlier *Mirrors* are somewhat oblique. Although its common thematic concerns with those *Mirrors* are minimal, it features a preface and postface that closely adhere to their conventions.[13] And despite the fact that its stance with regard to the past differs from those taken by the historiographic *Mirrors*, it is not without a sense of history, although it charts the movements of practices and beliefs, rather than individual human figures.

9. Gomi, *Shomotsu no chūseishi*, 463. Gomi's discussion of this is brief and simply points out a potential parallel between the idea of a history of China and one of the "East Country." He follows Ogawa Takeo in the work's dating (as do I) but proposes Shogunal Regent Hōjō Tokimune (1251–84) as its recipient.

10. Tonomura, "Kamakura bushi to Chūgoku koji," 115.

11. This is evident, for instance, in the entry for Kenchō 8 (1256).6.14, when the author is interpreting a celestial anomaly and contrasts the "original writings" (*honmon*) and those of "our sovereignty" (*honchō*) (Nagahara and Kishi, *Zen'yaku Azuma kagami*, 5:261).

12. In a further demonstration of the *Mirrors*' ongoing circulation, Yotsutsuji Yoshinari's (1329–1402) *Kakaishō* commentary to the *Genji* attests to the continued consumption of the *Mirrors* by educated males well beyond the time of composition for *The Mirror of the East*—he frequently cites both *The Great Mirror* and *The Water Mirror* by name ("Kakaishō").

13. Gustav Heldt's examination of "harmonization" in the practice of poetic composition at the early Heian court, one he defines as "the practice of 'harmonization' (*wa*) with a superior's words through their citation and other ritual observances," suggests that harmonization reproduces correlative cosmological relations (*Pursuit of Harmony*, 2; see also 34–36 and 55–58). From this perspective, too, including *Watchman*—which establishes links between poetry, music, and ritual—in a discussion of *Mirrors* as texts that aspire to produce political power makes sense.

Lastly, if anachronistically, both forms of the *Mirror* suggested by the two paths of *The Mirror of the East* and *Watchman* survive into the fourteenth century. There, *The Mirror of the Gods* borrows the format of *The Mirror of the East* even as it explicitly engages with *The Water Mirror.* Thus, it is imperative to consider the bigger picture, one that enables the location of lines that could connect these texts for medieval readers and writers, even if they have come to occupy different categories in the present. The first step in this process is to focus on the fork in the *Mirror* path that incorporating *The Mirror of the East* and *Watchman* into the genre reveals.

Embracing Orthodoxy: The Mirror of the East

There is no denying that *The Mirror of the East* superficially looks very different from the earlier *Mirrors*. Rather than attempting to prove that it actively draws inspiration from those *Mirrors*—an impossible task—this section will introduce some of the basic features of the work and consider how *The Mirror of the East* engages with elements common to the earlier *Mirrors*. This provides a way to think more broadly about what forms claims for authority take, particularly when presented as a *Mirror*: in the end, although the specific iterations are different, language, place, the past, and even principles are just as central to *The Mirror of the East* as they are to earlier *Mirrors*.

The exact circumstances of the composition of *The Mirror of the East*, including precisely which earlier works it draws from, are unclear.[14] Gomi points out that even the question of its original title is a matter of contention. He proposes that *The Mirror of the East* refers to a revised and expanded work dating to roughly the Einin period (1293–99) that is itself based on an earlier text.[15] Elaborating on the conventional editorial

14. For speculation on potential types of sources and close readings of several likely references, see Gomi, *Zōho Azuma kagami no hōhō*, 59–61 and 86–146, respectively.

15. For a summary of his conclusions on dating, including reference to a proposed earlier history titled *Kamakura jiki*, see Gomi, *Shomotsu no chūseishi*, 463–64. There are other theories about the dating, including one that the work was composed in two stages—which is why a broader range (1266–1306) for its composition is often pro-

attribution to Hōjō sympathizers, Gomi suggests that members of the Kanazawa branch of the Hōjō are the most likely candidates for its compilation.[16] It is this larger, later work of Kanazawa (Hōjō) editorship—in other words, the amalgamation of earlier texts that as a whole came to be known as a *Mirror*—that will be discussed here. In this form, *The Mirror of the East* that survives today covers the period from 1180 to 1266 and chronicles the founding of the Kamakura *bakufu* as well as the tenures of the first six shoguns, from Minamoto no Yoritomo (1147–99) through Prince Munetaka. Even without any extant entries for 1183, 1196–98, 1242, 1249, 1255, 1259, 1262, and 1264, it spans fifty-two scrolls in its most complete form, making it by far the longest of the medieval *Mirrors*.[17]

Like all of the *Mirrors* before it, *The Mirror of the East* charts the establishment and transmission of a type of authority. However, rather than presenting a history built out of biographies, as most of the *Mirrors* do, *The Mirror of the East* treats a given shogun's tenure as the defining unit of time.[18] This institutional orientation is highlighted by the format of the text. The entries for each new shogun are preceded by a formula that appears as a sort of certificatory summary (*sodegaki*) of what is to follow: a list of dramatis personae that includes (in chronological order) the names of any emperors, retired emperors, and shogunal regents or chancellors, with each name followed by a biography of a few lines. These are typically concluded by an entry explaining that "the aforementioned is, all in one place, an enumeration of the emperors and regents corresponding to the [X] generation of the [office of] shogun," accompanied by the dates of office. This, in turn, is followed by an equally short summary of the

vided. Gomi's scholarship is among the more recent on this matter, however. For a study that focuses on the varied nature of the source materials as reflected in notation style, see Takahashi, "Reikishi jojutsu to jikoku."

16. Gomi, *Zōho Azuma kagami no hōhō*, 58–59.

17. As Nagahara Keiji points out, there is also a textual lineage that contains forty-seven scrolls (Nagahara and Kishi, *Zen'yaku Azuma kagami*, 1:9). The entries in this edition for 1225–27 are reconstructions (ibid., 3:407).

18. Gomi seems to see the biography as the fundamental unit, although he is not explicit. It is perhaps more accurate to say he does not draw a line between the individual and the office in his analysis of sources as they might contribute to the records of a given shogun (*Zōho Azuma kagami no hōhō*, 129–41).

shogun's basic biography.[19] In perhaps the most dramatic example of the prioritization of office over biography, the entire work closes with the singularly nondramatic return of the ousted sixth shogun, Munetaka, to the capital. The minimalist entry for Bun'ei 3 (1266).7.20 simply reads: "*Kanoe-inu*. Clear skies. At the hour of the Dog, the former shogun returned to the capital and went to the residence of the Commissioner of the Imperial Bodyguards of the Left, Captain Lord (Hōjō) Tokishige [1241–70], in Rokuhara."[20] The reader is left with no information on the remaining eight years of Munetaka's life.

While *The China Mirror* accorded space to martial figures and exploits, the specifics of the Japanese office of shogun are, needless to say, new. The developing nature of the office of shogun and the *bakufu* are refracted through *The Mirror of the East*'s chief preoccupation with three things: the social and religious rituals of the *bakufu* (as well as the filling of secular and sacred posts when possible), the military feats of its partisans, and matters of administration. The latter are initially primarily land oriented but later expand to cover a range of concerns. By the final decades, without major military campaigns to record, social and ritual matters outweigh other activities being chronicled. The attention given to social and ritual matters also increases as the court rank of the shogun rises, and by the time of the sixth shogun, Prince Munetaka, substantial space is devoted to simply cataloguing the members of his retinue for any given event. Likewise, after the implementation of the *Goseibai shikimoku* (Kamakura Code of Governance) in 1232, administrative concerns expand notably.[21] By the 1250s, land disputes cede their virtual monopoly, and the text includes more general questions of legal procedure, commerce regulation, and infrastructure, as well as sundry matters of public order and safety. For instance, the deliberations from Kenchō 4 (1252).10.14 on measures to improve citizens' morale clearly illustrate this by including how to deal with arson, theft of horses, seduction of married women, armed disputes, illegally obtained goods, and the clandestine impregna-

19. See, for instance, the "cast list" and explanation preceding the Yoritomo years in Nagahara and Kishi, *Zen'yaku Azuma kagami*, 1:43–45.

20. Nagahara and Kishi, *Zen'yaku Azuma kagami*, 5:543.

21. The entry announcing the completion of the editing of the code is for Jōei 1 (1232).8.10 (Nagahara and Kishi, *Zen'yaku Azuma kagami*, 4:126).

tion of another's wife.[22] In these specifics of the institution, one thus sees something quite different from the earlier *Mirrors*, where administrative or ritual concerns featured rarely, if at all—and even then, only in service of a larger narrative. Nevertheless, despite the increased focus on administrative concerns, and the shift in the nature and amplitude of activities recorded, *The Mirror of the East* is at heart the history of an office or set of offices and thus reminiscent of *The China Mirror*, with the latter's ultimate commitment to tracing the mandate of heaven across genealogies to give a thorough history of China.

It is true that *The Mirror of the East* is the first *Mirror* to be written entirely in something close to the traditional prestige language of *kanbun*, but earlier *Mirrors* played with language mixing. *The Water Mirror*, with its regular insertion of miniature text in *kanbun*, was the first such instance. The scriptive variation in the earliest manuscript of *The China Mirror* likewise suggested movement between two distinct registers, one of which was visually close to *kanbun*. Much like the use of linguistic hybrids in earlier *Mirrors*, *The Mirror of the East*'s new exclusive deployment of *kanbun*, traditionally the purview of the court and clerical elite, has performative significance.[23] Its use speaks to an ongoing appreciation on the part of writers of the ability of language or register selection to impart an authority beyond that conveyed by a text's content. In this light, and given *The Mirror of the East*'s exclusive reliance upon *kanbun* and sheer scale, there seems to be little reason to dispute Minoru Shinoda's observation that "obviously [*Azuma kagami*] was intended by its sponsors to be an official history in the manner of the official histories of the imperial court."[24] When both the focus on the detailed chronicling of

22. Nagahara and Kishi, *Zen'yaku Azuma kagami*, 5:182. For a succinct introduction to the legal system during the Kamakura period, see Kiley, "Imperial Court as a Legal Authority." What I have called the "Kamakura Code of Governance," Kiley refers to as "the 1232 warrior code" (ibid., 30).

23. To understand how this could have worked, one can consider a slightly earlier observation on language and audience by Hōjō Yasutoki (1183–1242). Regent to the third Kamakura shogun and at the apex of warrior power, Yasutoki advises the use of Chinese characters for those who could read them and the deployment of *kana* in writings for warriors (Fukazawa, "Rekishi no 'gaibu' ni tatsu koto," 145–46). Yasutoki's letter is quoted in ibid., 146.

24. Shinoda, *Founding of the Kamakura Shogunate*, 8. According to Nagahara, the fourth Tokugawa shogun, Ietsuna, even commissioned a *kana* "translation" for "women

government activities, especially rites and bureaucracy, and the linguistic register are taken into account, it indeed seems to be an effort at writing a history from a position of institutional centrality. This makes *The Mirror of the East* by far the most "mainstream" of the *Mirrors*, a position that will be inherited by its Muromachi successor, *The Mirror of the Gods.*

Like *The Water Mirror* and *The China Mirror, The Mirror of the East* follows a chronicle format, though one that is much more richly developed than that of any earlier *Mirror.* It features a substantial increase in the number and nature of incidents recorded. No longer are entries primarily narrative: the seeming majority take note of ceremonies, divinations, celestial anomalies, sutra readings, stupa and/or temple construction projects, archery meets, poetry or kickball gatherings, government deliberations, and the like without offering much elaboration beyond an occasional list of participants or the most abbreviated explanation. Because the preponderance of entries focuses on mechanical notations of social, political, and religious ritual rather than "plot," *The Mirror of the East* moves away from the more narrative-centered earlier *Mirrors* and toward a more canonical mode of record keeping.

This suggests that even as real-world Kamakura sociopolitical structures were evolving to accommodate changing power players, the props required for performing authority were desired to be recognizably familiar. In this sense, *The Mirror of the East* achieves a perfect fusion of old and new in its finished form. It has the heft of an "official" chronicle-style history, but the cosmological imperative of the *Mirror*: whether or not *The Mirror of the East* owes its direct inspiration to a particular Heian or Kamakura *Mirror*, it almost certainly reflects the idea common to the earlier *Mirrors* that the past is a way to interpret and understand—or even validate—the present, much as Taizong's famous quote that was reworked in *The China Mirror* implies.[25] Thus, the work is meaningful not

---

and children" (Nagahara and Kishi, *Zen'yaku Azuma kagami,* 1:5). Yamashita Hiroaki similarly assesses it as "a work recorded to affirm the legitimacy of the *bakufu*" ("Kantō no <rekishi> kijutsu," 10).

25. The *Zhenguan zhengyao* (Fundamentals of Governance from the Zhenguan Era), the source for the original citation, also circulated among elites at this time. The third shogun, Minamoto no Sanetomo (1192–1219), spent at least four months—the seventh to the eleventh—reading the *Fundamentals* in Jōgen 5 (1211); and the fourth shogun, Kujō Yoritsune (1218–56), was presented with a copy by Hōjō Tokiyori (1227–63)

only as a repository of precedent, although that surely plays an important role, but also as a text that ought to be integrated within a larger cosmological discourse. The nature of that cosmology, however, differs dramatically from the discourse about the end of the world and general decline that are so dominant in the Heian *Mirrors*, and this results in a fundamentally different type of historiographic enterprise—as the following section demonstrates.

RHETORICAL MANEUVERS: PLACE, PRINCIPLE, AND AUTHORITY

Another way that *The Mirror of the East* differs markedly from its predecessors is in its lack of a preface. Thus, bereft of a framing story, the role of cosmologically derived historiographic imperatives is also much less obvious than in the case of the earlier *Mirrors*, with their careful deployment of temple settings and otherworldly narrators. There is no acknowledged setting at which to ground the narrative, nor is there a narrator who informs the reader exactly what it is that she or he is to learn from the text. Both of these matters have implications for the nature of the authority to which *The Mirror of the East* appeals.

Although *The Mirror of the East* has no obvious narrative setting or overt narrator or compiler, it is not without the occasional editorial comment, such as the characterizations of Hōjō Masako's (1157–1225) behavior as "spoiled" (*hoshiimama*) and the remark likening her court position, despite being tonsured, to that of the notorious monk Dōkyō.[26] Indeed, in a recent study, Yabumoto Katsuharu persuasively argues that an agenda can be extracted from the very editing and manipulation of the recording of events.[27] Still, without the preternatural narrator to explain the

---

in Kenchō 2 (1250). On Sanetomo's reading, see the entry for 7.4 for the first mention of the work and the entry for 11.20 for the completion of his study (Nagahara and Kishi, *Zen'yaku Azuma kagami*, 3:175 and 178, respectively). On Yoritsune, see the entry for 5.27 (ibid., 5:81).

26. For the former, see Nagahara and Kishi, *Zen'yaku Azuma kagami*, 2:123, the entry for Bunji 5 (1189).9.28. On the Dōkyō comparison, see ibid., 3:285, the entry for Kenpō 6 (1218).4.29.

27. Yabumoto, "'Azuma kagami' ni okeru 'rekishi' kōchiku no ichi hōhō." The article has a narrow focus in terms of incidents, but I suspect that its conclusions are relevant for the entire work.

work's charge or the Buddhist setting to give it a transcendent authority, the presence of a driving cosmological principle is not established for a reader at the work's outset. In other words, the lack of a preface has a significant influence on the presentation of the contents and raises several questions: What might the absence of a preface permit? Can one understand *The Mirror of the East* as engaging in cosmological discourse without a preface? Most importantly, what are the sometimes messy cosmological discourses and the external events of that time, and how might they be influencing the configuration of the past?

By and large, the earlier *Mirrors* confronted the idea of karmic causality and the urgent question of how to make sense of Japan within a final-age narrative. Even *The China Mirror*, though displacing the decline onto the Chinese past, acknowledged concern with the decay of the Buddha's teachings. Invariably, the foundations for these positions were laid out in the prefaces. The absence of a preface in *The Mirror of the East* enables two things: an uncoupling from the site-based authority seen in the earlier *Mirrors* and a less exclusive, if also much less overt, cosmological perspective.

To be clear, the jettisoning of a preface should not be understood as bringing *The Mirror of the East* into line with the implicit stylistic conventions of orthodox court histories, or "this sovereignty's histories" (*honchō shisho*). On the contrary, of the eight works that the roughly contemporary *Shaku Nihongi* (Exegesis of the Chronicles of Japan) lists as constituting the category of orthodox histories, six feature prefaces.[28] Therefore, not including any sort of preface is not a particularly orthodox move. Nor does the lack of a preface indicate a lack of interest in religious or cosmological matters. *The Mirror of the East* is replete with sutra offerings, lectures, and recitations. Buddha images are commissioned, enshrined, and reverenced to multiple ends, from ensuring safe childbirth to accruing posthumous benefit for the departed. Temple and shrine construction and repair are recurring concerns, and yin-yang diviners set dates for festivals, progresses, and household events, as well as administering countless rites and conducting divinations for matters as lofty as

28. These works are *Sendai kuji hongi*, *Nihon shoki*, *Nihon kōki*, *Shoku Nihon kōki*, *Nihon Montoku Tennō jitsuroku*, and *Nihon sandai jitsuroku* (Onoda, *Shaku Nihongi*, 17–19).

celestial anomalies and as lowly as the meaning of dog feces on tatami.[29] As Martin Collcutt has demonstrated, the late twelfth century is revealed in this work to have been an age replete with religious activity (broadly defined), in which the shogun and his officials were active participants.[30]

Nevertheless, by doing away with the prefatory framing device and removing the cosmologically charged setting that characterizes the rest of the *Mirrors* to date, the compilers of *The Mirror of the East* have removed the most typical opportunity to foreground the rhetoric of cosmological principles or their implied trajectories. Taking into consideration the foci of these earlier principles, this becomes less surprising. Over time, there has been a gradual shift from a principle of karmic cause and effect in *The Great Mirror* to a preoccupation with decline and the end of the world, most obviously in *The Water Mirror*. While it is unclear whether the decline that characterizes China in *The China Mirror* likewise threatens Japan, the risk is there. In this light, I would suggest that a new "upstart" regime such as that suggested by the *bakufu* had little to gain, regardless of the scope of its ambitions, in situating its founding in a larger discourse that emphasizes most change as negative. Mention of the final age or the decline of Buddhist law appears infrequently throughout the entire work, and nowhere does it exhibit the earnestness of, for instance, Tadachika's concern that the end of the world is imminent. In fact, nearly all use of terms specifying the world as in the "final age" vanishes right around the time of the Hōjō-dominated *bakufu*'s successful defeat of its strongest remaining rivals, the Miura family, in the Hōji Disturbance (1247).[31] Perhaps, thanks to the Hōjō, the world was no longer heading to its demise.

29. The celestial anomalies are too numerous to list, but see the entry for Kangi 1 (1229).5.21 for the discovery of the feces and the subsequent divination (Nagahara and Kishi, *Zen'yaku Azuma kagami*, 4:75).

30. Collcutt, "Religion in the Formation of the Kamakura Bakufu."

31. Only approximately three mentions postdate the Jōkyū Disturbance. These are comments on snow in Minō on Kangi 2 (1230).6.16; Yasutoki's understanding of appropriate behavior on night duty on Kangi 4 (1232).11.28; and a resurrection on Jōei 2 (1233).7.20 (Nagahara and Kishi, *Zen'yaku Azuma kagami*, 4:94, 134–35, and 143, respectively). This is not to suggest that most previous references are dire. Ashikaga Tadatsuna is described as "a warrior of unparalleled bravery in the final age" in the entry for Jishō 5 (1181).i2.25 (ibid., 1:101). An edict is assessed as the final age standard (literally, "tortoise mirror") for later generations on Kenkyū 3 (1192).8.5 (ibid., 2:252). Genshō has

Despite the absence of a preface, *The Mirror of the East* does possess a sense of cosmological imperative. Yet while the entire sociopolitical world of the *bakufu* is filled with religious practices—ceremonies, offerings, and so on—it is primarily the battles that surround its very existence that are actually discussed as being directly influenced by cosmological forces. Given the exclusivity with which this rhetoric is deployed, focusing on the cosmological forces in the narration of military conflicts in *The Mirror of the East* allows us to understand the ways in which the progression of events is justified and interpreted. This rhetoric reflects a move away from the earlier *Mirrors*' versions of the past, which were exclusively driven by Buddhist principles and focused on the world's downward trajectory, and toward an understanding of warrior successes as achieved with divine aid and the endorsement of both the *kami* and buddhas. This shift is most evident in the rhetoric of the Genpei War and, less explicitly, the Jōkyū Disturbance (1221) and Hōji Disturbance (1247).

In addition to the abovementioned campaigns, *The Mirror of the East* features an impressive array of military conflicts, including the Northern Expedition (1189), the Wada Rebellion (1213), and at least three attempted coups: one in the first month of Shōji 3 (1201), another in the intercalary fourth and fifth months of Kangen 4 (1246), and a final abortive uprising in the seventh month of 1266 that resulted in the deposition of the first of the princely shoguns, Munetaka, and his removal back to Kyoto. However, it is primarily the founding war and the imperial uprising of 1221 (and the 1247 war, to a lesser extent) that are treated in cosmological terms.[32] To discern whether there is a consistent cosmological

a preternatural encounter with a monk who refuses to instruct him in the advanced arts of calculation due to a lack of ability that characterizes the final age (ibid., 2:394–95, the entry for Shōji 2 [1200].12.3). Hōjō Yoshitoki (1163–1224) assesses the falconry skill of one Sakurai Gorō (dates unknown) as rare in the "final age" (ibid., 3:126, the entry for Genkyū 3 [1206].3.13). The copy Sanetomo receives of the *Kokin wakashū* is likewise dubbed "a treasure of the final age" (ibid., 3:142, the entry for Jōgen 2 [1208].5.29). The collapse of Suzaku Gate is speculated to be a sign of the final age (ibid., 3:178, the entry for Jōgen 5 [1211].11.4). An oracle at Enoshima predicts "a rare miracle in the final age" (ibid., 3:260, the entry for Kenpō 4 [1216].1.15). Lastly, Adachi Kagemori (died 1248) expresses uncertainty about his descendants, "should this be the final age" in the build-up to the Hōji Disturbance (ibid., 4:456, the entry for Hōji 1 [1247].4.11).

32. However, the chronicler wonders whether "devils haven't got a hold of people" in the lead-up to the clash with the Miura on Hōji 1 (1247).6.5 (Nagahara and Kishi,

principle (or set of principles) shaping the worldview of *The Mirror of the East*, it will be useful to consider how each of these three military campaigns is articulated.

The Genpei War narrative with which *The Mirror of the East* commences, as the origin story of the *bakufu* itself, is the account that has the most recourse to otherworldly authority and reveals the importance of a new, inclusive *kami*-Buddhist rhetoric. It does so, moreover, in ways that cleave to Sasaki Kaoru's characterization of "warrior authority" in the age of the *bakufu*'s establishment as based on a "*kami*-Buddha fusion" under a layer of yin-yang divination.[33] (That is, in a world where in addition to shogunal sponsorship of construction of temples and shrines alike, a reader will also see how both *kami* and buddhas are turned to in moments of need. And, as noted above, numerous matters from the celestial to the mundane frequently entail a consultation with one or more diviners.) Furthermore, the Genpei War is distinct from all other military encounters in *The Mirror of the East* because its cause is clearly framed in the document used as the rallying call that launches the war: the edict attributed to Prince Mochihito (1151–80), third son of Tonsured Retired Emperor Goshirakawa.

The narrative of *The Mirror of the East* opens with Minamoto no Yorimasa's (1104–80) secret nocturnal journey to the residence of the would-be rebel Prince Mochihito to accept the charge to help take back the realm from the Taira and their allies. Mochihito's plan is then transmitted to the Hōjō residence in Izu, where it finds a sympathetic ear in Yoritomo, the much aggrieved exile.[34] The reader learns of his accumulated (and just) resentment of Taira no Kiyomori's abuse of power, his sympathies with

Zen'yaku Azuma kagami, 4:463). Eight days later, Tokiyori also attributes the restoration of peace to the dharma (ibid., 4:470).

33. Sasaki Kaoru, *Nihon chūsei shisō no kichō*, 38. Sasaki, however, refers to this as the "age of Yoritomo" and the "religious world around [him]," which I am interpreting as referring to the *bakufu* religious climate. Collcutt likewise takes Yoritomo's beliefs as somewhat representative "of other eastern warriors" in that they were "a blend of devotion to Shinto and Buddhism, with considerable trust in divination as a guide in critical moments" ("Religion in the Formation of the Kamakura Bakufu," 68).

34. For a succinct synopsis of the factors that led to his exile, see Oyler, *Swords, Oaths, and Prophetic Visions*, 31–32.

the imperial cause, and his resolve to raise an army.[35] This is followed by the text of the charge, as copied by Yorimasa's son Minamoto no Nakatsuna (1126–80), in which the call to arms is set up as a divine command based on the *Sutra of the Most Triumphant King*.[36] After enumerating the abuses of power and perversions of rule by Kiyomori and his followers, the justification for rebellion culminates in a promise to "smite and eradicate those who would destroy Buddhist law."[37] Mochihito continues, "This is not to be [achieved] by relying on mustering human strength alone, but rather something for which I look solely to the aid of the ruler of heaven. Thereby, should I enjoy the numinous and unfathomable response of the Emperor, Three Treasures, and the Brilliant Sun Goddess, how could I not at once have the will of the realm?"[38] In other words, from the outset, the conflict that brings about the institution at the heart of *The Mirror of the East* is articulated in terms of cooperative divine forces: those of the imperial house, Buddhism, and the *kami*.[39] The last two overlap with the forces that Elizabeth Oyler has identified as being at play in a set of dream interpretations found in several other medieval texts that justify Yoritomo's rise. She cites the "Minamoto identity," including its "association with the royal family"; the "divine authority" derived from clan ties to Hachiman; and Yoritomo's "rise to the position of shogun" as the three keys to the dream narratives as tools of legitimation. The shared

35. Nagahara and Kishi, *Zen'yaku Azuma kagami*, 1:46–47.

36. This is an abbreviation for the *Sutra of the Golden Light Most Triumphant King*, which Bernhard Scheid identifies as "one of the 'three sutras of state protection'" already in the Nara period ("Shōmu Tennō and the Deity from Kyushu," 36n21). This article provides an overview of the multifaceted nature of the Hachiman deity and its early connection to the Nara state.

37. Nagahara and Kishi, *Zen'yaku Azuma kagami*, 1:47.

38. Nagahara and Kishi, *Zen'yaku Azuma kagami*, 1:47. For a complete English translation of the account, see Collcutt, "Religion in the Formation of the Kamakura Bakufu," 57–58. Although our wordings differ, the thrust of the translations is the same. The only significant variation is that where I take *shinmei* to refer to Amaterasu, Collcutt uses the broader meaning of "native gods" (ibid., 58). I suggest that in this instance, the import is more or less the same. Because of the focus on religion in Collcutt's study, this document plays a key role in the opening of his article as well.

39. Gomi's analysis of the opening likewise identifies three key elements: the call to arms; Yoritomo, as the scion of a warrior house with noble origins; and Hōjō Tokimasa (1138–1215), as a representative of one of the great warrior families of the East (*Zōho Azuma kagami no hōhō*, 39).

recourse to otherworldly forces and the imperial bloodline suggests that *The Mirror of the East* is not an outlier in its consistent use of this rhetoric.[40]

Mochihito's endorsements are echoed, albeit less dramatically, throughout the war. In the entry for Jishō 4 (1180).9.10, Ichijō Tadayori (died 1184) is reported to have received an oracle via the wife of a shrine priest from Amaterasu, urging the Genji westward.[41] Yoritomo likewise makes use of the rhetoric of divine favor in a petition submitted at Ise Shrine on Yōwa 2 (1182).2.8. First, he establishes his imperial lineage—a distant link to Emperor Seiwa (850–80)—and then attributes his escape from Kiyomori and his allies to divine assistance. Second, after noting that Kiyomori's death was surely due to "divine displeasure" (*shinryo fukai*), he turns to two destructive incidents at shrines in Ise as signs that the world is still imperiled. He then concludes the list of his aspirations by stating his wish to "humbly venerate divine matters and perpetuate the customs of the True Teachings."[42] A later prayer petition during the war, dating to Yōwa 2 (1182).12.2, is more succinct but still consistent with this logic. After expressing surprise that divine authority is behind him, he muses, "However, the gods heed principles" and concludes by noting his faith in the power of prayer to the gods and buddhas.[43]

Yoritomo's rhetoric in his long petition reflects the convergence of the three powers Mochihito is said to have invoked: the personal tie to the imperial lineage, the implicit blessing of the Sun Goddess, and a devotion to the Buddhist teachings.[44] The message is clear that these are the forces that should be mobilized behind a legitimate claim to authority.[45]

40. Oyler, *Swords, Oaths, and Prophetic Visions*, 46–59. On "Minamoto identity," see ibid., 47–49, and on "Divine Authority," see ibid., 49–51.

41. Nagahara and Kishi, *Zen'yaku Azuma kagami*, 1:69.

42. Nagahara and Kishi, *Zen'yaku Azuma kagami*, 1:121; see also 120.

43. Nagahara and Kishi, *Zen'yaku Azuma kagami*, 1:135.

44. Yamashita locates additional references to the aid of buddhas or *kami* in the account of Yoritomo's first battle, as well as noting the oracular exchange I also cite ("Kantō no <rekishi> kijutsu," 15). However, I have chosen to focus on the rhetoric presented in the petition, since it explains the origins of the war.

45. Even so, not everyone has equal potential access to this authority. Minamoto no Yoshitsune's (1159–89) claim that he, too, enjoys the protection of the *kami* and buddhas in this "land of the gods" and his vow upon the talismans of all of the shrines that his intentions are noble fall on deaf ears. For the text of his missive intended to persuade his brother of his innocence, see Nagahara and Kishi, *Zen'yaku Azuma kagami*, 1:215–17.

And indeed, while the rhetoric is not invoked in the narration of the later Northern Expedition, the design of its new banner attests to this: the names of both the Ise Grand Shrine and the Hachiman Bodhisattva are written at the top, with a pair of doves beneath them.[46]

Yet a sidelining of the "imperial" aspect is demonstrable in the account of the 1221 Jōkyū Disturbance, in which the forces of Hōjō Yasutoki (1183–1242) defeated those of Retired Emperor Gotoba and his supporters, even as the "divine" element remains significant. Although not as dramatic as Mochihito's call to arms, proof of divine endorsement is nonetheless provided to Masako in a dream—complete with an oracular mirror—that urges Yasutoki to bring peace to the realm.[47] The entry recording the initial decision to send Hōjō troops to the capital uses similar justification: after Hōjō Yoshitoki (1163–1224) learns that Masako has received similar advice from two separate quarters, he remarks, "Both counsels are of a single mind. How could this not be the aid of the *kami* and buddhas?"[48] And in the course of the campaign, an entry that details the warriors' rampage through the capital closes with the observation that "the engendering of the defeat of court forces of late must be a blessing of the unexhausted power of the gods and buddhas."[49] There is no attempt to otherwise legitimate the warrior position against imperial support (including that of two other retired emperors) for Gotoba.

46. For a description of the banner, see Nagahara and Kishi, *Zen'yaku Azuma kagami*, 2:92, the entry for Bunji 5 (1189).7.8.

47. The entry for Jōkyū 3 (1221).3.22 records: "Twenty-second day. *Hinoto-hitsuji*. Hatano Jirō Tomosada [dates unknown] set off for the Ise Grand Shrine as [Masako's] emissary of second rank. This was due to a dream that Masako had that morning. A mirror with a surface of roughly two *jō* was floating on the waves of Yui Bay. A voice spoke from it, saying: 'I am from Ise Shrine. When I reflect on the realm, the age is one of great chaos, and an army must be summoned. Should [Hōjō] Yasutoki polish me, he will achieve great peace'; given this [Masako's] faith was truly strengthened. Since Tomosada was the grandchild of a shrine official, he was the emissary and so forth" (Nagahara and Kishi, *Zen'yaku Azuma kagami*, 3:326).

48. Nagahara and Kishi, *Zen'yaku Azuma kagami*, 3:330. The translation is after William McCullough, "*Azuma kagami* Account," 110–11. McCullough provides an English translation of the entries that record the war (Jōkyū 3 [1221].5.20–i10.29). Their enemies later doubt their chances without similar aid. See Nagahara and Kishi, *Zen'yaku Azuma kagami*, 3:332, the entry for Jōkyū 3 (1221).5.26; McCullough, "*Azuma kagami* Account," 115.

49. Nagahara and Kishi, *Zen'yaku Azuma kagami*, 3:340, the entry for Jōkyū 3 (1221).6.15. The translation is after William McCullough, "*Azuma kagami* Account," 132.

Perhaps given their opponents and the warrior victory, it should be unsurprising that the narrative of this rebellion suggests a somewhat different priority than Yoritomo's. This narrative seems to foreshadow, to borrow Sasaki's characterization, post-Jōkyū warrior beliefs in "divine country" thought that disengage from the emphasis on the imperial house's "descent from the gods" while still taking broader *kami* worship seriously.[50] Sasaki persuasively argues that proof of this can be seen in the following otherwise puzzling passage from *The Mirror of the East*, in which the compiler muses: "Amaterasu is the original mistress of our bountiful land and the progenitrix of our imperial line. Why would she now, however, in the eighty-fifth generation of the line, change her vow to keep the land ordered for 100 reigns and cause three emperors and two princes to embrace the shame of the exile?"[51] In Sasaki's analysis, the remainder of the entry, which suggests that there were several signs that those in power failed to heed, is an effort to demonstrate the unsuitability of the "court authority" that results in its just displacement.[52] A brief exchange on Jō'ō 3 (1224).7.17 between Hōjō Masako and Miura Yoshimura (died 1239) illustrates the idea that divine favor is not the exclusive prerogative of the imperial line. Masako has caught wind of ill-fated "secret discussions" (*mitsudan*) between Miura Yoshimura and Hōjō Masamura (1205–73; a younger half-brother of Yasutoki), who hoped to seize control of the *bakufu*. She chides Yoshimura for failing to appreciate that the right to rule belongs to Yasutoki, attributing their victory in the Jōkyū Disturbance half to Yasutoki and half to the mandate of heaven itself![53] Be it the Genpei War or the Jōkyū Disturbance, neither is articulated as a sign of decline: instead, the *kami* and buddhas together enable deserved warrior successes.

50. For this description of post-Jōkyū thought, see Sasaki Kaoru, *Nihon chūsei shisō no kichō*, 127–29.

51. See Nagahara and Kishi, *Zen'yaku Azuma kagami*, 3:364, the entry for the Jōkyū 3 (1221).10.10. The translation is after William McCullough, "*Azuma kagami* Account," 154.

52. Sasaki Kaoru sees the refusal to take the dreams seriously as an attempt to explain warrior authority in the face of this vow (*Nihon chūsei shisō no kichō*, 127–28). This is reminiscent of the conversation between Duke Ai of Lu and Confucius cited by Shigenori in *The China Mirror* and discussed in chapter 3.

53. Nagahara and Kishi, *Zen'yaku Azuma kagami*, 3:398, the entry for Jō'ō 3 (1224).7.17.

The familiar framework of *kami* and buddhas returns yet again in the account of the Hōji Disturbance of 1247, in which *bakufu* forces defeat an uprising of Miura loyalist supporters of the deposed shogun, Kujō Yoritsune (1218–56). The Hōjō hero, Tokiyori (1227–63), initially learns of the uprising from a shrine head into whose hands a prayer petition has fallen. The petition asks the "miraculous gods" not to help the rebellion, but instead to aid in protecting stability and safety.[54] Roughly two weeks later, in his report to the *bakufu* on Hōji 1 (1247).6.13, Tokiyori is moved to attribute "this battle and the peace of the Kantō" as "all brought about by the efficacy of the dharma."[55] This lingering rhetoric serves as a reminder that despite the surge in reliance upon *kami* among warriors, this was complementary—not contradictory—to reliance upon assorted buddhas.

The obverse of this position vis-à-vis the undeserving is likewise explicit in instances where failure or censure is attributed to affronts to the gods and/or buddhas. On Jishō 5 (1181).1.21, shortly before Kiyomori's death, for instance, we find another catalogue of his faults, stated in terms that suggest he is not long for this world: in "an excess of pride," Kiyomori "scorns court governance, disregards the authority of the gods, destroys the Buddhist law, and brings suffering and chaos to the people."[56] As if this is not enough, he also orders the seizure of the military rice rations headed to the shrine of the Sun Goddess and the arrest of the people involved, an act "unprecedented in the hundreds and thousands of years since the Sun Goddess's [first] reposing [there]."[57] This is the perfect setup for Yoritomo's abovementioned observation that in his death, Kiyomori essentially got what he had coming to him.

Other less dramatic examples include the sudden death of the governor of Echigo on Yōwa 1 (1181).9.3, before he is able to carry out his plan to attack Kiso Yoshinaka (1154–84), which is interpreted as "divine punishment, perhaps?"; and the Yōwa 2 (1182) response to Minamoto no Yukiie's (died 1186) prayer in which he is informed that the gods are behind

54. Nagahara and Kishi, *Zen'yaku Azuma kagami*, 4:459, the entry for Hōji 1 (1247).5.26.

55. Nagahara and Kishi, *Zen'yaku Azuma kagami*, 4:470.

56. Nagahara and Kishi, *Zen'yaku Azuma kagami*, 1:95.

57. Nagahara and Kishi, *Zen'yaku Azuma kagami*, 1:95.

the Minamoto.[58] (And given this, the Hie monks are encouraged to fall in line.[59]) Even Retired Emperor Goshirakawa invokes the "resentment of the people and the curses of the gods" to urge Kamakura to get their stewards under control.[60]

Moreover, such threats are still potent a quarter of a century later, when Miura Yoshimura urges his siblings to abandon their agreement with the Wada family to support them in their revolt against the Hōjō-led *bakufu* forces, lest they incur "the punishment of heaven" (*tenken*) for their disloyalty. (Yoshimura points to his family's long service to the Minamoto and reminds his brother that the current shogun, Sanetomo, belongs to the same line.) In the same uprising, the Wada partisan Tsuchiya Yoshikiyo (died 1213) is felled by a stray arrow widely attributed to the gods.[61] In other words, just as the support of the *kami* was needed for success, divine censure was also seen as a real threat: without a divinely bestowed right and a commitment to Buddhism (far from incompatible allegiances in this period), one's cause could not triumph.[62]

While the idea of Buddhist principles influencing events is familiar from the earlier *Mirrors*, in the justifications for attributing how matters unfold to the gods, one can observe a reorientation away from concerns with imperial authority. As the *bakufu* grew in strength, it moved toward what Sasaki has described as typical of nonelite belief in the *kami*: the previously mentioned idea of Japan as a sacred land that enjoyed divine protection but without commitment to the notion of the emperor as divine.[63] Indeed, where one might expect the removal of an imperial prince from the office of shogun to cause at least some discomfiture—were his "divine origin" taken seriously—the record makes no mention of *kami* or buddhas in the quashed 1266 uprising that ends Munetaka's position

58. Nagahara and Kishi, *Zen'yaku Azuma kagami*, 1:112 and 126–27, respectively.

59. Nagahara and Kishi, *Zen'yaku Azuma kagami*, 1:127.

60. Fujiwara no Tsunefusa's transcription of this is included in Nagahara and Kishi, *Zen'yaku Azuma kagami*, 1:362, the entry for Bunji 3 (1187).10.3.

61. For the first exchange and for the arrow incident, see Nagahara and Kishi, *Zen'yaku Azuma kagami*, 3:208, the entry for Kenryaku 3 (1213).5.2, and 3:213, the entry for Kenryaku 3 (1213).5.3, respectively.

62. Conlan's work suggests that this logic continued unabated in the fourteenth century (*State of War*, 166–67).

63. Sasaki Kaoru, *Nihon chūsei shisō no kichō*, 126.

as shogun.[64] Instead, after Yoritomo's initial citation of his tie to the imperial house, there seems to be little concern about justifying uprisings (or crackdowns) with rhetoric that makes recourse to imperial ties. The gods and buddhas are enough.

All of the rhetoric of cosmological forces notwithstanding, however, there is no "principle" that is ever articulated as such. While the omnipresent Buddhist rituals suggest that karmic causality is still very much a part of the understanding of the universe, the lack of a frame story to remind readers to be on the lookout for a karma-driven explanation creates a certain vagueness in outlook. Similarly, the concept of "final age," most often rendered in this text as *matsudai*, is never treated in a sustained way: the range of events to which it is applied—from a miraculous resurrection to a copy of the *Kokin wakashū* (Anthology of Waka Old and New, written in 905)—suggests a different level of gravitas than was used in its earlier deployment. Nor is there any theorization of the involvement of *kami* in mundane affairs—again, something that the patterns of the earlier *Mirrors* would lead one to expect in a preface. To be sure, the victorious side in a military struggle is aided by *kami*, no doubt thanks to the many offerings and prayers made to them both annually and ad hoc, but no long-term trajectory is spelled out. In short, *The Mirror of the East* is not a text that derives its authority from a discourse on principles, nor does it make a clear statement on where the world is headed. Without the authority of place that the earlier *Mirrors* established through their settings at specific temples, there is no obvious concern in *The Mirror of the East* with situating its world on a well-delimited cosmological path.

Instead, various types of authority, which are mobilized in the treatment of military campaigns, are scattered throughout the work along with the more general movement of goods and people within the world of the text. I propose that by refraining from tying the text to a specific temple, the compilers of *The Mirror of the East* have created a narrative that is able to mobilize different strands of authority—strands that were unlikely to map to a single locus within the domain of the Kamakura shogunate in particular, even as Kamakura is the *de facto* center that both initiates and

64. For the entries that deal with the "mysterious" unrest in Kamakura, beginning on Bun'ei 3 (1266).6.23 and concluding with the former shogun's return to the capital on 7.20 of the same year, see Nagahara and Kishi, *Zen'yaku Azuma kagami*, 5:540–43.

serves as a destination for movement. This approach achieves multiple effects. First, by not allying the work with either the Ise Grand Shrine (with its imperial ties) or the Tsurugaoka Hachiman Shrine (with its strong warrior ties), *The Mirror of the East* manages to refrain from calling attention to the complicated relevance of imperial authority to its narrative. Second, just as earlier *Mirrors* featured settings at an increasing remove from the capital to consider other types of authority, not explicitly setting *The Mirror of the East* in either a Kyoto or Kamakura location allows one to sidestep the thorny issue of the *bakufu*'s putative and actual power relations with the court. Last, in the refusal to bind *The Mirror of the East* to one legitimating locus, the work's compilers create a network of authority rather than a particular fixed site. This move is unsurprising if one takes into account the close relationship between the *bakufu*'s performance of authority and its ability to mobilize literal traffic out of and into Kamakura, including trips to and from the capital, religious pilgrimages, punitive exhibitions, and pleasure outings. *The Mirror of the East* documents a world in which very little is stationary. Although the enumeration of each of these trips in a text that spans eighty years is beyond the scope of this chapter, the near-constant movement of the *bakufu* officials, emissaries, offerings, and even sometimes the shogun between the shrines and temples of the East (Mishima, Hakone, and so on), Ise, and Kyoto—or between the governmental centers or residences in Kamakura and Rokuhara or more central Kyoto—speaks to the impossibility (or inadvisability) of trying to metaphorically tie the authority of the *bakufu* to a single geographic site.[65]

This is not the only thing that the disaggregation of place and authority achieves: it also extricates *The Mirror of the East* from the relationship between more literary writing and historiographic authenticity present in all of the earlier *Mirrors*. The first three *Mirrors* tied themselves to Murasaki Shikibu and/or *The Tale of Genji* in explicit ways, often including the significance of the site. The fourth, *The China Mirror*, cre-

65. I suspect it would be a step too far to equate the frequent movement with a claim to "ubiquitously inhabit . . . a vast number of places all at once," as Terry Kawashima proposes to be the case in one of the roughly contemporary Suwa narratives (*Itineraries of Power*, 183). In *The Mirror of the East*, Kamakura is clearly a center of gravity, even if no one site is named. But such inconsistency simply attests to the multivalence of mobility in medieval texts.

ated an analogous tie with its references to Sugawara no Michizane and the continental literary tradition, the narrative setting at Anrakuji, the temple built atop Michizane's presumed grave.[66] Yet the surviving scrolls' lack of a direct tie to the *Genji* suggests a move away from a narrative of the past that defines its position in terms of that particular earlier work and its ideas on historiography.[67] Still, Michizane was recognized before his exile as one of the literary stars of the court. Thus, to identify with him, rather than Murasaki, is not a complete break with the literary tradition, but instead a reorientation. The first four *Mirrors* all hark back to prominent writers who served at court, even temporarily. The more significant cutting of ties with the literary culture of the court does not come until *The Mirror of the East*, with its refusal to acknowledge overtly any precedent in its composition. There is no suggestion anywhere that a courtly pedigree is required to affirm its historiographic legitimacy or its position as authoritative.

Taken together with the earlier discussion of Gomi's idea of the influence of *The China Mirror*, Tonomura's hypothesis about the involvement of Fujiwara no Shigenori's house, and the generally high level of literacy required to produce such a work, this refusal makes the absence of a preface in *The Mirror of the East* a significant choice. By doing away with any preface at all, the text navigates several complicated relationships: it simultaneously avoids the issue of presentation to the court or *bakufu* suggested by traditional imperial histories' prefaces, skirts the potential difficulties of committing to a particular place as the seat of its authority, and steers clear of any sort of literary "taint."[68] This is more than a question of morality; it can also be interpreted as a choice not to

66. For an overview of the relationship between this location, Michizane, and his "reincarnation" as Tenjin, see Borgen, "Michizane, Tenjin, and Dazaifu." On the connection between Michizane's interment and the temple, see ibid., 41.

67. This in no way meant that the *Genji* was not of interest to thirteenth-century readers: as noted above, Munetaka received instruction in "the tale of the Shining Genji" at his Kamakura residence on Kenchō 6 (1254).12.18 (Nagahara and Kishi, *Zen'yaku Azuma kagami*, 5:244).

68. The notion of tales as morally problematic was still operative at this time, as can be seen in Yotsutsuji, *Kakaishō*, 251. The author's explanation of the "Fireflies" chapter—noted in both the introduction and chapter 2 as the site of the "tales" versus "chronicles" discussion—centers on the lines in Genji's account of how tales function as "expedient means." Such emphasis suggests that this point was still both critical and contentious.

acknowledge court-centered writing as the standard against which all other writing is to define itself. Perhaps through this decision, together with the *bakufu*'s co-optation or mimicry of the institutions, rituals, and language of court authority, *The Mirror of the East* was intended to demonstrate that the authority of the warrior had arrived.

PASTS REFINED

One other casualty of the decision not to include a preface in *The Mirror of the East* is the overt thematization of the past. Whereas *The Great Mirror* and *The New Mirror* had promised that history would be revealed to be governed by (karmic) causality, *The Water Mirror* and *The China Mirror*, albeit in different ways, drew on a discourse about the past that characterized it as moving along a trajectory of decline. Yet *The Mirror of the East* remains silent on this matter. To consider how the work addresses the nature of the past and the ends to which it is put, I return to Paul Ricoeur's notion, introduced in chapter 2, of the relationship between any history and its "founding violence."[69] This offers a way to think through some of the implications of producing an institutionally focused history of the *bakufu*'s founding and development in the final decade of the thirteenth century.

Yamashita Hiroaki has pointed to the "precarity" of the *bakufu* in the wake of the attempted Mongol invasions of 1274 and 1281, which is near the time of the presumed composition of *The Mirror of the East*.[70] It is perhaps with this uncertainty in mind that the stakes behind narrating the history of the office of the shogun take on additional significance. Yamashita and others have called attention to the mythic nature of the founding narrative itself, and I will not retrace their work.[71] What I wish to focus on is the "founding violence" and the recurring smaller-scale battles that serve as continued reminders of the legitimacy of the *bakufu* as the legacy of that violence.[72] Unlike the narrative of violence

69. Ricoeur, *Memory, History, Forgetting*, 82.

70. Yamashita, "Kantō no <rekishi> kijutsu," 10.

71. Ibid.

72. In a reading that pairs *The Mirror of the East* with *Soga monogatari* (The Tale of the Soga Brothers), Gomi proposes regicide as a symbolic recurring motif in *The Mirror of the East* (*Zōho Azuma kagami no hōhō*, 48–51).

in *The Water Mirror* that downplayed the impact of the Genpei War, *The Mirror of the East* opens with the war that enables Yoritomo's rise to power and eventual occupation of the office of shogun. In this, I suggest it acknowledges the Kamakura regime's "original relation to war."[73]

Ricoeur's writing on "founding violence" emphasizes the contingency of such a result: "What we celebrate under the heading of founding events are, essentially, violent acts legitimated after the fact by a precarious state of right."[74] The logic of *The Mirror of the East* can be interpreted as an attempted refutation of a position such as this: what it celebrates should not be precarious, because it is endorsed by gods and buddhas alike. As already seen, otherworldly support is most dramatically invoked in the founding war, but it is also reaffirmed in those military clashes that unsuccessfully threaten to unseat the *bakufu*. Each time, cosmological aid works in favor of the Kamakura-based powers. Specifically, it rallies behind the regent, who is nominally acting on behalf of the shogun.

In fact, by recording the codification of the *bakufu*'s ritual, military, civil, and judicial practices, *The Mirror of the East* offers a means of self-legitimization that is derived from the "institutionalization" of *bakufu* authority in all of its facets. The repetition of ritual acts across the *bakufu*'s would-be sphere of authority can be read as intended, to borrow Ricoeur's words affirmatively this time, to "[tie] together values, norms, models of relations and behaviors, roles."[75] It reminds readers of *The Mirror of the East* that the law of the *bakufu* (in all senses) is the law of an increasing part of the land.

This is critical in light of fact that *The Mirror of the East* most likely appeared in the wake of the Mongol invasions and with instability on the rise. Ishii Susumu has demonstrated that the repeated Mongol assaults struck an already weakened Kamakura regime.[76] At the same time, the 1274 attack created an opportunity of sorts for the *bakufu*, which "enforced a series of measures designed to fortify the nation."[77] The reforms

73. Again, I borrow this wording from Ricoeur, *Memory, History, Forgetting*, 82.

74. Ricoeur, *Memory, History, Forgetting*, 82.

75. Ricoeur, *Memory, History, Forgetting*, 220. This paragraph is informed by Ricoeur's discussion of scale (see ibid., 209–21).

76. Ishii points to the 1263 demise of Hōjō Tokiyori as the beginning of the end ("Decline of the Kamakura Bakufu," 128–29).

77. Ishii, "Decline of the Kamakura Bakufu," 142.

that Ishii details, however, are primarily practical in nature, with the attempted construction of a defensive coastal wall being the most dramatic and concrete example.[78] Had the danger of the Mongols been the *bakufu*'s only test, that alone would have posed significant difficulties—in particular, the task of duly compensating those who had fought the invaders.[79] But challenges also came from within, including the jockeying for power that culminated in the Shimotsuki Disturbance of 1285, a coup led by Taira no Yoritsuna (died 1293) that wiped out the powerful Adachi family.[80]

Preoccupied with its survival in the face of these various threats, the *bakufu* seems to have let slide some of the more ritualistic performances of authority. The realization of this oversight may well have been an impetus for compiling *The Mirror of the East*.[81] After all, the *bakufu*'s inaction with respect to ritual stood in marked contrast to the court's effective capitalization on the ability to invoke divine assistance when confronted with the Mongols. Thomas Conlan characterizes the disparate approaches of the court and the *bakufu* in the face of threatened invasion as follows:

> Although courtiers and warriors alike prayed for success in war, Kyōto, and not Kamakura, took the lead in mobilizing the gods. The court ignored the initial Mongol missives of 1266, but began enacting esoteric rituals of destruction against foreigners (*ikoku chōbuku* 異国調伏) during the third month of 1268. . . . After the 1281 invasion, the court (and the retired sovereign Kameyama in particular) took the most active role in cursing the Mongols. The Kamakura *bakufu* belatedly promulgated prayers in eight of Japan's sixty-six provinces in 1283 and did not apparently start issuing nationwide prayers throughout Japan until 1290.[82]

78. Ishii, "Decline of the Kamakura Bakufu," 142–44.
79. Ishii, "Decline of the Kamakura Bakufu," 130, 141–42, and 148–49.
80. On the general tensions, see Ishii, "Decline of the Kamakura Bakufu," 148. On the Shimotsuki Disturbance, see ibid., 150–52.
81. Ishii suggests that advancing the *bakufu*'s position was a goal of the practical and strategic reforms, but he does not address this more performative type of authority ("Decline of the Kamakura Bakufu," 142). In terms of the collapse of Kamakura, Ishii credits the *bakufu*'s ill-fated involvement with succession issues at court as the final straw (ibid., 160–62).
82. Conlan, *In Little Need of Divine Intervention*, 273–74.

In other words, *The Mirror of the East*, which centralizes cosmological authority in the institution of the office of the shogun (or in the pair of offices of the shogun and regent) and its supporters, appears precisely at the instant when the *bakufu* begins to more actively assert and perform the cosmological basis for its authority.[83] This may also partially explain why *The Mirror of the East* stops when it does: the Mongol invasions are a moment when the *bakufu* fails to perform the ritual functions necessary to create a compelling narrative of divine support for its actions. Better to regroup and reframe the past in a way that demonstrates that, from the beginning, the gods and buddhas alike have guaranteed the *bakufu*'s legitimacy and authority. This allows any reader to infer that, by extension, the *bakufu* was surely supported by the same powers in the most recent conflicts, too.[84]

I am disinclined to think that the presumed gap between the years covered in *The Mirror of the East* and its time of compilation represents a concerted effort to break with the past and establish it as a distinct object. In my reading, there is no attempt to establish that the world has moved beyond the one depicted in *The Mirror of the East*—rather, the text represents an effort to reestablish a connection between a divinely sanctioned origin and its contemporary iteration.[85] The past—the age of a powerful *bakufu*—is again desired as the present. In this respect, *The Mirror of the East* exhibits an unexpected affinity with the earliest *Mirrors*. The world it relates is connected to that of the present, and it is tacitly centered at a site close to the home of authority. However, at the same time, I want to suggest that by breaking off its narrative before a challenge that the *bakufu* survived, the work ends on an optimistic note. *The Great Mirror* celebrated something that had already been lost by the time of its composition, and in this sense, its glory could never be other than ironic. *The Mirror of the East*, in contrast, can be read as seeking to persuade the reader that just as the *bakufu* is known to have survived the

83. In addition, it was also facing Fushimi (1265–1317), who was a more ambitious emperor. See Ishii, "Decline of the Kamakura Bakufu," 164–65.

84. Gomi reaches a similar conclusion about the desirability of a "reconsideration" of the past in the face of the *bakufu*'s challenges over the decades following Sanetomo's removal (*Zōho Azuma kagami no hōhō*, 311).

85. Therefore, the requisite distance to think of the past here as an object of knowledge is lacking. Compare Certeau, *Writing of History*, 36–37.

famous challenges that arose after the text's conclusion, so, too, can it be assumed to be able to survive into the future.

Thus, *The Mirror of the East* is at one end of the Kamakura *Mirror* spectrum: a text that cloaks its revolutionary stance in a conservative linguistic form as one way of legitimizing its position. At the same time, it is a text that refuses to openly tie itself to a single location. Even as Kamakura and, more precisely, Tsurugaoka clearly constitute its nexus, *The Mirror of the East* does not derive its authority from a specific teaching passed on at a particular temple or shrine. It gives its readers a world that is demonstrably governed by divine right—via the aid of the *kami* and buddhas—but it never reveals precisely how this works, beyond a combination of offerings and prayers. Despite duly recording the rituals of religion, in stopping short of offering a cosmological principle or even a historical trajectory, it is the most "secular" yet of the *Mirrors.* It is a work that features the external trappings of authority but lacks an explicit otherworldly grand narrative at its foundation.

To an extent, this is effective because the legitimacy of the institution does not require a specific historical trajectory; it only needs proof that the cosmos is behind its continued survival, and such proof is invariably provided in the pro-*bakufu* outcome of events. Nevertheless, this depiction of a relatively amorphous cosmological path hints at a potential reason for the demise of the *Mirror* as a productive genre for narrating medieval pasts. Without a cosmological principle to reconcile unwelcome historical developments with a desired future trajectory, the persuasive powers of the *Mirrors* are considerably weakened, a phenomenon explored in chapter 5. However, before moving on to how this plays out in fourteenth-century historiographic efforts, an examination of the *Mirror* occupying the other end of the spectrum is required.

Nostalgic Reflections: Mirror of the Watchman in the Fields

At roughly the same time as *The Mirror of the East*, another much smaller *Mirror* appeared, one that had little to do with the past overtly but that embraced the very conventions that *The Mirror of the East* eschewed: the use of a preface that followed the precedents of the earlier *Mirrors*, the reliance upon *wabun* as its idiom, and the embrace of an explicit religious position. As such, *Watchman* constitutes an antipode to *The Mirror of the East*. Despite its slight size and relative lack of concern with the past, it is tempting to see *Watchman*'s use of elements and techniques of the *Mirror* genre as an additional factor in the persistence of the bifurcation of the *Mirrors* in the fourteenth century.

A PLACE FOR POETRY AND THE PAST

Watchman is a compact two scrolls and has long been tentatively attributed to Minamoto no Arifusa (1251–1319, also known as Rokujō Arifusa).[86] The preface begins like those of the *Mirrors* that predate *The Mirror of the East*: there is a return to the narrative convention of a trip to a temple that leads to an instructive transmission. This time, the narrator's destination is the Tendai temple Engyōji (or Enkyōji) in Harima (modern-day Hyōgo Prefecture). When the narrator arrives there, an Indian monk who is about fifty years old shows him the clogs of the Holy Man Shōkū (910–1007), the temple's long-ago founder, and once the other visiting mendicants have dispersed, the narrator and the monk become involved in a night-long conversation that forms the body of the text.

As with the earlier *Mirrors*, the choices of both site and interlocutor are significant. In setting the narrative at Engyōji, Arifusa returns his *Mirror* to the world of temples with strong imperial connections. The "Harima-no-kuni Shosha-zan engi" (Account of the Origins of Mount Shosha in Harima Province), attributed to the monk Kairin (dates unknown), repeatedly notes imperial pilgrimages to the site and stresses the ties of its temple's founder, Shōkū, to the first to make the journey, Emperor Kazan (968–1008).[87] In addition to Kazan's trips in 986 and 1002, as well as his sponsorship of the construction of the lecture hall (completed in 987), the account also records visits by Retired Emperor Goshi-

86. This attribution is in the colophon to the text as it appears in *Nomori no kagami*, 514. For a brief look at competing theories of authorship, see Kimbrough, "*Nomori no kagami* and the Perils," 99.

87. The colophon to the *engi* dates to 1644, so the source is not unproblematic for discussing the site's valence in the Kamakura period. Thus, it will be used primarily in the context of historically verifiable occurrences (Kairin, "Harima-no-kuni Shosha-zan engi").

rakawa in 1174 and the receipt of an imperial commission from Retired Emperor Gosaga (1220–72) in 1249 among its examples of the temple's continued success, even after Shōkū's death in 1007.[88] Engyōji clearly understands its prestige as stemming at least in part from continued imperial patronage. This is the first indication that *Watchman* has very different allegiances than those of *The Mirror of the East*.

The preface also reinstates the familiar form of an exchange between an enlightened informant and his or her audience, albeit with a twist. The informant is the first Indian monk to appear in a *Mirror*, and it is easy to conjecture that his presence is intended to call to mind the well-known tale of an encounter between the Japanese monk Gyōki (668–749) and Bodhisena (704–60) that includes an exchange of *waka*.[89] Even if the connection is not explicitly intended, the resonances may still be there, because unlike the previous *Mirrors* that promise a transmission about the past, *Watchman* soon reveals that both the narrator and the foreign monk who joins him in a nighttime vigil are praying about *waka*. The narrator rationalizes this by pointing out that Murasaki Shikibu composed *The Tale of Genji* after "a vision of Kannon at Ishiyama[dera Temple] was granted in response to her prayer" and speculates on the possibility of a similar result.[90] In this regard, too, the relocation to Engyōji is felicitous: the temple's *engi* reveals that Shōkū, in addition to composing *waka* himself, was in poetic communication via both *kanshi* and *waka* with famed poets of his day. Although the examples are limited in number, they include works by the noted *kanshi* poet Yoshishige no Yasutane (died 1002), the famed poet-monk Jakushō (962–1034), and Retired Emperor Kazan.

Although poetry is a new topic for the *Mirrors*, Arifusa is nevertheless not entering completely uncharted territory. *The New Mirror* and *The*

88. Kairin, "Harima-no-kuni Shosha-zan engi," 34:113 (on the events of 986 and 987), 115–16 (on 1002), 117 (on Goshirakawa), and 118 (on Gosaga). In addition, Godaigo visits in 1333 (Hasegawa, *Taiheiki*, 1:552–54; Helen McCullough, *Taiheiki*, 317–18).

89. On the Bodhisena stories in this time period, see Huey and Matisoff, "Lord Tamekane's Notes on Poetry," 134–35n27. Whether one should assume that the narrator's interlocutor follows the precedent suggested by Bodhisena's *waka* on this occasion and equate him (the narrator) with Mañjuśrī is never made explicit, although it would certainly have further boosted the narrator's prestige. Indeed, Gyōki heads a subsequent list of holy figures who produced poetry (*Nomori no kagami*, 477).

90. *Nomori no kagami*, 476.

Water Mirror had both already engaged discourses on literature, if not always directly. Not only did the former have a narrator who worked for Murasaki Shikibu in her youth and end with speculation about Murasaki's afterlife, but the latter also concluded with a reference to Murasaki's work. And *The China Mirror* had made effective use of citations from both Chinese and Japanese poets, above all in its preface. Thus, this thematic shift, while dramatic, does not mark a complete break with the priorities of the other *Mirrors*.

Nevertheless, the ensuing content has very little in common with that of the historiographic *Mirrors*. Arifusa, an adherent of the Nijō poetry lineage, devotes much of the first scroll to skewering the work of the progenitor of the rival Kyōgoku line, Tamekane (1254–1332), with occasional digressions on the evils of the monk Ippen (1239–89), his popular dancing *nenbutsu* practice, and his followers. In this attack, the narrator's opening gambit is a complaint to his interlocutor that despite the supposed inviolability of *waka*, Tamekane "turns his back on poetic mores that go back generations to [*waka*'s] origins" (*senzo yoyo no kaze o somuki*).[91] This is met with the Indian monk's damning assessment that even sage rulers are not guaranteed clever descendants, followed by the observation that "the Buddha, also, already [recognized] that his disciples would inevitably lose his teachings"—a response that simultaneously elevates the status of *waka* while aligning its practice with the risk of decline.[92] The remainder of the first scroll is spent on a six-point attack on Tamekane's poetry, interwoven with occasional comparisons to Ippen's movement and teachings.[93]

The first part of the second scroll is devoted to establishing a relationship between *waka* and musical modes, but the remainder of the work then turns to a critique of both more general *nenbutsu* adherents and Zen,

91. *Nomori no kagami*, 478.

92. *Nomori no kagami*, 478.

93. The charges levied against Tamekane, as well as the specific rhetoric they use, make the most sense when read together with Tamekane's poetic treatise of roughly a decade before, *Tamekane wakashō* (Tamekane's *Waka* Essentials, ca. 1285–87). For an annotated translation, see Huey and Matisoff, "Lord Tamekane's Notes on Poetry." See also Kimbrough, "*Nomori no kagami* and the Perils," 103n15. Kimbrough's essay provides an accessible overview of the criticisms leveled against Tamekane.

interspersed with ongoing criticism of Tamekane's verse.[94] At some urging from the narrator, the monk relates that he has lived in the mountains for the past thirty years, lamenting the decline of poetry.[95] He equates *waka* with Confucian virtues, in addition to their Buddhist properties and potential, and assigns them a "helping" role in the context of ritual music (*reigaku o tasuketsutsu*) before explaining how contemporary poetic form—in other words, Tamekane's—deviates from all of these.[96] The speaker then switches to a careful mapping of the relationship among ritual, music, and the pacification of people, including one's enemies. In a rare recourse to the extrapoetic world, he bolsters this position with both textual and historical precedents, including an account of how the Indian ruler King Pasenadi (sixth century BCE) repelled an attack with a virtuous drum performance.[97] Chinese music, in contrast, is charted as having been in a state of decline since its inception.[98] Superior music, the narrator concludes, is what enables the triumph of the "small country" over the "great." It is because of (the correct cultivation of) *waka* that Japan has been well governed and never invaded, and it is due to the lack of *waka* that China has lost the eight schools of Buddhism and been overrun by foreign brigands.[99]

Although historical events are likewise sporadically referred to in the ensuing discussion of preaching practices, this is largely in their role of origins or precedents, rather than a consideration of the past as such.[100] The general critiques of excessive devotion to chanting the *nenbutsu* and

94. For an account of *Nomori no kagami* that explicates this relationship between music and poetry, see Bialock, "From *Heike* to *Nomori no kagami*," 184–88. For a discussion of the criticism of Ippen's dancing *nenbutsu* (in particular) and Zen as representatively reactionary positions, see Gomi, *Shomotsu no chūseishi*, 487–89 and 494–96; for a discussion of poetry and authorship, see ibid., 498–502. Bialock also refers to the negative valence of *nenbutsu* and earlier scholarship on it ("From *Heike* to *Nomori no kagami*," 183, especially note 56). Marra also offers a brief summary of *Nomori no kagami* that characterizes it as grounded in Tendai thought (*Representations of Power*, 25–27).

95. *Nomori no kagami*, 495–96.

96. *Nomori no kagami*, 496.

97. *Nomori no kagami*, 497.

98. *Nomori no kagami*, 498.

99. *Nomori no kagami*, 498. See also Kimbrough, "*Nomori no kagami* and the Perils," 108n25. Zen is also blamed for the schools' loss (*Nomori no kagami*, 504).

100. *Nomori no kagami*, 499–502.

the spread of Zen both follow a similar pattern. The outbreak of the Jōkyū Disturbance and the "decline of the kingly way" are due to the proliferation of the practice of chanting the *nenbutsu*, which is likened to the "sounds of a dying state."[101] The "long ago" (mythical) military expedition to Silla and the successful 940 defeat of Masakado (mentioned in the introduction) are likewise ultimately attributed to the "promulgation of Tendai Law."[102] It is only in the occasional citation of a series of events that the text provides any sense of historical progression, as in Arifusa's attribution of a chain of disasters largely to the spread of Zen:

> The spread of the Zen sect throughout the provinces is thanks to the construction of Kenchōji Temple in the East. This was truly an instance of straying from the will of the *kami*, was it not? The horror of the famines in the Kenchō [1249–56], Shōka [1257–59], and Shōgen [1259–60] years and the suffering and death of the people! Because there were many who still did not know what to blame for this, even though a comet appeared in the Bun'ei [1264–75] period, and the Hakozaki palace burned down, without anyone who understood the gist of the oracle, we encountered the troubles with foreign kingdoms. From that time on through the present, the land has been in a state of unrest.[103]

Even when there is some sense of diachronic development, the text does not move beyond a narrative of currently occupying the final age of the dharma, with the targets of *Watchman*'s criticism as proof of the decline, and the dangers of failing to follow suitable teachings as well as the will

101. *Nomori no kagami*, 499 and 502. For more instances of the link between poetry and the Mongols, see Kimbrough, "*Nomori no kagami* and the Perils," 108–9. On "the sounds of a dying state" (or "a state going to ruin" per Bialock) more generally, see Bialock, "From *Heike* to *Nomori no kagami*," 177–79 and 183. For his discussion of how it relates to *Nomori no kagami* specifically, see ibid., 185–88, esp. 188 for a translation of the longer passage on the *nenbutsu* referred to above. For a short look at medieval discourse on such music, especially as it pertains to the *Heike*, see Bialock, "Biwa Masters and Musical Hierophanies," 127–33.

102. *Nomori no kagami*, 507. The vilification of Zen and the *nenbutsu*, especially the deleterious effects of both on the ability of a country to resist the Mongols, is not new. It can be found at least as far back as Nichiren's writing in 1270. On Nichiren, see Saeki Koji, "Mōko shūrai ikō no Nihon no tai-Kōrai kankei," 14.

103. *Nomori no kagami*, 509.

of the *kami* the ultimate warning. In other words, within *Watchman*, the past functions most often as a source of precedents, referred to only in the context of poetry or specific Buddhist practices. The declines of poetry and the Buddhist teachings that are the focus of the text are positioned against a backdrop in which the present age is understood to be inferior to the past, but rather than interpreting the past—the project of the earlier *Mirrors*—Arifusa's work treats the past as beyond contestation.

Watchman evinces a worldview in which things are irredeemably and inarguably worsening. To repeat, this is manifest in the decline of the Way of Poetry (*uta no michi*) and its imperiled existence in the final age, as well as the proliferation of corrupt teachings.[104] Arifusa bluntly characterizes the latter situation as follows: "Because basically, both Zen and the *nenbutsu* sects are truly teachings that circulate in the final age, they only have ignorant students."[105] Yet the latter days rhetoric is not used to suggest a larger historical trajectory; instead, it is used to interpret specific social and religious currents. This is a major difference from the historiographic *Mirrors*, where the course of history is inevitably mapped out in recognition of a larger cosmological logic in which the fate of the sovereignty or the polity is a manifestation of a bigger pattern. In contrast, Arifusa's use of this apocalyptic rhetoric is much more functionalist. He seems to be saying, with a shrug, "Tamekane's poetry, Zen, and the dancing *nenbutsu* are all terrible, but what do you expect? We're in the final age." He takes the forces that govern change as self-evident and directs the reader to consider the challenges the resulting condition poses.

PATTERNS AND PRINCIPLES

Although *Watchman*'s author evinces little interest in the past as such, the work nevertheless exhibits an engagement with language, as well as a usage of the mirror metaphor that is fairly consistent with the Heian *Mirrors*. As noted, *Watchman* is a *Mirror* that returns to the familiar pattern of a dialogue-based transmission written in *wabun*. This development makes sense, given the work's subject matter, yet Arifusa clarifies at one

104. On poetry's presumed fate, see *Nomori no kagami*, 484.
105. *Nomori no kagami*, 513.

point that there is more behind this decision than simply using Classical Japanese (*yamatokotoba*) to write about *waka* (or *uta*). This point is explicated as part of his larger discussion of Tamekane's inept and inappropriate use of language. Emphasizing the need for suitable and engaging language, the speaker explains: "Also, although expressions of inner thoughts and feelings are all the same, the language (*buntai*) thereof always varies, from sutras and their commentaries to Confucian texts, petitions to communiqués, Chinese characters (*mana*) to the syllabary (*kana*), vernacular tales to Classical Chinese verse. How on earth could *waka* and vulgar speech use the same [idiom]?!"[106] Here is an echo of the "Fireflies" argument from the *Genji* discussed in the introduction and chapter 2 that pointed to a clear correlation between form and content, or language (or even register) and meaning. As with the other *Mirrors*, *Watchman*'s use of a particular form of Japanese to narrate its teachings is meaningful. Language selection remains a way to "pattern" the message.[107]

The *Mirror* metaphor and the engagement with a principle-governed cosmos it is repeatedly used to suggest also appear in *Watchman*. Admittedly, the first use appears in the midst of Arifusa's repudiation of Tamekane's poetry and seems relatively free of cosmological portents. At the end of his criticism of Tamekane's "poetic form" (*sugata*) is a poem:[108]

Samazama ni	Despite the forms
miyuru sugata mo	variously reflected in you,
masukagami	clear mirror,
hitotsu omoi no	you have
kake ni zo arikeru.	but a single wish![109]

Considering that this comes in the wake of a charge that Tamekane neglects the proper form, a relatively straightforward reading of this as a mirror reflecting a (desired) reality is possible.

106. *Nomori no kagami*, 486–87. I have broken the list into what I read as implied contrasting pairs; the punctuation added to the typeset version is ambiguous.

107. "Pattern" in the sense of *mon* (Chinese *wen*). See the discussion of Kūkai in "What Is a *Mirror*?" in the introduction.

108. I follow Kimbrough in translating *sugata* as "poetic form" ("*Nomori no kagami* and the Perils," 102).

109. *Nomori no kagami*, 493.

The remaining imagery, however, has obvious Buddhist significance, which brings *Watchman* back to the rhetorical territory of the earliest *Mirrors.* Following his ten-point attack on Zen, Arifusa reminds the reader that the partnership between the buddhas and the *kami* is what safeguards Japan, with Ise Shrine as the central site of this cooperation.[110] Ise's inner and outer precincts are mapped to the Womb and the Diamond Realms of Esoteric Buddhism, and a mirror is located in the stream that flows through the grounds of the shrine.[111] This mirror, the reader is told, "is the Great Mirror of Perfect Cognition."[112] Subsequently, Arifusa reminds the reader that Tendai and Shingon are best suited to "manifesting Buddhist virtue and ensconcing the authority of the gods."[113] In this way, although the mirror here is not invoked for its specific power to reflect the past (or even the present), its ability to reveal an ultimate understanding of reality is nonetheless reaffirmed. Moreover, as Sasaki points out, this rhetoric replicates the divine country discourse espoused by the court (which included the idea of divine descent).[114] In this respect, too, *Watchman* takes a conservative stance.

This revelatory attribute to the mirror metaphor is, indeed, the last image with which the reader is presented. Although perhaps not obvious from the preceding discussion, the cosmological logic underpinning Arifusa's text is based on the interdependence of buddhas and *kami* in ways not entirely dissimilar to that in *The Mirror of the East.* This blend of veneration for buddhas and *kami* and the religiously charged symbol of the mirror converge in a brief postface. There, after first confessing that his pilgrimage to the temple was inspired by a dream oracle from none other

110. *Nomori no kagami*, 505.

111. This seems to be the same mirror that *The Mirror of the East* records on Jōkyū 3 (1221).3.22 as having appeared in Masako's dream (Nagahara and Kishi, *Zen'yaku Azuma kagami*, 3:326).

112. *Nomori no kagami*, 507. Because it is specified as one of five (rather than four), it is likely that Arifusa is referring to an Esoteric Buddhist context. This is consistent with the larger trend during the age of the Mongol invasions as described by Andreeva (*Assembling Shinto*, 181).

113. *Nomori no kagami*, 507.

114. Sasaki Kaoru, *Nihon chūsei shisō no kichō*, 134. It also is similar to the rhetoric of Ryōbu Shinto, which would become influential in the fourteenth century. However, given *Watchman*'s Tendai leanings, there is perhaps no direct connection. For a brief overview of Ryōbu and Ise Shinto, see Itō Satoshi, "Kami Merge with Buddhism," 84–88.

than *waka*'s patron *kami*, the Sumiyoshi deity—a gesture that draws a neat parallel between Murasaki Shikibu's divinely inspired work and his own—Arifusa explains his title.[115] He suggests that it refers to the unanticipated departure and reappearance of a hunting hawk, although his reference is elliptical: in the full version of the story, the hawk's reflection appears in a puddle of water in the field where its imperial owner is hunting.[116] He then offers that the mirror might be a reflection by the mind of one of lowly status like a field watchman (who, again unmentioned, spots the hawk's reflection), and he concludes that "it must mean the revelation of the 'original mind' mirrored in the pure waters of a field in the long-ago past."[117] The closing imagery once more firmly ties the mirror to the context of a cosmologically inspired transmission.

In summary, *Watchman* is at the other end of the spectrum of late thirteenth-century *Mirror* writing, a markedly conservative end. It suggests a concept of the *Mirror* in which the structure of the tale—above all, the presence of a conventional preface and postface—are indispensable elements. Furthermore, in contrast to *The Mirror of the East*, in *Watchman* the fixed setting at a temple plays a significant role by allowing the narrator to frame the work as a divine (or divinely inspired) transmission. While the temple is not in the *kinai* provinces, it does have imperial ties and is considerably closer to the court than the most recent *Mirror(s)*, suggesting a recentering of the imagined geography of the *Mirror* in the vicinity of older bodies of power. Most significant, despite the relatively narrow timeframe of its immediate focus and general lack of thematization of the past, *Watchman* offers a fundamentally pessimistic appraisal of the present in relation to it, which brings it in line with the *New Mirror*'s valorization of the past discussed in chapter 1. In short, whereas *The Mirror of the East* takes the reader to Kamakura with the implicit hope for the *bakufu*'s continued survival, *Watchman* returns the reader to a site that has its best days behind it, in a world filled with heterodox poetic prac-

115. For a short history of the Sumiyoshi deity's connection with poetry, see Klein, *Allegories of Desire*, 190–98.

116. This tale often features Emperor Yūryaku on a hunting expedition. A fuller account of the incident can be found, for instance, as an explanation for a *waka* in Kawamura, *Shūchūshō*, 195.

117. *Nomori no kagami*, 514.

tices and degenerate teachings. Both this formal division and the contrasting expectations that the two texts embody will find counterparts in the final two medieval historiographic *Mirrors*, the subject of chapter 5.

Conclusion

Looking back at the *Mirrors* before the Mongol invasions, we see that the genre has undergone gradual developments that continue to be relevant for understanding the late Kamakura *Mirrors*. These include a decline in the overt rhetoric of a specific cosmological principle that defines the historical trajectory, a move from circular to linear ordering of the reader's experience of time, and an increasing experimentation with the insertion of *kanbun* or *kanbun*-like text at regular intervals. In a comparison of the earlier *Mirrors* with the two immediately post-Mongol *Mirrors*, a difference in two traits stands out: the use of a temple as setting and the focus on the past as legible in terms of cosmological logic as subject matter. In *Watchman* and *The Mirror of the East*, these two elements are disaggregated. The latter retains the commitment to narrating the past, while the former assumes the rhetorical trappings of the temple setting.

Despite the two different forms taken by the late thirteenth-century *Mirrors*, their shared indifference to any specific rhetoric of principles is significant and deserves a bit more examination. In chapter 3, the look at Jien's *My Humble Thoughts* suggested some of the potential difficulties with "principle" rhetoric. One particular stumbling block appeared to be the challenge involved in producing a coherent yet sufficiently flexible principle-based discursive framework for a project more complicated than an effort to provide an alternative trajectory to final age decline. For *The Mirror of the East*, it is possible to postulate two elements that render "principle" rhetoric superfluous. First, as noted above, if "principles" rhetoric is most effective as an antidote to apocalyptic concerns, quite simply, *The Mirror of the East* does not seriously engage in a discourse of decline. Second, its world is clearly subject to cosmological principles, even if they are never named as such. But the principles are precisely those that sunk Jien's text into chaos—a world in which the will of the *kami* and buddhas is determinative, but in which these forces are also amenable to persuasion. As *My Humble Thoughts* demonstrated, this relationship does not readily yield a clear one-size-fits-all principle for interpreting historical development or establishing a clear authoritative trajectory.

This is still more noteworthy in the case of *Watchman*, precisely because it clearly rests on notions that there are rules for the views that it espouses. Yet rather than relying on "principles," Arifusa's rhetoric is based on the notion of "propriety" (*gi*) that governs the Way of Poetry and other laudable practices, as well as the "violations" (*ayamari*) that imperil them. But the term principle (*dōri*) does not occur even once. This may be because despite Arifusa's frequent references to the final age, he does not offer a way out, as it were. Or it may be that a more abstract principle-based rhetoric would have blunted his ability to make very specific, pointed attacks. As Jien's writing demonstrates, a proliferation of principles does not necessarily result in a more effective set of tools.

The obsolescence of principle rhetoric within the *Mirrors* even in a world that was still believed to be subject to cosmological logic was neither temporary nor limited. In the historiographic *Mirrors* that appear in the Muromachi period, there is no sign of this rhetoric at all, with the result that what sets a *Mirror* apart from other historiographic modes of writing becomes increasingly unclear. Nevertheless, even as the *Mirror* will cede its primacy over the historiographic landscape, as an authoritative voice, it has clearly arrived. These developments and their outcome can best be understood in the larger context of the wars, reshufflings of power, and instability that beset the Ashikaga shogunate, to which chapter 5 turns.

CHAPTER 5

Memories of *Mirrors*

Nostalgia for a Unified Realm

Main texts (in chronological order)

***Jinnō shōtōki* (A Chronicle of Gods and Sovereigns)**
Author: Kitabatake Chikafusa
Date: circa 1339–43
Language: mix of Chinese characters and *kana*
Preface: no
Setting: none specified
Time covered: the age of the gods–early reign of Emperor Gomurakami (1328–68)

***Baishōron* (Discussion on Plums and Pines)**
Author: unknown
Date: circa 1351
Language: mix of Chinese characters and *kana*
Preface: yes
Setting: Kitano Tenmangū Shrine (Kyoto)
Time Covered: the reign of Emperor Keikō (traditionally first or second century CE)–the enthronement of Emperor Sukō (1334–98)

***Masukagami* (The Clear Mirror)**
Author: attributed to Nijō Yoshimoto
Date: circa 1368–75
Language: *wabun*
Preface: yes
Setting: Seiryōji Temple (Kyoto)
Time covered: the abdication of Emperor Takakura Emperor (1161–81)–the 1333 return to the capital of Emperor Godaigo (1288–1339)

***Shinmeikyō* (The Mirror of the Gods)**
Author: unknown
Date: late fourteenth century, added to through 1434
Language: *hentai kanbun*
Preface: no
Setting: none stated; the implied center is Kyoto
Time covered: the reign of Emperor Jinmu (traditionally seventh century BCE)–the early reign of Emperor Gohanazono (1419–1470)

Just as the *Mirrors* had survived the Genpei War and the Mongol invasions, they also withstood the fall of the Kamakura *bakufu*. The last of the medieval historiographic *Mirrors* breaks off in 1434, just decades before the Ōnin War (1467–77) ushered Japan into roughly a century of conflict now referred to as the Warring States period. Returning to where chapter 4 left off, the first two-thirds of the fourteenth century—the time that would pass before the appearance of the two Muromachi historiographic *Mirrors*—saw substantial changes both domestically and abroad. To the west, the fall of the Yuan (1271–1368) and establishment of the Ming (1368–1644) meant that China was again under Chinese rule. Within Japan, the Kamakura shogunate collapsed in 1333, to be succeeded by the short-lived Kenmu Restoration (1333–36). The failure of the latter, in turn, led to the dissolution of the imperial house into the competing Northern (Kyoto) and Southern (Yoshino) Courts (1336–92), with each championing its own imperial line. Although Ashikaga Takauji (1305–58) was named shogun in 1338, marking the official founding of the Ashikaga (or Muromachi) *bakufu*, this did not signal an end to instability.[1] Further unrest followed only a short while later in the form of the Kannō Disturbance (1350–52).[2] With so many competitions for power, it is not unexpected that the half-century of shake-ups and armed struggle after the Mongol attacks saw a burst of historiographic production, much of it *Mirror*-inspired, as various parties attempted to stake their claims to legitimacy.

1. An overview of these developments can be found in Hall, "Muromachi Bakufu," especially 175–93. On the date of Takauji's appointment, see ibid., 187.

2. I follow Thomas Conlan in the translation of *Kannō no jōran* and in the assessment thereof. For a brief comparison of the impact of the Kenmu Restoration and the Kannō Disturbance in terms of casualties, see Conlan, *State of War*, 57.

Among these developments, the creation of rival courts and the fundamental disunity that embodied seems to have been the catalyst for the production of several of the textual efforts to order the past. Certainly emperors had been exiled before, including the expulsion of Godaigo, the founder of the Yoshino Court, to the Oki Islands in 1332, but having two separate contending courts was unprecedented. Godaigo's bitter verse plaint—selected from "among those poems composed at the temporary palace in Yoshino" by his son, Prince Munenaga (born 1311–12), for inclusion in the *Shin'yō wakashū* (New Leaves Waka Collection, compiled in 1381)—effectively evokes a sense of displacement and distress that may well have resonated with many partisans of the Yoshino Court:

Fushiwabinu	Unable to sleep,
shimo samuki yo no	my pallet in shambles
toko wa arete	beneath the chill night's frost,
sode ni hageshiki	my sleeves blown
yamaoroshi no kaze	by blustering mountain gales.[3]

The imagery is evocative of a disordered hostile environment and inadequate defense against outside powers. This is surely not how the keeper of the imperial regalia should be, buffeted by forces beyond his control and removed from the palace proper. In fact, the anxiety and precarity of a divided court that Godaigo effectively captures in this poem seem to underlie both of the final *Mirrors* and their split allegiances—*The Clear Mirror* (circa 1368–75) and *The Mirror of the Gods* (late fourteenth or early fifteenth century)—as well as other contemporary attempts at narrativizing the past, including Kitabatake Chikafusa's *Jinnō shōtōki* (A Chronicle of Gods and Sovereigns, written circa 1339–1343) and the *Baishōron* (Discussion on Plums and Pines, written circa 1351).[4]

3. Fukatsu and Kimishima, *Shin'yō wakashū*, 89.

4. Ōmori Kitayoshi sees the fourteenth century as a turning point in historiography ("'Masukagami' no rekishi jojutsu," 9). The dating of the *Baishōron* is from Uyenaka and Conlan, "Baishoron," 21. Their assessment is based on a 2005 study. More recently, Takeda Masanori has proposed consideration of a date as late as 1354 ("Ashikaga no ken'i," 76).

Despite the variety of perspectives and genres suggested by the above four titles, these works are all written with an awareness of earlier *Mirrors*, demonstrating that however marginal its origins, by the early fourteenth century the *Mirror* genre had become one of the, if not the, major means of refracting the past. These works, *Mirrors* and non-*Mirrors* alike, also share characteristics that make it profitable to consider them together. Each faces the challenge of chronicling a past that has, in a sense, failed. Both *Gods and Sovereigns* and *The Clear Mirror* culminate in the imperial restoration, albeit from a time when the restoration had already collapsed. *Plums and Pines*, in contrast, concludes with the Ashikaga victory but dates from an age in which Ashikaga authority was already imperiled by the fraternal conflict between Ashikaga Takauji, the first shogun, and his increasingly powerful younger brother Tadayoshi (1306–52). *The Mirror of the Gods* concludes awkwardly with a series of trouble-filled entries from after the reunification of the Northern and Southern Courts.

This chapter examines these developments from two main perspectives. It begins by looking at the *Mirror*-influenced historiographic projects that emerge between the last of the Kamakura *Mirrors* and their two Muromachi counterparts. In the century or so covered in chapters 1–3, the *Mirrors* seemed to be gaining in stature, taking on increasingly ambitious subject matter and replicating ever more obviously the narrative structure and language of orthodox historiography, while at the same time maintaining an overt commitment to understanding the past in terms of cosmological theories. However, chapter 4 demonstrated that even as the concerns that were common to all of the earlier *Mirrors*—the articulation of the cosmos, the geographical site of legitimation, the negotiation between old and new languages and forms of political authority, and the relation to the past—persisted, the late thirteenth-century *Mirrors* exhibited major differences from their predecessors. The most striking change was the polarization of the manifestation of these concerns: a *kanbun-wabun* divide, a divergence between court and *bakufu* orientations, and possibilities for either pessimistic or optimistic readings of the past. In addition to this bifurcation, the genre also witnessed the complete abandonment of clearly articulated principle-derived historical trajectories. I suggest that it is this breakdown of the principle-place-language-past framework that comes to limit the *Mirrors'* specific cachet as productive historiographic tools, even as it reflects greater sociohistorical realities. One result of this, as this chapter will argue, is that both of the *Mirrors'* final medieval iterations are primarily legible as expressions of a historiographic nostalgia. Ironically, the true indication of the *Mirrors'* attainment of mainstream status is their use in precisely this capacity: the genre that originated as a celebration of the past as meaningful on multiple levels becomes part of the past that is desired.

To assess the legacies of this breakdown more broadly, as well as to highlight how central to historiography the *Mirrors* and their concerns had become, this chapter first turns to the two alternative historiographic approaches suggested by the abovementioned *Gods and Sovereigns* and *Plums and Pines.*[5] Early historiographic projects from the age of the Ashikaga shoguns, both of these works adopt some of the *Mirror* techniques with uneven results. This chapter will then consider their respective appropriations of *Mirror* elements in comparison with the rhetorical strategies suggested by the preface to the more popular *Tale of the Heike.* Lastly, in light of the varied receptions of these works and their techniques, the chapter will turn to *The Clear Mirror* and *The Mirror of the Gods* to examine how the disaggregation of cosmological principle, place, and the past has impacted the ability of a *Mirror* or a similarly inspired text to present a persuasive account of the events it relates. In this light, the *Mirrors* become more meaningful for their remembered prestige than as powerful or persuasive tools for interpreting history.

In Between: Gods, Plums, *and the* Heike

Appearing approximately sixty years after the last of the Kamakura *Mirrors* and several years after the overthrow of the Kamakura *bakufu*, *Gods and Sovereigns* and *Plums and Pines* are the mid-fourteenth century's earliest answers to *The Mirror of the East.* Both predate *The Clear Mirror* and

5. *Gods and Sovereigns* is probably the best known of the fourteenth-century historiographic projects today. This is due in part, I suspect, to the success of H. Paul Varley's English translation (*Chronicle of Gods and Sovereigns*).

the likely beginning of *The Mirror of the Gods* by three to four decades, dovetailing with these last two of the medieval historiographic *Mirrors* in ways that further contextualize the latter's formal and thematic nostalgia. All four, in turn, are products of the period of the Northern and Southern Courts in a post-Mongol-invasions Japan, a time in which "self-awareness of their country's uniqueness" had been "ignited."[6] Most significantly for the fate of the *Mirrors*, especially as a type of writing that primarily defined historical trajectories in terms of, or in reaction to, Buddhist principles of decline, it was also an age in which divine country thought experienced "unprecedented expansion" and Shinto began to emerge as a more powerful force, thanks to the proactive theorization occurring at Ise Shrine.[7]

These developments in the intellectual climate notwithstanding, why, after an apparent move to the center, did the *Mirrors* all but disappear from the historiographic scene after the mid-fifteenth century until the seventeenth century? After all, the genre had shown itself to be malleable and resilient. Some explanation for this can be found in the following look at *Gods and Sovereigns*, *Plums and Pines*, and the opening to the *Heike*. It reveals the possibility of deeper problems with ordering the past—specifically, the reliance upon narrative place and cosmological authority—in an increasingly factious age. *Gods and Sovereigns* and *Plums and Pines* take different approaches to establishing order, but neither successfully resolves the difficulties. Their imperfect solutions in particular foreshadow the final turn toward the past that the Muromachi historiographic *Mirrors* take.

CHRONICLES OF THE PAST: GODS AND SOVEREIGNS

The rhetoric and cosmological logic of both *Gods and Sovereigns* and *Plums and Pines* suggests that it was precisely these challenges—how to synthesize changing scales of place, principle, and the past—that fourteenth-

6. Sasaki Kaoru, *Nihon chūsei shisō no kichō*, 140. On the impact of the Mongol invasions, see ibid., 133–35.

7. On the spread of divine country thought, see Sasaki Kaoru, *Nihon chūsei shisō no kichō*, 137. On Shinto, see ibid., 139.

century historiographers were confronting.[8] In Sasaki Kaoru's analysis, both works also promote Confucian notions of rule by virtue, even as they embody different positions. *Gods and Sovereigns* speaks to the Southern Court's values and its allegiance with the traditional court elite; *Plums and Pines* reflects the Northern Court's position, including its reliance upon warrior power.[9] The challenge underlying each work at a basic level is that of winning readers to its cause in an unstable polity with two courts competing for legitimacy. The differing rhetorical strategies are reminiscent of those seen in *The Mirror of the East* and *The Mirror of the Watchman in the Fields*: *Gods and Sovereigns* has no place but promises an amorphous principle, while *Plums and Pines* offers no explicit principle but grounds its narrative in a very particular place.

Kitabatake Chikafusa's *Gods and Sovereigns* relates the imperial genealogy from the age of the gods through the reign of the Southern Court emperor Gomurakami (1328–68). In returning its reader to a world familiar from the earliest *Mirrors* (the imperial court), it also takes up a familiar genre (the chronicle) for asserting an orthodox position. There are few obvious commonalities with the other *Mirrors* beyond a broad interest in narrativizing historical events: for instance, *Gods and Sovereigns* appears unconcerned with the prestige gained or lost through its selected linguistic medium, with the oldest manuscripts in mixtures of Chinese characters and *kana*.[10] Yet given Chikafusa's claim in the first section that

8. There are conflicting assessments of the fate of *Gods and Sovereigns*, depending in part on its presumed original audience. Iwasa Masashi, for instance, assumes an imperial audience and conjectures a wide reading in the Southern Court and among the warriors of the East, with the latter claim based on the proliferation of errors that resulted in a revised edition of 1343 (*Jinnō shōtōki*, 12). On later medieval engagement with and additions to the work, see ibid., 21–24. Conlan attributes the revisions to an effort "to further persuade eastern warriors to support the Southern Court," without suggesting that these were successful (*From Sovereign to Symbol*, 71). Varley mainly skirts the issue of contemporary reception, other than noting that Chikafusa did not manage to persuade Yūki Chikatomo to back the Southern Court (Kitabatake Chikafusa and H. Paul Varley, *Chronicle of Gods and Sovereigns*, 5–6). Shuzo Uyenaka provides the harshest characterization, observing, "The *Jinnō shōtōki* apparently failed to perform its immediate function of rallying north-eastern warriors to the loyalist cause" ("Study of *Baishōron*," 63).

9. Sasaki Kaoru, *Nihon chūsei shisō no kichō*, 137–38.

10. On the various manuscripts, see Iwasa, *Jinnō shōtōki*, 13–18. This being said, if part of its purpose was to reach a warrior audience, writing in *kanbun* would have seemed ill-advised. Compare Fukazawa, "Rekishi no 'gaibu' ni tatsu koto," 145–46.

he will "save [us] from disorder born of ignorance" and "discuss the principles of direct succession to the throne from the age of the gods," it is worth taking a closer look at the role that principles (and other *Mirror* features) do or do not play in his account.[11]

To begin with, reminiscent of *The Mirror of the East*, *Gods and Sovereigns* has no preface to invoke a site that enhances its claims. In light of the political situation at the time, it is not safe to assume that not assigning an explicit setting to the narrative is equivalent to considering the setting to be unimportant. Rather, this move is perhaps to be expected: *Gods and Sovereigns* is loyal to the Yoshino Court, a setting that its adherents hoped was temporary (as seen in the preface to Godaigo's poem above in this chapter). The work opens simply with the assertion that "Japan is the land of the divine," a move that can easily be read as implying a position that speaks for all of Japan.[12] While this suggests a claim to polity-wide authority that may also be a goal of *The Mirror of the East*, there is no obvious direct connection.

However, further examination shows *Gods and Sovereigns* to be a text that is indisputably aware of earlier *Mirrors*, even if it stops short of acknowledging them openly. This is discernible in an oblique refutation of an account of events during the reign of Emperor Seiwa, as well as, I suggest, in a later admonition to "regard the gains and losses of recent times and use them as a mirror for the future."[13] This rhetoric is reminiscent of

11. Iwasa, *Jinnō shōtoki*, 49. The translation is after Kitabatake Chikafusa and H. Paul Varley, *Chronicle of Gods and Sovereigns*, 61. I have relied heavily on Varley's translation in this discussion. Shimokawa Ryōko points out that Chikafusa sets all of this forth as a means of favorably distinguishing Japanese history from Chinese ("'Jinnō shōtōki' no rekishi jojutsu," 440 and 446–48). She also attributes Chikafusa's interest in "principles" to Sima Guang and even more so to Zhu Xi, before arguing for engagement with the *Chunqiu*, as well (for Sima Guang and Zhu Xi, see ibid., 452–54; for the *Chunqiu*, see ibid., 454–57). This does not, however, preclude the possibility of influence from the *Mirrors*, of which Chikafusa was clearly aware.

12. Iwasa, *Jinnō shōtoki*, 41. The translation is after Kitabatake Chikafusa and H. Paul Varley, *Chronicle of Gods and Sovereigns*, 49.

13. Iwasa, *Jinnō shōtoki*, 164. The translation is after Kitabatake Chikafusa and H. Paul Varley, *Chronicle of Gods and Sovereigns*, 231. On Seiwa, see Iwasa, *Jinnō shōtoki*, 120n13; Kitabatake Chikafusa and H. Paul Varley, *Chronicle of Gods and Sovereigns*, 168n119. On the interpretation of the warning, Iwasa simply cites a Ming dynasty dictionary (*Jinnō shōtōki*, 164n5). Wei Zheng, the advisor to Taizong mentioned in chap-

the lines of Tang Taizong that were echoed in *The China Mirror*. However, the most obvious *Mirror* reference turns up in the discussion of the practice of writing histories that appears in the middle of the entry on the reign of Emperor Kōkō (830–87). Without preamble, Chikafusa follows up a remark on the sovereign's death with a larger mission statement for his work. In it, he emphasizes that divine will is ultimately behind all matters of succession, while at the same time positioning his project in a larger historiographic context: "There have since ancient times been many writings in the possession of the great families that trace in general terms the history of imperial succession. My writing this book, therefore, is in no way exceptional. It has simply been my intent to discuss the basic reason why there has been no disruption of the legitimate line of imperial succession . . . from the time of the age of the gods."[14] For the present study, what is more significant than the promise that imperial succession always eventually works out as it should is that in these lines Chikafusa explicitly positions his work vis-à-vis not only imperially commissioned histories, but also unofficial histories: those "in the possession of the great families," such as the *Mirrors*, that deal with matters of succession.[15] In other words, even if the more recent *Mirrors* are not acknowledged, *Gods and Sovereigns* is nevertheless being written in a world in which the legacy of the *Mirrors* continues to be recognized.

It is also a text that makes recourse to cosmological forces, most specifically the will of the *kami* (although Buddhism is also addressed). However, the repeated nods to living in a degenerate age, the refrain that succession is governed by the will of the gods, and the concern with the preservation of the "imperial regalia" notwithstanding, Chikafusa's sometimes vague principle of succession does not allow for much in the way of interpretive history.[16] Early on, when explaining the diminution of the

---

ter 3, appears in Emperor Gouda's biography (see Iwasa, *Jinnō shōtōki*, 167; Kitabatake Chikafusa and H. Paul Varley, *Chronicle of Gods and Sovereigns*, 236).

14. Iwasa, *Jinnō shōtoki*, 124. The translation is after Kitabatake Chikafusa and H. Paul Varley, *Chronicle of Gods and Sovereigns*, 173.

15. Iwasa takes this as not only referring to the *kagamimono* but also potentially including a range of "private" histories, among them the *Gukanshō* (*Jinnō shōtōki*, 205n32).

16. For a very explicit statement on the indispensability of the regalia, see Iwasa, *Jinnō shōtoki*, 66; Kitabatake Chikafusa and H. Paul Varley, *Chronicle of Gods and Sov-*

human life span, he avers, "The Way of the Gods is impossible to understand."[17] Later, in a similarly problematic moment, he declares that the matter might have been "decided by Amaterasu herself, in which event its purpose cannot be comprehended by mortal minds."[18] In short, Chikafusa's history does invoke cosmological forces, not unlike the *Mirrors* before him, but he does so in a way that is reminiscent of the challenges that Jien's *My Humble Thoughts* faced. Whereas Jien is prepared to offer seemingly unlimited principles to accommodate historical change, Chikafusa takes the opposite tack: there is only one principle, but it is often illegible to his reader. I suppose this to be indicative both of an ongoing effort to render the cosmos as governed by logic on the part of writers and of the limitations of the specific rhetorical device of the principle when required to impart a clear order to an increasingly unstable picture. Nevertheless, the device's persistence in historiographic projects other than the *Mirrors* suggests that the ability to interpret the logic behind the past, rather than simply recording events, continued to attract medieval thinkers.

Chikafusa's focus on the imperial institution, one might argue, is analogous to the focus on the office of the shogun seen in *The Mirror of the East*. In this sense, the aspirations of *Gods and Sovereigns* (recognition of lasting imperial legitimacy), like those of *The Mirror of the East*, do not demand a specific historical trajectory. They merely demand plausible proof of correctness, which Chikafusa gamely supplies through interpretations of varying clarity.[19] Perhaps this is one reason why *Gods and Sovereigns*, like *The Mirror of the East*, met with enthusiastic readers later. Yet even as it probably found sympathetic ears among contemporary imperial loyalists, it is unsurprising that it failed to rally warriors to its

---

ereigns, 84. Even if one takes into account the defining role of Confucian virtue in determining legitimacy, this does not alleviate the abstruseness of Chikafusa's logic much. On Chikafusa's rhetoric as a fusion of Shinto myths and (Neo-)Confucianism, see Shimokawa, "'Jinnō shōtōki' no rekishi jojutsu," 438–48.

17. Iwasa, *Jinnō shōtoki*, 66. The translation is modified from Kitabatake Chikafusa and H. Paul Varley, *Chronicle of Gods and Sovereigns*, 84.

18. Iwasa, *Jinnō shōtoki*, 90. The translation is from Kitabatake Chikafusa and H. Paul Varley, *Chronicle of Gods and Sovereigns*, 120.

19. Michele Marra proposes that "on the premises that Japan is located in the sphere of eternity and that evil is the product of human activity, Chikafusa can reject completely the theory of historical decline (*mappō*)" ("Conquest of Mappō," 333).

cause.[20] If nothing else, it is missing two of the elements of the earlier successful *Mirrors* that spawned imitation: a specific locus of authority and a clear historical trajectory grounded in cosmological logic. There is no divine transmission to prove that Yoshino is the site to which the cosmologically discerning should flock to move forward along a divinely endorsed path.

To be sure, all that this demonstrates is a particular technique that does not work well. To see what Ashikaga partisans thought would be effective, these absences must be read against the appropriations of early *Mirror* writing found in *Plums and Pines*. As it turns out, *Plums and Pines* similarly misses the mark when it comes to attracting a broad contemporary readership. However, its *Mirror*-inspired position suggests that much like appeals to an ordered cosmos, ties to an authority of place continued to exert a powerful, if inconsistent, pull.[21]

DISCUSSIONS OF THE PAST: PLUMS AND PINES

Plums and Pines, a pro-Ashikaga work of uncertain authorship, recalls in many ways the more traditional *Mirrors*:[22] the language is a variety of Classical Japanese (Chinese characters interspersed with *katakana*),[23] and the narrative is an exchange between an elderly informant and an inquisitive interlocutor set at a temple.[24] The occasion is an observance of the anniversary of Sugawara no Michizane's death, and thus it is not entirely unexpected that the setting is the Bishamondō Hall on the grounds of Kyoto's Kitano Shrine. As for the *Mirrors* before it, for *Plums and Pines*, the return to Kyoto is about more than simply following the geographi-

20. As noted above, there is not complete consensus on the early readerships of these works.

21. Uyenaka and Conlan, "Baishoron," 18.

22. Conlan argues that the author is most likely from the Munakata family (Uyenaka and Conlan, "Baishoron," 21–26).

23. This is based on the image of the oldest surviving manuscript from Kanshō 7 (1466) (see Yashiro and Kami, *Baishōron*, second unnumbered plate).

24. Indeed, Fukuda Akimichi points out how the work's rhetoric pays homage to *The Great Mirror*, both in explicit metaphorical uses of the mirror image and in similar locutions to those found in the earlier work ("Rekishi monogatari toshite no 'Baishōron,'" 2–3). Fukuda also notes the structural similarities with the *Mirrors* and other *wakumonogatari* (framed tales).

cal relocation of *bakufu* authority to the capital. Rather, Kitano Shrine was a site of major significance for the Ashikaga, as demonstrated by Hosokawa Taketoshi's observation of the close ties to the shrine and its deity that the Ashikaga maintained from Takauji onward.[25] Moreover, Matthew Stavros's recent discovery that the Tōji'in Temple (site of the graves of the first two Ashikaga shoguns at the time of *Plums and Pines*' composition), Yoshimitsu's (later) palace, and the shrine align "along an east-west axis" suggests that the decision to relate the origin story of the Ashikaga shogunate at that particular site, a clear Ashikaga "power spot" (for lack of a better term), was a deliberate one.[26]

To return to the events of the preface, as is soon revealed, one of the audience members has a nagging wish to learn "the full story of how the present Shogun [Ashikaga Takauji] came to overthrow his predecessor and, after establishing the basis of his good fortune, to surpass all others in glory."[27] A learned priest volunteers to explain, and what follows is the history of the founding of the Ashikaga *bakufu*. The first thing provided is an enumeration of all of the shoguns—a history of the office that stretches back to the origins of Japan, in which the shogun is inevitably presented as working in tandem with the emperor prior to the Jōkyū Disturbance.[28] What follows is an event-driven history that concludes with the enthronement of Emperor Sukō (1334–98) in 1348, in what turned out to be a temporary calm before the Ashikaga turned on each other in 1350.

Like *The Mirror of the East* and *Watchman*, *Plums and Pines* subscribes to a view of the cosmos as governed by the powers of the *kami* and buddhas. In addition to numerous references to particular events determined

25. Hosokawa, "Ashikaga Yoshimitsu no kitayama shintoshin kōsō," 97. On the contested sites of authority early in the Muromachi period, see Stavros, "Sanjō bōmon Temple-Palace Complex."

26. Stavros, "Monuments and Mandalas in Medieval Kyoto," 351, figure 4. The extension of "Axis 1" to Kitano does not appear in the article but is the subject of a "field note" available on YouTube (Stavros, "Kitano Shrine and Muromachi"). For a discussion of some of the other buildings along this axis, see Stavros, "Monuments and Mandalas in Medieval Kyoto," 349–50.

27. Yashiro and Kami, *Baishōron*, 36. The translation is from Uyenaka and Conlan, "Baishoron," 29.

28. As Fukuda points out, while not all of those listed as shoguns actually held that rank, the individuals in question are all known for martial exploits (Rekishi monogatari toshite no 'Baishōron,'" 4).

by divine favor (or lack thereof), there are more dramatic episodes as well. These include a series of divine battlefield manifestations recorded in the entry for Kenmu 3 (1336).5.15, when "the spirit of Tenjin's messenger appeared, shining, in each battle, inspiring great confidence in Takauji's men,"[29] and an oracular dream ordering that battles on Mount Hie must be avoided, lest "the Buddhism of my [the dream deity's] mountain . . . be destroyed."[30] Such isolated instances of otherworldly intervention notwithstanding, *Plums and Pines* cannot be said to have a driving cosmological principle that reveals a trajectory for historical events. In this, too, it is similar to both *The Mirror of the East* and *Watchman*.

Whereas the absence of an explicit cosmological principle does not undermine the aspirational institutional focus of *The Mirror of the East*, it may be what limits the suasive potential of *Plums and Pines*, which is ostensibly a celebration of the unity and stability achieved by Takauji and a testament to his enduring legacy.[31] After all, Takauji's peace had already dissolved into war by the time *Plums and Pines* was completed, making the work, in Conlan's words, "ideologically obsolescent" from the outset.[32] In this regard, *Plums and Pines* faces a conundrum similar to that of *The Water Mirror*: how to order the past in a way that is not undermined by recent events. *The Water Mirror* achieved this by recourse to a vast cosmological framework. *Plums and Pines* simply avoids the question. These very different responses may be indicative of why *The Water Mirror* continued to be read over two centuries later, while *Plums and Pines* fell into nearly immediate neglect.[33] At the same time, the inability

29. Yashiro and Kami, *Baishōron*, 116. The translation is from Uyenaka and Conlan, "Baishoron," 98.

30. Yashiro and Kami, *Baishōron*, 129. The translation is from Uyenaka and Conlan, "Baishoron," 110.

31. See Yashiro and Kami, *Baishōron*, 141. For the corresponding events in English, see Uyenaka and Conlan, "Baishoron," 120.

32. Uyenaka and Conlan, "Baishoron," 17. The incommensurability of its stance with reality is further heightened if one accepts Kitamura Masayuki's suggestion that the "fraternal bond" between Takauji and Tadayoshi is a leitmotif in *Plums and Pines*, with rhetoric possibly intended to encourage a "reappraisal" of Tadayoshi ("'Baishōron' no seijisei," 296 and 308–10).

33. The mid-fourteenth-century narrator of *The Clear Mirror* admits, for instance, to a passing familiarity with *The Water Mirror*. See Kidō, *Masukagami*, 7; Perkins, *Clear Mirror*, 28.

of a principle-free, place-grounded narrative to win readers may point to the limited ability of a narrowly confined geographical site, particularly one associated with the power of a family whose members were at war with each other, to resonate with a broad audience in an age of upheaval.

TALES OF THE PAST: THE HEIKE

The limited medieval readership of both *Gods and Sovereigns* and *Plums and Pines* should not be mistaken for an indication that either cosmological logic or the symbolism of place was no longer of concern. Both elements appear in the preface to *The Tale of the Heike*, a work that deals with events central to many of the *Mirrors* and that was taking shape in the interim between the Kamakura and Muromachi *Mirrors*.[34] And unlike either of the *Mirror*-influenced experiments just discussed, the *Heike* seized the medieval imagination.[35] Although a full treatment of the *Heike* falls outside the scope of this chapter, the work deserves mention both as a way of contextualizing its fourteenth-century status—its subsequent popularity notwithstanding, the *Heike* was but one experiment among many with narrativizing the past in this time period—and to show what the basic rhetorical strategies on view in its preface may reflect about a gap between medieval audience expectations and developments within *Mirror* rhetoric.

From the perspective of *Mirror* writing, the *Heike*'s representation of the cosmos as governed by principles and its invocation of place, both of which occur in its opening lines, are the most striking elements. There is no evidence that the *Heike* was influenced by any of the *Mirrors*, but both of these aspects demonstrate how far-reaching the concerns that underpin the *Mirrors* continued to be in the mid- to late fourteenth century. To begin with, like the *Mirrors*, the *Heike* promises a cosmological ex-

34. For a short summary of the dating of the (now canonical) Kakuichibon and (earliest known) Engyōbon versions of the *Heike*, see Selinger, *Authorizing the Shogunate*, 8–9n15; for a fuller account, see ibid., 17–20. See also Tyler, *Tale of the Heike*, xxii–xxiii.

35. This is not to attribute canonical status to it, but rather to call attention to its wide performance and consumption in various forms, as well as to its usefulness as source material for other medieval works, such as *nō* plays. I also do not wish to imply that there was a single set version of the *Heike* at this time. David Bialock documents the *Heike*'s modern canonization as well as diverse premodern practices of its performance ("Nation and Epic," especially 164–68).

planation for historical change. This works on multiple levels. It can be seen most obviously in the rhetoric of precedent and promise of causality that are featured in the preface. The famous opening lines read: "The Jetavana Temple bells/ ring the passing of all things./ Twinned sal trees, white in full flower,/ declare the great man's certain fall./ The arrogant do not long endure:/ They are like a dream one night in spring./ The bold and brave perish in the end:/ they are as dust before the wind."[36] The audience knows at once that the tale to follow will be illustrative of the timeless truths set forth here.[37] These are very basic principles that order all historical change.

At the same time, however, as Vyjayanthi Selinger demonstrates in her analysis of the *Heike* texts' "representational mechanisms," this is more than just the promise of laws that the early *Mirrors* in particular offer. Instead, multiple elements of the work can be read as generative of "order."[38] The specifics of Selinger's analysis are nontextual phenomena and the implied belief systems that render their treatment in the *Heike* meaningful: bodies, behaviors, symbolically charged weaponry, and even modes of movement. Closely examining the depiction of these objects and practices, she shows them to be "expressive devices through which historical change is explained," an approach that highlights the deeply political nature of textualizing the past.[39] The sheer variety of means for manifesting order that Selinger interrogates demonstrates that the *Heike* texts attest to or enable a regulated world in ways that do not always dovetail with the methods of the *Mirrors*. Yet in the commitment to historical change as fundamentally principled—discernible not only in the legitimating orders that Selinger locates but also explicitly in the *Heike*'s opening lines, the work's vision of the past accords with the positions

36. Ichiko, *Heike monogatari*, 19. The translation is from Tyler, *Tale of the Heike*, 3.

37. Hyodo Hiromi builds on a close reading of the preface to argue that seeming pairs of mutually constitutive "relativized" perspectives or principles run throughout the *Heike* ("'Heike monogatari' joshōron"). The central role Hyodo accords to the preface in establishing this mode of reading is most germane to the present analysis, as it attests to the convention of reading the preface for a key as to how to interpret the entire *Heike*.

38. On "representational mechanisms," see Selinger, *Authorizing the Shogunate*, 12. For a clear summary of these claims, see ibid., 167. On the tension between "reflecting" and "producing" in her reading, see ibid., 169.

39. Selinger, *Authorizing the Shogunate*, 2.

taken by several of its contemporaries, be they the Kamakura *Mirrors* or the variation on *Mirror* writing from the early thirteenth century found in *Gods and Sovereigns*.

In addition to the promise to teach a lesson—reflecting a cosmological principle, even if that specific rhetoric is not used—the opening lines of the *Heike* also firmly place the story within a geography that is related to the tale's lesson. The tale's preface follows the transmission of Buddhism itself, and hence of the principles it promotes, beginning with India as a site. The assertion that "the Jetavana Temple bells/ ring the passing of all things," while "twinned sal trees, white in full flower,/ declare the great man's certain fall," firmly locates an origin for the tale's lessons at a site believed to have hosted none other than the historical Buddha.[40] From there, it moves eastward to China, listing several precedents of profligate power wielders "far away in the Other Realm," all of whom "spurned the governance established/ by their lords of old, by sovereigns past,/ sought pleasure and ignored all warnings,/ blind to ruin threatening the realm,/ deaf to suffering people's cries./ So it was that they did not last:/ Their lot was annihilation."[41] The preface's journey concludes with arrival in "our sovereignty" and one last enumeration of men brought low before alighting on its true focus: "Yet all still pale beside that man/ among us in the recent past:/ the novice monk of Rokuhara,/ former chancellor, his lordship/ Taira no Kiyomori."[42] In this way, the preface's geographic progression works to enhance its claims to a truth that the text will then transmit within a Buddhist geography. As its narrative moves ever closer to its audience, "our sovereignty" becomes one site among several that provide proof of the transcendence of the lesson to follow.

Although stylistically the *Heike* preface is unlike the prefaces of the earlier *Mirrors*, the rhetorical strategy analyzed here suggests the continued importance of both place and principle to effective narrativization of the past, as well as their symbiotic relationship. The decades that saw the

40. Ichiko, *Heike monogatari*, 19. The translation is from Tyler, *Tale of the Heike*, 3. The identification of the location is according to the annotation to the Japanese edition used here (Ichiko, *Heike monogatari*, 19n1). See also Tyler, *Tale of the Heike*, 3n1.

41. Ichiko, *Heike monogatari*, 19. The translation is from Tyler, *Tale of the Heike*, 3.

42. Ichiko, *Heike monogatari*, 19. Except for the rendering of *honchō* as "our sovereignty," the translation is from Tyler, *Tale of the Heike*, 3–4.

production of *Gods and Sovereigns* and *Plums and Pines*, as well as the development of the *Heike* narratives, was an age that Conlan describes as one in which "every success and failure; life and death; victory and defeat unfolded according to divine plan."[43] Given this, the *Heike* preface's promise to demonstrate an order to the past resonates with broader currents. At the same time, its skillful use of an inclusive polity-wide setting within an even more expansive geography governed by Buddhist law removes, intentionally or not, the risk of precarity attendant upon selecting a given site within the capital. This is a concern particularly germane to the late fourteenth century, when, in Terry Kawashima's words, "the ontological significance of the capital as a space that houses the pinnacle of national authority, and the very existence of such an authority itself, were constantly being called into question."[44] "Our sovereignty" reasserts that existence, enforced and contained within a broader Buddhist geographical framework but without being tied to a particular, potentially compromised, site. By drawing on both principles and place, the *Heike* reproduces the very rhetorical strategies that seem to have made the early *Mirrors* so successful, and the partial abandonment of which does not seem to have done *Gods and Sovereigns* or *Plums and Pines* any favors.

These "in between" years in *Mirror* production thus saw continued experimentation with some of the concerns that had so shaped the *Mirrors'* Heian and Kamakura iterations. What is remarkable in hindsight is how despite this experimentation and its mixed results, the final two medieval historiographic *Mirrors* faithfully reproduce the contrasting models and the ideological divergence set forth by their Kamakura predecessors as though none of the intervening fourteenth-century texts were of any concern.[45] In more than one way, this move suggests that the value of the *Mirrors* in the late fourteenth century derives at least as much from

43. Conlan, *State of War*, 172.

44. Kawashima is writing here specifically about the context for the *Heike* Kakuichibon, the earliest version of which dates to 1371 (*Itineraries of Power*, 146).

45. What is also curious is that in so doing, each mimics the early fourteenth-century historiographic experiment least similar to it. Thus, the pro-Godaigo *Clear Mirror* adopts a conversational style and particular setting reminiscent not only of *Watchman* but also of the pro-Ashikaga *Plums and Pines*. The pro-Ashikaga *Mirror of the Gods*, in contrast, adopts a written register and unspecified setting reminiscent not only of the pro-*bakufu Mirror of the East*, but also of the pro-Godaigo *Gods and Sovereigns*.

their longevity and an inherited symbolic authority to speak to the idea of a unified polity as from their ability to interpret the past.

Gazing Backward through Mirrors

Roughly twenty years after *Gods and Sovereigns* and *Plums and Pines*, the penultimate medieval historiographic *Mirror* appeared: *The Clear Mirror*. Some two decades after that, an initial version of *The Mirror of the Gods* was likely completed. Together, the works mark the twilight of the medieval historiographic *Mirror*. Like their direct genre predecessors, the two are near polar opposites in form and sympathies (see figs. 5.1 and 5.2). *The Clear Mirror* takes on the language, structure, and setting of the earliest *Mirrors* that was replicated by *Watchman* to retell the events that culminate in the Kenmu Restoration, although written some forty years after its failure. *The Mirror of the Gods* uses the language, structure, and unspecified setting of *The Mirror of the East* to recount the entire history of Japan, beginning with Emperor Jinmu and reaching a narrative present just before the reign of Emperor Gokomatsu (1377–1433) and the triumphant unification of the courts—although ominous later accretions that run through the early years of the reign of Emperor Gohanazono (1419–70) cast a gloomy pall over the final reigns.

Their disparate forms and allegiances notwithstanding, to a certain extent both of the final *Mirrors* gesture to the memory of a unified court. Thus, both can also be characterized as celebrations of the past, although not uncomplicatedly so. Most importantly of all, both, I argue, self-consciously seek to capitalize on the accrued prestige of the earlier *Mirrors* they imitate, even as this strategy marks them as backward-oriented projects at heart.

COURTWARD BOUND: THE CLEAR MIRROR

Most often attributed to the prolific poet Nijō Yoshimoto (1320–88), *The Clear Mirror* dates approximately to the years in which Yoshimoto was in a paradoxical position.[46] He occupied the highest rank in the Northern

46. Kidō Saizō offers this dating based on internal textual evidence combined with speculation about when circumstances would best have suited his presumed author, Nijō

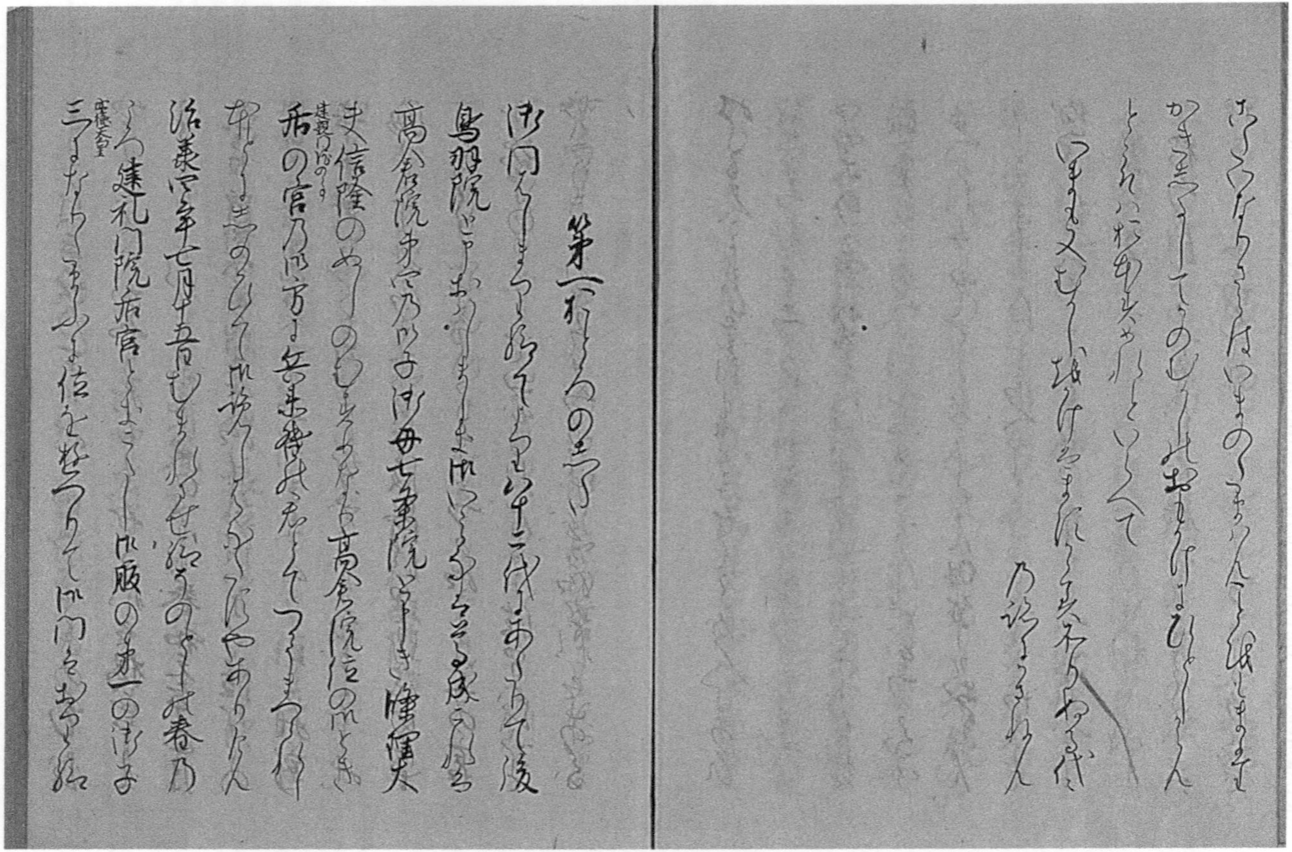

FIGURE 5.1. Conclusion of the preface and opening lines on Emperor Gotoba's reign in *The Clear Mirror* in a 1402 manuscript copy of a 1375 original. Photograph courtesy of the Main Library, Kyoto University–*Masukagami: Ōeibon* (image 6), adapted.

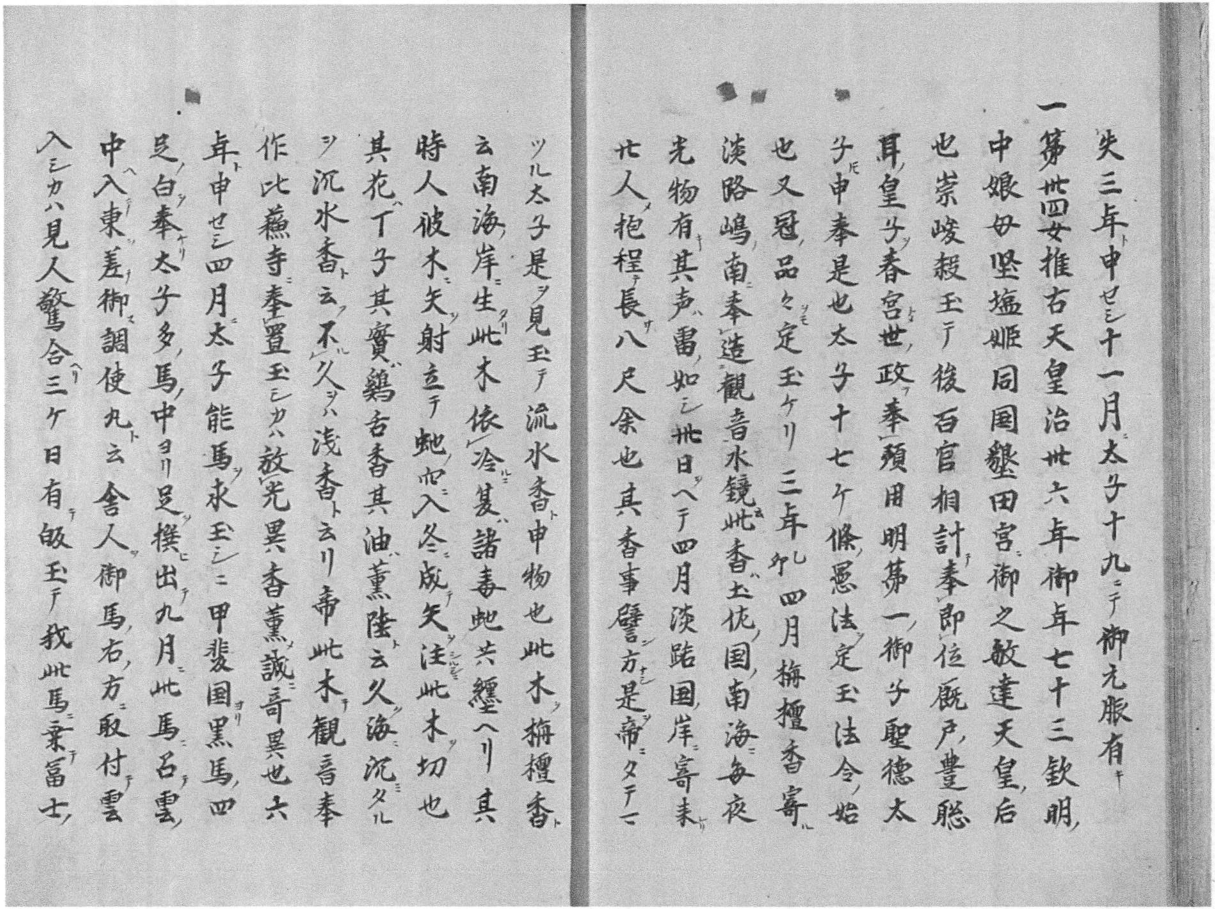

FIGURE 5.2. Excerpt from Empress Suiko's biography in *The Mirror of the Gods*, including a citation of *The Water Mirror* in the eighth line from the right, in a 1540 manuscript. Reprinted with permission from the National Diet Library Digital Collections—*Shinmeikyō* (frame 20).

Court that a nonimperial person could hold—*jugō* (ranking on par with an empress)—under a regime with increasingly limited authority.[47] At the same time, he also must have enjoyed at least some actual power, thanks to the favor of the young third shogun, Ashikaga Yoshimitsu (1358–1408), who had taken office in 1368 at the age of ten.[48] This position informs the main contradiction of *The Clear Mirror*: the superficial acceptance of the traditional *Mirror* rhetoric and framework without the trademark grounding in a cosmologically governed historical trajectory.[49] As shown below, however, *The Clear Mirror* does not require a principle to explain historical trajectories or even a redoubling of temporal loops in the fashion of *The New Mirror*, because the world that it celebrates is already lost. Thus, *The Clear Mirror*—a formal return to the center that is devoid of any far-reaching cosmologically grounded promises about history—can be taken on one level as a textual refraction of the reality

---

Yoshimoto (*Masukagami*, 298). George Perkins, though not an unquestioning advocate of the hypothesis that Yoshimoto is the author, proposes similar dating (*Clear Mirror*, 224).

47. Helen McCullough notes that "equality with the three (classes of) Empresses (*junsangū* or *jusangū*) was an economic privilege entitling the recipient to annual ranks and offices equivalent to those awarded the three categories of Empresses (Empress, Grand Empress, Senior Grand Empress)—i.e., to three annual offices and one annual rank" (*Ōkagami*, 91n3).

48. The biographical information is drawn from Kidō, *Masukagami*, 295–97. For an accessible overview of the mechanics of centralization under Ashikaga Yoshimitsu, see Imatani and Kozo, "Not for Lack of Will or Wile." While *The Clear Mirror* dates from Yoshimitsu's youth and predates the earliest sources discussed there by roughly twenty years, the article gives an implicit sense of the norms that made Yoshimitsu's moves possible. For an older study on the early days of the Muromachi *bakufu*, see Grossberg, "From Feudal Chieftain to Secular Monarch." Stavros characterizes Yoshimoto's relationship with Yoshimitsu as that of "tutor and close confidant" ("Monuments and Mandalas in Medieval Kyoto," 328).

49. However, this should not be understood as saying the work has no ideological bias. Both Kidō and Perkins point to its clear sympathy for or allegiance to the court and "court culture" (Kidō, *Masukagami*, 299–300; Perkins, *Clear Mirror*, 16–17 and 24). As Bialock has pointed out, with reference to Gustav Heldt's work, *The Clear Mirror* is not without any relation to cosmological discourses in its content (personal communication, March 2018). Kidō and Perkins also both discuss the devotion of the first third of the tale to Gotoba and the last third to Godaigo (Kidō, *Masukagami*, 299–300; Perkins, *Clear Mirror*, 17). Much of the remainder of Perkins's introduction consists of an examination of the literary techniques found in *The Clear Mirror* (ibid., 18–25).

that produced it: a court at its traditional base in Kyoto, but with its actual power increasingly diminished.

With its setting at Kyoto's Seiryōji Temple and the framing device of the twilight exchange between a narrator and a preternaturally aged informant, *The Clear Mirror* returns to both the capital-centered geography and the literary tropes of its earliest predecessors. As with those *Mirrors*, the choice of site is significant. The elderly informant explains to the narrator, "This temple was the only place that survived such unprecedented and ne'er-to-be-seen-again unrest unscathed."[50] The notes to the Japanese edition clarify that this comment primarily refers to the Genkō Disturbance (1331–33), Emperor Godaigo's uprising that hastened the end of the Kamakura *bakufu*.[51] The identification makes sense, since *The Clear Mirror* concludes with Godaigo's triumph. However, what is also made explicit from the outset is that the history transmitted in *The Clear Mirror* is very much past: a long ago time, likened to the world of "ancient *waka*" by the narrator or "vain dreams" by her informant.[52] If the narrative present is roughly the same as the time of composition, then what follows are reminiscences of a bygone age from the perspective of a time in which the Southern Court's authority had already been vastly eroded.[53]

The Clear Mirror's site represents more than a mere return to the capital and realignment with the court. Seiryōji Temple, formerly the mountain villa of Minamoto no Tōru (822–95), is popularly believed to be the inspiration for the temple Genji erects in Saga in *The Tale of Genji*, and Tōru is conventionally regarded as a possible inspiration for the character of Genji.[54] For a work that "might equally be described as a nostalgic celebration of Heian-style court life, a treasure trove of elegant anecdote, which seeks to re-create the romantic world of *The Tale of the Genji*," this is unlikely to be a coincidence.[55] Rather, it marks a return to the practice

50. Kidō, *Masukagami*, 6. The translation is modified from Perkins, *Clear Mirror*, 27.

51. See also Perkins, *Clear Mirror*, 230n4.

52. Kidō, *Masukagami*, 6. The translation is from Perkins, *Clear Mirror*, 27–28.

53. For a brief overview of the final decades of the Southern Court, see Conlan, *State of War*, 222–25.

54. This tidbit about the temple is, in fact, the first thing noted on the introductory page of its website. Seiryōji ("Seiryōji ni tsuite").

55. Perkins, *Clear Mirror*, 2. On specific similarities with the *Genji* (which do not include any connection with its setting), see ibid., 16–21.

of the earliest *Mirrors* of defining themselves in relation to the *Genji* or evaluating their efforts in contrast with those of Murasaki Shikibu. For *The Clear Mirror*, then, the reassertion of "place" carries multiple meanings that firmly return it to traditional (in multiple senses) grounds.[56]

In tone and language, too, *The Clear Mirror* is a throwback to an earlier age: other than the odd citation, *wabun* dominates. It is particularly reminiscent of *The New Mirror*, meandering between members of the imperial family in a narrative that moves forward but is punctuated largely by poems, social gatherings, and clothing descriptions (rather than violence, as in *The Water Mirror*, or rituals of statecraft, as in *The Mirror of the East*). Nevertheless, it acknowledges three major instances of upheaval: the Jōkyū Disturbance, the two attempted Mongol invasions, and the Genkō Disturbance.[57] Although the significance of each is inscribed in the narrative in different ways, all are critical for the remembered historical arc that the tale transmits.

The Jōkyū Disturbance initially receives minimal attention: "When the Jōkyū Disturbance erupted the members of Retired Emperor Gotoba's family scattered, and even the young boys who remained in the city became outcasts."[58] The following commentary assesses the event primarily as an opportunity for the next emperor and then immediately drops the topic. However, the Jōkyū era is repeatedly referred to in ways that suggest a lingering resentment over the rebellion's outcome. The earliest such instance is the succession crisis of 1242, when the sudden death of Emperor Shijō (1231–42) necessitates the *bakufu*'s selection of the next emperor. Hōjō Yasutoki is euphemistically referred to as "the warrior who had come to the capital in the Jōkyū era," an understated description of the general who led marauding shogunal troops into Kyoto.[59] Some ninety

56. This is in contrast to the "critique" of a place-centered view that Kawashima locates in the Suwa origin stories contained in the roughly contemporary *Shintōshū* (*Itineraries of Power*, 159; see also 151–204). Perhaps even in the use of this technique, *The Clear Mirror* is enacting its nostalgic position.

57. Ōmori also sees the depiction of the Jōkyū and Genkō Disturbances as significant and one of the unique features of *The Clear Mirror* ("'Masukagami' no rekishi jojutsu," 9).

58. Kidō, *Masukagami*, 46. The translation is from Perkins, *Clear Mirror*, 60.

59. Kidō, *Masukagami*, 62; see also 61–63. The translation is from Perkins, *Clear Mirror*, 68–69.

years later, in 1331, the current regent is similarly traced back to "Yoshitoki, the regent who had held office in the Jōkyū era."[60] Even the origins of Ashikaga Takauji's traitorous ways are traced to Jōkyū.[61] Thus, the year 1221 is clearly positioned as a defining moment for configurations of power that would play out over the next century.

At the same time, Jōkyū is the default point of reference for succession disputes. It is referred to in the aftermath of an attempted coup traced back to Retired Emperor Kameyama (1249–1305), but the strongest condemnation of the Jōkyū legacy appears in the explanation of Emperor Gouda's (1267–1324) desire to abdicate:[62]

> Since his [the emperor's] sole desire was now to devote himself to religion, he found people gathering to report worldly matters to him irksome—so much so that he sent Major Counselor [Yoshida] Sadafusa [1274–1338] to Kamakura around the summer of that year, apparently in order to inform the shogunate of his desire to yield the realm to Emperor Godaigo. What a world it had become! Shouldn't it have been a simple matter for a father to suit himself about assigning that degree of responsibility to an imperial son? People were astounded. But there was nothing new in the situation. Things had been exactly the same ever since the Jōkyū era.[63]

Thus, although the disturbance is accorded minimal treatment when it actually occurs, through repeated gestures that direct our attention to its players and subsequent impact, *The Clear Mirror* elevates it to a position of importance.[64]

60. Kidō, *Masukagami*, 249. The translation is from Perkins, *Clear Mirror*, 192.

61. Kidō, *Masukagami*, 285. For the corresponding events in English, see Perkins, *Clear Mirror*, 216.

62. On the coup, see Kidō, *Masukagami*, 173–76; Perkins, *Clear Mirror*, 141–43.

63. Kidō, *Masukagami*, 214. The translation is modified from Perkins, *Clear Mirror*, 169. Ōmori also cites this passage as proof of the importance accorded the Jōkyū Disturbance in in *The Clear Mirror*, and he cites the passage on Godaigo's (temporary) exile as a means of establishing ties to the earlier Jōkyū Disturbance ("'Masukagami' no rekishi jojutsu," 9–10).

64. It may have an intended ominous valence, too. *The Mirror of the Gods* notes that Godaigo's exile follows the precedent set after the Jōkyū Disturbance (*Shinmeikyō*, 177).

The Mongol invasions also feature prominently, albeit in a much more temporally contained manner. While the earlier invasion is noted only as an interference with the Gosechi dance performances,[65] the second is recounted with a much greater sense of crisis and notes the efforts of the retired emperor in particular. The defeat of the Mongols is attributed to "a mighty typhoon" stirred up by a "humming-bulb arrow" let loose from the heavens "just as the *Great Wisdom* recitations at Iwashimizu reached their climax."[66] In this instance, the governing cosmological logic is revealed to be similar to that of *The Mirror of the East* and *Watchman*: namely, that a dual-pronged appeal to *kami* and Buddhist authorities results in victory. Yet this is nowhere explicitly addressed, at least not beyond the observation that the victory by typhoon is once again due to the fact that "after all, ours is a land of the gods."[67] Instead, the record draws to a close with an almost comical image of the defeated "Mongol chieftain," who "is said to have succumbed with a vow on his lips: 'I intend to depart this world, return as king of Japan, and drag that country down to destruction.'"[68]

The Genkō Disturbance is the violence that enables the restoration of imperial rule, and as such, it occupies a major place in *The Clear Mirror*—from the fifteenth chapter through the conclusion of the work.[69] The second half of the fifteenth chapter is devoted to the outbreak of the disturbance and Godaigo's ignominious return to the capital;[70] the exiles of the major participants and the melancholic aftermath dominate most of the sixteenth chapter;[71] and the final seventeenth chapter relates the battles leading up to Godaigo's later triumphant return, as well as the

65. Kidō, *Masukagami*, 126. For the corresponding events in English, see Perkins, *Clear Mirror*, 111.

66. Kidō, *Masukagami*, 149–50. The translation is from Perkins, *Clear Mirror*, 124.

67. Kidō, *Masukagami*, 150. The translation is modified from Perkins, *Clear Mirror*, 125.

68. Kidō, *Masukagami*, 150–51. The translation is from Perkins, *Clear Mirror*, 125–26.

69. It is also possible, as Ōmori does, to include in this mix the fourteenth chapter and its account of the preempted Shōchū coup of 1324 ("'Masukagami' no rekishi jojutsu," 12–17).

70. Kidō, *Masukagami*, 242–56. For the corresponding events in English, see Perkins, *Clear Mirror*, 188–96.

71. Kidō, *Masukagami*, 257–81. For the corresponding events in English, see Perkins, *Clear Mirror*, 197–212.

imperial procession back to the palace. There the narrative abruptly breaks off, without any return to the frame story.[72] There is only a final poem:

Sumizome no	Even black robes
iro o mo kaetsu	change with time;
tsukikusa no	changing as the dayflower
utsureba kawaru	transfers its hue
hana no koromo ni	onto a brilliant robe.[73]

Given the repetition in the poem of verbs of change, as well as the long-familiar trope of the colors of the flower to signify "inconstancy,"[74] this is perhaps not as auspicious a note upon which to end as the conversion of dark robes into colorful ones might otherwise seem. Although a return to the framing story could have resolved this ambiguity in tone, the narrative elephant in the room for *The Clear Mirror*'s readers (or what George Perkins calls "unpalatable realities") is the fact that Godaigo's victory was short-lived, lasting only three years before the country was split between two courts—a victory, in other words, that was over well before the composition of *The Clear Mirror*.[75]

The gap between the narrative present at the conclusion of *The Clear Mirror* and the historical present of its composition, in other words, invites a reading of the work as fundamentally pessimistic. Without the circular recuperative structure of *The New Mirror*, the glory of Godaigo's restoration and the possibilities it represents at the end of *The Clear Mirror* can only recede ever further into the past. Read in this way, *The Clear Mirror* speaks to a relationship between narrative and power similar to the one that Kawashima postulates for the roughly coeval Kakuichibon of the *Heike* (1371), which likewise attributes weight to the latter's choice

72. Kidō, *Masukagami*, 282–93. For the corresponding events in English, see Perkins, *Clear Mirror*, 214–20.

73. Kidō, *Masukagami*, 293. The translation is after Perkins, *Clear Mirror*, 220.

74. Perkins reaches the same conclusion, pointing to the dayflower specifically as "a metaphor for inconstancy" and supplying an eighth-century poem as an early example (*Clear Mirror*, 25).

75. Perkins, *Clear Mirror*, 25. Perkins similarly speculates that the short life of the restoration could explain the decision to end *The Clear Mirror* where it does (ibid., 11–12; also 16–17).

of concluding events. As Kawashima observes regarding the Kakuichibon: "It is likely not an accident that the last named major incident in the main body of the text is the Jōkyū rebellion of 1221, instigated by Gotoba. The failure of the retired emperor's plot to overthrow the Kamakura *bakufu* and to reconsolidate power under the imperial court is an ominous reminder that a return to Heian-style courtier rule is likely impossible."[76] In short, this version, at least, of the *Heike* promotes a worldview in which there is no going backward. This is a reality that *The Clear Mirror* likewise recognizes.

Kawashima's analysis of the Kakuichibon in the particular moment of the late fourteenth century emphasizes the potential of texts to powerfully reconfigure their written and cultural antecedents to new ends. Her particular focus here is on traditionally prestigious poetic languages, but the characterization of the Kakuichibon as a work that "seal[s] the constituent parts of this bedrock [the courtly tradition] . . . as relics of the past that need to be fundamentally recast in order to play a useful role amidst the power plays of the post-Genpei era" can usefully be considered more broadly.[77] If the Kakuichibon shows elements of court culture to be susceptible to containment and appropriation to new ends, *The Clear Mirror* is the refutation of such a position. Although *The Clear Mirror* likewise sees the past as past, it does not suggest the potential for a productive repositioning of its elements. *The Clear Mirror* instead avoids the question of what comes next. Its retreat into a structural and linguistic conservatism is well suited for a narrative that is ultimately marked by nostalgia and loss.

The concluding lines of *The Clear Mirror* invite comparison with the earlier *Mirrors* precisely because of how, in not returning to the frame story, they enable a resolutely nostalgic gaze. Had *The Clear Mirror* followed the conventions of the earlier *Mirrors*, a return to the world of the framing story would have required a totalizing explanation of these events: the narrative postface is where *The New Mirror* and *Water Mirror* (as well as *Watchman*) summarize the import of their transmissions, reemphasizing their otherworldly sources as a means of enhancing the value of their

76. Kawashima, *Itineraries of Power*, 146.
77. Kawashima, *Itineraries of Power*, 147.

interpretations of the past.[78] *The New Mirror*, while stopping short of reemphasizing karmic causality in its postface, embarks on a final discussion of the morality of writing. In contrast, *The Water Mirror* is explicit, if typically pessimistic, when the narrator reports her source's final utterance as follows: "On the whole, having been born after the Buddha's death in this small country at the end of a *kalpa* of destruction, it's precisely the badness of things that is the true principle."[79] This reminds the reader yet again of the historical trajectory upon which the events of *The Water Mirror* are to be placed. (Even *The China Mirror* similarly, though indirectly, suggests a path of decline in its surviving portions.) Yet *The Clear Mirror* offers no interpretation of history as a teaching tool. Unlike the quasi-oracular Heian *Mirrors*, it makes no promises to shed light on anything beyond "what happened next."[80] In short, the account offers a what, but not a why.[81]

To be sure, the author of *The Clear Mirror* would face a dilemma similar to *The Water Mirror*'s were he to address the problem of cosmological logic. Like *The Water Mirror*, *The Clear Mirror* reflects the perspective of the (relatively) disenfranchised. And as in *Plums and Pines*, the state of affairs celebrated in *The Clear Mirror*'s narrative has already been consigned to the past. What would the principle be that enabled both the Kenmu Restoration and its collapse? How persuasive could an institutional focus be when its strongest proponent, Emperor Godaigo, was dead? Given such dramatic developments, *The Clear Mirror* may mark an epistemological shift, with the actual division of the court suggesting that the former ways of understanding the world could not be productively applied to interpreting a new reality.[82] If this is the case, then the

78. Perkins observes that a return to the framing story "would have diminished its [the ending poem's] impact," although he does not elaborate beyond that (*Clear Mirror*, 25).

79. Kaneko et al., *Mizukagami zen chūshaku*, 449.

80. Kidō, *Masukagami*, 8. The translation is from Perkins, *Clear Mirror*, 28.

81. Perkins writes, "His [the author's] basic aim, like Emon's [author of *Tale of Flowering Fortunes*], was to tailor historical writing to the taste of an aristocratic readership by employing the elegant devices of the fictional tale, and in that he succeeded better than any of his peers" (*Clear Mirror*, 16).

82. Watase Sigeru similarly sees *The Clear Mirror* as the end of a genre, albeit the genre of the "historical tale" ("Rekishi monogatari no shūen"). He attributes this to the irreconcilability of language and topic. Watase's analysis rests on the traditional categorizations

decision to write the history of the events that led to the Kenmu Restoration as a *Mirror* becomes a doubly nostalgic gesture, one that celebrates not only the court culture that Godaigo represented, but also the age in which the world was still legible via the *Mirror* genre. In this light, it is unsurprising that *The Clear Mirror* marks the end of the writing of the medieval court-oriented historiographic *Mirrors*.

BAKUFU TIES: THE MIRROR OF THE GODS

The Mirror of the Gods is the last of the medieval historiographic *Mirrors*, the final stop on the path set by *The Mirror of the East*. Although *The Mirror of the Gods* has not received much scholarly attention, the fact of its composition attests to how mainstream the *Mirror* had become as a vehicle for narrating the past.[83] After the varying results of the early fourteenth-century experimentation with *Mirrors* and their features that resulted in chronicles, discussions, and even tales of the past, it was a *Mirror* that was selected late in the fourteenth century to narrate an account of history legitimating the Ashikaga-backed Northern Court. And as with *The Clear Mirror*, the composition of *The Mirror of the Gods* seems to have initially been inspired by the divided court. The first sovereign listed as the "current emperor" (*kinjō*) is Goen'yū (1358–93), which dates the work's initial composition to the rule of the third shogun, Ashikaga Yoshimitsu.[84] That said, *The Mirror of the Gods* is also a work that continued to be added to well into the fifteenth century: each of the subsequent entries,

---

of the genre: Classical Japanese only, exclusive focus on the court, and so on. Although framed in discursive terms that do not line up with the goals of the present study, Hyōdō Hiromi's characterization of this development also resonates: "The fact that historical tales of the court, which ran from *The Great Mirror* to *The New Mirror*, *The Water Mirror*, and *The Clear Mirror*, concluded with Emperor Godaigo's attack on the *bakufu* signifies, in a nutshell, that the age in which the relation of the history of court society as 'Japanese' history was possible ended with the age of Emperor Godaigo" (*Godaigo tennō*, 4).

83. Sasaki Kiichi identifies three manuscript lineages for this text, as well as the typeset *Zoku Gunsho ruijū* edition, and one other (unseen) version in the possession of Sokō Bunko as the forms in which it survives today ("'Shinmeikyō' denpon [jō]," 16–17).

84. Goen'yū reigned in 1371–82, which could mean that *The Mirror of the Gods* was being compiled or composed even as Yoshimitsu's mentor, Nijō Yoshimoto, was writing *The Clear Mirror*.

which run through Emperor Gohanazono, refers to its subject as currently occupying the throne. And with the latest dated event a large earthquake in Eikyō 6 (1434), the work clearly contains later additions.[85]

This obviously layered composition is unprecedented in the *Mirrors*. On the one hand, it may indicate that *The Mirror of the Gods* had enough lingering prestige to not be supplanted by a new history of the reunified courts. On the other hand, the fact that it inspired no known successors as well as the way the final entry seems to end in the middle of Emperor Gohanazono's reign can be interpreted as signs that the *kanbun*, *bakufu*-sympathetic *Mirror*, like its *wabun* court-oriented counterpart, had outlived its usefulness as a productive means of narrating the past.

As with many of the predecessors to *The Mirror of the Gods*, the text's authorship is unclear—although the work follows the emperors of the Northern Court as the legitimate line, which suggests a pro-Ashikaga orientation. Sasaki Kiichi argues for the involvement of the Satake family in addenda to the work.[86] His painstaking comparison of surviving manuscripts leads him to conclude that a reconstruction of the original text, particularly at a detailed level, is impossible at present. Therefore, the following discussion focuses on broader points that are consistent across the extant versions.

Like *The Mirror of the East*, *The Mirror of the Gods* has no preface, and in this way, it shares the "placelessness" of the other shogunal *Mirror*; but also like *The Mirror of the East*, the site of the institution that forms its framework is central to its authority. As a work that at least structurally focuses on the imperial line, while at the same time implicitly bowing to the authority of the Muromachi *bakufu*, its implied normative site of authority is Kyoto, the capital, home to both the imperial palace and the shogunate. Thus, like all of the *Mirrors* before it, there is an

85. For the entry on Goenyū, see *Shinmeikyō*, 200. This is the primary edition used for the present study. I have also made use of the National Diet Library manuscript dating to Tenbun 9 (1540)—the oldest surviving version—for comparative purposes. Sasaki Kiichi offers a nearly identical assessment of the dating ("'Shinmeikyō' denpon [jō]," 16). See also Sasaki Kiichi, "'Shinmeikyō' denpon (ge)," 29–30.

86. Sasaki Kiichi, "'Shinmeikyō' denpon (ge)," 22–23. Specifically, he makes a strong case for the involvement of the Satake retainer Okamoto Zentetsu (died 1583) or his father (ibid., 23–29). His conclusion argues for transmission and editing in Hitachi (ibid., 29–33).

intimate connection between the geographic site at the narrative center and the authority it invokes or promotes. Yet rather than explicitly position itself, the account simply begins with the biography of Emperor Jinmu, before advancing in chronological order through 105 imperial reigns spread across two scrolls of approximately equal length. The biographies typically open with the emperor's date of accession to the throne and parentage. Alternative names are also often provided, and for the early emperors before the establishment of a stable capital in Nara, palace names and locations are noted. (The flip side of this listing of palaces is the superfluity of naming the current capital, implied to be stable by not being listed.)

Other significant elements from the reign—the logic of which is not always obvious—are appended to this information, followed in several cases by selected contemporary events from China and India. The peninsular kingdoms occupy an ambiguous status and are often interwoven with the "Japanese" narrative, but they are nevertheless present. The first eighty reigns are covered in the first scroll, most often in fairly brief terms. But plenty of space is given to the struggles around Crown Prince Shōtoku's promotion of Buddhism and the fighting that followed, as well as the buildup to the Genpei War during Emperor Takakura's reign. The last twenty-five reigns are covered in the second scroll, which goes into great detail about battles of the Genpei War, the Mongol invasions, the Genkō Disturbance, Godaigo's Kenmu Restoration and its aftermath, and eventually the Kannō Disturbance. Yet although the narrative action often takes place on the battlefield, the framework of the imperial biography repeatedly calls the reader back to the capital. In the narrative's implied base in Kyoto, the site of both the Muromachi *bakufu* and the Northern Court it backed, *The Mirror of the Gods* makes a case for its own centrality in a way reminiscent of that used by *The Mirror of the East.* And to repeat, as with all of the earlier *Mirrors*, the imagined geography of power that *The Mirror of the Gods* reflects is key to understanding the nature of the authority it seeks to project.

The Mirror of the Gods also shares with the later *Mirrors*—in particular, *The Mirror of the East* and *The Clear Mirror*—a lack of a clearly articulated cosmological principle that defines a historical trajectory or provides a logic to events. Its tenor is especially close to that of *The Mirror of the East*, the *Mirror* it also resembles most closely structurally, with manifestations of *kami* and buddhas and the divine origins of the imperial house duly recorded, but without any discussion of cosmological principles. The work is also bookended by calculations that position the opening and closing entries along a timeline related to the Buddha's death, which likewise speaks to a continued engagement with an ultimately Buddhist timeframe: Jinmu ascends the throne 290 years after the Buddha passes away, and the final entry concludes with the observation that the year Ōei 34 (1427) marks 2,379 years since the Buddha's death.[87] Yet as with the other later *Mirrors*, karma and the final age are scarcely mentioned.[88]

This move, too, is consistent with the shift in *The Mirror of the East*—and, arguably, *The China Mirror*—away from an emphasis on offering models for historical interpretation and toward one on the longevity of an office. Just as *The China Mirror* offers as complete a record of dynastic rulers as its informants can recall and *The Mirror of the East* recounts the founding of the Kamakura *bakufu* from its origins up almost to the present, *The Mirror of the Gods* presents a history of the imperial house that runs from its first emperor to the time that *The Mirror of the Gods* was composed. In other words, as with *The China Mirror* and *The Mirror of the East*, it makes a case for the longevity of an institution and does so by covering that institution's development in its entirety.

The Mirror of the Gods' composition primarily in variant *kanbun* is another feature it shares with *The Mirror of the East*, and it lends itself to a similar interpretation: the decision to write *The Mirror of the Gods* in this form of the language can also be understood as a performative gesture intended to denote the perspective of the center. This is especially

87. While this does not tally with current positions that date the historical Buddha's lifetime to the fifth or sixth century BCE, it is consistent with the calculations found in *The China Mirror*, in which the Buddha's death is dated to the reign of King Mu of Zhou in the tenth century BCE. See *Shinmeikyō*, 203; Hirasawa and Yoshida, *Kara kagami: Shōkōkanbon*, 53.

88. Two exceptions to the former are when Crown Prince Shōtoku remarks that Mononobe no Moriya was ignorant of the workings of karma and the point at which the author characterizes Kō no Moronao's (died 1351) burning of temples and shrines in Yoshino as resulting in *asamashiki zaigō* (dreadfully wicked karma) (*Shinmeikyō*, 107 and 198, respectively). The terms for "final age" are scattered throughout the work, but not with regard to interpreting a trajectory or chain of events.

striking when one realizes that some of the text's material derives from *wabun* sources—specifically, *The Water Mirror*. Whereas *The Water Mirror* recounted the earliest ages of the imperial house primarily in *wabun* as part of an effort to create a new center outside of a compromised system, *The Mirror of the Gods* covers the same ground in *kanbun* from the official and actual seats of power within the dominant system.

Nonetheless, to reiterate, *The Mirror of the Gods* did not spawn successors, and its current form suggests a somewhat haphazard cessation in composition. Nor does it seem to have drawn a later audience, unlike the other *Mirrors*. All of this suggests that despite its formal orthodoxy, the more chronicle-style *kanbun* historiographic *Mirror*—like its neoclassical *wabun* counterpart, *The Clear Mirror*—was already at or nearing the end of its line when work on *The Mirror of the Gods* began. The existence of the latter raises the question of why, after almost a century of historiographic experimentation and development, there was a return to the *Mirror* genre at all. Why take up a form that resembled the history of the previous shogunate to present a presumably self-legitimizing account of the past?

Similar to the case of *The Clear Mirror*, in that of *The Mirror of the Gods* one possible reason for the appeal of ordering the past through the logic of a *Mirror* is the very idea that the *Mirror* might well have been perceived as an artifact of a previous age. David Spafford argues that Japan's mid-fifteenth through early sixteenth centuries—roughly the time of the final appended entries to *The Mirror of the Gods*—were marked by a "persistent medieval" in strategies for land management.[89] I would suggest that *The Mirror of the Gods* is a historiographic analogue to this.[90] In Spafford's analysis, a common recourse was "to find not a new pragmatism, or a search for new solutions, but a dogged attachment to the old."[91] It is tempting to infer from this that the early medieval had a conservative cachet that may have gone beyond an administrative reliance upon

89. Spafford, *Sense of Place*, 12.

90. Following the observation on the Buddha's death mentioned above, the *Zoku gunshoruijū* edition closes with a list of twenty-one dates from 1425 to 1570, without explanation, that may indicate the production of copies. Since some predate the final entry of the work, this is problematic. Even so, this expanded date range overlaps with the time period that Spafford discusses.

91. Spafford, *Sense of Place*, 12.

medieval precedent and extended into the exercise of other types of intellectual authority.[92] If the elite were "backward-looking" in their "search for solutions to novel problems in ancient texts and precedents" with regard to land administration,[93] it is not much of a stretch to imagine that this orientation could have easily pertained to the inherently political project of textually ordering the past, too. In a climate such as this, casting the past as a *Mirror* becomes an unsurprising move, one that could have been a gesture with multiple meanings. Revisiting the framing of history as a *Mirror* not only enabled reaching back to a romanticized picture of the first shogunate and its *Mirror*. It also created a link with the ongoing project common to all of the *Mirrors*: presenting some type of authority—be it cosmological laws, governing institutions, or even the principles of good poetry—as immutable, regardless of the instability of the extratextual world that so often constituted the backdrop for *Mirror* production. Read in such a way, *The Mirror of the Gods* simultaneously attests to the genre's "arrival" as well as to a perception of it as belonging to the past.

In the end, in my reading, the very quality of "pastness" becomes central to understanding the creation of both of the Muromachi *Mirrors*, despite their different ends. Where the *Mirror* reflects a contained irrecoverable past in *The Clear Mirror*, it has an aspirational valence in *The Mirror of the Gods*. Perhaps the imperial house, supported by the shogun, will live on beyond the confines of the text, just as the Kamakura *bakufu* continued for the better part of a century after the final years related in *The Mirror of the East*. Yet in either case, the *Mirror*'s value then derives from its nature as an established form of historiography rather than its having a unique ability to offer a key to unlock the lessons of the past to understand where the world is headed. In other words, even as the *Mirror* became meaningful as precedent, its forfeiture of the exegetical imperative—no longer will it tell the reader from a position of authority how the cosmos works—may, in part, explain its apparent loss of appeal as a productive medieval historiographic tool.

92. Compare Spafford, *Sense of Place*, 12–14.

93. Spafford, *Sense of Place*, 14.

Conclusion

This chapter took *The Clear Mirror* and *The Mirror of the Gods* as the outgrowths of the two divergent models for *Mirror* writing in the 1290s discussed in chapter 4. Yet whereas the late Kamakura *Mirrors*, particularly *The Mirror of the East*, seemed to be fruits of a vibrant and evolving historiographic development, both *The Clear Mirror* and *The Mirror of the Gods* mark the end of their respective paths. As such, they offer an opportunity to think about why, as a historiographic tool, the *Mirrors* lapse into disuse.

One explanation for this may lie in the changing ends to which the later *Mirrors*, especially the Muromachi compositions, were put. The old *Mirrors* answered questions: Where was the world headed? How had it gotten where it was? In earlier and contemporary works, the appeal of a clearly demonstrated cosmological logic seems to have been very powerful. Not only had the *Mirrors* themselves demonstrated this; other works revealed the absence of such a logic as problematic. One only needs to think of those historiographic experiments that did not garner a substantial contemporary readership to see this: Jien's proliferation of ad hoc principles in *My Humble Thoughts* (chapter 3), Chikafusa's abstruse principle that mortals could not hope to understand in *Gods and Sovereigns*, and *Plums and Pines*' abandonment of any claims to a cosmological framework. Nonetheless, neither of the *Mirrors* of the late thirteenth and fourteenth centuries addresses issues of the fate of the world or the reasons for its current condition—at least, not overtly.

At the same time, the earlier *Mirrors*, as well as other texts, illustrated the value of a specific narrative setting that served to buttress their claims to authority. This, too, is only erratically taken up in the fourteenth-century texts discussed above. *Plums and Pines*, with its limited readership, and *The Clear Mirror*, which survived to eventually become valorized for its neoclassical style, both retained the use of place. *Gods and Sovereigns*, which eventually garnered a readership, and *The Mirror of the Gods*, which seems to have languished in obscurity, did not.

The move away from a single authoritative site, as in *The Mirror of the Gods*, is perhaps less unexpected: what site would speak to all of a fractured polity? The rationale behind the shift in narrative approach away from explaining the whys of the past is more difficult to infer. But the break with offering cosmological justifications for historical trajectories and/or chains of events—especially in a world fraught with political instability and changing ideas of the power of otherworldly forces—marks a choice that was perhaps to the detriment of the *Mirrors* and their imitators, judging by the muted immediate reception of nearly all of the works that are discussed in this chapter. (The *Heike* is the one exception in this regard, and as shown, it did promise rules for understanding historical change as well as a geography to back up its claims.)

Contrasting the Muromachi *Mirrors*' principle-free histories with a text that was demonstrably effective in creating a narrative that drew broad support clarifies the significance of cosmological rhetoric in particular. If, for instance, one turns to the beginning of *The Mirror of the East* and Prince Mochihito's 1180 petition to rise up against the Taira—the petition that is credited with rallying the Minamoto and their supporters—it is rife with talk of cosmological continuity (and threats to it). The severing of the line of the "Hundred Sovereigns," the "destruction of Buddhist law," and the "break with antiquity" are among the imminent dangers. Following the "traces of Prince Shōtoku" and relying on aid of "the laws of Heaven" together with the "protection of the Emperor, Three Treasures, and the Gods" are the strategies that will shape the course of events.[94]

Yet none of these defining forces or principles, nor even the long-familiar threat of the end of the world, plays a major role in the *Mirrors* of the fourteenth century. On the one hand, there is a substantial chronological gap between Mochihito's petition and *The Clear Mirror*. On the other hand, "affairs of the divine," in Conlan's words, "permeated the fabric of life throughout the fourteenth century."[95] This makes the absence of such a "plan" in *The Clear Mirror* and *The Mirror of the Gods* striking. Moreover, the fact that *The Clear Mirror*'s account of the past begins in 1180 suggests that the Genpei War continued to exert a powerful hold on the early medieval historical imagination. Thus, the rhetoric of Mochihito's petition might not have been as remote as a two-century break could otherwise suggest.

94. Nagahara and Kishi, *Zen'yaku Azuma kagami*, 1:47.
95. Conlan, *State of War*, 165.

Nevertheless, to restate: even though the impetus to populate historiographic works with otherworldly powers, or to attribute individual events to them, continued across the late Kamakura and early Muromachi *Mirrors*, there was no longer any larger instructive interpretive framework. Whether this is tied to or reflective of the "disintegration of overwhelming hegemonic authority," the gradual decentralization of authority that spans much of the later fourteenth century in particular, or even a decreasing warrior interest in early medieval precedent is impossible to say.[96] It may simply be that in an increasingly fragmented and unstable order, the discourse of cosmological principles had outlived its usefulness in lending clear shape to historical trajectories. To accommodate the vicissitudes of the late thirteenth and fourteenth centuries, perhaps a principle would have required so much breadth and flexibility as to be meaningless.

In any case, this represents a lost opportunity of sorts for the *Mirrors*, for it was precisely in the "chaos of the Northern and Southern Court wars" that a broader "hope for divine protection above and beyond that of . . . [popular] veneration of the gods" that extended outside of the metropolitan population arose.[97] It seems, then, that there should have been a growing audience for a grounded, ordered representation of the past. Instead, however, the *Mirrors* ceased to make effective recourse to cosmological principles in a symbolically powerful setting as a way to interpret history. Once they did so, they ceded their otherworldly endorsed authority to narrate the past. The lingering value they enjoyed can instead be understood as due to the memory of their earlier power and perhaps even a nostalgia for the world that they had once been in a position to order.

96. Conlan, *State of War*, 217. Conlan is referring here specifically to the fallout from the Kannō Disturbance. The more general trends are summarized in ibid., 223–31. On the changing attitude toward precedent in particular, see ibid., 231.

97. Sasaki Kaoru, *Nihon chūsei shisō no kichō*, 141.

EPILOGUE

Mirror *Legacies for Early Modern Japan*

Mirror writing explodes in the seventeenth century. A search of the "illustrated book" holdings of the Boston Museum of Fine Arts, known for its impressive collection of Japanese materials (including the original of *An Illustrated Scroll of Minister Kibi's Trip to China* mentioned in chapter 3), gives a sense of the numbers, yielding approximately twenty-four examples of works labeled as *kagami* (mirror) and definitively dated to the Edo period alone.[1] These range from the *Yoshiwara kagami* (Mirror of the Yoshiwara [Pleasure Quarters], 1660) to *Ehon taka kagami* (An Illustrated Mirror of Falconry, circa 1863–68), and they also include *Mirrors* that pun on the titles of their medieval predecessors, despite little or no obvious overlap in content. Instead of *The Clear Mirror*, there is *Ehon masukagami* (The Complete [ten-tenths] Illustrated Mirror, 1748), and in a new spin on *The Mirror of the East*, there is *Ehon Azuma kagami* (The Illustrated Mirror of Eastern Wives, 1787).[2]

1. Boston Museum of Fine Arts ("Illustrated Books/kagami/Asia"). This is a somewhat artificial limitation, since other printed materials, including *ukiyo-e*, Kabuki playbills, and references to plays such as *Ashiya dōman ōuchi kagami* (1734), *Natsu matsuri: Naniwa kagami* (1745), and *Sugawara denju tenarai kagami* (1746) also bore *Mirror* designations, attesting to the now-protean possibilities for a *Mirror*.

2. The website for the Thomas J. Waston Collection of the Metropolitan Museum of Art lists an alternative title for *Ehon masukagami* that is more indicative of the work's contents: *True Reflections on the Life and Manners of a Woman* (Metropolitan Museum of Arts, Digital Collections).

Moreover, as hinted by the titles that appear in this limited search, the sheer numbers are not the only development. The most cursory glance at *Mirrors* from the early Edo period likewise reveals an expansion in their subject matter that would challenge any attempt to identify a commonality in the works beyond that of didacticism (ironic or earnest). In addition to the *Mirrors* noted above, there are *Mirrors* that narrate the past, particularly Hayashi Razan's (1583–1657) massive *Honchō tsugan* (A Comprehensive Mirror of Our Sovereignty, written circa 1670);[3] and *Mirrors* that relate the present, such as *Shikidō ōkagami* (The Great Mirror of the Erotic Way, written and edited circa 1678–1688).[4] From the title alone, Razan's aspirations for the scope of *A Comprehensive Mirror of Our Sovereignty* are clear; but *The Great Mirror of the Erotic Way* likewise uses the mirror as a metaphor to suggest the exhaustive treatment of a topic rather than an explanation based on principles, cosmological or otherwise.[5] In the latter vein, one also finds Ihara Saikaku's *Nanshoku ōkagami* (The Great Mirror of Male Love, published in 1687).[6] Some *Mirrors* offer

3. According to Kondō Shigekazu, it is also in the Edo period that we first see the *kagami* of *Azuma kagami* written with the character 鑒 (Japanese: *kan*, Chinese: *jian*) rather than 鏡 (Japanese: *kyō*, Chinese: *jing*). Kondō attributes the change to new trends in Edo-period Sinology (personal communication, August 2018).

4. My understanding of *Shikidō ōkagami* is based on the work of Lawrence Rodgers, whom I also follow in terms of the dating and title translation ("She Loves Me. She Loves Me Not").

5. This is evident in the preface, where the narrator likens his *Mirror* to the *San du fu* (Three Capitals Rhapsody), Zuo Si's (250–305) famous prose poem that attempts to exhaustively and accurately recount the features of the Shu, Wu, and Wei capitals (Fujimoto, *Shinpan shikidō ōkagami*, 3). For David Knechtges's English translation of the rhapsody, see Zuo Si, "Three Capitals Rhapsody." Related to the issue of comprehensive treatment, Michael Kinski observes that the early Edo turn of the eighteenth century saw an increasing appetite for texts that offered a totality of knowledge, or at least a totality with regard to a given topic or topics ("Treasure Boxes, Fabrics, and Mirrors," 73). He takes up three editions of a *Mirror*, complete with title variations, in his subsequent discussion to conclude that the designation had no exclusive genre significance (ibid., 79–80). Whether or not one is persuaded by this example, Kinski's study indirectly offers support for the notion of the semantic shift behind the idea of *Mirror* suggested above.

6. Based on the title, one might also suppose Saikaku's *Shoen ōkagami* (The Great Mirror of the Several Charms, published in 1684) to fall into this category. I follow Rodgers on the dating and translation of the title for *Shoen ōkagami* ("She Loves Me. She Loves Me Not," 37). *Nanshoku ōkagami*'s preface does not feature the conventional

cribs for the classics, such as *Genji binkagami* (Hand-Mirror for the Genji, published in 1660), which Peter Kornicki describes as "a condensed version of the tale that included an illustration and a haiku for each of the fifty-four chapters."[7] Other *Mirrors* focus on more practical matters, such as the slightly later *Onna fūzoku tamakagami* (Jeweled Mirror of Manners for Women, published in 1732), which the Kyoto Institute, Library and Archives website characterizes as "an illustrated instructive manual on personal appearance for women."[8] In addition to works such as these, the historiographic *Mirrors* discussed in the present study continued to be copied and/or printed in this period as well.

How did this happen? What is the relationship between the medieval historiographic *Mirrors* and this overwhelming diversity of early modern *Mirrors*? Although answering this rests on speculation, retracing the development of the historiographic *Mirrors* offers some potential clues as to how the mirror metaphor may have come to primarily signal a didactic position (or at least the ironic pose of one), as well as a preference for an exhaustive scope. The *Mirrors* began with a relatively limited aim: a promise to relate the history of one man's success, even if that man was the exceptional Fujiwara no Michinaga, in the vernacular as a narrative. Yet they evolved in ways that allowed for the incorporation of the prestige register of *kanbun*, more orthodox forms of record keeping in some works, and increasingly ambitious chronological spans.[9] The impact of

setting of the earlier *Mirrors*, but it invokes *The Chronicles of Japan* in the opening lines. Munemasa Isō, Matsuda Osamu, and Teruoka Yasutaka, *Nanshoku ōkagami*, 291. I have relied on Paul Schalow's translation thereof (Ihara Saikaku and Paul Gordon Schalow, *The Great Mirror of Male Love*, 49 [unnumbered page]). For Schalow's discussion of Saikaku's nods to and twists on *The Great Mirror*, see ibid., 3–4. The editors of the *Shinpen Nihon koten bungaku zenshū* edition of *The Great Mirror of Male Love* suggest that *The Great Mirror of the Erotic Way* (rather than *The Great Mirror*) was a model for Saikaku (Munemasa, Matsuda, and Teruoka, *Nanshoku ōkagami*, 294–95, unnumbered note).

7. Kornicki, "Unsuitable Books for Women?," 167.

8. Kyoto Institute, Library and Archives ("Shiryō gaido: 'Onna fūzoku tamakagami' to 'Jochū fūzoku tsuyakagami'").

9. The shift toward "full" histories—of China, the shogunate, the imperial house, and so on—is an intriguing development, because it suggests that even if Sima Guang's *Zizhi tongjian* (A Comprehensive Mirror for Assisting Governance) was the inspiration for *Honchō tsugan*, there was already an audience eager for texts that claimed to provide

this first becomes legible when all of the medieval historiographic *Mirrors*—not only those familiar from their canonization as "historical tales"—are taken into account. Therefore, after briefly retracing the medieval journey of the present book's inclusive category of *Mirrors* in terms of principle, place, and language, this epilogue will step back to consider the *Mirrors* more broadly in their world—a world in which it was increasingly not just the past that they were tasked with revealing, but an ever growing array of human concerns and experiences.

To begin with the rhetoric of cosmological principles, across the eight *Mirrors* examined—*The Great Mirror*, *The New Mirror*, *The Water Mirror*, *The China Mirror*, *The Mirror of the East*, *The Mirror of the Watchman in the Fields*, *The Clear Mirror*, and *The Mirror of the Gods*—one can observe a gradual disengagement from defining a historical trajectory in Buddhist terms. Even as cosmological forces in the form of *kami* and buddhas continue to populate the *Mirrors*, there appears to be a diminishing concern with depicting historical change as subject to an overt, well-defined cosmological principle. In contrast to the earliest *Mirrors*, which struggle to explain (or in some instances escape) a perceived decline, the final *Mirrors* offer no indication of a vision beyond that of charting change. For lack of a better term, a gradual secularization of the genre occurs.

To be sure, the *Mirrors* never completely eschew a preternatural guarantor of order. Although references to karmic causation and/or "principles" as such disappear, the appeal of attributing outcomes to a greater divine right—the power of the *kami* and buddhas—remains. Yet revealing a particular shape to the past defined by divine or cosmological logic is a different enterprise from proposing that otherworldly forces influenced the past. In progressing from the former position to the latter, the *Mirrors* move away from the principle-underpinned discourse that governs their earliest iterations toward a more amorphous relationship with the forces that determine the course of events. The final two *Mirrors* focus primarily on recording, rather than explaining, and become nostalgic meditations, in an abstract sense, on the history of the *Mirror* genre itself. Even as this trend suggests a gradual divergence from medieval audiences'

---

a thorough account of the "big picture." On the transmission of Sima Guang's work, see the annotation to "What Is a *Mirror*?" in the introduction.

expectations for accounts of the past, it may well have lent itself to the eventual use of a *Mirror* to explain a vast array of subjects, a development returned to below.

Throughout the *Mirrors*, narrative geography and place play a central role. As a group, the *Mirrors* begin in Kyoto but gradually move through various more distant sites before returning to the capital. The first three *Mirrors* take advantage of one or more settings in the Kyoto or Nara region, and *The China Mirror* is the first to move beyond the traditional *kinai* provinces, going all the way to Dazaifu, and to take up a subject other than the Japanese court. The *Mirrors*' path is then complicated by the genre's bifurcation following *The China Mirror*. The subsequent *Mirrors* that are sympathetic to a *bakufu*—*The Mirror of the East* and *The Mirror of the Gods*—both revolve around central sites implied to be the locations of the Kamakura and Muromachi shogunates, respectively. Yet neither makes use of a preface to specify this. This can be at least partially explained in terms of the fact that each celebrates an idea of warrior authority that derives some of its power from directing movement. For these *Mirrors*, the move away from authority grounded in a particular site and to authority based on a (potentially mobile) institution suggests the limitations of a widespread appeal based on a specific place.[10] Instead, the symbolic preservation of institutions as authoritative—the office of shogun, the imperial throne, and so on—and their intimated future survival become the focus of the historiographic enterprise in this time of growing instability and disunity. Meanwhile, the later court-oriented *Mirrors*—*Watchman* and *The Clear Mirror*—continue to rely on temples in or near the *kinai* region to ground their narratives. There they wage losing battles against the forces of historical change, retreating into memories of how the world once was. These diverging paths for the *Mirrors* reflect real-world shifts in power structures, and each location, named or not, is intimately connected to the nature of the authority the related *Mirror* projects. As with the evolving discourse on cosmological principles, this engagement with place resonates across and beyond the world of the medieval *Mirrors*.

10. On mobility as key to the exercise of authority in this time period, see Spafford, *Sense of Place*, 12.

As part of their journey from the historiographic margins to the center, over time the *Mirrors* engage in an increasingly complicated relationship with linguistic form and its implicit ties to orthodoxy. With the earliest two *Mirrors* written in *wabun*, the genre appears at first to be one that will define itself mostly in terms of a concern with veracity and the eyewitness. *The Water Mirror* begins to complicate that via the introduction of *kanbun* in a pattern that suggests an interdependent, but not redundant, relationship with the work's *wabun* content; there are then echoes of this in *The China Mirror*. The picture is further complicated with the subsequent split marked by the *wabun* court *Mirrors* on the one hand, and the *kanbun bakufu Mirrors* on the other hand. *Wabun* becomes synonymous with cultural conservatism and nostalgia, while *kanbun* signals aspirations that have no place in the traditional "historical tale" driven account of the development of Japanese historiography. This is where the inclusion of *The Mirror of the East* is particularly valuable. Traditionally, it has been seen as a breed apart, with its attempts to mark its new claims to authority—the use of variant *kanbun*, the grounding in an amorphous but powerful cosmology, and the complete recentering around warrior institutions of government—regarded as an isolated phenomenon, unrelated to court-generated narratives of the past (such as the *wabun Mirrors*).[11] *The Mirror of the Gods*, however, exposes the problematic nature of this narrative. As a preface-free *Mirror* that centers on the imperial line (and its *bakufu* support), but that structurally and linguistically resembles *The Mirror of the East*, *The Mirror of the Gods* attests to the riskiness in assuming a particular mode of reading or genre to be monolingual. This is not because it collapses the topics of imperial succession and *bakufu* exploits into a single history, but because it does so in explicit dialogue with *The Water Mirror*, one of only two texts that it names as a source and the only one that is cited more than once.[12] This is striking not only because it attests to the longevity and circulation of

11. That said, *The Mirror of the East* famously found an enthusiastic reader in Tokugawa Ieyasu (1543–1616) (Nagahara and Kishi, *Zen'yaku Azuma kagami*, 1:3).

12. *The Water Mirror* is overtly cited three times: in the reigns of Emperor Keikō, Empress Iitoyo (traditionally fifth century), and Empress Suiko (*Shinmeikyō*, 98, 103, and 109). This is still more intriguing given that *The Mirror of the Gods* in fact draws upon numerous sources, most of which go unnamed. See Sasaki Kiichi for a quick partial list of these presumed sources that includes both *Tale of the Heike* and *Taiheiki* ("'Shinmeikyō' denpon [ge]," 33). The fact that the Yoshino-oriented *Taiheiki*'s content

The Water Mirror, but even more so because it exposes how intertwined *kanbun* and *wabun* writing could be in this period. Moreover, *The Water Mirror*, despite being mostly in *kana*, is shown to be a perfectly acceptable source of material for a history that aims at orthodoxy.[13] This suggests that *Mirrors*, regardless of their written register, have achieved a certain stature as a genre for articulating the past. It also demonstrates their potential for ongoing engagement with one another, providing further evidence that content, or a particular intellectual commitment—the presentation of the ordered transmission of power within an institution—rather than language, is what makes a *Mirror* a "Mirror."

Integrating these developments into a broader picture that includes other fourteenth- and fifteenth-century writings provides additional useful context for understanding the *Mirrors*' development. These centuries witness a shift in expectations of what *Mirrors* might reveal, as they move gradually from apologetic presentations of partially remembered transmissions with a contained chronological scope to detailed, expansive presentations of information. This appears to be connected to a semantic widening with regard to the nature of what a *Mirror* is intended to reflect. Looking back at the ways actual mirrors were deployed in the *Mirrors* and other texts under discussion, it is never the case that the surface reflects the object directly in front of it. There is Masako's dream vision of the magic mirror in *The Mirror of the East*; and before that, in *The China Mirror*, Taizong's mirror is alluded to as something that provides lessons from the past, not an image of what stands before it. Although Mujū Ichien's (1226–1312) *Tsuma kagami* (Mirror for Women, written in 1300) does not use the past to teach, it likewise frames a longer meditation on Buddhist teachings as a *Mirror* of "precepts."[14] Physical mirrors

is subsumed and unacknowledged is particularly noteworthy. My understanding of the *Taiheiki* derives from Helen McCullough, *Taiheiki*.

13. Moreover, the passages from *The Water Mirror* are visually indistinct from the rest of the text in *hentai kanbun*.

14. Mujū Ichien, *Mujū tsuma kagami*, 264. See also Morrell, "Mirror for Women: *Tsuma Kagami*," 75. Designating the work a "popular religious tract (*kana hōgo*)," Morrell also suggests that its title may be a reference to *The Mirror of the East*, but the work's similarities with the historiographic *Mirrors* end with the name and the general Buddhist orientation ("Mirror for Women: Mujū Ichien's *Tsuma Kagami*," 45 and 48). *Honchō shojaku mokuroku* includes a listing of an eight-scroll *Hōkyō* (Mirror of the Law) under the "Miscellany" heading, but I have been unable to identify the text or its putative author, Taikaku (Fujiwara no Sanefuyu, *Honchō shojaku mokuroku*, 179).

are also depicted as capable of channeling something other than what is before them to reflect geographically or metaphysically distant realities, as a scene toward the end of *The Tale of Matsura* (introduced in chapter 3) illustrates. There, the hero, Ujitada, draws out a mirror given to him by his erstwhile lover, the Chinese dowager empress, whereupon "the world he had known was clearly reflected."[15] This is by no means presented as an ordinary event, but Ujitada is not alarmed by the sight, only pained. He does not cast aside the mirror as something sinister but rather cries over it as the light gradually fades, until at last he puts it away. Although the particulars of the reflections are different, mirrors in each of these texts function as conduits, but not as a way to recognize the immediate object, person, or event before them.

This valence for the mirror metaphor continues to hold at least into the early Muromachi period, as can be seen in the appearance of another magical mirror in the *nō* play "Shōkun" (Zhaojun), attributed to the fourteenth-century playwright Konparu Gonnokami (dates unknown) and presumably dating from roughly the same time period as *The Clear Mirror*. The play is based loosely on the first-century figure of Wang Zhaojun (Japanese: Ō Shōkun) who was married off in a diplomatic arrangement with the Xiongnu, and it focuses on the grief of Shōkun's parents after the loss of their daughter. In the play's sixth scene, Shōkun's father explains the situation to a male villager, who in turn suggests using a magic mirror to see an image of their far-off daughter. What the parents do not realize is that Shōkun is dead, but her ghost is nonetheless able to send an image of her to them via the mirror. (The same mirror also reveals to her "barbarian" husband his true nature as a demon.) The play concludes with the chorus commenting on the image briefly visible to Shōkun's parents as they huddle around the mirror: "Since hers *is* an unsullied heart, this is a mirror that reflects the truth, this is a mirror that reflects the truth."[16] In the world of the play at least, the mirror continues to have

15. Higuchi and Kuboki, *Matsuranomiya monogatari*, 135. An alternative translation is, "In the mirror was reflected, with vivid clarity, the world he had left behind in China" (Fujiwara Teika and Wayne P. Lammers, *Tale of Matsura*, 160).

16. Yokomichi and Omote, "Shōkun," 173 (my discussion is based on this work). Similarly, Mujū's work contains an account of a deluded woman who is unable to see herself in the mirror she is gazing into (*Mujū tsuma kagami*, 258–59). See also Morrell, "Mirror for Women: *Tsuma Kagami*," 68.

significance for what truths it can transmit rather than simply for reflecting what is right in front of it.

The lingering preternatural valence of the mirror metaphor notwithstanding, already in the Muromachi period there are at least two didactic *Mirrors* that have nothing to do with history or cosmology: *Genji ōkagami* (The Great Mirror of the Genji, possibly written in the fourteenth century) and *Genji kokagami* (The Small Mirror of the Genji, possibly written in the early fifteenth century).[17] Neither of these *Genji*-related *Mirrors* explains its title or offers any sort of narrative framework.[18] *The Small Mirror* provides a table of contents and then launches directly into a chapter-by-chapter commentary on the *Genji*. If the opening explanation of the "Paulownia Pavilion" (Kiritsubo) chapter (the first) is representative, these are largely a combination of explanatory glosses and simplified recapitulations of the content.[19] *The Great Mirror of the Genji* operates along similar lines.[20] Their existence suggests a perpetuation of the schism observed in chapter 4 between *The Mirror of the East* as a historiographic *Mirror* and *Watchman* as a *Mirror* devoted primarily to literary (and religious) criticism. In short, both the trend up to this time within the *Mirrors* and the appearance of commentaries such as these indicate a decreasing interest in using Buddhist principles to govern the meaning of the mirror metaphor, even as *Mirrors* retain their claims to edify.

The *Mirrors* as a historiographic genre are comparatively few in number—only seven (or eight, if one includes *Watchman*). But in terms of their span of production, from the late eleventh through the mid-fifteenth centuries, the genre displays a remarkable longevity. Even as

17. Kornicki characterizes the latter as a "digest" of the *Tale of Genji* ("Unsuitable Books for Women?," 149). Given the presence of these and seemingly similar works about the *Genji* that appear throughout Kornicki's article, the trope of the *Mirror* as corrective and/or instructive seems to be a common one in the seventeenth century.

18. For a fuller description of both of these *Genji* "Mirrors," see Goff, "The Reception of the *Genji*," 31–33.

19. I base this statement upon a limited inspection of Nakano, *Genji kokagami: Keichō kokatsujibon/Genji kokagami: Meireki hanpon*. On the translation of the title, I follow Tyler's translation: Murasaki Shikibu, *Tale of Genji*.

20. I base this statement upon a limited inspection of the Koten bunko version of *Genji ōkagami* (Ishida and Kayaba, *Genji ōkagami*).

the specifics for how *Mirror* writers presented the past evolved, the enduring commitment to rendering events as fundamentally subject to a cosmic order, if not always an obvious one, remained. This enabled the creation of a body of works that in their ascendancy promised much: a morality for ordering the past in the tumultuous years of the late Heian period, the survival of the world beyond the Genpei War, the intellectual mastery of the Chinese past, and the establishment and longevity of the *bakufu* in the face of internal and external threats. In later iterations, they took on an increasingly nostalgic function, romanticizing the imperial restoration and asserting the legitimacy of the Northern Court and its eventual reintegration of its southern rival. Throughout, they promised—or remembered—a Japan that was somehow ordered, despite all of the this-worldly signs to the contrary. While not all "worked" equally well in their respective moments—some clearly enjoyed a broader readership and richer afterlife than others—as a type of teaching text, the appeal of the *Mirror* endured. Perhaps it was this mix of flexible specifics with a recognizably consistent frame (or pair of frames, if one thinks of the genre as becoming bifurcated) that enabled the *Mirrors* to establish a generic authoritative voice that could ultimately teach nearly anything in the early modern world, from the dawn of Japanese civilization to mastery of the pleasure quarters. Although this cannot be attributed to the history of Japanese *Mirrors* alone, the fact remains that if one wished to teach something, and teach it with authority in early modern Japan, the *Mirror* would be a wildly popular vehicle to use. As surely as Sima Guang's (1019–86) *Mirror* played an important role in early modern ideas of how to narrate history as a *Mirror*, the twisting and forked path traced by Japan's medieval *Mirrors* helped create a prominent indigenous historiographic tradition in which a *Mirror* was to be taken seriously and an audience whose members knew to look to *Mirrors* for answers.[21]

Releasing the *Mirrors* from twentieth-century ideas of what determines genre and instead engaging with the texts as they cross linguistic and stylistic lines, blend and borrow formal structures, and unfailingly endeavor to order the past reveals the *Mirror* genre as one that came to

21. For a discussion of historiography in early modern Japan that indirectly reveals the longevity of modes of reading and writing the past that the *Mirrors* participated in and promoted, see Thomas Keirstead, "The Romance of the Middle Ages."

be the preferred tool in its day for interpreting or processing the past and guaranteeing future survival. In voices that are at some times nostalgic for a lost world and at other times hopeful for an eventual triumph, the medieval *Mirrors* as a group formed an intellectual institution that had the flexibility and resourcefulness to create continuities with successive pasts and to offer promises for a future. This enabled their survival for nearly three and a half centuries despite the frequent war, unrest, and re-structuring that shaped Japan's medieval world.

Character List

Akazome Emon 赤染衛門
Anrakuji 安楽寺
Ashikaga Tadayoshi 足利直義
Ashikaga Takauji 足利尊氏
Ashikaga Yoshimitsu 足利義満
Ashiya dōman ōuchi kagami 芦屋道満大内鑑
Azuma kagami 吾妻鏡

Bailian jing 百練鏡
Baishōron 梅松論
Bishamondō 毘沙門堂
Bunkyō hifuron 文鏡秘府論
buntai 文体
butsumyōe 仏名会

Dōkyō 道鏡
dōri 道理
dōri monogatari 道理物語

Ehon Azuma kagami 絵本吾嬬鏡
Ehon masukagami 絵本十寸鑑
Ehon taka kagami 絵本鷹かがみ
Eiga monogatari 栄花物語
ekō or *egō* 壊劫
Engyōji or Enkyōji 円教寺
Ennin 円仁

Fujiwara no Fusasaki 藤原房前
Fujiwara no Kamatari 藤原鎌足
Fujiwara no Michinaga 藤原道長
Fujiwara no Michinori 藤原通憲
Fujiwara no Momokawa 藤原百川
Fujiwara no Moronaga 藤原師長
Fujiwara no Nakamaro 藤原仲麻呂
Fujiwara no Shigenori 藤原成範 (1135–1187)
Fujiwara no Shigenori 藤原茂範 (circa 1204–circa 1294)
Fujiwara no Sumitomo 藤原純友
Fujiwara no Tadamichi 藤原忠通
Fujiwara no Tadazane 藤原忠実
Fujiwara no Takanori 藤原孝範
Fujiwara no Tametsune 藤原為経
Fujiwara no Tokihira 藤原時平
Fujiwara no Yorinaga 藤原頼長

Genji binkagami 源氏鬢鏡
Genji kokagami 源氏小鏡
Genji ōkagami 源氏大鏡
gi 義
gohō 御報
gonge 権化
gongen 権現
Goseibai shikimoku 御成敗式目

Gukanshō 愚管抄
gunki monogatari 軍記物語
Gyōki 行基

Hachiman gudōkun 八幡愚童訓
Harima-no-kuni Shosha-zan engi 播磨国書写山縁起
Hasedera 長谷寺
Hayashi Razan 林羅山
Heihanki or Hyōhanki 兵範記
hentai 変体
Hōbutsushū 宝物集
Hōjō Masako 北条政子
Hōjō Masamura 北条政村
Hōjō Tokiyori 北条時頼
Hōjō Yasutoki 北条泰時
Hōjō Yoshitoki 北条義時
honchō 本朝
honchō shisho 本朝史書
Honchō shojaku mokuroku 本朝書籍目録
Honchō tsugan 本朝通鑑
honmon 本文
Huainanzi (Japanese: Enanji) 淮南子

Ichijō Tadayori 一条忠頼
Imakagami 今鏡
Ippen 一遍

Jakushō 寂照
Jien 慈円
Jikkunshō or Jikkinshō 十訓抄
Jinnō shōtōki 神皇正統記
jōkō 成劫
Jōkyūki 承久記
jugō 准后
jūkō 住劫

kagamimono 鏡物
kahō 果報
Kakaishō 河海抄
kakikudashi 書き下し
kami 神
kana hōgo 仮名法語
kanbun 漢文
kan'i jūni-kai 冠位十二階
Kara kagami 唐鏡
karidono 仮殿
Katsuragi or Kazuraki 葛城
kemari (Chinese: *cuju*) 蹴鞠
Kenchōji 建長寺
Kibi no Otodo nittō emaki 吉備大臣入唐絵巻
kidentai 紀伝体
kinai 畿内
kinjō 今上
Kiso Yoshinaka 木曽義仲
Kitabatake Chikafusa 北畠親房
Kō no Moronao 高師直
kokon or *kokin* 古今
Kokon chomonjū 古今著聞集
kokuō heiran 国王兵乱
Kong Anguo (Japanese: Kō Ankoku) 孔安國
Konparu Gonnokami 金春権守
Kujō Yoritsune 九条頼経
Kūkai 空海
kūkō or *kūgō* 空劫
Kyōgoku Tamekane 京極為兼
Kyōkai or Keikai 景戒

Liu Yu 劉裕

mana 真名
mappō (Chinese: *mo fa*) 末法
masse 末世
Masukagami 増鏡
matsudai 末代
Matsuranomiya monogatari 松浦宮物語
meyasushi 目安し
mimijikashi 耳近し
Minamoto no Arifusa 源有房
Minamoto no Arihito 源有仁
Minamoto no Mitsuyuki 源光行
Minamoto no Nakatsuna 源仲綱
Minamoto no Sanetomo 源実朝
Minamoto no Tōru 源融
Minamoto no Yorimasa 源頼政
Minamoto no Yoritomo 源頼朝
Minamoto no Yukiie 源行家
mitsudan 密談
Miura Yoshimura 三浦義村
Mizukagami 水鏡
Mochihito [Ō] 以仁[王]

Mōko shūrai ekotoba 蒙古襲来絵詞
mōgo 妄語
mon 文 (Chinese: *wen*)
monogatari 物語
Mononobe no Moriya 物部守屋
Mujū Ichien 無住一円
Mumyōzōshi 無名草子
Munenaga [Shinnō] 宗良[親王]
Munetaka [Shinnō] 宗尊[親王]

Nakayama Tadachika 中山忠親
Nanshoku ōkagami 男色大鑑
Natsu matsuri: Naniwa kagami 夏祭浪花鑑
nenbutsu 念仏
Nenjū gyōji emaki 年中行事絵巻
Nihon kōki 日本後記
Nihon Montoku Tennō jitsuroku 日本文徳天皇実録
Nihon ryōiki 日本霊異記
Nihon sandai jitsuroku 日本三代実録
Nihon shoki 日本書紀
Nijō Yoshimoto 二条良基
Nomori no kagami 野守鏡

Ōe no Asatsuna 大江朝綱
Ōe no Masafusa 大江匡房
Ōkagami 大鏡
Onna fūzoku tamakagami 女風俗玉鏡

rekishi monogatari 歴史物語
Rokuhara 六波羅
Ruiju myōgishō 類聚名義抄
Ryūgaiji 龍蓋寺

Saichō 最澄
San du fu (Japanese: San to no fu) 三都賦
Seiryōji 清凉寺
Sendai kuji hongi 先代旧事本紀
Shaku Nihongi 釈日本紀
Shikidō ōkagami 色道大鏡
shinmei 神明
Shinmeikyō or Shinmei kagami 神明鏡
shinryo fukai 神慮不快
shōbō (Chinese: *zheng fa*) 正法
Shoen ōkagami 諸艶大鑑
Shōkū 性空
Shoku Nihon kōki 続日本後紀
Shōmonki 将門記
Sima Guang (Japanese: Shiba Kō) 司馬光
sodegaki 袖書
Soga no Emishi 蘇我蝦夷
Soga no Iruka 蘇我入鹿
Soga no Umako 蘇我馬子
Sugawara denju tenarai kagami 菅原伝授手習鑑
Sugawara no Fumitoki 菅原文時
Sugawara no Michizane 菅原道真
sukuse 宿世

Taira no Kiyomori 平清盛
Taira no Masakado 平将門
Taira no Nobunori 平信範
Taira no Yoritsuna 平頼綱
tenken 天譴
Tsuchiya Yoshikiyo 土屋義清
tsūkō 通好
Tsuma kagami 妻鏡
Tsurugaoka Hachimangū 鶴岡八幡宮

Urin'in or Unrin'in 雲林院
uta 歌

wabun 和文
wago 和語
Wang Zhaojun (Japanese: Ō Shōkun) 王昭君
Wei Zheng (Japanese: Gi Chō) 魏徴

yamatokotoba 倭詞
Yoshishige no Yasutane 慶滋保胤
Yoshiwara kagami 吉原鏡

zasshō 雑抄
Zhang Heng (Japanese: Chō Kō) 張衡
Zheng Xuan (Japanese: Jō Gen) 鄭玄
Zhenguan zhengyao (Japanese: Jōgan seiyō) 貞観政要
Zizhi tongjian (Japanese: Shiji tsugan) 資治通鑑
zōbō (Chinese: *xiang fa*) 像法

Bibliography

Unpublished Manuscripts

Fusō ryakki: *Scrolls 22, 24, 25, and 28* 扶桑略記：巻 22, 24, 25, 28. Kōen. 1600/early Edo. NDLBibID 000010555025. National Diet Library. Accessed September 8, 2019. http://dl.ndl.go.jp/info:ndljp/pid/2532533.

Kara kagami: *Tameujibon* 唐鏡：為氏本. Traditionally attributed to Fujiwara no Tameuji (1222–86). Doc. 108-67. Nagoya-shi hakubutsukan, Hosa Bunko.

Masukagami: Ōeibon 増鏡：応永本. 1402. Doc. 5-07/マ/1貴. Main Library, Kyoto University.

Mizukagami: Ōeibon 水鏡：応永本. 1402. Doc. 107-25. Nagoya-shi hakubutsukan, Hosa Bunko.

Shinmeikyō 神明鏡. 1540. NDLBibID 000007298731. National Diet Library. Permanent link: http://dl.ndl.go.jp/info:ndljp/pid/2606917.

Published Works

Adolphson, Mikael S. *Gates of Power: Monks, Courtiers, and Warriors in Premodern Japan*. Honolulu: University of Hawai'i Press, 2000.

Agency for Cultural Affairs. "Kokushi bunkazai nado dētabēsu." Accessed September 24, 2019. http://kunishitei.bunka.go.jp/heritage/detail/201/8787.

Amsler, Mark. *Affective Literacies: Writing and Multilingualism in the Late Middle Ages*. Turnhout, Belgium: Brepols, 2011.

Andreeva, Anna. *Assembling Shinto: Buddhist Approaches to Kami Worship in Medieval Japan*. Cambridge, MA: Harvard University Asia Center, 2017.

Aoki Kengō 青木賢豪. "Fujiwara no Shigenori nenpyō-kō" 藤原成範年評孝. In *Kōza Heian bungaku ronkyū* 3, edited by Satō Akihiro, 261–305. Tokyo: Kazama Shōbo, 1986.

Asai Mineji 浅井峯治, ed., and Fujiwara no Shigenori 藤原成範, au. *Kara monogatari shinshaku* 唐物語新釈. Tokyo: Yushodo Shuppan, 1940; 1989 printing.

Asami Kazuhiko 浅見和彦, ed. *Jikkunshō* 十訓抄. Tokyo: Shōgakukan, 1997.

Atsuta Kō 熱田公. "Rekishi toshite no kagamimono" 歴史としての鏡物. In *Ōkagami/Masukagami*, edited by Yamagishi Tokuhei, 301–9. Tokyo: Kadokawa Shoten, 1976; 1977 printing.

Bailey, Don Clifford. "Early Japanese Lexicography." *Monumenta Nipponica* 16, nos. 1–2 (April–June, 1960): 1–52.

Batten, Bruce L. *Gateway to Japan: Hakata in War and Peace, 500–1300*. Honolulu: University of Hawai'i Press, 2006.

Benjamin, Walter. "Über den Begriff der Geschichte." In *Illuminationen*, edited by Siegfried Unseld, 51–61. Frankfurt, Germany: Suhrkamp Taschenbuch Verlag, 1977.

Bialock, David T. "Biwa Masters and Musical Hierophanies in the *Heike monogatari* and Other Medieval Texts." *Journal of Religion in Japan* 2 (2013): 119–51.

———. *Eccentric Spaces, Hidden Histories: Narrative, Ritual, and Royal Authority from* The Chronicles of Japan *to* The Tale of the Heike. Stanford, CA: Stanford University Press, 2007.

———. "From *Heike* to *Nomori no kagami*: Onmyōdō and the Soundscapes of Medieval Japan." *Cahiers d'Extrême Asie* 21 (2012): 165–99.

———. "Nation and Epic: *The Tale of the Heike* as Modern Classic." In *Inventing the Classics: Modernity, National Identity, and Japanese Literature*, edited by Haruo Shirane and Tomi Suzuki, 151–78. Stanford, CA: Stanford University Press, 2000.

Blair, Heather. *Real and Imagined: The Peak of Gold in Heian Japan*. Cambridge, MA: Harvard University Asia Center, 2015.

Bodeman, Richard. "Poetics and Prosody in Early Medieval China: A Study and Translation of Kūkai's *Bunkyō Hifuron*." PhD diss., Cornell University, 1978.

Borgen, Robert. "Michizane, Tenjin, and Dazaifu." In *Hakata: The Cultural Worlds of Northern Kyushu*, edited by Andrew Cobbing, 25–42. Leiden, the Netherlands: Brill, 2013.

Boston Museum of Fine Arts. "Illustrated Books/kagami/Asia." Accessed March 1, 2018. https://collections.mfa.org/search/Objects/classifications%3AIllustrated%20books%3Btitle%3Akagami%3BcollectionTerms%3AAsia/*/images?page=1.

Brightwell, Erin L. "*The Mirror of China*: Language Selection, Images of China, and Narrating Japan in the Kamakura Period (1185–1333)." PhD diss., Princeton University, 2014.

Brown, Delmer M. "Buddhism and Historical Thought in Japan before 1221." *Philosophy East and West* 24, no. 2 (April 1974): 215–25.

Brown, Delmer M., and Ichirō Ishida. *The Future and the Past: A Translation and Study of the Gukanshō, an Interpretive History of Japan Written in 1219*. Berkeley: University of California Press, 1979.

Brownlee, John S. *Political Thought in Japanese Historical Writing: From* Kojiki *(712) to* Tokushi Yoron *(1712)*. Waterloo, ON: Wilfred Laurier University Press, 1991.

Brownstein, Michael C. "From Kokugaku to Kokubungaku: Canon-Formation in the Meiji Period." *Harvard Journal of Asiatic Studies* 47, no. 2 (December 1987): 435–60.

Burns, Susan L. *Before the Nation: Kokugaku and the Imagining of Community in Early Modern Japan*. Durham, NC: Duke University Press, 2003.

Carpenter, John T. "Chinese Calligraphic Models in Heian Japan." In *The Culture of Copying in Japan: Critical and Historical Perspectives*, edited by Rupert Cox, 156–95. London: Routledge, 2008.

Certeau, Michel de. *The Writing of History*. Translated by Tom Conley. New York: Columbia University Press, 1988.

Chino Kaori 千野香織. "Gender in Japanese Art." Translated by Martha J. McClintock, Ikumi Kamanishi, and Judith Stubbs. In *Gender and Power in the Japanese Visual Field*, edited by Joshua S. Mostow, Norman Bryson, and Maribeth Graybill, 17–34. Honolulu: University of Hawai'i Press, 2003.

———. "Nihon bijutsu no jendā" 日本美術のジェンダー. In *Chino Kaori chosakushū*, edited by Chino Kaori chosaku henshū iinkai, 517–39. Tokyo: Buryukke, 2010.

Collcutt, Martin. "Religion in the Formation of the Kamakura Bakufu: As Seen through the 'Azuma kagami.'" *Japan Review* 5 (1994): 55–86.

Conlan, Thomas D. *From Sovereign to Symbol: An Age of Ritual Determinism in Fourteenth-Century Japan*. Oxford: Oxford University Press, 2011.

———. *In Little Need of Divine Intervention: Takezaki Suenaga's Scrolls of the Mongol Invasions of Japan*. Ithaca, NY: East Asia Program, Cornell University, 2001.

———. *State of War: The Violent Order of Fourteenth-Century Japan*. Ann Arbor: University of Michigan Center for Japanese Studies, 2003.

———. "Traces of the Past: Documents, Literacy, and Liturgy in Medieval Japan." In *Currents in Medieval Japanese History: Essays in Honor of Jeffrey P. Mass*, edited by Gordon M. Berger, Andrew E. Goble, Lorraine F. Harrington, and G. Cameron Hurst III, 19–50. Los Angeles: Figueroa Press, 2009.

Dykstra, Yoshiko K. "Notable Tales Old and New: Tachibana Narisue's *Kokon Chomonjū*." *Monumenta Nipponica* 47, no. 4 (Winter 1992): 469–93.

Endō Keita 遠藤慶太. "Chokusen shisho no seijisei: Futatsu no Kanmu tenki o meguri" 勅撰史書の政治性—ふたつの桓武天紀をめぐり. *Rekishigaku kenkyū* 826 (April 2007): 10–17.

Eubanks, Charlotte. *Miracles of Book and Body: Buddhist Textual Culture and Medieval Japan*. Berkeley: University of California Press, 2011.

Friday, Karl. *The First Samurai: The Life and Legend of the Warrior Rebel, Taira Masakado*. Hoboken, NJ: John Wiley and Sons, 2008.

Fujimoto Kizan 藤本箕山 (1628–1704). *Shinpan shikidō ōkagami* 新版色道大鏡. Tokyo: Yagi Shoten, 2006.

Fujiwara no Sanefuyu 藤原実冬 (1243–1303). *Honchō shojaku mokuroku* 本朝書籍目録. In *Gunshoruijū*, vol. 28, edited by Hanawa Hokinoichi (1746–1821), 166–81. Tokyo: Yagi Shoten, 2014.

Fujiwara no Sanesuke 藤原実資 (957–1046). *Shōyūki*: vol. 5 小右記：五. Tokyo: Iwanami Shoten, 1969.

Fujiwara Teika and Wayne P. Lammers. *The Tale of Matsura: Fujiwara Teika's Experiment in Fiction*. Ann Arbor: University of Michigan Center for Japanese Studies, 1992.

Fukatsu Mutsuo 深津睦夫 and Kimishima Aki 君嶋亜紀, eds. *Shin'yō wakashū* 新葉和歌集. Tokyo: Meiji Shoin, 2014.

Fukazawa Tōru 深沢徹. "Rekishi no 'gaibu' ni tatsu koto—'Gukanshō' ni okeru 'ichininshō' hyōgen no kanōsei" 歴史の＜外部＞に立つこと–『愚管抄』における「一人称」表現の可能性. In *'Gukanshō' no 'uso' to 'makoto'—rekishi monogatari no jikogenkyūsei o koedete*, 124–62. Tokyo: Shinwasha, 2006.

Fukuda Akimichi 福田景道. "Rekishi monogatari no han'i to keiretsu (ge)" 歴史物語の範囲と係列(下). *Shimane Daigaku kyōikubu kiyō (jinbun/shakai)* 27, no. 2 (March 1994): 17–27.

———. "Rekishi monogatari no han'i to keiretsu (jō)" 歴史物語の範囲と系列(上). *Shimane Daigaku kyōikubu kiyō (jinbun/shakai)* 27, no. 1 (December 1993): 25–34.

———. "Rekishi monogatari no katarite settei no keishō to tenkai" 歴史物語の語り手設定の継承と展開. *Shimane Daigaku shakai fukushi ronshū* 3 (March 2010): 1–16.

———. "Rekishi monogatari toshite no 'Baishōron'" 歴史物語としての『梅松論』. *Shimane Daigaku kyōiku gakubu kiyō* 28 (December 1994): 1–13.

Fukunaga Susumu 福長進. "Kagamimono to setsuwa" 鏡物と説話. In *Setsuwa no kōza 6: Setsuwa to sono shūen—monogatari, geinō*, edited by Honda Yoshinori, Ikegami Junichi, Komine Kazuaki, Mori Masato, and Abe Yasurō, 70–90. Tokyo: Benseisha, 1993.

Geddes, Ward. *Kara monogatari: Tales of China*. Tempe, AZ: Center for Asian Studies, 1984.

Goff, Janet. "The Reception of the *Genji* in the Middle Ages." In *The Tale of Genji: Japanese Literature in English*, vol. 3, edited by H. Richard Okada, 19–37. London and New York: Routledge, 2011.

Gomi Fumihiko 五味文彦. "Kyō, Kamakura no ōken" 京・鎌倉の王権. In *Kyō, Kamakura no ōken*, 7–113. Tokyo: Yoshikawa Kōbunkan, 2003.

———. *Shomotsu no chūseishi* 書物の中世史. Tokyo: Misuzu Shobō, 2003; 2004 printing.

———. *Zōho Azuma kagami no hōhō: Jijitsu to shinwa ni miru chūsei* 増補吾妻鏡の方法：事実と神話に見る中世. Tokyo: Yoshikawa Kōbunkan, 2000; 2006 printing.

Grossberg, Kenneth A. "From Feudal Chieftain to Secular Monarch: The Development of Shogunal Power in Early Muromachi Japan." *Monumenta Nipponica* 31, no. 1 (Spring 1976): 29–49.

Haga Yaichi 芳賀矢一. "Rekishi monogatari to sono genryū" 歴史物語とその源流. In *Haga Yaichi senshū*, vol. 3, edited by Haga Yaichi senshū henshū iinkai, 293–98. Tokyo: Kokugakuin Daigaku, 1982.

Hagiwara Tatsuo 萩原龍夫. "Hachiman gudōkun (kō)" 八幡愚童訓(甲). In *Nihon shisō taikei 20: Jisha engi*, edited by Sakurai Tokutarō, Hagiwara Tatsuo, and Miyata Noboru, 169–205. Tokyo: Iwanami Shoten, 1975.

Hakamada Mitsuyasu 袴田光康. "Genji ippon kyō" 源氏一品経. In *Genji monogatari to Bukkyō: Butten, koji, girei*, edited by Hinata Kazumasa, 217–34. Tokyo: Seikansha, 2009.

Hall, John W. "The Muromachi Bakufu." In *The Cambridge History of Japan*, vol. 3, edited by Yamamura Kozo, 175–230. Cambridge: Cambridge University Press, 1990.

Hambrick, Charles H. "The 'Gukanshō': A Religious View of Japanese History." *Japanese Journal of Religious Studies* 5, no. 1 (March 1978): 37–58.

Harper, Thomas. "Obsequies for *Genji*." In *Reading the Tale of Genji: Sources from the First Millennium*, edited by Haruo Shirane and Thomas Harper, 177–206. New York: Columbia University Press, 2015.

Hasegawa Tadashi 長谷川端, ed. *Taiheiki* 太平記, vol. 1. Tokyo: Shōgakukan, 1994.

Heldt, Gustav. *The Pursuit of Harmony: Poetry and Power in Early Heian Japan*. Ithaca, NY: Cornell University East Asia Program, 2008.

Higuchi Yoshimaro 樋口芳麻呂 and Kuboki Tetsuo 久保木哲夫, eds., and Fujiwara no Shunzei no musume 藤原俊成女, au. *Mumyōzōshi* 無名草子. In *Matsuranomiya monogatari: Mumyōzōshi*, 167–285. Tokyo: Shōgakukan, 1999

Higuchi Yoshimaro and Kuboki Tetsuo, eds., and Fujiwara no Teika 藤原定家 (1162–1241), au. *Matsuranomiya monogatari* 松浦宮物語. In *Matsuranomiya monogatari: Mumyōzōshi*, 7–166. Tokyo: Shōgakukan, 1999.

Hiraizumi, H. "Der Einfluss der Mappō-Lehre in der Japanischen Geschichte." *Monumenta Nipponica* 1, no. 1 (January 1938): 58–69.

Hirasawa Gorō 平澤五郎. "*Kara kagami* no denpon oyobi shutten kō" 唐鏡の傳本及び出典考. *Shidō bunko ronshū* 4, no. 3 (1965): 309–418.

Hirasawa Gorō. *Kara kagami: Kōi hen* 唐鏡校異編. Tokyo: Koten Bunko, 1967.

Hirasawa Gorō and Yoshida Kōichi 吉田幸一 eds., and Fujiwara no Shigenori 藤原茂範 (circa 1204–circa 1294), au. *Kara kagami: Shōkōkanbon* 唐鏡: 彰考館本. Tokyo: Koten Bunko, 1965.

Hosokawa Taketoshi 細川武稔. "Ashikaga Yoshimitsu no Kitayama shintoshin kōsō" 足利義満の北山新都心構想. In *Toshi o kugiru*, edited by Chūsei toshi kenkyūkai, 89–101. Tokyo: Yamakawa Shuppansha, 2010.

Huey, Robert N., and Susan Matisoff. "Lord Tamekane's Notes on Poetry: Tamekanekyō Wakashō." *Monumentica Nipponica* 40, no. 2 (Summer 1985): 127–46.

Hurst, G. Cameron, III. "Insei." In *The Cambridge History of Japan*, vol. 2, edited by Donald H. Shively and William McCullough, 576–643. Cambridge: Cambridge University Press, 1999.

———. "The Kōbu Polity: Court-Bakufu Relations in Kamakura Japan." In *Court and Bakufu in Japan: Essays in Kamakura History*, edited by Jeffrey P. Mass, 3–28. Stanford, CA: Stanford University Press, 1982.

Hyodo Hiromi 兵藤裕己. "'Heike monogatari' joshōron: Rekishi no ronri to monogatari no ronri" 平家物語序章論 : 歴史の論理と物語の論理. *Nihon bungaku* 35, no. 1 (1986): 9–24.

———[as Hyōdō Hiromi]. *Godaigo tennō* 後醍醐天皇. Tokyo: Iwanami Shoten, 2018.

Ichiko Teiji 市古貞次, ed. *Heike monogatari* 平家物語, vol. 1. Tokyo: Shōgakukan, 1994.

Ihara Saikaku and Paul Gordon Schalow. *The Great Mirror of Male Love*. Stanford, CA: Stanford University Press, 1990.

Ikeda Shinobu 池田忍. "'Heiji monogatari emaki' ni miru risō no bushi-zō" 「平治物語絵巻」に見る理想の武士像. *Bijutsushi* 44, no. 2 (1995): 255–59.

Imatani, Akira, and Kozo Yamamura. "Not for Lack of Will or Wile: Yoshimitsu's Failure to Supplant the Imperial Lineage." *Journal of Japan Studies* 18, no. 1 (Winter 1992): 45–78.

Imperial Household Agency. "Genealogy of the Emperors of Japan." Accessed September 8, 2019. http://www.kunaicho.go.jp/e-about/genealogy/img/keizu-e.pdf.

Ishida, Ichirō. "Structure and Formation of *Gukanshō* Thought." In *The Future and the Past: A Translation and study of the* Gukanshō, *an Interpretive History of Japan Written in 1219*, Delmer M. Brown and Ichirō Ishida, 420–450. Berkeley: University of California Press, 1979.

Ishida Jōji 石田穰二 and Kayaba Yasuo 茅場康雄, eds. *Genji ōkagami* 源氏大鏡. Tokyo: Koten Bunko, 1989.

Ishii, Susumu. "The Decline of the Kamakura Bakufu." In *The Cambridge History of Japan*, vol. 3, edited by Yamamura Kozo, 128–74. Cambridge: Cambridge University Press, 1990.

Ishikawa Tōru 石川徹, ed. *Ōkagami* 大鏡. Tokyo: Shinchōsha, 1989.

Itō, Satoshi. "The Medieval Period: The Kami Merge with Buddhism." Translated by Mark Teeuwen. In *Shinto: A Short History*, edited by Inoue Nobutaka, Endō Jun, Mori Mizue, and Itō Satoshi; translated and adapted by Mark Teeuwen and John Breen, 63–107. London: Routledge Curzon, 2003.

Itō Takako 伊藤孝子. "Murasaki Shikibu dagoku setsuwa tsuiseki-kō (1)—*Ima kagami* to *Genji ippon kyō*" 紫式部堕獄説話追跡考 (一) 一今鏡と源氏一品経. *Kokubungaku shiron* 10 (March 1985): 57–64.

Iwasa Masashi 岩佐正, ed., and Kitabatake Chikafusa 北畠親房 (1293–1354), au. *Jinnō shōtōki* 神皇正統記. In *Jinnō shōtōki/Masukagami*, edited by Iwasa Masashi, Tokieda Motoki, and Kidō Saizō, 3–211. Tokyo: Iwanami Shoten, 1965.

Kairin 快倫. "Harima-no-kuni Shosha-zan engi" 播磨国書写山縁起. In *Zoku gunsho ruijū*, vol. 34, edited by Hanawa Hokinoichi and Ōta Tōshirō, 109–18. Tokyo: Yagi Shoten, 2014.

Kamens, Edward. *The Buddhist Poetry of the Great Kamo Priestess*. Ann Arbor: University of Michigan Center for Japanese Studies, 1990.

Kamo no Chōmei. "An Account of a Ten-Foot-Square Hut (Hōjōki, 1212)." Translated by Anthony H. Chambers. In *Traditional Japanese Literature: An Anthology, Beginnings to 1600*, edited by Haruo Shirane, 624–35. New York: Columbia University Press, 2007.

Kaneko Dairoku 金子大麓. "'Mizukagami' no setsuwa bungakusei shiron" 『水鏡』の説話文学性試論. In *Rekishi monogatari ronshū*, edited by Matsumoto Haruhisa, 109–26. Tokyo: Shintensha, 2001.

Kaneko Dairoku, Matsumoto Haruhisa 松本治久, Matsumura Takeo 松村武夫, and Katō Utako 加藤歌子, eds. *Mizukagami zen chūshaku* 水鏡全注釈. Tokyo: Shintensha, 1998.

Kanō Shigefumi 加納重文. "Imakagami kenkyūshi" 今鏡研究史. In *Rekishi monogatari kōza 4: Imakagami*, edited by Rekishi monogatari kōza kankō iinkai, 59–74. Tokyo: Kazama Shobō, 1997.

———. "Rekishi monogatari no seikaku" 歴史物語の性格. *Kokubungaku: kaishaku to kanshō* 54, no. 3 (1989): 16–23.

Katō Shizuko 加藤静子. "Kaisetsu" 解説. In *Ōkagami* 大鏡, 433–67. Tokyo: Shōgakukan, 1996.

Kawakita Noboru 河北騰. "'Mizukagami' ni tsuite no tokushoku nado jūni kō"「水鏡」についての特色など十二項. In *Mizukagami zen hyōshaku*, 2–6. Tokyo: Kasama Shoin, 2011; 2012 printing.

———. "Rekishi monogatari no seiritsu to tokushoku—iwayuru 'kagamimono' o chūshin to shite" 歴史物語の成立と特色いわゆる「鏡物」を中心として. *Dokkyō Daigaku kyōyō shogaku kenkyū* 18 (September 1983): 1–20.

Kawamura Teruo 川村晃生, ed., and Kenshō 顕昭 (flourished 1160–1206), au. *Shūchūshō* 袖中抄. Tokyo: Miyai Shoten, 2000.

Kawashima, Terry. *Itineraries of Power: Texts and Traversals in Heian and Medieval Japan*. Cambridge, MA: Harvard University Asia Center, 2016.

Keirstead, Thomas. "The Romance of the Middle Ages: Discovering the Past in Early Modern Japan." In *A Companion to Global Historical Thought*, edited by Prasenjit Duara, Viren Murthy, and Andrew Sartori, 47–62. Chichester: Wiley Blackwell, 2014.

Kidō Saizō 木藤才蔵, ed., and Nijō Yoshimoto 二条良基 (1320–88), au. *Masukagami* 増鏡. Tokyo: Meiji Shoin, 1969; 2008 edition.

Kiley, Cornelius J. "The Imperial Court as a Legal Authority in the Kamakura Age." In *Court and Bakufu in Japan: Essays in Kamakura History*, edited by Jeffrey P. Mass, 29–44. Stanford, CA: Stanford University Press, 1995.

Kimbrough, R. Keller. "*Nomori no kagami* and the Perils of Poetic Heresy." *Proceedings of the Association for Japanese Literary Studies* 4 (Summer 2003): 99–114.

Kinski, Michael. "Treasure Boxes, Fabrics, and Mirrors: On the Contents and the Classification of Popular Encyclopedias from Early Modern Japan." In *Listen, Copy, Read: Popular Learning in Early Modern Japan*, edited by Matthias Hayek and Annick Horiuchi, 70–88. Leiden, the Netherlands: Brill, 2014.

Kitabatake Chikafusa and H. Paul Varley. *A Chronicle of Gods and Sovereigns: Jinnō Shōtoki* of Kitabatake Chikafusa. New York: Columbia University Press, 1980.

Kitamura Masayuki 北村昌幸. "'Baishōron' no seijisei—Tatarahama kassen no igi o megutte" 『梅松論』の政治性−多々良浜合戦の意義をめぐって. In *Gunki monogatari no mado*, vol. 4, edited by Kansai gunki monogatari kenkyūkai, 295–313. Osaka: Izumi Shoin, 2012.

Klein, Susan Blakely. *Allegories of Desire: Esoteric Literary Commentaries of Medieval Japan*. Cambridge, MA: Harvard University Asia Center, 2002.

Kobayashi Yasuharu 小林保治, ed., and Fujiwara no Shigenori 藤原成範 (1135–87), au. *Kara monogatari zenshaku* 唐物語全釈. Tokyo: Kasama Shoin, 1998.

Kōen 皇円 (died 1169?). *Fusō ryakki: Kinshōinbon* 扶桑略記：金勝院本. In *Tenri toshokan zenpon sōsho washo no bu*, vol. 13, edited by Tenri toshokan zenpon sōsho washo no bu iinkai, 389–504 and appended 39–52. Tokyo: Yagi Shoten, 1975.

Koizumi Hiroshi 小泉弘 and Yamada Shōzen 山田昭全, eds., and Taira no Yasuyori 平康頼 (flourished in the twelfth century), au. "Hōbutsushū" 宝物集. In *Hōbutsushū/Kankyo no tomo/Hirasan kojin reitaku*, 1–373. Tokyo: Iwanami Shoten, 1993.

Kokubota Kaaki 小久保崇明. "Shikyō no bunshō—tairitsu suru wabungo to kanbun kundokugo o tsūshite" 四境の文章−対立する和文語と漢文訓読語を通して. *Ōmon ronsō* 79 (2011): 1–28.

Komatsu Shigemi 小松茂美. *Nihon no emaki 3: Kibi no Otodo nittō emaki* 日本の絵巻3：吉備大臣入唐絵巻. Tokyo: Chūō Kōronsha, 1987.

———. *Nihon no emaki 13: Mōko shūrai ekotoba* 日本の絵巻 13: 蒙古襲来絵詞. Tokyo: Chūō Kōronsha, 1988.

Komine Kazuaki 小嶺和明. "Chūsei no rekishi jojutsu kenkyū no kiseki to tenbō" 中世の歴史叙述研究の軌跡と展望. *Kaishaku to kanshō* 54, no. 3 (March 1989): 159–64.

———. "*Kara monogatari* no hyōgen keisei" 唐物語の表現形成. In *Chūko bungaku to kanbungaku II*, edited by Wakan hikaku bungaku kai, 195–215. Tokyo: Kyūko Shoin, 1987

———. "*Kara monogatari shōkō*" 唐物語小考. *Chūsei bungaku kenkyū* 12 (August 1986): 28–42.

———. "Ōkagami-ron" 大鏡論. In *Inseiki bungaku-ron*, 527–633. Tokyo: Kasama Shoin, 2006.

———. *Setsuwa no gensetsu: Chūsei no hyōgen to rekishi jojutsu* 説話の言説—中世の表現と歴史叙述. Tokyo: Shinwasha, 2002.

Konoe Kanetsune 近衛兼経 (1210–59). *Okanoya kanpakuki* 岡屋関白記. Tokyo: Iwanami Shoten, 1988.

Kornicki, Peter. "Unsuitable Books for Women? 'Genji monogatari' and 'Ise monogatari' in Late Seventeenth-Century Japan." *Monumenta Nipponica* 60, no. 2 (Summer 2005): 147–93.

Koselleck, Reinhart. *Futures Past: On the Semantics of Historical Time*. Translated by Keith Tribe. New York: Columbia University Press, 2004.

Kubota Jun 久保田淳. *Chūsei bungaku no jikū* 中世文学の時空. Tokyo: Wakakusa Shobō, 1998.

Kuroita Katsumi 黒板勝美, ed., and Kōen, au. *Fusō ryakki* 扶桑略記. Tokyo: Yoshikawa Kōbunkan, 1932.

Kyōkai. *Record of Miraculous Events in Japan: The Nihon Ryōiki*. Translated by Burton Watson. New York: Columbia University Press, 2013.

Kyoto Institute, Library and Archives ("Shiryō gaido: 'Onna fūzoku tamakagami' to 'Jochū fūzoku tsuyakagami'"). Accessed March 1, 2018. http://www.archives.kyoto.jp/?introduction=『女風俗玉鏡』と『女中風俗艶鏡』〜江戸時代女.

LaFleur, William R. *The Karma of Words: Buddhism and the Literary Arts in Medieval Japan*. Berkeley: University of California Press, 1986.

LaMarre, Thomas. *Uncovering Heian Japan: An Archaeology of Sensation and Inscription*. Durham, NC: Duke University Press, 2000.

Liu An 劉安 (d. 122 BCE). *Huainanzi* 淮南子. Taibei, Taiwan: Xin Wenfeng, 1978.

Lurie, David. "The Origins of Writing in Early Japan: From the 1st to the 8th Century CE." PhD diss., Columbia University, 2001.

———. *Realms of Literacy: Early Japan and the History of Writing*. Cambridge, MA: Harvard University Asia Center, 2011.

Marra, Michele. "The Conquest of Mappō: Jien and Kitabatake Chikafusa," *Japanese Journal of Religious Studies* 12, no. 4 (December 1985): 319–41.

———. "The Development of Mappō Thought in Japan (I)." *Japanese Journal of Religious Studies* 15, no. 1 (March 1988): 25–54.

———. "The Development of 'Mappō' Thought in Japan (II)." *Japanese Journal of Religious Studies* 15, no. 4 (December 1988): 287–305.

———. *Representations of Power: The Literary Politics of Medieval Japan*. Honolulu: University of Hawai'i Press, 1993.

Masamune Atsuo 正宗敦夫, ed. *Ruiju myōgishō* 類聚名義抄. 2 vols. Tokyo: Kazama Shobō, 1962.

Matsubara Shigeru 松原茂. "'Heiji monogatari ekotoba' no denrai to seiritsu"「平治物語絵詞」の伝来と成立. In *Heiji monogatari ekotoba: Nihon emaki taisei*, vol. 13, edited by Komatsu Shigemi, 82–100. Tokyo: Chūō Kōronsha, 1977.

Matsubayashi Yasuaki 松林靖明, ed. *Jōkyūki* 承久記. Tokyo: Gendai Shichōsha, 1974.

Matsueda Shigeo 松枝茂夫 and Wada Takeshi 和田武司, eds., and Tao Yuanming 陶淵明 (365–427), au. *Tō Enmei zenshū (jō)* 陶淵明全集(上). Tokyo: Iwanami Shoten, 1990.

Matsumoto Shinpachirō 松本新八郎. "Rekishi monogatari to shiron" 歴史物語と史論. In *Iwanami kōza Nihon bungakushi 6: chūsei*, 3–48. Tokyo: Iwanami Shoten, 1959.

Matsumura Hiroji 松村博司, ed. *Ōkagami* 大鏡. Tokyo: Iwanami Shoten, 1960.

Matsumura Takeo 松村武夫. "Mizukagami no shohon" 水鏡の諸本. In *Rekishi monogatari kōza 5: Mizukagami*, edited by Rekishi monogatari kōza kankō iinkai, 63–92. Tokyo: Kazama Shobō, 1997.

McCullough, Helen Craig. *Ōkagami, the Great Mirror: Fujiwara Michinaga (966–1027) and His Times*. Ann Arbor: University of Michigan Center for Japanese Studies, 1991.

———. *The Taiheiki: A Chronicle of Medieval Japan*. Rutland, VT: Charles E. Tuttle, 1979; 1992 printing.

McCullough, William. "The *Azuma Kagami* Account of the Shōkyū War." *Monumenta Nipponica* 23, nos. 1–2 (1968): 102–55.

———. "The Heian Court." In *The Cambridge History of Japan*, vol. 2, edited by Donald H. Shively and William H. McCullough, 20–96. Cambridge: Cambridge University Press, 1999.

McCullough, William H., and Helen Craig McCullough. *A Tale of Flowering Fortunes: Annals of Japanese Aristocratic Life in the Heian Period*. Vol. 1. Stanford, CA: Stanford University Press, 1980.

Metropolitan Museum of Art. Digital Collections. Accessed March 1, 2018. http://libmma.contentdm.oclc.org/cdm/ref/collection/p16028coll7/id/1379.

Miller, Roy Andrew. "Writing Systems." In *The Japanese Language*, 90–140. Chicago: University of Chicago Press, 1967.

Misumi Yōichi 三角洋一. "Kanbun-tai to wabun-tai no aida: Heian chūsei no bungaku sakuhin" 漢文体と和文体の間：平安中世の文学作品. In *Koten Nihongo no sekai: Kanji ga tsukuru Nihon*, edited by Tokyo daigaku kyōyō gakubu kokubun kanbun gakubukai, 99–123. Tokyo: Tokyo Daigaku Shuppansha, 2007.

Mori Masato 森正人. "Ōkagami ni okeru 'monogatari no ba' to Hokkekyō" 大鏡における＜物語の場＞と法華経. *Kokugo to kokubun* 67 (September 1990): 15–27.

Morishita Yōji 森下要治. "'Kara monogatari' no shinshō sekai—dai 18-wa 'Yōkihi' o megutte"『唐物語』の心象世界—第十八話「楊貴妃」をめぐって—. *Bunkyō kokubungaku* 50 (2006): 16–30.

Morita Tsurayuki 森田貫之. "Jidō setsuwa to gohō riron" 慈童説話と護法理論. *Kyōtō Daigaku kokubungaku ronsō* 24 (September 2010): 53–74.

———. "'Kara kagami'-kō (shōzen)" 『唐鏡』考(承前). *Kyōtō Daigaku kokubungaku ronsō* 27 (March 2012): 39–54.

Morrell, Robert E. "Mirror for Women: Mujū Ichien's *Tsuma Kagami*." *Monumenta Nipponica* 35, no. 1 (Spring 1980): 45–50.

———. "Mirror for Women: *Tsuma Kagami*." *Monumenta Nipponica* 35, no. 1 (Spring 1980): 51–75.

Mujū Ichien 無住一円 (1226–1312). *Mujū tsuma kagami* 無住妻鏡. In *Zoku gunsho ruijū*, vol. 28-2, edited by Hanawa Hokinoichi and Ōta Tōshirō, 243–64. Tokyo: Yagi Shoten, 2014.

Munemasa Isō 宗政五十緒, Matsuda Osamu 松田修, and Teruoka Yasutaka 暉峻康隆, eds., and Ihara Saikaku 井原西鶴, au. *Nanshoku ōkagami* 男色大鑑. In *Shinpen Nihon koten bungaku zenshū* 67, Tokyo: Shōgakukan, 1996; 2000 printing.

Murasaki Shikibu and Royall Tyler. *The Tale of Genji*. Vol. 1. New York: Viking, 2001.

Nagahara Keiji 永原慶二 and Kishi Shōzō 貴志正造, eds. *Zen'yaku Azuma kagami* 全訳吾妻鏡, 6 vols. Tokyo: Shin Jinbutsu Ōrai-Sha, 2011.

Nakada Norio 中田祝夫, ed., and Kyōkai 景戒 (ninth century), au. *Nihon ryōiki* 日本霊異記. Tokyo: Shōgakukan, 1975.

Nakajima Etsuji 中島悦次, ed., and Jien 慈円 (1155–1225), au. *Gukanshō: Zen chūkai* 愚管抄全註解. Tokyo: Yuseido, 1969.

Nakano Kōichi 中野幸一, ed. *Genji Kokagami: Keichō Kokatsujibon/Genji Kokagami: Meireki Hanpon* 源氏小鏡：慶長古活字本・源氏子鏡：明暦版本. Tokyo: Bensei Shuppan, 2009.

Nakayama Tadachika 中山忠親 (1131–95). *Kirei mondō* 貴嶺問答. In *Gunsho ruijū*, vol. 9, edited by Hanawa Hokinoichi, 438–59. Tokyo: Yagi Shoten, 2014.

———. *Mizukagami [Senjūjibon]* 水鏡[専修寺本]. Kyoto: Kichō Tosho Eihon Kankōkai, 1938.

——— [as Fujiwara Tadachika]. *Sankaiki:* 1–3 山槐記：一～三. Kyoto: Rinsenshoten, 1965; 1975 printing.

National Institute of Japanese Literature. "'Kara kagami': Hizen Matsudairabon." Accessed October 25, 2019. https://kotenseki.nijl.ac.jp/biblio/100182414/viewer.

Nattier, Jan. *Once Upon a Future Time: Studies in a Buddhist Prophecy of Decline*. Berkeley, CA: Asian Humanities Press, 1991.

Nishio Kōichi 西尾光一 and Kobayashi Yasuharu 小林保治, eds., and Tachibana no Narisue 橘成季 (thirteenth century), au. *Kokon chomonjū (ge)* 古今著聞集(下). Tokyo: Shinchōsha, 1986.

———. *Kokon chomonjū (jō)* 古今著聞集(上). Tokyo: Shinchōsha, 1983.

Nishio Yōtarō 西尾陽太郎. "Heian jidai gōki no rekishi shisō—Yotsugi, kyōrui to Gukanshō" 平安時代後期の歴史思想—世継ぎ・鏡類と愚管抄. In *Nihon ni okeru rekishi shisō no tenkai*, edited by Nihon shisōshi kenkyūkai, 75–99. Sendai, Japan: Tōhoku Shuppan, 1961.

Nomori no kagami 野守鏡. In *Gunshoruijū*, vol. 27, edited by Hanawa Hokinoichi, 474–514. Tokyo: Yagi Shoten, 2014.

Ogawa Takeo 小川剛生. "Fujiwara no Shigenori-den no kōsatsu—'Kara kagami' sakusha no shōgai" 藤原茂範伝の考察—『唐鏡』作者の生涯. *Wa-Kan hikaku bungaku* 12 (1994): 27–38.

Ogawa Toyō 小川豊夫. "Sangai o kenritsu suru kami: Chūsei Nihon ni okeru kiki no shingaku" 三界を建立する神–中世日本における危機の神学. *Nihon bungaku* 55, no. 7 (July 2006): 43–55.

Okamura Shigeru 岡村繁, ed., and Bai Juyi 白居易 (772–846), au. *Hakushi monjū*, vol. 1 白氏文集：一. Tokyo: Meiji Shoin, 1988; 2017 printing.

———. *Hakushi monjū*, vol. 4 白氏文集：四. Tokyo: Meiji Shoin, 1990.

Ōki Masayoshi 大木正義. "Imakagami no buntai" 今鏡の文体. In *Rekishi monogatari kōza 4: Imakagami*, edited by Rekishi monogatari kōza kankō iinkai, 141–63. Tokyo: Kazama Shobō, 1997.

———. "'Ōkagami' to 'Imakagami'" 『大鏡』と『今鏡』. *Kokubungaku: kaishaku to kanshō* 68, no. 2 (2003): 126–32.

Ōmori Kitayoshi 大森北義. "'Masukagami' no rekishi jojutsu" 『増鏡』の歴史叙述. *Koten issan* 55 (December 2005): 7–19.

Onoda Mitsuo 小野田光雄, ed., and Urabe Kanekata 卜部兼方 (flourished 1274–1301), au. *Shaku Nihongi* 釈日本紀 Tokyo: Shintō taikei hensankai, 1986.

Onoue Hachirō 尾上八郎. "Kaidai" 解題. In *Kōchū Nihon bungaku taikei: Dai 12-kan*, edited by Kokumin tosho kabushiki kaisha, 1–60. ed. Tokyo: Kokumin Tosho, 1916; 1928 printing.

Otagiri Fumihiro 小田切文洋. "'Kara kagami' ni okeru Kanseki juyō no ichi kōsatsu: Chūsei Nihon no rekishi jojutsu to Kanbun sekai" 『唐鏡』における漢籍受容の一考察中世日本の歴史叙述と漢文世界. *Studies in International Relations (Intercultural Relations 22)* 20, no. 2 (1999): 179–221.

———. "'Kara kagami' ni okeru Kanseki juyō no ichi kōsatsu (zoku)" 『唐鏡』における漢籍受容の一考察(続). *Omon ronsō* 51 (August 2000): 1–16.

Oyamada Kazuo 小山田和夫. "'Mizukagami' to 'Fusō ryakki'" 水鏡と扶桑略記. In *Rekishi monogatari kōza 5: Mizukagami*, edited by Rekishi monogatari kōza kankō iinkai, 93–112. Tokyo: Kazama Shobō, 1997.

———. "Shisen kokushi to wa nani ka: 'Fusō ryakki' no seiritsu to sono tokuchō" 私撰国史とは何か：『扶桑略記』の成立とその特徴. *Rekishi tokuhon* 45, no. 9 (June 2000): 156–61.

Oyler, Elizabeth. *Swords, Oaths, and Prophetic Visions: Authoring Warrior Rule in Medieval Japan*. Honolulu: University of Hawai'i Press, 2006.

Ozaki Isamu 尾崎勇. "'Gukanshō' no hōhō to 'Mizukagami'" 『愚管抄』の方法と『水鏡』. *Kumamoto tandai ronshū* 43, no. 1 (October 1992): 1–37.

———. "'Gukanshō' to 'Ōkagami'—sono setsuwa ni tsuite" 『愚管抄』と『大鏡』—その説話について. *Kokubungaku ronsō* 29 (March 1984): 19–38.

Perkins, George W. *The Clear Mirror: A Chronicle of the Japanese Court During the Kamakura Period (1185–1333)*. Stanford, CA: Stanford University Press, 1998.

Rabinovitch, Judith N. *Shōmonki: The Story of Masakado's Rebellion*. Tokyo: Monumenta Nipponica, Sophia University, 1986.

Rhodes, Robert F. "*Ōjōyōshū* and Pure Land Discourse in Heian Japan." *Japanese Journal of Religious Studies* 34, no. 2 (2007): 249–70.

Ri Yuri 李裕利. "Chōsenbon 'Tōkoku tsugan' no Nihon de no ryūden oyobi kankō" 朝鮮本『東国通鑑』の日本での流伝及び刊行. In *Umi o wataru shisho*, edited by Kim Shiduck and Hamano Seiichirō, 81–100. Tokyo: Bensei shuppan, 2016.

Ricoeur, Paul. *Memory, History, Forgetting*. Translated by Kathleen Blamey and David Pellauer. Chicago: University of Chicago Press, 2006.

Rodgers, Lawrence. "She Loves Me. She Loves Me Not. Shinjū and Shikidō Ōkagami." *Monumenta Nipponica* 49, no. 1 (Spring 1994): 31–60.

Rohlich, Thomas H. "In Search of Critical Space: The Path to *Monogatari* Criticism in the *Mumyōzōshi*." *Harvard Journal of Asiatic Studies* 57, no. 1 (June 1997): 179–204.

Saeki Koji 佐伯弘次. "Mōko shūrai ikō no Nihon no tai-Kōrai kankei" 蒙古襲来の日本の対高麗関係. *Shien* 153 (2016): 1–28.

Saeki Shin'ichi 佐伯真一, ed. *Chūsei no gunki monogatari to rekishi jojutsu* 中世の軍記物語と歴史叙述. Tokyo: Chikurinsha, 2011.

Sakakibara Kunihiko 榊原邦彦. "Imakagami no shisō" 今鏡の思想. In *Rekishi monogatari kōza 4: Imakagami*, edited by Rekishi monogatari kōza kankō iinkai, 117–140. Tokyo: Kazama Shobō, 1997.

Sakamoto Tarō. *The Six National Histories of Japan*. Translated by John S. Brownlee. Vancouver: University of British Columbia Press, 1991.

Sakurai Hironori 桜井宏徳. "'Ōkagami' ni hajimaru mono—'Imakagami' to 'Mumyōzōshi' o chūshin to shite" 『大鏡』に始まるもの－『今鏡』と『無名草子』を中心として. *Kokubungaku: kaishaku to kanshō* 76, no. 8 (2011): 51–59.

Sakurai Yoshirō 桜井好朗. *Chūsei Nihon no shinwa to rekishi jojutsu* 中世日本の神話と歴史叙述. Tokyo: Iwata Shoin, 2006.

Sasaki Kaoru 佐々木馨. *Nihon chūsei shisō no kichō* 日本中世思想の基調. Tokyo: Yoshikawa Kōbunkan, 2006.

Sasaki Kiichi 佐々木紀一. "'Shinmeikyō' denpon no seiri to seiritsi ni tsuite (ge)" 『神明鏡』伝本の整理と成立について(下). *Kokugo kokubun* 69, no. 2 (February 2000): 20–36.

———. "'Shinmeikyō' denpon no seiri to seiritsi ni tsuite (jō)" 『神明鏡』伝本の整理と成立について(上). *Kokugo kokubun* 69, no. 1 (January 2000): 16–33.

Scheid, Bernhard. "Shōmu Tennō and the Deity from Kyushu: Hachiman's Initial Rise to Prominence." *Japan Review* 27 (2014): 31–51.

Seiryōji 清凉寺. "Seiryōji ni tsuite." Accessed July 27, 2017. http://seiryoji.or.jp/introduce.html.

Selinger, Vyjayanthi R. *Authorizing the Shogunate: Ritual and Material Symbolism in the Literary Construction of Warrior Order*. Leiden, the Netherlands: Brill, 2013.

Shields, Anna M. "Remembering When: The Uses of Nostalgia in the Poetry of Bai Juyi and Yuan Zhen." *Harvard Journal of Asiatic Studies* 6, no. 22 (December 2006): 321–61.

Shimokawa Ryōko 下川玲子. "'Jinnō shōtōki' no rekishi jojutsu." In *Chūsei no gunki monogatari to rekishi jujutsu*, edited by Saeki Shin'ichi, 438–460. Tokyo: Chikurinsha, 2011.

Shinmeikyō 神明鏡. In *Zoku gunsho ruijū*, vol. 29-1, edited by Hanawa Hokinoichi and Ōta Tōshirō, 95–203. Tokyo: Yagi Shoten, 2014.

Shinoda, Minoru. *The Founding of the Kamakura Shogunate, 1180–1185: with Selected Translations from the* Azuma Kagami. New York: Columbia University Press, 1960.

Shirane, Haruo. "Introduction: Issues in Canon Formation." In *Inventing the Classics: Modernity, National Identity, and Japanese Literature*, edited by Haruo Shirane and Tomi Suzuki, 1–27. Stanford, CA: Stanford University Press, 2000.

Shukaku Hosshinō 守覚法親王 (1150–1202). *Saki* 左記. In *Gunsho ruijū*, vol. 24, edited by Hanawa Hokinoichi, 665–72. Tokyo: Yagi Shoten, 2014.

———. *Uki* 右記. In *Gunsho ruijū*, vol. 24, edited by Hanawa Hokinoichi, 673–88. Tokyo: Yagi Shoten, 2014.

Smits, Ivo. "China as Classic Text: Chinese Books and Twelfth-Century Japanese Collectors." In *Tools of Culture: Japan's Cultural, Intellectual, Medical, and Technological Contacts in East Asia, 1000–1500s*, edited by Andrew Edmund Goble, Kenneth R. Robinson, and Haruko Wakabayashi, 185–210. Ann Arbor, MI: Association for Asian Studies, 2009.

———. "The Way of the Literati: Chinese Learning and Literary Practice in Mid-Heian Japan." In *Heian Japan: Centers and Peripheries*, edited by Mikael Adolphson, Edward Kamens, and Stacie Matsumoto, 105–28. Honolulu: University of Hawai'i Press, 2007.

Spafford, David. *A Sense of Place: The Political Landscape in Late Medieval Japan*. Cambridge, MA: Harvard University Asia Center, 2013.

Stavros, Matthew. "Kitano Shrine and Muromachi (A Field Note with Matthew Stavros)." March 2017. https://youtu.be/V3-DPfeyEUU.

———. "Monuments and Mandalas in Medieval Kyoto: Reading Buddhist Kingship in the Urban Plan of Ashikaga Yoshimitsu." *Harvard Journal of Asiatic Studies* 77, no. 2 (December 2017): 321–61.

———. "The Sanjō bōmon Temple-Palace Complex: The First Locus of Ashikaga Authority in Medieval Kyoto." *Japan Review* 22 (2010): 3–29.

Stockdale, Jonathan. *Imagining Exile in Heian Japan: Banishment in Law, Literature, and Cult*. Honolulu: University of Hawai'i Press, 2015.

Suyama Yuko 陶山欲有子. "'Imakagami' ni okeru Kannon shinkō—rekishi no katarite wa Kannon no kegen ka" 『今鏡』における観音信仰—歴史の語り手は観音の化現か. *Gakushūin Daigaku jinbunkagaku ronshū* 17 (2008): 119–36.

Taira no Nobunori 平信範 (1112–87). *Heihanki: Vol. 2* 兵範記(二). Kyoto: Rinsen Shoten, 1965.

Takahashi Hideki 高橋秀樹. "Reikishi jojutsu to jikoku—Azuma kagami genshiryō zokkō" 歴史叙述と時刻—吾妻鏡原史料続考. In *Chūsei no gunki monogatari to rekishi jojutsu*, edited by Saeki Shin'ichi, 406–36. Tokyo: Chikurinsha, 2011.

Takeda Kō 武田孝, ed., and Kamo no Chōmei 鴨長明 (circa 1155–1216), au. *Hōjōki zenshaku* 方丈記全釈. Tokyo: Kasama Shoin, 1995.

Takeda Masanori 武田昌憲. "Ashikaga no ken'i—'Baishōron' no yukue, shōkō" 足利の権威—『梅松論』の行方・少考. *Gunki to Katarimono* 43 (March 2007): 75–77.

Takehana Isao 竹鼻績, ed., and Fujiwara no Tametsune 藤原為経, au. *Imakagami: Zen yakuchū* 今鏡：全訳注. 3 vols. Tokyo: Kōdansha, 1984.

Terada Takanobu 寺田隆信. "Shijin no shiteki kyōyō ni tsuite—arui wa 'Shiji tsugan' no rufu ni tsuite" 士人の史的教養についてーあるいは「資治通鑑」の流布について. *Rekishi* 82 (April 1994): 1–17.

Tōmatsubon ōkagami 東松本大鏡. Tokyo: Kichōkotensekikankōkai, 1953.

Tonomura Hisae 外村久江. "Kamakura bushi to Chūgoku koji" 鎌倉武士と中国故事. In *Kamakura bunka no kenkyū—sōka sōzō o megutte*, 103–19. Tokyo: Miyai Shoten, 1996.

Tyler, Royall. *Before* Heike *and After:* Hōgen, Heiji, Jōkyūki. Charleston, SC: CreateSpace, 2012.

———. *The Tale of the Heike.* New York: Viking, 2012.

Uwayokote Masataka 上横手雅敬. "'Jikkunshō' no hensha o megutte" 『十訓抄』の編者をめぐって. *Bukkyō bungaku* 31 (March 2007): 66–77.

Uyenaka, Shuzo. "A Study of *Baishōron:* A Source for the Ideology of Imperial Loyalism in Medieval Japan." PhD diss., University of Toronto, 1978.

Uyenaka, Shuzo and Thomas Conlan. "Baishoron." In *From* Baishoron *to* Nantaiheiki *(Fourteenth Century Voices* 2), edited by Royall Tyler, 15–120. N.p.: Blue-Tongue Books, 2016.

Vande Walle, Willy. "Japan: From Petty Kingdom to Buddha Land." *Japan Review* 5 (1994): 87–101.

Watanabe, Takeshi. "Buried Mothers: Exhuming Memories of Heian Families through *Eiga Monogatari.*" PhD diss., Yale University, 2005.

Watase Sigeru 渡瀬茂. "Rekishi monogatari no shūen—'Masukagami' ni okeru buntai no kiki ni tsuite." 歴史物語の終焉ー『増鏡』における文体の危機について. *Nihon bungaku* 40 (June 1991): 34–42.

White, Hayden. *Metahistory.* Baltimore, MD: Johns Hopkins University Press, 1975.

———. "The Value of Narrativity in the Representation of Reality." In Hayden White, *The Content of the Form: Narrative Discourse and Historical Representation*, 1–26. Baltimore, MD: Johns Hopkins University Press, 1987.

Wilkinson, Endymion. *Chinese History: A New Manual.* 4th ed. Cambridge, MA: Harvard University Asia Center, 2015.

Wu Jing 呉兢 (670–749). *Zhenguan zhengyao* 貞觀政要. Shanghai: Shanghai guji chubanshe, 1978.

Yabumoto Katsuharu 藪本勝治. "'Azuma kagami' ni okeru 'rekishi' kōchiku no ichi hōhō: Nogimiya kassen kiji o chūshin ni" 『吾妻鏡』における＜歴史＞構築の一方法—野木宮合戦記事を中心に. *Kokugo to Kokubungaku* 91, no. 9 (September 2014): 17–31.

Yamada Naoko 山田尚子. *Chūgoku koji juyō ronkō: Kodai chūsei Nihon ni okeru keishō to tenkai* 中国故事受容論考:古代中世日本における継承と展開. Tokyo: Bensei Shuppan, 2009.

———. "'Kara kagami'-kō—rekishi monogatari toshite no sokumen o megutte" 『唐鏡』考—歴史物語としての側面をめぐって. *Kokugo kokubungaku kenkyū (Kumamoto Daigaku)* 43 (2008): 29–43.

Yamada Yoshio 山田孝雄, Yamada Tadao 山田忠雄, Yamada Hideo 山田英雄, and Yamada Toshio 山田俊雄, eds. *Konjaku monogatarishū*: vol. 3 今昔物語集：三. Tokyo: Iwanami Shoten, 1961; 1963 printing.

Yamanaka Yutaka 山中裕. "Rekishi to bungaku" 歴史と文学. *Kokubungaku: kaishaku to kanshō* 54, no. 3 (1989): 6–13.

Yamashita Hiroaki 山下宏明. "Kantō no <rekishi> kijutsu—'Azuma kagami' Yoritomo Shōgun-ki o megutte" 関東の＜歴史＞記述ー『吾妻鏡』頼朝将軍記をめぐって. *Nihon bungaku* 34, no. 5 (May 1985): 10–18.

Yanai Shigeshi 柳井滋, Murofushi Shinsuke 室伏信助, Ōasa Yūji 大朝雄二, Suzuki Hideo 鈴木日出男, Fujii Sadakazu 藤井貞和, Imanishi Yūichirō 今西祐一郎, eds., and Murasaki Shikibu 紫式部 (circa 937–circa 1014), au. *Genji monogatari* 源氏物語. Vol. 2. Tokyo: Iwanami Shoten, 1994.

Yashiro Kazuo 矢代和夫 and Kami Hiroshi 加美宏, eds. *Baishōron* 梅松論. Tokyo: Gendai Shichō Shinsha, 2010.

Yokomichi Mario 横道萬里雄 and Omote Akira 表章, eds. "Shōkun" 昭君. In *Yōkyokushū (jō)*, 166–73. Tokyo: Iwanami Shoten, 1960; 1973 printing.

Yotsutsuji Yoshinari 四辻善成 (1329–1402). "Kakaishō" 河海抄. In *Kakaishō, Kachō yojō, Shijo shichi-ron*, edited by Muromatsu Iwao, 1–455. Tokyo: Kokugaku-in Daigaku Shuppanbu, 1908.

Zuikei Shūhō and Charlotte von Verschuer. "Japan's Foreign Relations 1200 to 1392 AD: A Translation from 'Zenrin Kokuhōki.'" *Monumenta Nipponica* 57, no. 4 (Winter 2002): 413–45.

Zuo Si. "Three Capitals Rhapsody." Translated by David R. Knechtges. In *Wen Xuan, or Selections of Refined Literature*, 1:337–477. Princeton, NJ: Princeton University Press, 1982.

Zürcher, Erik. *The Buddhist Conquest of China: The Spread and Adaptation of Buddhism in Early Medieval China*. 3rd ed. Leiden, the Netherlands: Brill, 2007.

Index

Page numbers for figures are in italics.